The New
500
LOW-CARB
RECIPES

Over 125
New and
Revised
Recipes

DANA CARPENDER

The New
500
LOW-CARB
RECIPES

500 Updated Recipes for
Doing Low-Carb Better
and More Deliciously

FAIR WINDS

Inspiring | Educating | Creating | Entertaining

Brimming with creative inspiration, how-to projects, and useful information to enrich your everyday life, Quarto Knows is a favorite destination for those pursuing their interests and passions. Visit our site and dig deeper with our books into your area of interest: Quarto Creates, Quarto Cooks, Quarto Homes, Quarto Lives, Quarto Drives, Quarto Explores, Quarto Gifts, or Quarto Kids.

23 22 21 20 19   1 2 3 4 5

ISBN: 978-1-59233-863-4

Digital edition published in 2019
eISBN: 978-1-63159-651-3

Library of Congress Cataloging-in-Publication Data is available

Cover Design: Megan Jones Design
Page Layout: Megan Jones Design

Printed in China

The information in this book is for educational purposes only. It is not intended to replace the advice of a physician or medical practitioner. Please see your health-care provider before beginning any new health program.

MIX
Paper from
responsible sources
FSC® C008047

To my husband, Eric Schmitz, who has unfailingly helped me, supported me, and believed in me. I couldn't have done it without you. I love you with all my heart.

And to the readers of my long-gone Internet newsletter, *Lowcarbezine!*, my books, my blog, and my Facebook fan page. You have taught me how much enthusiasm, humor, intelligence, caring, and love can come through a fiber-optic cable. You have also taught me my job. This book is for you, and for low carbers everywhere.

CONTENTS

INTRODUCTION

Welcome to Low-Carbohydrate Variety!

What's the hardest thing about your low-carb diet? And what's the most common reason that people abandon their low-carb way of eating and all the health benefits and weight loss that come with it?

Boredom. People just plain get bored. After a few weeks of scrambled eggs and bacon for breakfast, a hamburger with no bun for lunch, and a steak—no baked potato—for dinner, day after day, people get fed up and quit. They just can't face a life of food monotony. Sound familiar?

If you've been getting bored with your low-carb diet, this is the book for you. You'll find dozens of exciting ways to vary a hamburger, a steak, pork chops, chicken, and fish. You'll find a wide variety of side dishes and salads. You'll find snacks and party foods that you can eat without feeling like you're depriving yourself. You'll even find recipes

for bread, not to mention muffins, waffles, pancakes, and granola. In short, this book has recipes for all sorts of things you never dreamed you could have on a low-carb diet.

Did I come up with these recipes for you? Heck, no! I came up with these recipes for me.

Who am I? I'm a person who, through circumstances that surely could have happened to anyone, has spent the past several years writing about low-carbohydrate dieting. In fact, I spent so much time answering questions for the curious that I finally wrote a book, *How I Gave Up My Low Fat Diet and Lost Forty Pounds!* To supplement the book, I started an "e-zine"—an Internet newsletter—for low-carb dieters, called *Lowcarbezine!* Knowing that recipes had been instrumental in my success, I included one or two in every issue. *Lowcarbezine!* is gone, but I'm still coming up with recipes!

I've always loved to cook, and I've always been good at it. My friends long ago dubbed me "The God of Food." So when low-fat, high-carb mania hit in the 1980s, I learned how to make a killer low-fat fettuccine Alfredo, curried chicken and mixed grain pilau, black beans and rice, blue corn pancakes, low-fat cheesecake—you name it.

And I got fat. Really fat. And sick. And tired. Thank heavens, in 1995 I got smart and tried going low carb, instead. Within two days my energy levels skyrocketed and my clothes were looser. It was overwhelmingly clear that this was the way my body wanted to be fed and that this was the way of eating that would make me well. I had set my foot upon a path from which there was no turning back. I was low carb for life.

The only thing that nearly derailed me was a terrible sense of Kitchen Disorientation. I had to discard the vast majority of my recipes when I dropped the grains, beans, potatoes, and such from my diet. For the very first time in my life, I'd walk into my kitchen and have no idea what to cook—and I had always known what to cook and how to put together a menu. It really was pretty scary, and it certainly was depressing. But I set out to become as good a low-carb cook as I had been a low-fat cook.

By 2002 that mission was accomplished, and then some! What you hold in your hands is the end result of those first years of trial and error, of learning what works and what doesn't, of experimenting to find out which substitutes are yummy and which are just plain lame.

This is not, for the most part, a gourmet cookbook, which for many of you means that the recipes you find here are recipes you'll actually use. You'll find a lot of fairly simple recipes and a few more complex ones for special occasions. There's lots of family fare here—pork chops and meat loaf, burgers and chicken. You'll find lots of meals you can cook on the stove top in a simple skillet and plenty of salads you can make ahead and stash in the refrigerator, ready to be pulled out and served when you dash in the door at a quarter-to-dinnertime. You'll find many one-dish meals that are protein and vegetables combined, from main dish salads to thick, hearty soups to casseroles. You'll also find ethnic flavors from around the world right alongside comfort foods you won't believe are low carb!

WHY IS THERE SUCH A WIDE RANGE OF CARB COUNTS IN THE RECIPES IN THIS BOOK?

If carbs are your problem, then they're going to be your problem tomorrow, and next week, and next year, and when you're old and gray. If you hope to keep your weight off, you cannot think in terms of going on a low-carb diet, losing your weight, and then going off your diet—you'll gain back every ounce, just as sure as you're born. You'll also go back to blood-sugar swings, energy crashes, and nagging, insatiable hunger, not to mention all the health risks of hyperinsulinemia. In short, you are in this for life.

When I first wrote this book, I'd been eating this way for seven years. As I revise it, it's been almost twenty-three. If you are to have any hope of doing this forever, you're going to need to enjoy what you eat. You're going to need variety, flavor, color, and interest. You're going to need festive dishes, easy dishes, and comfort foods—a whole world of things to eat. You're going to need a *cuisine*.

Because of this, I have included everything from very low-carb dishes, suitable for folks in the early, very low-carb "induction" stage of their diet, not to mention for those who are maintaining ketosis, to "splurge" dishes, which would probably make most of us gain weight if we ate them every day, but which still have far fewer carbs than their "normal" counterparts and are unlikely to awaken old food addiction demons.

There's another reason for the range of carb counts: Carbohydrate intolerance comes in degrees, and different people can tolerate different daily carbohydrate intakes. Some of you, no doubt, need to or will choose to stay in that twenty-grams-a-day-or-less range. Many others—lucky souls—can have as much as 90 to 100 grams a day and stay slim. This cookbook is meant to serve you all.

Only you can know, through trial and error, how many grams of carbs you can eat in a day and still lose weight. It is up to you to pick and choose among the recipes in this book while keeping an eye on the carbohydrate, protein, and fat counts provided. That way, you can put together menus that will please your palate and your family while staying below that critical carb level.

However, I do have this to say: Always, always, always the heart and soul of your low-carbohydrate diet should be meat, fish, poultry, eggs, healthy fats, and low-carb vegetables. This book will teach you a boggling number of ways to combine these things, and you should try them all. Don't just find one or two recipes that you like and make them over and over. Try at least one new recipe every week. That way, within a few months, you'll have a whole new repertoire of familiar low-carb favorites!

You will, as I just mentioned, find recipes in this book for what are best considered low-carb treats. Do not take the presence of a recipe in this book to mean that it is something that you can eat every day, in unlimited quantities, and still lose weight. I can tell you from experience that even low-carb treats, if eaten frequently, will put weight on you. Recipes for breads, cookies, muffins, cakes, and the like are here to give you a satisfying, varied diet that you can live with for life, but they should not become the new staples of your diet. *Do not try to make your low-carbohydrate diet resemble your former Standard American Diet.* That's the diet that got you in trouble in the first place, remember?

One other thought: It is entirely possible to have a bad reaction to a food that has nothing to do with its carbohydrate count. Gluten, a protein from wheat that is essential for baking low-carb yeast bread, causes bad reactions in a fair number of people. Soy products are problematic for many folks, as are nuts. Whey protein, used extensively in these recipes, contains lactose, which some people cannot tolerate. And surely you've heard of people who have bad reactions to artificial sweeteners of one kind or another. I've also heard from diabetics who get blood-sugar spikes from eating even small quantities of onions or tomatoes.

I have, as much as possible, eliminated gluten, grains, and soy products other than soy sauce from these recipes. I have also given you options on sweeteners. Indeed, this was the biggest reason for the reboot of this book.

Pay attention to your body. If you add a new food to your diet and you gain weight (and you're pretty certain it's not tied to something else, like your menstrual cycle or a new medication) or you find yourself unreasonably hungry, tired, or "off" despite having stayed within your body's carbohydrate tolerance, you may want to consider avoiding that food. One man's meat is another man's poison, and all that.

WHAT'S A "NET CARB COUNT?"

You may or may not be aware of the concept of the net carb count, sometimes called the "effective carb count." Drs. Michael and Mary Dan Eades introduced the idea in their book *Protein Power*. If you're not familiar with the concept, here it is in a nutshell:

Fiber is a form of carbohydrate and is, at least in American nutritional breakdowns, included in the total carbohydrate count. However, fiber is made of molecules so big that you can neither digest nor absorb them. Therefore fiber, despite being a carbohydrate, will not push up your blood sugar and will not cause an insulin release. Even better, by slowing the absorption of the starches and sugars that occur with it, fiber actually lessens their bad influence. This is very likely one of the reasons that high-fiber diets appear to be so much better for you than "American Normal."

For these reasons, many low-carb dieters subtract the grams of fiber in a food from the total grams of carbohydrate to determine the number of grams of carbohydrates that are actually a problem. These are the "net carbs" or the "effective carb count." For many, these non-fiber carbs are what they limit. This approach allows a much wider variety of foods and especially lots more vegetables.

I feel this approach is valid. However, you know how people are—show them a loophole and they start trying to game the system. Especially the food processors! As soon as the net carbs concept became popular, the food industry started subtracting all kinds of things from their total carb counts. Fiber, sure, but they also decided they could subtract maltitol (see About Polyols, page 18), "resistant starch," "low glycemic monosaccharides" (a.k.a. fructose), glycerine—all sorts of things. One pasta manufacturer marketed a "low-carb" pasta with nearly the same ingredients as regular pasta, claiming that their proprietary technology sequestered the starch and kept the human gut from digesting and absorbing it. They wound up paying $8 million in a fraud suit.

Since I originally wrote this book, there has been a swing back to counting total carbs, as recommended by Robert Atkins, M.D. in his original *Dr. Atkins' Diet Revolution*. That's fine, too! This book is useful whether you're counting net carbs or total carbs—or just avoiding eating concentrated carb foods.

I have listed net carb counts for these recipes. To get those figures, I have subtracted only two things: fiber and erythritol. See "About Erythritol," page 19.

HOW MANY GRAMS OF CARBOHYDRATE SHOULD I EAT IN A DAY?

"How the heck should I know?" she asked with a wise-acre grin. People restrict carbs for various reasons—to lose weight, to control blood sugar, to improve—yes, improve—athletic performance, to slow aging, to control seizures, to improve cognitive function, to reduce the risk of heart disease and/or cancer, to reduce hunger, or because they just plain feel better eating this way, plus a bunch more reasons I can't think of right now. The longer I pay attention to carbohydrate restriction, the more benefits are found.

The various reasons for reducing carbohydrate intake require differing degrees of restriction. When I started on this adventure at age thirty-six, I just cut all obviously starchy and sugary foods out of my diet, but didn't count anything. I ate all the non-starchy vegetables I wanted, plus grain products like fiber crackers, low-carb breads, and tortillas. I lost weight easily and felt immensely better, both physically and mentally. When I tested, I generally found I was in ketosis. To a great degree, this book is representative of that original approach to carb control.

But you may be trying to get into the deep ketosis needed to control seizures. If so, you'll want to eat the lowest-carb, highest fat recipes in the book, which is why we have provided expanded nutritional breakdowns for you. Or, you may be a person who was slim in youth and is just looking to keep the middle-aged bulge at bay now that you're forty-something and have a desk job. You very likely can use every recipe in the book, at least now and then.

Too, carb tolerance varies quite a lot. Some people, especially natural athletes, will lose weight if they drop below 100 grams per day. Others have to drop to 50 grams, 20 grams, or even lower. It's your body. You'll have to experiment.

ARE THESE RECIPES KETOGENIC?

Yes and no. Nothing like a decisive answer, huh?

What is dietary ketosis? It's a state where the body shifts from using glucose for most of its energy needs to burning free fatty acids and ketones.

What's a ketone? It's a by-product of fat burning. Just as burning coal at the proper temperature will drive off impurities, creating coke, which burns hotter and cleaner, the burning of free fatty acids creates ketones, a fuel that can be used by tissues that cannot burn free fatty acids, most importantly the brain.

It's important to know that testing positive for ketosis means that you are burning fat and ketones for fuel, but does not tell you whether you're burning dietary fat—fat you've just eaten—or body fat. *It is possible to be in ketosis without burning any body fat at all.*

To get back to the recipes: If you have excess body fat, you are likely to go into ketosis so long as you keep your carb count low enough—for most people, between 20 and 50 grams of total carbs per day, though there's wiggle room on either end. You'll be burning partly dietary fat, partly body fat.

You need to make sure you get enough protein—about 1 gram per kilogram of healthy body weight. For those of us who don't think in grams, divide your healthy body weight (not the weight that would make you look like a stick-thin model) in pounds by two. That's roughly how many grams of protein you need per day. You can eat a little more, but be aware: Your body will convert excess protein into glucose, and it may kick you out of ketosis. (I wish I'd known this sooner. When I started, I, like so many, was thinking "high-protein diet." Turns out my liver is really good at converting protein to glucose.)

Let's say your healthy body weight would be 140 pounds. That means you need about 70 grams of protein per day. At 4 calories per gram of protein, that's just 280 calories—hardly sufficient. (Of course, protein usually brings fat along with it—think steak, part protein, part fat.) If you eat 30 grams of carbohydrate, that's another 120 calories, for a total of 400 calories. The rest of your calories should be coming from fat—with the caution that, again, you can eat enough fat that all your ketones will be coming from dietary fat, not body fat.

On the other hand, if you're not looking to lose weight, but rather to get into the deepest possible state of ketosis for therapeutic reasons, again, you'll want to eat sufficient protein but no more, very little carbohydrate, but you can eat virtually unlimited fat.

In general, a ratio of 75 to 80 percent of calories from fat, 10 to 15 percent of calories from protein, and 5 percent of calories from carbohydrate should result in dietary ketosis, though, again, bodies differ. These ratios are sometimes called "macros," short for "macronutrients."

Back to the original question: Are these recipes ketogenic? Some fall within those ratios, some do not. Combining two dishes—say, a very low-carb fish dish that only has 20 percent fat paired with a very low-carbohydrate vegetable in a fatty sauce or a salad with a rich dressing—can yield the ratios desired.

But not everyone is paying attention to ketones. Some people just want to keep their carb load low. There are recipes here that run as high as 15 to 17 or so grams of carbohydrate per serving, but are still far lower carb than standard versions. Some of you will eat these as a matter of course; others are meant only as occasional treats, for special occasions.

We have chosen to label as "ketogenic" recipes that derive 75 percent or more of their calories from fat *and* have 7 grams total carbohydrate or fewer per serving. As a moment's thought will make clear, if a recipe has, say, 80 percent fat but has 9 grams of carb per serving, a smaller serving will make that recipe fit our ketogenic macros.

USING THIS BOOK

I can't tell you how to plan your menus. I don't know if you live alone or have a family, if you have hours to cook or are pressed for time every evening, or what foods are your favorites. I can, however, give you a few pointers on what you'll find here that may make your meal planning easier.

There are a lot of one-dish meals in this book—main dish salads, skillet suppers that include both meat and vegetables, and hearty soups that are a full meal in a bowl. I include these because they're some of my favorite foods, and to my mind, they're about the simplest way to eat. I also think they lend a far greater variety to low-carb cuisine than is possible if you're trying to divide up your carbohydrate allowance for a given meal among three or four different dishes. If you have a carb-eating family, you can appease them by serving something on the side, such as whole-wheat pitas split in half and toasted, along with garlic butter, a tortilla or two, rice, or a baked potato or sweet potato. (Of course, I don't recommend that you serve them canned biscuits, Tater Tots, or Minute Rice, but that shouldn't surprise you.)

When you're serving these one-dish meals, remember that most of your carbohydrate allowance for the meal is included in that main dish. Unless you can tolerate more carbohydrates than I can, you probably don't want to serve a dish with lots of vegetables in it with even more vegetables on the side. Remember, depending on what low-carbohydrate plan you follow, it's either the total carb or net carb count for the whole meal you have to keep an eye on. Complement simple meat dishes—such as roasted chicken, broiled steak, or pan-broiled pork chops—with the more carbohydrate-rich vegetable side dishes.

There's one other thing I hope this book teaches you to do: break out of your old ways of looking at food. There's no law that you eat eggs only for breakfast, have tuna salad for lunch every day, and serve some sort of meat and two side dishes for dinner. Short on both time and money? Serve eggs for dinner a couple of nights a week; they're fast, cheap, and unbelievably nutritious. Having family video night or game night? Skip dinner and make two or three healthy snack foods to nibble on. Can't face another fried egg at breakfast? Throw a pork chop or a hamburger on the electric tabletop grill while you're in the shower, and you've got a fast-and-easy breakfast. (Or eat leftovers. Since writing the first edition of this book, I have learned that when I am in recipe development, I must eat leftovers for breakfast. It's quick, easy, and good!) Sick of salads for lunch? Take a protein-rich dip in a snap-top container and some cut-up vegetables to work with you.

HELPFUL GENERAL HINTS

- If you're not losing weight, go back to counting every carb. Remember that snacks and beverages count, even if they're made from recipes in this book. A 6-gram muffin may be a lot better for you and your waistline than a convenience store muffin, but it's still 6 grams, and it counts! Likewise, don't lie to yourself about portion sizes. If you make your cookies really big, so that you only get two dozen instead of four dozen from a recipe, the carb count per cookie doubles, and don't you forget it.

- Beware of hidden carbohydrates. It's important to know that the government lets food manufacturers put "0 grams of carbohydrates" on the label if a food has less than 0.5 gram per serving, and "less than 1 gram of carbohydrate" if a food has between 0.5 gram and 0.9 gram. Even some diet sodas contain trace amounts of carbohydrates! These amounts aren't much, but they do add up if you eat enough of them. If you're having trouble losing, count foods that say "0 grams" as 0.5 gram and foods that say "less than 1 gram" as 1 gram.

- As mentioned previously, cast a skeptical eye on "net carb" claims on food labels. In particular, do not be snookered into believing that maltitol—used in sugar-free candy—doesn't count at all. You'll absorb about half of it. (The other half will be turning to gas in your gut. You have been warned.)

- Be aware that European food labeling law differs from American food labeling law. Their "total carbohydrate counts" already have the fiber subtracted. Subtract the fiber again, and you'll wind up thinking that food is far lower in net carbs than it is.

- Remember that some foods you may be thinking of as carb-free actually contain at least traces of carbohydrates. Eggs contain about 0.5 gram apiece, shrimp have 1 gram per 4-ounce (115 g) portion, natural cheeses have about 1 gram per ounce (28 g), and heavy cream has about 0.5 gram per tablespoon (15 ml). And coffee has more than 1 gram in a 10-ounce (280 ml) mug before you add cream and sweetener. (Tea, on the other hand, is carb-free.) If you're having trouble losing weight, get a food counter book and use it, even for foods you're sure you already know the carb counts of.

HOW ARE THE CARBOHYDRATE COUNTS IN THESE RECIPES CALCULATED?

These carbohydrate counts have been calculated using MasterCook software. This very useful program allows you to enter the ingredients of a recipe and the number of servings it makes, and it then spits out the nutritional breakdown for each serving. My MasterCook database has been expanded over the years by many low-carb ingredients I have added.

The carb counts for these recipes are as accurate as we can make them. However, they are not, and cannot be, 100 percent accurate. MasterCook gets its nutritional information from the USDA Nutrient Database, and my experience is that the USDA's figures for carbohydrate content tend to run a bit higher than the food count books. This means that the carbohydrate counts in this book are, if anything, a tad high, which beats being too low!

Furthermore, every stalk of celery, every onion, every head of broccoli is going to have a slightly different level of carbohydrates in it because it grew in a specific patch of soil, in specific weather, and with a particular kind of fertilizer. You may use a different brand of vanilla whey protein powder than I do. You may be a little more or a little less generous with how many bits of chopped green pepper you fit into a measuring cup.

Don't sweat it. These counts are, as the old joke goes, close enough for government work. You can count on them as a guide to the carbohydrate content in your diet. And do you really want to get obsessed with getting every tenth of a gram written down?

In this spirit, you'll find that many of these recipes call for "1 large rib of celery," "half a green pepper," or "a clove of garlic." This is how most of us cook, after all. These things do not come in standardized sizes, so they're analyzed for the average. Again: Don't sweat it! If you're really worried, use what seems to you a smallish stalk of celery, or green pepper, or clove of garlic, and you can count on your cumulative carb count being a hair lower than what is listed in the recipe.

LOW-CARB SPECIALTY FOODS

When I went low carb in 1995, it was a radical concept. Low-fat, high-carb diets were practically scriptural, and although there were loads and loads of low-fat specialty foods in every grocery store, from Healthy Choice dinners to Snackwells cookies, there were virtually no low-carb specialty foods to be found. As a result, eating a low-carbohydrate diet back then virtually forced me to eat real, unprocessed foods. Meat, poultry, fish, vegetables, low-sugar fruits, nuts and seeds, cheese, and butter were pretty much the whole of the diet.

By the time I wrote the first edition of *500 Low-Carb Recipes*, low-carb specialty products were appearing like mushrooms after a rainstorm. Some were good, some were bad, and some were middlin', pretty much like products in every other category. Some have survived and some have disappeared in the intervening years.

I saw and see this proliferation of low-carb specialty products as a double-edged sword. On the one hand, anything that helps carbohydrate-intolerant people remain happily on their diets is a good thing. On the other hand, most of these specialty products are highly processed foods, and they do not equal genuine foodstuffs in nutritional value. I fear that too many people eat these things as staples of their diet, displacing the real foods that should be the bedrock of any healthy low-carb diet.

Too, low-carb specialty foods tend to be expensive. Don't mistake what I'm saying—these products are not, in general, a rip-off. Low-carb products are more expensive to make, partly because they call for more expensive ingredients and partly because they are made in smaller quantities by smaller companies than are regular processed foods. These are specialty foods, and you're going to pay specialty prices for them. But I'd hate for you to start basing your diet on specialty products, decide that a low-carb diet is too expensive, and go back to eating junk. Use these products wisely to add a little variety, to provide an occasional treat, or to fight off cravings, but not as a major part of your diet.

And again, I must warn you: food processors have taken the "net carbs" concept to ridiculous, and, in my view, sometimes dishonest lengths. For example, most sugar-free candy is made with the sugar alcohol (polyol) maltitol, and food processors like to subtract it from total carbs to show a low net carb count. Yet maltitol is a carb, and although it is only partially and slowly absorbed, it is, indeed, absorbed to some degree—about half of it, actually. When you see that sugar-free candy claiming you can subtract all 20 grams of maltitol from the total carbs, realize that you really can only subtract about 10 grams.

The only things I subtract to get a net carb count are fiber and erythritol (page 11).

Here's a taste of the variety of low-carb specialty products now available on the market:

- **Breads.** Some are okay; some are wretched. Many, though not all, contain gluten. Be aware that "gluten-free" is not the same thing as low-carb. Most gluten-free breads are high-carb.

- **Tortillas and flatbreads.** These are useful not only for eating with fajitas and burritos and for making quesadillas and wraps, but also in place of Chinese mu shu pancakes. Be aware that low-carb tortillas, although tasty, are not identical to either flour or corn tortillas in either flavor or texture. Again, most contain gluten.

- **Jams, jellies, and condiments.** These contain the carbohydrates from whatever fruit or vegetable was used to make them, but not added sugars. I like the Polaner "sugar-free with fiber" line. Be aware that "all-fruit" preserves generally are no lower in sugar than regular jams and jellies; they just get their sugar from fruit juice. Sugar from fruit is still sugar.

- **Pastas.** Most low-carb pastas I've tried have been dreadful, and, as mentioned previously, some are not even low carb. The only low-carb pasta I use is shirataki noodles, more about which in the Ingredients section (page 22).

- **Cauliflower products.** I knew we'd cracked the mainstream when first Trader Joe's, then regular grocery stores, started selling "riced" cauliflower—cauliflower in tiny bits, to be steamed and used in place of rice. Both Green Giant and Birds Eye have started selling frozen pureed cauliflower, long loved by low carbers as "Fauxtatoes." And cauliflower-based pizza crust, invented by my friend Jamie Saal VanEaton, now is being made commercially. (I wish I thought Jamie was getting royalties.)

- **Protein bars.** These seem to be everywhere these days. They range from pretty good to wretched, sometimes within the same brand. You'll have to try a few brands and flavors to see which ones you like. Be aware that there is a lot of controversy about low-carb protein bars. Many contain glycerine to make them moist and chewy. The controversy is over whether or not glycerine acts like a carbohydrate in some ways in the body. Many people find that these bars knock them out of ketosis, whereas others don't have a problem. So, I'll say it again: Pay attention to your body!

- **Cookies and brownies.** I've had some I liked pretty well. Nui brand cookies are quite nice, but I rarely eat cookies, and if I do, I make them myself.

- **Chocolate.** There are a fair number of sugar-free chocolates available these days. I like ChocoPerfection and the sugar-free Reese's mini-cups and Hershey's Dark mini-bars are indistinguishable from the sugary stuff, while Russell Stover sugar-free English toffee is a dead ringer for Heath bars. However, since 85 percent dark chocolate has only a few grams in 1 or 2 squares, I'm as likely to eat that as the sugar-free stuff. Remember: If you eat sugar-free candy with maltitol, you have to count at least half the maltitol carbs. (Also remember that if you eat more than a modest portion, you will become socially offensive, or even give yourself gut trouble.)

  Lily's brand makes sugar-free chocolate chips sweetened with erythritol and stevia. They are my chocolate chips of choice; I order them through my health food store, though no doubt you can also buy them online.

- **Other sugar-free candy.** You can, if you look, find sugar-free taffies, hard candies, marshmallows, jelly beans, gummy bears, and other sweet treats. Again, the quality of these tends to be excellent. However, there are risks here, ranging from stalling your weight loss to serious diarrhea. Read "About Polyols," page 18, before you try these.

ABOUT POLYOLS

Polyols, also known as sugar alcohols, are widely used in sugar-free candies and other sweets. There are a variety of polyols; their names end with "tol"—lactitol, maltitol, mannitol, sorbitol, xylitol, erythritol, and the like. (I am aware of one exception: isomalt.) Polyols are indeed carbohydrates, but they are carbohydrates that are made up of molecules that are too big for humans to digest or absorb easily.

Polyols, especially maltitol, are used in commercial sugar-free sweets because, unlike sucralose and other artificial sweeteners, or stevia and monkfruit, they will give the same kinds of textures that can be achieved with sugar. Maltitol, in particular, can be used to make crunchy toffee, chewy jelly beans, slick hard candies, chewy brownies, and creamy chocolate, just as sugar can. Yet, they are easier on your carbohydrate metabolism and on your teeth, as well.

Since writing the first edition of this book, I have learned that most of the polyols are partially absorbed in the human gut, contributing roughly half the calories—and therefore carbs—as sugar.* This means that they cannot be completely discounted. Divide the maltitol number in half, add it to the net carb count listed, and you'll be closer to the truth. I still think that if one or two sugar-free Reese's mini-cups are what make it possible for you turn your back on your old way of eating, they're a useful adjunct to the diet.

The bigger problem with polyols: they can cause gas and diarrhea. For this reason, I cannot recommend that you consume more than 1 to 2 small pieces of commercial sugar-free candy in a day. (Funny story: Years ago, a friend said she just couldn't eat sugar-free chocolate, it upset her gut. I said that I found that a half a small bar a day or so gave me no trouble. "Half a bar!" she exclaimed. "I've been eating five or six bars!" Uh, I think I found your problem . . .)

Once we get past chocolate, things get dicier. Why?

Much of the mass of chocolate is made up of chocolate; the maltitol is only used to add sweetness, just as sugar is only used to add sweetness to regular chocolate bars. However, many other candies are made *mostly* of sugar—hard candies, taffies, jelly beans, marshmallows, gummy bears—and therefore their sugar-free counterparts consist largely of maltitol. Think of them less as food and more as remarkably tasty laxative tablets.

What we have here, then, are excellent quality sweets that rigidly enforce moderation. This not a bug, but a feature.

The bottom line is, I wouldn't eat sugar-free candies at all if you have an important meeting or a hot date a few hours later or if you'll be getting on an airplane. (Altitude can make gas swell very uncomfortably in your gut, plus you should be considerate of your fellow travelers.) In all situations, proceed with caution.

* What's the Deal With Sugar Alcohols?
http://www.foodinsight.org/articles/sugar-alcohols-fact-sheet

About Erythritol:
The One Polyol Exception

Erythritol is the one big exception in the polyol family: It is passed through the body whole, virtually unabsorbed, and it has little to no gastric effect. You'll learn more about it in the Ingredients section (page 33).

WHERE TO FIND LOW-CARBOHYDRATE SPECIALTY PRODUCTS

Hah! When I wrote the original edition of this book, I had several paragraphs on how to hunt down low-carb specialty products. That's longer needed! Google is your friend. Both Amazon and Netrition have tons of low-carb and sugar-free stuff. If you have an Internet connection and a credit card, you've got this.

ON THE IMPORTANCE OF READING LABELS

Do yourself a favor and get in the habit of reading the label on every food product, and I do mean *every* food product, that has one. I have learned from long, hard, repetitive experience that food manufacturers can, will, and do put sugar, corn syrup, cornstarch, and other nutritionally empty, carb-laden garbage into every conceivable food product. I have found sugar in everything from salsa to canned clams, for heaven's sake! (Who it was who thought that the clams needed sugaring, I'd love to know.) You will shave untold thousands of grams of carbs off your intake in the course of a year simply by looking for the product that has no added junk.

Be particularly wary when you see "New and Improved!" on the label of a product you have long considered safe. Too often it means, "Now with corn syrup!"

There are classes of food products to which sugar is virtually always added—the cured meats come to mind. There is almost always sugar in sausage, ham, bacon, hot dogs, liverwurst, and the like. You will look in vain for sugarless varieties of these products, which is one good reason why you should mostly eat fresh meats. However, you will find that there is quite a range of carb counts among cured meats because some manufacturers add more sugar than others do. I have seen ham that has 1 gram of carbohydrate per serving, and I have seen ham that has 6 grams of carbohydrates per serving—that's a 600 percent difference! Likewise, I've seen hot dogs that have 1 gram of carbohydrate apiece, and I've seen hot dogs that have 5 grams of carbohydrates apiece.

If you're in a position where you can't read the labels (for instance, at the deli counter at the grocery store), ask questions. The nice deli folks will be glad to read the labels on the ham and salami for you—they may even have a handout. They also can tell you what goes into the various items they make themselves. You'll want to ask at the meat counter, too, if you're buying something they've mixed up themselves, such as Italian sausage or marinated meats. I've found that if I simply state that I have a medical condition that requires me to be very careful about my diet—and I don't come at the busiest hour of the week—folks are generally very nice about this sort of thing.

In short, you need to become a food sleuth. After all, you're paying your hard-earned money for this stuff, and it is quite literally going to become a part of you. Pay at least as much attention as you would if you were buying a car or a computer.

REGARDING MICROWAVE OVENS

I use my microwave all the time, not just for reheating leftovers, but for cooking, especially for steaming vegetables. I know of no simpler nor more satisfactory method, and my Tupperware microwave steamer is out of the cabinet more often than in it. Further, I have seen some fairly convincing arguments for microwave steaming of vegetables retaining more nutrients than most other cooking methods. I also often cook bacon in the microwave; I haunted the local Goodwill until I found a circular microwave bacon tray that would go around on my microwave's turntable.

However, I suspect that at least some of you will be appalled that I would even consider using a microwave. There is a faction that considers them, and all food cooked in them, to be horribly dangerous.

I'm not going to argue the point here. Just take it as given that anything I cook in my microwave, you are welcome to cook on your stove top.

CHAPTER 1

Ingredients You Need to Know About

This is by no means an exhaustive rundown of every single ingredient used in this book; these are just the ones I thought you might have questions about. I've grouped them by use, and within those groupings they're alphabetized, so if you have a question about something used in a recipe, flip back here and read up on whatever you're curious about.

EGGS

You will find a few recipes in this book calling for raw eggs. This runs directly counter to the food safety information we've had drummed into our heads for the past couple of decades. According to the Egg Board, only one out of every 20,000 uncracked, properly refrigerated eggs is actually contaminated. As one woman with degrees in public health and food science put it, "The risk is less than the risk of breaking your leg on any given trip down the stairs." And that's with factory-farmed eggs; I consider small-farm eggs—and the eggs from my backyard—even safer.

It's not that there's no risk in eating raw eggs; there's a risk to everything. But I'm increasingly convinced that people worry about the wrong things. They get panicky about raw eggs while consuming Coca-Cola, Lucky Charms, and Wonder Bread. For what it's worth, I've never gotten sick from a raw egg. But your risks are your own to take.

If you're really unhappy about raw eggs, you can pasteurize them. You'll need a digital thermometer or one of the new electronic induction burners. Bring a saucepan of water to 140°F (60°C)—you'll need a thermometer. Keep it at that temperature for a couple of minutes, to make sure it's not climbing. Immerse room-temperature egg, and hold them at that temperature—and no hotter—for 3 minutes. Then, immediately pour off the hot water and flush the eggs with several changes of cold water. Use the eggs right away or store them in the refrigerator until needed.

SHIRATAKI

I mentioned that these are the only noodles I eat. So what are they? Shirataki are a traditional Japanese noodle made from *glucomannan*, a fiber extracted from the konjac or *konyaku* root. Because of this, shirataki pretty much consist of fiber and water. They are very low calorie and very low carb; I sometimes call them "nothing noodles."

There are two basic varieties of shirataki: traditional and tofu shirataki. Traditional shirataki are made only of the glucomannan fiber. They are translucent and somewhat gelatinous in texture. For lack of a better word, they are very Asian. I like them in Asian-style dishes, but find them odd in Western dishes.

Tofu shirataki, as the name suggests, have a little tofu added to them—by my math, about 2 teaspoons worth per packet. It makes tofu shirataki white and lends them a tenderer texture than the traditional shirataki. I like tofu shirataki in everything from fettuccini Alfredo to tuna casserole.

Both of these kinds of shirataki come in various shapes, just like the noodles you're used to. I like House Foods brand tofu shirataki, which come in spaghetti, angel hair, fettuccini, and macaroni shapes, some easier to find than others. (As always, Google is your friend.) Miracle Noodles is the most widely distributed traditional shirataki, and they also make Miracle Rice—the same substance, but in small pellets, about the size of short-grain rice. But new brands of shirataki crop up often.

It is important to know how to prepare shirataki since so many bad reviews of these noodles come from improper preparation. Shirataki come pre-hydrated in a pouch of liquid, so they do not need to be cooked soft. They do, however, need a little prep. Here's how:

Put a strainer in the sink, snip open your packet of shirataki, and dump them in. You will notice the liquid in the pouch smells fishy. Panic not. Rinse your shirataki well and put them in a microwaveable bowl. Microwave them on high for two minutes then drain them again. Put them back in the bowl, microwave them for another two minutes, and drain them one more time. You will be surprised at how much liquid cooks out of them! This microwaving and draining renders your noodles bland and not-fishy. It also keeps them from oozing liquid that would dilute any sauce, ruining your supper and causing you to curse.

If you're using your shirataki in soup, you needn't be quite so assiduous about cooking all the excess liquid out.

If you hate microwaves and everything they stand for, you'll need to drain and rinse your shirataki and then heat them, stirring, in a dry skillet over low heat for a good five minutes or so, to drive out the excess liquid.

Oh, and if you're using one of the long-skinny types, be aware that long noodles are considered good luck in Japan, so they tend to be really long. I snip across mine a few times with my kitchen shears before I microwave 'em.

FATS AND OILS

Lard: Yes, lard. Until Americans were sold a bill of goods about vegetable oils and hydrogenated shortening, lard was the most-used fat in the American diet, not only for frying and sautéing, but also as shortening in baked goods. My grandma used it in pie crust. It is lard that Crisco and other hydrogenated shortenings supplanted in American cooking. Lard was also spread on bread, just like butter, and still is in much of the world.

Yet, lard has been so defamed that it has become symbolic of "artery clogging saturated fat," though, ironically, it has slightly more unsaturated than saturated fat—about 57 percent. Most of that unsaturated fat in lard is in the form of monounsaturates, the same sort of fat that is considered healthful when found in olive oil.

Unfortunately, most of the lard in grocery stores cannot be considered a good fat. Not only does it come from animals raised on the cheapest, nastiest feed, much of it is hydrogenated, specifically because lard is unsaturated enough to be soft at room temperature.

Seek out a local small farm that produces pasture-raised pork and buy a bucket of unprocessed lard. This is glorious stuff, bland yet rich, wonderful for all kinds of sautéing, basting, and even baking. At this writing, I pay about $15 for a 4-pound (1.8 kg) bucket of lard from locally raised pastured pigs. It's worth it.

Because lard is rich in monounsaturates, it will go rancid eventually. Scoop out enough for a week or so, put it in a clean old jar, and freeze the rest.

Bonus: Pigs, like us, create vitamin D in their skin when exposed to sunlight, that vitamin D is stored in their fat. This means that lard from pasture-raised pigs is one of the few naturally rich food sources of vitamin D. (The vitamin D in milk has been added.)

Bacon Grease: Lard with a salty, smoky, amazing flavor, bacon grease is pure culinary gold. If you shell out the money for good, small-farm bacon from pastured hogs, then throw out the grease, I will personally come to your house and dope-slap you. Around here, we keep the stuff from cheap grocery store bacon, too. I pour it into an old salsa jar, keep it by the stove, and use it for all sorts of things, from frying eggs to roasting vegetables. I'd refrigerate it, but I use it up too fast for it to go bad.

Butter

When a recipe says butter, use butter, will you? Margarine is nasty, unhealthy stuff, full of hydrogenated oils, trans fats, and artificial everything. It's terrible for you. So use the real thing. If real butter strains your budget, watch for sales and stock up; butter freezes beautifully. Shop around, too. In my town I've found stores that regularly sell butter for anywhere from $2.25 a pound (455 g) to $4.59 a pound (455 g). That's a big difference, and one worth going out of my way for.

Regarding Oils in General

Here's my rough rule of thumb: If I can figure out how they got the oil out of the source, I'm probably willing to use it, at least in limited quantity. If you rub a piece of coconut or a walnut meat or an avocado on a piece of paper, you'll get a grease

spot. Heck, you can practically squeeze the oil out of olives right there in your kitchen.

Can you figure out how you'd get oil out of a soybean? An ear of corn? I've never found those things to be oily, have you? I'm not even sure what a safflower is.

Coconut Oil

Coconut oil is very healthful stuff. Coconut oil is very saturated, far more so than lard, beef fat, or butter. It turns out this is a good thing. Saturated fats barely oxidize, you see, eliminating the risk of rancid fats. Even at room temperature, coconut oil will keep as long as a year.

It raises your HDL cholesterol levels (the good stuff), increases immunity, improves insulin sensitivity, and stimulates the thyroid gland. Most of the saturated fat in coconut oil is in the form of *medium chain triglycerides* (MCT), a fat that can be used directly by the muscles for fuel—it's true energy food. MCTs are also highly ketogenic.

Coconut oil is solid below 76°F (24°C), making it inappropriate for salad dressings. It's great for all sorts of cooking applications, though.

Because coconut oil is solid up to 76°F (24°C), it makes a terrific substitute for hydrogenated shortenings (Crisco and the like) in baking. When coconut oil is called for in a baking recipe, it is meant to be used in solid form, unless "melted" is specified.

I find two kinds of coconut oil in my local stores: some is labeled "extra-virgin coconut oil," while the rest is simply labeled "coconut oil." Extra-virgin is nutritionally superior, but it has a mild but distinct coconut fragrance and flavor. Depending on the recipe and your taste, this may or may not work for you. The stuff labeled "coconut oil" has been refined and is bland. While it is not as nutritionally pristine as the extra-virgin stuff, I still consider plain old coconut oil to be a healthful fat and keep it on hand.

Feel free to substitute another bland fat like lard or chicken fat for sautéing. Who am I to judge?

In my area, extra-virgin coconut oil is found in health food stores, while the refined stuff is found in big grocery stores, sometimes in the international aisle—it's a staple of Indian cookery—and sometimes with the other oils. Costco also now carries it in big buckets. I mean, it is Costco.

I also buy coconut oil cooking spray. I can get this in my local grocery stores, alongside the PAM cooking spray.

Medium Chain Triglyceride Oil (MCT)

Derived from coconut oil, MCT oil has been popular with athletes for a while. It can be burned directly by the muscles, offering a quick burst of energy without the crash that sugar would bring. It is also used for people who need concentrated nutrition; it can be particularly useful in cancer patients, for instance. Too, because MCTs are highly ketogenic, it is a great choice for keto dieters.

Because it is concentrated, MCT oil is even more ketogenic than coconut oil. Unlike coconut oil, MCT oil is liquid at room temperature, making it useful for salad dressings and the like. It has become my oil of choice for making mayonnaise.

A word to the wise: I just bought a whole gallon (3.8 L)—two half-gallon (1.9 L) jugs—of MCT oil for under $50 through Amazon.com. In the meanwhile, my pharmacy has a 1-liter (1 qt) bottle of the stuff behind the counter with a price tag of $91. Shop around.

Olive Oil

It surely will come as no surprise to you that olive oil is a healthy fat, but you may not know that there are various kinds. Extra-virgin olive oil is the first pressing. It is deep green, with a full, fruity flavor, and it makes all the difference in salad dressings. If you want a milder flavor, light olive oil is available in any grocery store.

Be aware that if you refrigerate olive oil it will become solid. This is no big deal, as it will be fine once it warms up again. If you need it quickly, you can run the bottle under warm water. Or, if the container has no metal and will fit in your microwave, microwave it for a minute or so on low power.

FLOUR SUBSTITUTES

As you are no doubt aware, flour is out, for the most part, in low-carb cooking. Flour serves a few different purposes in cooking, from making up the bulk of most baked goods and creating stretch-iness in bread dough to thickening sauces and "binding" casseroles. In low-carb cooking, we use different ingredients for these various purposes. Here's a rundown of flour substitutes you'll want to have on hand for low-carb cooking and baking:

Brans

When I first started cooking low carb, I used brans fairly often in cooking. As I've moved away from grains in general, they've fallen out of my cuisine. There are a few recipes in here that call for wheat bran or oat bran. Both should be available at your local grocery store.

Ground Almonds and Hazelnuts

Another change that time has wrought: I can now buy finely ground almond meal, called "almond flour," at both my local health food stores, Bloomingfoods and Sahara Mart, and in grocery stores. I buy Bob's Red Mill brand and think it's great.

Bob's Red Mill also makes hazelnut flour, however, I still grind it myself. It's simple: Put them in your food processor with the S-blade in place and run until the nuts are the texture of cornmeal. Done.

Guar and Xanthan Gums

These sound just dreadful, don't they? But they're in lots of your favorite processed foods, so how bad can they be? If you're wondering what the heck they are, anyway, here's the answer: They're forms of water-soluble fiber, extracted and purified. Guar and xanthan are both flavorless white powders; their value to us is as low-carb thickeners. Technically speaking, these are carbs, but they're all fiber, nothing but, so don't worry about using them.

You'll find guar or xanthan used in small quantities in a lot of these recipes. Don't go dramatically increasing the quantity of guar or xanthan to get a thicker product because in large quantities, they make things gummy. But in these tiny quantities, they add oomph to sauces and soups without using flour.

In some of these recipes, I tell you to put the guar or xanthan through the blender with whatever liquid it is that you're using, and this is a fine method, though it results in a blender that needs washing. You can also use a stick blender.

More and more, though, I use the shaker method, like this: put your guar or xanthan in a salt shaker. Start whisking your dish first and then lightly sprinkle the guar or xanthan, bit by bit, over your sauce or soup, whisking madly all the while. Stop when your dish is a little less thick than you wish; it will continue to thicken a bit on standing.

My local health food stores carry guar and xanthan—I marginally prefer xanthan. You can also find suppliers online. Keep either one in a jar with a tight lid, and it will never go bad. The first time I bought guar I bought an entire pound (455 g) and took more than fifteen years to use it up! It kept just fine.

Vital Wheat Gluten

Gluten is a grain protein. It's the gluten in flour that makes bread dough stretchy so that it will trap the gas released by the yeast, letting your bread rise. We are not, of course, going to use regular, all-purpose flour, with its high carbohydrate content. Fortunately, it is possible to buy concentrated wheat gluten. This high-protein, low-starch flour is absolutely essential to making low-carbohydrate yeast breads.

Buying vital wheat gluten can be a problem, however, because the nomenclature is not standardized. Some packagers call this "vital wheat gluten" or "pure gluten flour," whereas others simply call it "wheat gluten." Still others call it "high-gluten flour." This is a real poser since the same name is frequently used for regular flour that has had extra gluten added to it; that product is something you definitely do not want.

To make sure you're getting the right product, you'll simply have to read the label. The product you want, regardless of what the packager calls it, will have between 75 and 80 percent protein, or about 24 grams in ¼ cup (30 g). It will also have a very low carbohydrate count, somewhere in the neighborhood of 6 grams of carbohydrates in that same ¼ cup (30 g). If your health food store has a bulk bin labeled "high-gluten flour" or "gluten flour" but there's no nutrition label attached, ask to see the bulk food manager and request the information off of the sack the flour came in. If the label on the bin says "vital wheat gluten" or "pure gluten flour," you can probably trust it.

At this writing, the most widely distributed brand of vital wheat gluten in the United States is Bob's Red Mill. More and more grocery stores are beginning to carry this line of products. If your grocery store doesn't yet, you might request that they start.

Whey Protein Powder

Whey is the liquid part of milk. If you've ever seen yogurt that has separated, the clearish liquid on top is the whey. Whey protein is of extremely good quality, and the protein powder made from it is tops in both flavor and nutritional value. For any sweet recipe, the vanilla whey protein powder is best, and it's readily available in health food stores. (Yes, this is the kind generally sold for making shakes with.) Keep in mind that protein powders vary in their carbohydrate counts, so look for the one with the fewest carbohydrates—and if you're gluten-free make sure to check the label just to be safe. Also beware of sugar-sweetened protein powders, which can be higher in carbs. I have tried several, all sweetened with stevia, and all with less than 1 gram of carbohydrate per serving. I have liked them all.

Natural whey protein powder is just like vanilla whey protein powder, except that it has not been flavored or sweetened. Its flavor is bland, so it is used in recipes where a sweet flavor is not desirable. Natural whey protein powder is called for in some of the recipes that other folks have donated to this book; I generally use rice protein powder when a bland protein powder is called for.

LIQUIDS

Beer

A few recipes in this book call for beer. The lowest carbohydrate beers I've been able to find are Michelob Ultra, with Miller Lite and Milwaukee's Best Light just a little higher. If you're avoiding gluten, Corona Lite is 5 grams of carbs a bottle and Corona Premier is only 2.6 g.

Broths

Canned or boxed chicken and beef broths are very handy items to keep around, and it's certainly quicker to make dinner with these than it would be if you had to make your own from scratch. However, the quality of most of the canned broth you'll find at your local grocery store is appallingly bad. The chicken broth has all sorts of chemicals in it and often sugar, as well. The "beef" broth is worse, frequently containing no beef whatsoever. I refuse to use these products, and you should, too.

However, there are a few canned and boxed broths worth buying. Many grocery stores now carry a brand called Kitchen Basics, which contains a little sugar, but no chemicals at all. It's packaged in 1-quart (946 ml) boxes, and it's available in chicken, beef, and seafood varieties.

Costco's Kirkland line has organic beef and chicken stocks, which I also have used.

Health food stores also have good-quality canned and boxed broths. Both Shelton's and Health Valley brands are widely distributed in the United States. Whichever brand you choose, if you're gluten-free, be sure to check the label.

All packaged broths are frailer-flavored than my homemade bone broth (page 258), so I often simmer them down—called "reducing"—to about two-thirds their original volume to make them stronger.

One last note: You will also find canned vegetable broth, particularly at health food stores. This is tasty, but it runs much higher in carbohydrates than the chicken and beef broths. I'd avoid it.

Vinegar

Various recipes in this book call for wine vinegar, cider vinegar, sherry vinegar, rice vinegar, tarragon vinegar, white vinegar, balsamic vinegar, and even raspberry vinegar, for which you'll find a recipe. If you've always thought that vinegar was just vinegar, think again! Each of these vinegars has a distinct flavor all its own, and if you substitute one for the other, you'll change the whole character of the recipe. Add just one splash of cider vinegar to your Asian Chicken Salad (page 251), and you've traded your Chinese accent for an American twang. Vinegar is such a great way to give bright flavors to foods while adding very few carbs that I keep all of these varieties on hand. This is easy to do, because vinegar keeps well.

As with everything else, read the labels on your vinegar. I've seen cider vinegar that has 0 grams of carbohydrates per ounce (28 ml) and I've seen cider vinegar that has 4 grams of carbohydrates per ounce (28 ml)—a huge difference. Beware, also, of apple cider–flavored vinegar, which is white vinegar with artificial flavors added. I bought this once by mistake. (You'd think someone who constantly reminds others to read labels would be beyond such errors, wouldn't you?)

Wine

There are several recipes in this cookbook calling for either dry red or dry white wine. I find the inexpensive box wines, which come in a plastic bag inside a cardboard box, very convenient to keep on hand for cooking. They don't go bad because the contents are never exposed to air. These are not fabulous vintage wines, but they're fine for our modest purposes, and they certainly are handy. I generally have dry red of some kind on hand because that's what we drink. But neither my husband nor I is a fan of white wine. Boxed Chablis or Chardonnay let me keep cooking wine on hand.

Be wary of any wine with "added flavors." Too often, one of those flavors will be sugar. Buy wine with a recognizable varietal name, such as Shiraz, Cabernet Sauvignon, Rhine, Chablis, Pino Grigio, and the like, rather than stuff like "Chillable Red," and you'll get better results with fewer carbs.

Coconut Milk

Since writing the first edition, I have come to use coconut milk more and more, both the thick, rich canned stuff and the "pourable" coconut milk in cartons that you find along with the soymilk and almond milk in the nondairy case at the grocery store. Writing *500 Paleo Recipes*, I learned that canned coconut milk worked as a substitute for heavy cream in most applications, though of course the flavor is different, and a 50/50 mixture of canned and pourable coconut milks works as a substitute for half-and-half. If you're avoiding dairy, feel free to use these; I suspect you'll find the results satisfactory.

Just be careful to buy unsweetened pourable coconut milk! Much of the stuff in cartons has added sugar. As for canned, buy the full-fat stuff instead of the "lite" coconut milk, okay?

Oh, and if you refrigerate a can of coconut milk overnight, then turn it over and poke two holes in it, you can drain off the liquid. When you open the can, you'll find unsweetened coconut cream. You can whip this with a little vanilla and sweetener as a substitute for whipped cream.

NUTS, SEEDS, AND NUT BUTTERS

Nuts and Seeds

Low in carbohydrates and high in healthy fats, protein, and minerals, nuts and seeds are great foods for us. These ingredients can be pricey, and you'll want to shop around. In particular, health food stores often carry nuts and seeds in bulk at better prices than you'll find at the grocery store. I have also found that specialty ethnic groceries often have good prices on nuts and seeds. I get my best deal on almonds at my wonderful Middle Eastern grocery, Sahara Mart.

By the way, along with pumpkin and sunflower seeds, you can buy sesame seeds in bulk at health food stores for a fraction of what they'll cost you in a little shaker jar at the grocery store. You can also get unsweetened coconut in shreds and flakes at health food stores.

Flaxseed Meal

Here's another ingredient that has become widely available in the past decade-and-a-half! I use Bob's Red Mill Golden Flaxseed Meal, and like it fine. Store flaxseed meal in the freezer; the fats in it go over all too readily.

Nut Butters

The only peanut butter called for in this cookbook is "natural" peanut butter, the kind made from ground, roasted peanuts; peanut oil; salt; and nothing else. Most big grocery stores now carry natural peanut butter; it's the stuff with the layer of oil on top. The oil in standard peanut butter has been hydrogenated to keep it from separating out (that's what gives big name-brand peanut butters that extremely smooth, plastic consistency), and it's hard to think of anything worse for you than hydrogenated vegetable oil—except for sugar, of course, which is also added to standard peanut butter. Stick to the natural stuff.

There are now some natural peanut butters that do not separate. These have palm oil added. This is not a nutritional problem, but involves ecological devastation and the slaughter of orangutans. I won't buy it.

Health food stores carry not only natural peanut butter but also almond butter, sunflower butter, and sesame butter, generally called "tahini." All of these are useful for low carbers. Keep all natural nut butters in the refrigerator unless you're going to eat them up within a week or two.

SEASONINGS

Bouillon or Broth Concentrates

Bouillon or broth concentrate comes in cubes, crystals, or liquids. It is generally full of salt and chemicals, and it doesn't taste notably like the animal it supposedly came from. It definitely does not make a suitable substitute for good-quality broth if you're making a pot of soup. However, these products can be useful for adding a little kick of flavor here and there, more as seasonings than as soups, and for this, I keep them on hand. I prefer Better Than Bouillon, a paste that comes in a jar. It has actual beef or chicken or whatever in it. It is widely available. Refrigerate after opening; I learned this the hard way.

Fresh Ginger

Many recipes in this book call for fresh ginger, sometimes called gingeroot. Fresh ginger is an essential ingredient in Asian cooking, and dried, powdered ginger is not a substitute. Fortunately, fresh ginger freezes beautifully; just drop your whole ginger (called a "hand" of ginger) into a zipper-lock freezer bag and toss it in the freezer. When the time comes to use it, pull it out, peel enough of the end for your immediate purposes, and grate it. (It will grate just fine while still frozen.) Throw the remaining root back in the bag and toss it back in the freezer.

Ground ginger in oil is available in jars at some very comprehensive grocery stores. I like freshly grated ginger better, but this jarred ginger will also work in these recipes.

Garlic

Garlic is a borderline vegetable. It's fairly high in carbohydrates, but it's very good for you. Surely, you've heard all about garlic's nutritional prowess by now. Garlic is also, of course, an essential seasoning in many recipes. However, remember that there is an estimated 1 gram of carbohydrates per clove, so go easy. A "clove," by the way, is one of those little individual bits you get in a whole garlic bulb. If you read "clove" and use a whole bulb (also called a "head") of garlic, you'll get lots more carbs—and a lot stronger garlic flavor—than you expected.

I mostly use fresh garlic, except for in the occasional recipe that calls for a sprinkle-on seasoning blend. Nothing else tastes like the real thing. To my taste buds, even the jarred, chopped garlic in oil doesn't taste like fresh garlic. And we won't even talk about garlic powder. You may use jarred garlic if you like; ½ teaspoon should equal about 1 clove of fresh garlic. If you choose to use powdered garlic, well, I can't stop you, but I'm afraid I can't promise the recipes will taste the same, either. Figure that ¼ teaspoon of garlic powder is roughly equivalent to 1 clove of fresh garlic.

By the way, the easiest way to crush a clove or two of garlic is to put the flat side of a big knife on top of it and smash it with your fist. Pick out the papery skin, which will now be easy, chop your garlic a bit more, and toss it into your dish. Keep in mind that the distinctive garlic aroma and flavor only develops after the cell walls are broken (that's why a pile of fresh garlic bulbs in the grocery store doesn't reek), so the more finely you crush or mince your garlic, the more flavor it will release.

Soy Sauce

If you're avoiding gluten, be aware that most soy sauce has wheat in it. San-J brand is gluten-free, and that's what I use. Recipes with soy sauce in them that are marked "GF" (gluten-free) assume you will use San-J or a similar sauce.

If you are avoiding soy, coconut aminos, available at health food stores and online, are remarkably similar to soy sauce.

Vege-Sal

If you've been reading my stuff, you know that I'm a big fan of Vege-Sal. What is Vege-Sal? It's a salt that's been seasoned, but don't think "seasoned salt." Vege-Sal is much milder than traditional seasoned salt. It's simply salt that's been blended with some dried, powdered vegetables. The flavor is quite subtle, but I think it improves all sorts of things.

I've given you the choice between using regular salt or Vege-Sal in a wide variety of recipes. Don't worry, they'll come out fine with plain old salt, but I do think Vege-Sal adds a little something extra. Vege-Sal is also excellent sprinkled over chops and steaks in place of regular salt. Vege-Sal is made by Modern Products and is widely available in health food stores. Recently, Modern Products has appended the name of its most popular product, Spike, (another seasoned salt), to Vege-Sal, so it is officially "Spike Vege-Sal."

If you decide you like Vege-Sal as much as I do, you might want to order it in the 20-ounce (560 g) box. This is far cheaper than paying for a shaker every time you purchase it! Be aware that as I wrote this section, I googled "Spike Vege-Sal" and found the 20-ounce (560 g) box selling for anywhere from $10 to $22. As ever, it pays to shop around.

SWEETENERS

The Sweetener Wars are the bane of my professional existence. No matter what sweetener I use, someone will complain. I use sucralose? How can I use an artificial sweetener?! Don't I know they're evil?! I call for stevia? Why? It's so expensive, and it tastes bad. Can't I just use Splenda? Why don't I use xylitol instead of erythritol? Etc. I am sidestepping the issue by giving you options wherever possible.

If I specify a sweetener in a recipe, it's because that's the sweetener that works. If it's not vital, I've listed "Sweetener to equal X sugar in sweetness," and you may choose for yourself from the sweeteners listed.

More and more, I use liquid sweeteners. Unlike granular Splenda or Stevia In The Raw, liquids don't have carby maltodextrin fillers. But liquid or granular, here's the vital thing: *You must know the sweetness equivalence of your particular kind and brand of sweetener.* In other words, you must know how many drops of your sweetener equal a teaspoon (4 g) of sugar in sweetness, or a tablespoon (13 g), or a cup (200 g). Once you know this, you're golden. Most sweeteners have this information on their labels. If yours doesn't, check the company's website.

- Liquid sucralose. I like EZ-Sweetz brand, available through Amazon.com or Netrition.com. It's reat stuff. You can get teeny bottles that fit nicely in purse or pocket, if you'd like to keep it on hand for coffee. You need to know the sweetness equivalency of your liquid sucralose. EZ-Sweetz comes in two strengths: 1 drop = 2 teaspoons (8 g) sugar and 2 drops = 2 teaspoons (8 g) sugar. They offer free samples! Go to: www.ez-sweetz.com/free-sample

Splenda also puts out a liquid version. I have no objection to it, but find it hard to control how much comes out. I want a bottle that lets me drip single drops.

- **Stevia.** If you've missed it, stevia is an herbal sweetener derived from the South American herb *Stevia rebaudiana*. While the dried leaves have been used for centuries, it is only with various extracts that stevia has become a major force in the low-carb/sugar-free community.

  The form of stevia I like best is liquid stevia extract. I use NOW and SweetLeaf brands, both of which come in a wide variety of flavors, making this a tremendously versatile ingredient. In these recipes, you'll find vanilla, chocolate, English toffee, and lemon drop flavored liquid stevia. I also keep plain—just sweet—liquid stevia on hand. In particular, I use English toffee stevia more than any other kind because it allows me to add a brown sugar–like note to all kinds of recipes.

  Liquid stevia is far sweeter than sugar; it is important to know the sweetness equivalency. The NOW and SweetLeaf brands run roughly 6 drops = 1 teaspoon (4 g) sugar, so 18 drops = 1 tablespoon (13 g) sugar. I start with ¼ teaspoon to replace ¼ cup (50 g) sugar, and ½ teaspoon to replace ½ cup (100 g) sugar. I also have both NuNaturals brand—6 drops = 1 teaspoon (4 g) sugar—and EZ-Sweetz brand, 4 drops = 2 teaspoons (8 g) sugar. If you use a different brand, you'll have to check their sweetness equivalence.

- **Monk Fruit, a.k.a. Lo Han Guo.** Just cracking the American market, Monk Fruit or *lo han guo* is the Asian equivalent of stevia: a concentrated sugarless sweetener derived from a naturally

sweet plant, in this case a melon. EZ-Sweetz makes a liquid stevia/monkfruit sweetener that I like. 4 drops = 2 teaspoons (8 g) sugar.

The "In The Raw" company now makes Monk Fruit In The Raw, similar to Stevia In The Raw in that it is bulked with maltodextrin so that it measures like sugar. This means you'll need to count 0.5 grams of carbohydrate per teaspoon (0.5 g), 24 grams per cup (24 g). I'd go with liquid.

About Calculating How Much Sweetener to Use

It's all well and good to say, "2 drops = 1 teaspoon (4 g) sugar," but what if you need the equivalent of ½ cup (100 g) of sugar? Arithmetic time.

> 1 tablespoon = 3 teaspoons
> 4 tablespoons = ¼ cup

So, in this case, if you needed sweetener to equal ½ cup (100 g) of sugar in sweetness, you'd multiply $2 \times 3 = 6$, and $8 \times 6 = 48$. You'd need 48 drops of that particular sweetener to equal ½ cup (100 g) sugar in sweetness.

This can become tedious. Once you've settled on a sweetener you like, I recommend you get out your measuring spoons and drip sweetener into them, counting as you go, and writing down the results on a card you then tape to the inside of the cabinet where you keep your sweeteners. I, by way of example, have figured out from trial and error that with the two brands of flavored liquid stevia I use—NOW and SweetLeaf—¼ teaspoon is roughly equal to ¼ cup (50 g) sugar, ½ teaspoon = ½ cup (100 g), etc. This saves a lot of dripping and counting. (I have also figured out that these two stevias run about 6 drops = 1 teaspoon [4 g] sugar, so 18 drops = 1 tablespoon [13 g] sugar.)

- **Erythritol.** A member of the polyol or sugar alcohol family, erythritol is technically a carbohydrate. However, unlike maltitol, which is absorbed, if slowly and incompletely, erythritol is passed through the body unchanged. Erythritol does not raise blood sugar, and unlike maltitol, sorbitol, and some of the other sugar alcohols, it has little to no gastric effect. Occurring in nature in some fruits and fermented foods, erythritol, while made industrially, can be considered at least passingly "natural." It is available at health food stores or online. There are brands boasting that they are non-GMO, if that concerns you.

  Erythritol comes with a couple of challenges: It is only 60 to 70 percent as sweet as sugar. It is also *endothermic*, meaning that when it hits the moisture in your mouth it absorbs energy and creates a cooling sensation. This is fine in ice cream, but disconcerting in a cookie. Because of these two properties, I have long combined erythritol with liquid stevia extract. I generally start with half the erythritol, by volume, as the quantity of sugar called for in the original recipe. Then, I add liquid stevia to bring it up to full sweetness. This works well, and the flavored liquid stevias let me add other flavor notes to the dish.

  Look for erythritol at health food stores or online. I also like Swerve, a blend of erythritol and *oligosaccharides*, which are sweet fibers, especially since it comes in confectioner's style.

  Full disclosure: While erythritol is a carbohydrate, because it is passed through the body unchanged, it is not included in the carb counts in this book.

Erythritol Blends

Clearly, I'm not the only one who thinks mixing erythritol with more concentrated sweeteners is a good idea. Erythritol/stevia and erythritol/monkfruit blends are the up-and-coming sweeteners. Truvia, an erythritol/stevia blend, is the best known and available in many grocery stores. I prefer erythritol/monkfruit blends. I've tried two—Virtue and Natural Mate, both available through Amazon.com. They claim different sweetness equivalences, but I find them interchangeable, about twice the sweetness of sugar. Truvia Spoonable is about the same.

I now use these erythritol/monkfruit blends anywhere I want some of the textures of sugar—in baked goods, glazes, and the like.

Molasses

What the heck is molasses doing in a low-carb cookbook? It's practically all carbohydrates, after all. Well, yes, but I've found that combining other sweeteners with a very small amount of molasses gives a good brown-sugar flavor to all sorts of recipes. Always use the darkest molasses you can find; the darker it is, the stronger the flavor and the lower the carb count. If you can get it, blackstrap—the darkest, strongest molasses—is also where all the minerals they take out of sugar end up. At least it's not a nutritional wasteland. Still, I only use small amounts.

Most health food stores carry blackstrap molasses, but if you can't find it, always buy the darkest molasses available, keeping in mind that most grocery store brands come in both light and dark varieties.

Why not use some of the artificial brown sugar–flavored sweeteners out there? Because I've tried them, and I haven't tasted even one I would be willing to buy again. Ick.

About Xylitol

I get queries about xylitol, which is popular in low-carb and Paleo circles. Like erythritol, it is a member of the polyol or sugar alcohol family. However, according to a table in the Sugar Alcohol Fact Sheet at foodinsight.org, we absorb xylitol at ten times the rate we do erythritol. Too, xylitol is highly toxic to dogs, and I have three. I can't risk it.

These Sweeteners Are Not Low Carb

Be aware that these sweeteners are not low carb:
- agave nectar
- organic sugar, organic cane sugar
- honey
- coconut sugar
- palm sugar
- date sugar
- crystalline fructose
- maple syrup
- Sucanat

These are all simply different forms of sugar.

I put agave nectar first because I consider it to be the greatest fraud perpetrated on the nutrition-conscious public since I started paying attention in the 1970s. There is nothing "natural" about agave nectar; it is manufactured by a process remarkably similar to that used to make high fructose corn syrup. But it is actually worse than corn syrup because it is higher in fructose—often as much as 90 percent.

Yes, agave nectar has a low glycemic index because it is high in fructose—fructose cannot be absorbed directly into the bloodstream as glucose is, but rather must be processed by the liver. For this reason, fructose is the biggest cause of non-alcoholic fatty liver disease. It also jacks up triglycerides like nobody's business and appears to be uniquely fattening.

VEGETABLES

"Eat your vegetables!" is the refrain of everyone's childhood supper memories. Vegetables play a big part in low-carbohydrate cuisine. They are the source of the majority of the carbs in my diet.

That is the irony: Vegetables have many positive qualities, but depending on your individual carbohydrate tolerance, it may be possible to eat enough vegetables to knock you out of ketosis, even spike your blood sugar. It's important to know your own body.

(My friend, William Douglas, M.D., author of *Wheat Belly* and *Undoctored*, recommends that you take your blood sugar one hour after eating. If it's above 120, Bill says, you should avoid that food in future or at least moderate your portions.)

Here's a rundown on some of the players:

Carrots

Because carrots have a higher glycemic index than many vegetables, some low carbers have started avoiding them with great zeal. But while carrots do have a fairly high blood sugar impact, you'd have to eat pounds of them to enough to jack up your blood sugar. So, don't freak when you see a carrot used here and there in these recipes, okay? I've kept the quantities small, just enough to add flavor, color, and a few vitamins, but not enough to torpedo your diet.

Frozen Vegetables

You'll notice that many of these recipes call for frozen vegetables, particularly broccoli, green beans, and cauliflower. I use these because I find them convenient, and I think that the quality is good. If you like, you may certainly substitute fresh vegetables in any recipe. You will need to adjust the cooking time, and if the recipe calls for the vegetable to be used thawed, but not cooked, you'll need to "blanch" your vegetables by boiling them for just three to five minutes.

It's important to know that frozen vegetables are not immortal, no matter how good your freezer. Don't buy more than you can use up in four to six weeks, even if they're on sale. You'll end up throwing them away.

Onions

Onions are borderline vegetables. They're certainly higher in carbohydrates than, say, lettuce or cucumbers. However, they're loaded with valuable phytochemicals, so they're healthful, and of course, they add an unmatched flavor to all sorts of foods. So, I use onions a lot, but I try to use the smallest quantity that will give the desired flavor. Indeed, one of the most common things I do to cut carb counts on "borrowed" recipes is to cut back on the amount of onion used. If you have diabetes, you'll want to watch your quantities of onions pretty carefully and maybe even cut back further on the amounts I've given.

If you're not an accomplished cook, you need to know that different types of onions are good for different things. There are mild onions, which are best used raw, and there are stronger onions, which are what you want if you're going to be cooking them. My favorite mild onions are sweet red onions; these are widely available, and you'll see I've used them quite a lot in the recipes here. You can substitute Vidalia or Bermuda onions anywhere I've specified sweet red onions. Scallions, also known as green onions, also are mild and are best eaten raw or quickly cooked in stir-fries. To me, scallions have their own flavor, and I generally don't substitute for them, but your kitchen won't blow up or anything if you use another sort of sweet onion in their place.

When a recipe simply says "onion," what I'm talking about is good old yellow globe onions, the ones you can buy 3 to 5 pounds (1.4 to 2.3 kg) at a time in net sacks. You'll be doing yourself a favor if you pick a sack with smallish onions in it so that when a recipe calls for just a ¼ or ½ cup (40 or 80 g) of chopped onion, you won't be left with half an onion. For the record, when I say "small onion," I mean one about 1½ inches (3.8 cm) in diameter, or about ¼ to ⅓ cup (40 to 55 g) when chopped. A medium onion would be about 2 inches (5 cm) in diameter and would yield between ½ and ¾ cup (80 and 120 g) when chopped. A large onion would be 2½ to 3 (6 to 7.5 cm) inches across and would yield about a cup (160 g) when chopped. I'm not so obsessive about exact carb counts that I bother to measure every scrap of onion I put in a dish; I think in terms of small, medium, and large onions, instead. If you prefer to be more exact, go for it.

Tomatoes and Tomato Products

Tomatoes are another borderline vegetable, but like onions they are so nutritious, so flavorful, and so versatile that I'm reluctant to leave them out of low-carb cuisine entirely. After all, lycopene, the pigment that makes tomatoes red, has been shown to be a potent cancer-fighter, and who wants to miss out on something like that?

You'll notice that I call for canned tomatoes in a fair number of recipes, even in some where fresh tomatoes might do. This is because fresh tomatoes aren't very good for much of the year, whereas canned tomatoes are all canned at the height of ripeness. I'd rather have a good canned tomato in my sauce or soup than a mediocre fresh one. Since canned tomatoes are generally used with all the liquid that's in the can, the nutritional content doesn't suffer the way it does with most canned vegetables.

I also use plain canned tomato sauce, canned pizza sauce, canned pasta sauce, and jarred salsa. When choosing these products, you need to be aware that tomatoes, for some reason, inspire food packers to flights of sugar-fancy. They add sugar, corn syrup, and other carb-laden sweeteners to all sorts of tomato products, so it is very important that you read the labels on all tomato-based products to find the ones with no added sugar. And keep on reading them, even after you know what's in them. The good, cheap brand of salsa I used for quite a while showed up one day with "New, Improved!" on the label. Can you guess how they improved it? Right—they added sugar. So I found a new brand.

YOGURT AND BUTTERMILK

Yogurt and buttermilk both fall into the category of "cultured milks"—milk that has deliberately had a particular bacteria added to it and then been kept warm until the bacteria grows. These bacteria give yogurt and buttermilk their characteristic thick textures and tangy flavors.

If you look at the label of either of these cultured milk products, you'll see that the nutrition label claims 12 grams of carbohydrates per cup (235 ml) (and, by the way, 8 grams of protein). This is the same carbohydrate count as the milk these products are made from. For this reason, many low carbers avoid yogurt and buttermilk.

However, in *GO-Diet*, Dr. Goldberg and Dr. O'Mara explain that in actuality, most of the lactose (milk sugar) in the milk is converted into lactic acid by the bacteria. This is what gives these foods their sour taste. The labels say "12 grams carbohydrate" largely, they say, because carbohydrate count is determined by "difference." What this means is that the calorie count is determined first. Then, the protein and fat fractions are measured, and the number of calories they contribute is calculated. Any calories left over are assumed to come from carbohydrate.

However, Goldberg and O'Mara say, this is inaccurate in the cases of yogurt and buttermilk, and they say we should count just 4 grams of carbohydrates per cup (235 ml) for these cultured milks.

Accordingly, I have added them back to my diet, and I have had no trouble with them, meaning no weight gain and no triggering of "blood sugar hunger." Based on this, the carb counts in this book are calculated using that 4-grams-of-carbohydrates-per-cup figure.

Keep in mind that these numbers only apply to plain yogurt. The sweetened kind is always higher in carbohydrate. If you like fruit-flavored yogurt, flavor it yourself. You'll find a recipe for making your own plain yogurt, easy as pie, in the Eggs and Dairy chapter, but any store-bought plain yogurt is fine.

Since I wrote the first edition of this book, Greek yogurt has become popular. This is modestly lower in carbs than regular plain yogurt. If you're buying yogurt to eat by itself, or with liquid stevia and a few berries, full-fat Greek yogurt is a fine choice. However, the recipes in this book were standardized with regular, not Greek, yogurt.

ICONS USED

 Keto

 Gluten-Free

 Grain-Free

 Dairy-Free

CHAPTER 2

Hors D'oeuvres, Snacks, and Party Nibbles

Unlike most snack and party foods, the recipes in this chapter are actually nutritious and filling. This means two things: One, that if you serve one or two of these items before dinner, you may want to cut back a bit on quantities at the meal itself, and two, that you can actually use many of these recipes as light meals. This is a particularly nice idea for family movie night—just put out a big tray of cut-up vegetables and dip, some wings, and a bowl of nut mix and call it supper.

WICKED WINGS*

These are a bit messy and time-consuming to make, but they're worth every minute. They'll impress the heck out of your friends, too, and you'll wish you'd made more of them. They also taste great the next day.

4 pounds (1.8 kg) chicken wings

1 cup (100 g) grated Parmesan cheese (the cheap stuff in the green shaker)

2 tablespoons (3 g) dried parsley

1 tablespoon (3 g) dried oregano

2 teaspoons paprika

1 teaspoon salt

½ teaspoon pepper

½ cup (112 g) butter

1. Preheat the oven to 350°F (180°C, or gas mark 4).

2. Cut the wings into drumsticks, saving the pointy tips.

   TIP: Not sure what to do with those wing tips? Freeze them for soup—they make great broth. (Or just buy cut-up "party wings.")

3. Combine the Parmesan cheese and the parsley, oregano, paprika, salt, and pepper in a bowl.

4. Line a shallow baking pan with foil. (Do not omit this step, or you'll still be scrubbing the pan a week later.)

5. Melt the butter in a shallow bowl or pan.

6. Dip each drumstick in butter, roll in the cheese and seasoning mixture, and arrange in the foil-lined pan.

7. Bake for 1 hour—and then kick yourself for not having made a double recipe!

* This recipe is known and loved—and much-pirated—under the name "Heroin Wings." We decided that given the current problem with opioid addiction, we'd change it. New name, same great recipe!

YIELD: About 50 pieces, each with: 68 Calories; 5 g Fat (73.1% calories from fat); 4 g Protein; trace Carbohydrate; trace Dietary Fiber; 0 net carbs

CHINESE PEANUT WINGS

If you love Chinese barbecued spareribs, try making these.

¼ cup (60 ml) soy sauce

1 tablespoon (15 g) erythritol/stevia or erythritol/monkfruit blend OR 1 tablespoon (15 ml) erythritol PLUS liquid stevia, monkfruit, or sucralose to equal 1 tablespoon (13 g) of sugar in sweetness

3 tablespoons (48 g) natural peanut butter

2 tablespoons (28 ml) dry sherry

1 tablespoon (15 ml) melted coconut oil

1 tablespoon (15 ml) cider vinegar

2 teaspoons Chinese five-spice powder

¼ teaspoon red pepper flakes (or more, if you want them hotter)

1 clove of garlic, crushed

12 chicken wings or 24 drumettes

½ cup (120 ml) chicken broth

1. Preheat the oven to 325°F (170°C, or gas mark 3).

2. Put the soy sauce, sweetener, peanut butter, sherry, oil, vinegar, spice powder, red pepper flakes, and garlic in a blender or food processor and blend well.

3. If you have whole chicken wings and want to cut them into drumsticks, do it now. (This is a matter of preference and is not essential.)

4. Arrange the wings in a large baking pan, pour the blended sauce over them, and then turn them over to coat on all sides.

5. Put the wings in the fridge and let them sit for at least half an hour (an hour is even better).

6. Bake the wings for an hour, turning every 20 minutes during baking.

7. When the wings are done, put them on a serving platter. Add the chicken broth to the pan and stir it around. Then, scrape the sauce from the pan back into the blender or food processor. Blend again for just a moment to make it smooth and serve with the wings.

YIELD: About 24 pieces, each with: 75 Calories; 5 g Fat (67.3% calories from fat); 5 g Protein; 1 g Carbohydrate; trace Dietary Fiber; 1 g net carbs

HOT WINGS

If you want to simplify this recipe, use store-bought Buffalo wing sauce instead of the mixture of dry spices. Most wing sauces don't have any sugar in them and are quite low in carbs.

1 teaspoon cayenne pepper

2 teaspoons dried oregano

1 teaspoon curry powder

2 teaspoons paprika

2 teaspoons dried thyme

2 pounds (910 g) chicken wings, cut into single joints

1. Preheat the oven to 375°F (190°C, or gas mark 5).

2. Combine the cayenne pepper, oregano, curry powder, paprika, and thyme well in a bowl.

3. Arrange the wings in a shallow baking pan and sprinkle the mixture evenly over them, turning to coat both sides.

4. Roast for 45 to 50 minutes or until crisp. Serve with the traditional accompaniments of ranch or blue cheese dressing and celery sticks, if desired.

YIELD: About 24 pieces, each with: 47 Calories; 3 g Fat (64.2% calories from fat); 4 g Protein; trace Carbohydrate; trace Dietary Fiber; 0 net carbs

PAPRIKA WINGS

I have become a huge paprika enthusiast, keeping at least three or four varieties on hand at all times. Try these with the familiar sweet paprika, sure, but how about smoked paprika, either sweet or hot?

20 cut-up chicken wing pieces

3 tablespoons (45 ml) olive oil

2 cloves of garlic, crushed

Salt

Pepper

Paprika

1. Preheat the oven to 350°F (180°C, or gas mark 4).

2. Arrange the wings in a baking pan so that they are not touching.

3. Combine the olive oil and garlic and spoon the mixture over the wings. Make sure you get a little of the crushed garlic on each piece.

4. Sprinkle the wings with salt and pepper to taste and then with enough paprika to make them reddish all over.

5. Roast for 15 to 20 minutes and then turn them over and sprinkle the other side with salt, pepper, and paprika.

6. Roast for another 45 minutes to 1 hour, turning every 15 to 20 minutes.

YIELD: 20 pieces, each with: 73 Calories; 6 g Fat (74.3% calories from fat); 5 g Protein; trace Carbohydrate; trace Dietary Fiber; 0 g net carbs

Stuffed Eggs

Don't save these recipes for parties: If you're a low-carb eater, a refrigerator full of stuffed eggs is a beautiful thing. Here are six varieties. Feel free to double or triple any of these recipes—you know they'll disappear.

CLASSIC DEVILED EGGS

These are everybody's potluck supper favorite.

6 hard-boiled eggs

⅓ cup (75 g) mayonnaise

2 teaspoons spicy brown or Dijon mustard

¼ teaspoon salt or Vege-Sal

Paprika

1. Slice the eggs in half and carefully remove the yolks into a mixing bowl.
2. Mash the yolks with a fork. Stir in the mayonnaise, mustard, and salt and mix until creamy.
3. Spoon the mixture back into the hollows in the egg whites. Sprinkle with a little paprika for color.

YIELD: 12 pieces, each with: 83 Calories; 8 g Fat (83.1% calories from fat); 3 g Protein; trace Carbohydrate; trace Dietary Fiber; 0 net carbs

ONION EGGS

This tiny bit of onion brings a whole new interest. You could substitute a minced scallion or two if you like, but the red onion looks pretty.

6 hard-boiled eggs

⅓ cup (75 g) mayonnaise

1 teaspoon spicy brown or Dijon mustard

2½ teaspoons (8 g) very finely minced sweet red onion

5 drops of Tabasco

¼ teaspoon salt or Vege-Sal

1. Slice the eggs in half and carefully remove the yolks into a mixing bowl.
2. Mash the yolks with a fork. Stir in the mayonnaise, mustard, onion, Tabasco, and salt and mix until creamy.
3. Spoon the mixture back into the hollows in the egg whites.

YIELD: 12 pieces, each with: 83 Calories; 8 g Fat (83.0% calories from fat); 3 g Protein; trace Carbohydrate; trace Dietary Fiber; 0 g net carbs

FISH EGGS

That's eggs with fish, not eggs from fish. If you thought stuffed eggs couldn't go to an upscale party, these will change your mind.

6 hard-boiled eggs

3 tablespoons (42 g) mayonnaise

3 tablespoons (45 g) sour cream

¼ cup (34 g) moist smoked salmon, mashed fine

1 tablespoon (15 g) jarred, grated horseradish

2 teaspoons finely minced sweet red onion

⅛ teaspoon salt, or to taste

1. Slice the eggs in half and carefully remove the yolks into a mixing bowl.

2. Mash the yolks with a fork. Stir in the mayonnaise, sour cream, salmon, horseradish, onion, and salt and mix until creamy.

3. Spoon the mixture back into the hollows in the egg whites.

YIELD: 12 pieces, each with: 75 Calories; 6 g Fat (76.5% calories from fat); 4 g Protein; 1 g Carbohydrate; trace Dietary Fiber; 1 g net carbs

KALI'S EGGS

These eggs are curried and buttery and good! If you'd like these to be dairy-free, feel free to use olive or coconut oil instead.

6 hard-boiled eggs

1 tablespoon (14 g) butter

1 teaspoon curry powder

1 clove of garlic, crushed

1 scallion, including the crisp part of the green shoot, finely minced

⅓ cup (75 g) mayonnaise

¼ teaspoon Tabasco

½ teaspoon salt

1. Slice the eggs in half and carefully remove the yolks into a mixing bowl.

2. In a small, heavy skillet over low heat, melt the butter. Add the curry powder and garlic and stir for 2 minutes.

3. Scrape the butter mixture into the yolks. Stir in the scallion, mayonnaise, Tabasco, and salt and mix until creamy.

4. Spoon the mixture back into the hollows in the egg whites.

YIELD: 12 pieces, each with: 92 Calories; 9 g Fat (83.8% calories from fat); 3 g Protein; 1 g Carbohydrate; trace Dietary Fiber; 1 g net carbs

HAMMOND EGGS

Deviled ham gives these eggs a country sort of kick.
Underwood Deviled Ham doesn't have any obvious
gluten, but because of the risk of cross-contamination,
Underwood does not guarantee that it's gluten-free. If
you have celiac disease, you might skip it.

6 hard-boiled eggs

1 can (2¼ ounces, or 64 g) of deviled ham

4 teaspoons (20 g) spicy brown mustard

¼ cup (60 g) mayonnaise

¼ teaspoon salt

Paprika

1. Slice the eggs in half and carefully remove the yolks into a mixing bowl.

2. Mash the yolks with a fork. Stir in the deviled ham, mustard, mayonnaise, and salt and mix until creamy.

3. Spoon the mixture back into the hollows in the egg whites. Sprinkle with a little paprika for color.

YIELD: 12 pieces, each with: 86 Calories; 8 g Fat (78.8% calories from fat); 4 g Protein; 1 g Carbohydrate; trace Dietary Fiber; 1 g net carbs

CAJUN EGGS

This is just one good reason to keep Cajun Seasoning
on hand. You could use Tony Chachere's Creole
Seasoning instead, if you like.

6 hard-boiled eggs

⅓ cup (75 g) mayonnaise

2 teaspoons horseradish mustard

1 teaspoon Cajun Seasoning (page 276)

1. Slice the eggs in half and carefully remove the yolks into a mixing bowl.

2. Mash the yolks with a fork. Stir in the mayonnaise and mustard and mix until creamy.

3. Add the Cajun Seasoning and blend well.

4. Spoon the mixture back into the hollows in the egg whites.

YIELD: 12 pieces, each with: 83 Calories; 8 g Fat (83.1% calories from fat); 3 g Protein; trace Carbohydrate; trace Dietary Fiber; 0 g net carbs

ARTICHOKE PARMESAN DIP

Serve this party favorite with pepper strips, cucumber rounds, celery sticks, pork rinds, or low-carb crackers. Should you have leftovers, make omelets! It's good made with half mayo, half cream cheese, too.

1 can (13½ ounces, or 380 g) of artichoke hearts

1 cup (225 g) mayonnaise

1 cup (100 g) grated Parmesan cheese

1 clove of garlic, crushed, or 1 teaspoon of jarred, chopped garlic

Paprika

1. Preheat the oven to 325°F (170°C, or gas mark 3).

2. Drain and chop the artichoke hearts.

3. Mix the artichoke hearts with the mayonnaise, Parmesan cheese, and garlic, combining well.

4. Put the mixture in a small, ovenproof casserole, sprinkle a little paprika on top, and bake for 45 minutes.

YIELD: 4 servings, each with: 522 Calories; 53 g Fat (86.7% calories from fat); 11 g Protein; 7 g Carbohydrate; trace Dietary Fiber; 7 g net carbs

SPINACH ARTICHOKE DIP

This is a great, equally yummy variation of the previous recipe, but keep in mind that it does make twice as much dip. This is good made with half mayo, half softened cream cheese, too. Again, serve with vegetable dippers, pork rinds, and/or low-carb crackers. And again, leftovers are great in omelets!

1 can (13½ ounces, or 380 g) of artichoke hearts

1 package (10 ounces, or 283 g) of frozen chopped spinach, thawed and drained

2 cups (450 g) mayonnaise

2 cups (200 g) grated Parmesan cheese

2 cloves of garlic, crushed, or 2 teaspoons jarred, chopped garlic

Paprika

1. Preheat the oven to 325°F (170°C, or gas mark 3).

2. Drain and chop the artichoke hearts.

3. Combine the spinach, mayonnaise, Parmesan cheese, and garlic in a large casserole (a 6-cup [1.4-L] dish is about right). Sprinkle with paprika.

4. Bake for 50 to 60 minutes.

YIELD: 8 servings, each with: 522 Calories; 53 g Fat (86.7% calories from fat); 11 g Protein; 7 g Carbohydrate; trace Dietary Fiber; 7 g net carbs

GUACAMOLE

This is a very simple guacamole recipe, without sour cream or mayonnaise, that lets the flavor of the avocados shine through. Eat on pork rinds, vegetable dippers, or in an omelet with Monterey Jack cheese. It's also great spread on a steak, or in Guacamatoes! (page 160) This recipe contains lots of healthy fats and almost three times the potassium found in a banana.

4 ripe black avocados

2 tablespoons (20 g) minced sweet red onion

3 tablespoons (45 ml) lime juice

3 cloves of garlic, crushed

¼ teaspoon hot sauce (I'd go with Cholula or another Mexican-style sauce.)

Salt or Vege-Sal

1. Halve the avocados and scoop the flesh into a mixing bowl. Mash coarsely with a fork.
2. Mix in the onion, lime juice, garlic, hot sauce, and salt to taste, stirring to blend well and mashing to the desired consistency.

YIELD: 6 servings, each with: 221 Calories; 21 g Fat (76.5% calories from fat); 3 g Protein; 11 g Carbohydrate; 3 g Dietary Fiber; 8 g net carbs

DILL DIP

This easy dip tastes wonderful with all sorts of raw vegetables. Try serving it with celery, peppers, cucumber, broccoli, or whatever else you have on hand.

1 pint (473 ml) sour cream

¼ of a small onion

1 heaping tablespoon (about 3 g) dry dill weed or 2–3 tablespoons (8–12 g) minced fresh dill weed

½ teaspoon salt or Vege-Sal

1. Put the sour cream, onion, dill, and salt in a food processor and process until the onion disappears. (If you don't have a food processor, mince the onion very fine and just stir everything together.)
2. You can serve this right away, but it tastes even better if you let it chill for a few hours.

YIELD: 12 servings, each with: 83 Calories; 8 g Fat (85.5% calories from fat); 1 g Protein; 2 g Carbohydrate; trace Dietary Fiber; 2 g net carbs

CLAM DIP

With some celery sticks and pepper strips for scooping, this would make a good lunch. Of course, you can serve it at parties, too, with celery, green pepper, cucumber rounds, or pork rinds for you and crackers or chips for the non-low-carbers.

2 packages (8 ounces, or 225 g each) of cream cheese, softened

½ cup (115 g) mayonnaise

2–3 teaspoons (10–15 ml) Worcestershire sauce

1 tablespoon (15 g) Dijon mustard

8 to 10 scallions, including the crisp part of the green shoot, minced

2 cans (6½ ounces, or 180 g each) of minced clams, drained

Salt or Vege-Sal

Pepper

1. Combine all the ingredients well. A food processor or blender works well for this, or if you prefer to leave chunks of clam, you could use an electric mixer.

2. Chill in the refrigerator before serving.

YIELD: 12 servings, each with: 200 Calories; 22 g Fat (83.0% calories from fat); 8 g Protein; 2 g Carbohydrate; trace Dietary Fiber; 2 g net carbs

NORTHWEST DIP

Reader Pat Moriarty says, "This is my all-time favorite!" Pat says to serve this with cucumber rounds, celery sticks, and/or pork rinds. And consider it as an omelet filling!

1 package (8 ounces, or 225 g) of cream cheese, softened

¼ cup (60 ml) heavy cream

1 scallion, thinly sliced

2 teaspoons freshly squeezed lemon juice

1 dash of red pepper sauce

4 ounces (115 g) smoked salmon, gently shredded

1 ripe avocado, mashed

1. In a large mixing bowl, combine the cream cheese and heavy cream together until smooth and creamy.

2. Stir in the scallion, lemon juice, and red pepper sauce. Gently fold in the smoked salmon and mashed avocado, being careful not to overmix.

YIELD: 6 servings, each with: 243 Calories; 23 g Fat (81.9% calories from fat); 7 g Protein; 4 g Carbohydrate; 1 g Dietary Fiber; 4 g net carbs

KATHY'S PORK RIND DIP

When she gets tired of eating plain pork rinds, reader Kathy Rice makes this dip to go with them.

3 ounces (85 g) cream cheese, softened

2 tablespoons (32 g) salsa

Blend and enjoy—that's all there is to it.

YIELD: 2 servings, each with: 153 Calories; 15 g Fat (85.8% calories from fat); 3 g Protein; 2 g Carbohydrate; trace Dietary Fiber; 2 g net carbs

AVOCADO CHEESE DIP

This dip used to make my mom very popular at parties. Dip with pork rinds, vegetables, or low-carb crackers. It can also be served over steak, and it makes perhaps the most elegant omelets on the face of the earth.

2 packages (8 ounces, or 225 g each) of cream cheese, softened

1½ cups (173 g) shredded white Cheddar or Monterey Jack cheese

1 ripe black avocado, peeled and seeded

1 small onion

1 clove of garlic, crushed

1 can (3 to 4 ounces, or 85 to 115 g) of green chilies, drained, or jalapeños, if you like it hot

1. Combine all the ingredients in a food processor and process until very smooth.

2. Scrape into a pretty serving bowl and place the avocado seed in the middle. For some reason, placing the seed in the middle keeps the dip from turning brown quite so quickly while it sits out. But if you're making this a few hours ahead of time, cover it with plastic wrap, making sure the wrap is actually touching the surface of the dip. Don't make this more than a few hours before you plan to serve it.

YIELD: 18 servings, each with: 148 Calories; 14 g Fat (81.1% calories from fat); 5 g Protein; 3 g Carbohydrate; trace Dietary Fiber; 3 g net carbs

SMOKED GOUDA VEGGIE DIP

This is great with celery, peppers, or any favorite raw veggie. Combine your ingredients with a mixer, not a food processor, so you have actual little bits of Gouda in the dip.

1 package (8 ounces, or 225 g) of cream cheese, softened

⅔ cup (150 g) mayonnaise

1 cup (120 g) shredded smoked Gouda

6 scallions, including the crisp part of the green shoot, sliced

2 tablespoons (10 g) grated Parmesan cheese

½ teaspoon pepper

1. Using an electric mixer, beat the cream cheese and mayonnaise together until creamy, scraping the sides of the bowl often.

2. Add the Gouda, scallions, Parmesan cheese, and pepper and beat until well blended.

3. Chill and serve with raw vegetables.

YIELD: 8 servings, each with: 290 Calories; 30 g Fat (89.0% calories from fat); 7 g Protein; 2 g Carbohydrate; trace Dietary Fiber; 2 g net carbs

KIM'S CRAB DIP

We have my sister to thank for coming up with this delicious, low-carb treat. She loves to entertain and invented this for a party.

1 package (8 ounces, or 225 g) of cream cheese, softened

½ cup (115 g) sour cream

1 can (6 ounces, or 170 g) of crabmeat, drained

1 teaspoon horseradish

2 tablespoons (6 g) fresh chives, or dried if fresh are unavailable

¼ teaspoon dry mustard

⅛ teaspoon salt

⅛ teaspoon pepper

1. Use your electric mixer to beat the cream cheese and sour cream together at a high speed until very smooth.

2. Set the beater to a low speed and mix in the crabmeat, horseradish, chives, dry mustard, salt, and pepper.

3. Chill. Serve with raw vegetables.

YIELD: 12 servings, each with: 101 Calories; 9 g Fat (77.7% calories from fat); 5 g Protein; 1 g Carbohydrate; trace Dietary Fiber; 1 g net carbs

BACON CHEESE SPREAD

This recipe is from Jen Eloff's book *Splendid Low-Carbing*. Jen says, "Your friends will beg you for this recipe!" Jen's original recipe called for light cream cheese; use it, if you prefer.

1 package (8 ounces, or 225 g) of cream cheese, softened

½ cup (115 g) mayonnaise

1½ cups (173 g) shredded Cheddar cheese

2 tablespoons (6 g) chopped fresh chives or (12 g) scallions

1 teaspoon dried parsley

¼ teaspoon garlic powder

8 slices of bacon, cooked until crisp

1. Preheat the oven to 350°F (180°C, or gas mark 4).

2. In a food processor with the S-blade in place or in a blender, process the cream cheese and mayonnaise until smooth.

3. In a medium bowl, combine the cream cheese mixture, Cheddar cheese, chives, parsley, and garlic powder until well combined. Spread the mixture evenly on the bottom of a 9-inch (23 cm) glass pie plate.

4. Use a pair of kitchen scissors to cut the cooked bacon into small pieces. Garnish the top of the cheese spread with the bacon pieces and bake for 15 minutes. Serve with low-carb crackers.

YIELD: 12 servings, each with: 213 Calories; 21 g Fat (86.9% calories from fat); 6 g Protein; 1 g Carbohydrate; trace Dietary Fiber; 1 g net carbs

DUKKAH

My friend Lou Anne brought this Turkish "dry dip" along on a campout, and I've been nagging her for the recipe ever since. Although dukkah is traditionally eaten with bread, it also adds an exotic, fascinating flavor to simple raw vegetables.

⅓ cup (33 g) almonds or (38 g) hazelnuts, chopped

¼ cup (20 g) coriander seeds

¼ cup (36 g) white sesame seeds

¼ cup (24 g) cumin seeds

Salt and pepper

1. Toast the nuts, sesame seeds, coriander seeds, and cumin seeds over high heat for 1 minute, stirring constantly.

2. Use a food processor, coffee grinder, or mortar and pestle to crush the toasted mixture, and then season it with salt and pepper to taste. (Don't overgrind; you want a consistency similar to coarse-ground cornmeal.)

3. Put your dukkah in a bowl next to a bowl of olive oil and set out cut-up raw vegetables. Dip the vegetables first into the oil, then into the dukkah, and eat.

YIELD: 10 servings, each with: 36 Calories; 3 g Fat (58.3% calories from fat); 1 g Protein; 3 g Carbohydrate; 1 g Dietary Fiber; 2 g net carbs

TUNA PÂTÉ

If you throw in some veggies for dipping, this versatile dish makes a great snack, first course at a dinner party, or even a fine brown bag lunch. SweetLeaf makes the Valencia orange liquid stevia. I can get it at Sahara Mart, my local health/international/gourmet grocery, but if you're not so blessed, Amazon has it.

2 tablespoons (28 g) butter

2 cloves of garlic, crushed

½ of a medium onion, chopped

1 can (4 ounces, or 115 g) of mushrooms, drained

18 drops of Valencia orange flavor liquid stevia, OR 18 drops of plain liquid stevia plus ½ teaspoon orange extract OR liquid monk fruit to equal 1 tablespoon (13 g) of sugar plus ½ teaspoon orange extract

1 package (8 ounces, or 225 g) of cream cheese, softened

1 can (5 ounces, or 140 g) of tuna, drained (I'd use olive oil–packed.)

2 tablespoons (8 g) fresh parsley

Grated rind of half an orange

¼ teaspoon salt

¼ teaspoon pepper

Cut-up vegetables and crackers (optional for serving)

1. In a small, heavy skillet over medium heat, melt the butter and sauté the garlic, onion, and mushrooms until the onion is limp. Add the sweetener and stir well. Cool.

2. Place the cream cheese, tuna, parsley, orange rind, salt, and pepper in a food processor with the S-blade in place. Pulse to blend. Add the sautéed mixture and pulse until smooth and well blended.

3. Spoon into a serving bowl and chill. Serve with celery sticks, pepper strips, cucumber rounds, and crackers (for the carb-eaters).

YIELD: 6 servings, each with: 240 Calories; 21 g Fat (77.8% calories from fat); 10 g Protein; 3 g Carbohydrate; trace Dietary Fiber; 3 g net carbs

MARINATED MUSHROOMS

The quality of the vinaigrette dressing makes all the difference here, so use the best you can make or buy.

8 ounces (225 g) small, fresh mushrooms	Lettuce leaves to line plate
1½ cups (355 ml) vinaigrette dressing (page 162 and 163)	

1. Thoroughly wipe the mushrooms clean with a soft cloth.

2. Place them in a saucepan, cover them with the dressing, and simmer over medium-low heat for 15 minutes.

3. Chill and drain the mushrooms, saving the dressing to store any leftover mushrooms in. (You can even simmer another batch of mushrooms in it when the first batch is gone.) Arrange the mushrooms on lettuce with toothpicks for spearing.

YIELD: About 15 pieces, each with: 116 Calories; 13 g Fat (94.6% calories from fat); trace Protein; 1 g Carbohydrate; trace Dietary Fiber; 1 g net carbs. These numbers are actually high since you'll drain off most of the dressing. Still, most of the calories are going to come from fat.

CHEESE COOKIES

This recipe requires a food processor, so if you only have a tiny one, cut the recipe in half. Despite the name, these are not sweet; they have the flavor of cheese crackers with the texture of cookies.

½ pound (225 g) processed American loaf cheese, such as Velveeta (store brand works fine)	¼ pound (115 g) butter
	1 cup (80 g) unflavored whey protein powder
½ pound (225 g) sharp Cheddar cheese	About 6 dozen pecan or walnut halves (optional)

1. Preheat the oven to 400°F (200°C, or gas mark 6).

2. Cut the loaf cheese, Cheddar cheese, and butter into chunks.

3. Put the cheese chunks, butter, and whey protein powder in the food processor and pulse until the dough is well combined.

4. Coat a cookie sheet with nonstick cooking spray. Drop spoonfuls of dough onto the cookie sheet and press half a pecan or walnut in the top of each one (if using).

5. Bake for 8 to 10 minutes or until the cookies are just getting brown around the edges.

YIELD: About 70, each with: 58 Calories; 4 g Fat (68.5% calories from fat); 4 g Protein; 1 g Carbohydrate; trace Dietary Fiber; 1 g net carbs

SNAPS

These are similar to the Cheese Cookies on previous page, but they bite back! Feel free to add extra hot sauce or cayenne to this if you're a serious chili-head.

1 pound (455 g) processed jalapeño Jack cheese

¼ pound (115 g) butter

1 cup (80 g) unflavored whey protein powder

1. Preheat the oven to 400°F (200°C, or gas mark 6).
2. Cut the Jack cheese and butter into chunks.
3. Put the cheese, butter, and whey protein powder in the food processor and pulse until the dough is well combined.
4. Coat a cookie sheet with nonstick cooking spray. Drop spoonfuls of dough onto the cookie sheet.
5. Bake for 8 to 10 minutes or until the cookies are just getting brown around the edges.

YIELD: About 70, each with: 48 Calories; 3 g Fat (62.8% calories from fat); 4 g Protein; trace Carbohydrate; trace Dietary Fiber; 0 g net carbs

ROASTED NUTS

Of course you can buy these in a can at the grocery store, but they're much better—and cheaper—when you roast them fresh at home. If you're dairy-free, make sure to use coconut oil.

4 tablespoons (55 g) butter or bland coconut oil

Salt

2 cups shelled nuts of your choice (almonds, pecans, walnuts, or a combination; weight will vary)

1. Preheat the oven to 300°F (150°C, or gas mark 2). Put the butter or coconut oil in a shallow roasting pan and put it in the oven as it heats.
2. When the butter or oil is melted, pull the pan out of the oven and add the nuts. Stir them to coat.
3. Roast for 20 to 25 minutes. Remove from the oven and salt to taste.

YIELD: 8 servings, per ¼ cup (weight will vary) serving:

Almonds: 260 Calories; 24 g Fat (79.2% calories from fat); 7 g Protein; 7 g Carbohydrate; 4 g Dietary Fiber; 3 g net carbs

Pecans: 231 Calories; 24 g Fat (88.4% calories from fat); 2 g Protein; 5 g Carbohydrate; 2 g Dietary Fiber; 3 g net carbs

Walnuts: 241 Calories; 23 g Fat (82.2% calories from fat); 8 g Protein; 4 g Carbohydrate; 2 g Dietary Fiber; 2 g net carbs

SOY AND GINGER PECANS

I gave away tins of these for Christmas one year and got rave reviews. Use coconut oil if you're dairy-free.

4 tablespoons (55 g) butter or coconut oil

3 tablespoons (45 ml) soy sauce

2 cups (200 g) shelled pecans

1 teaspoon ground ginger

1. Preheat the oven to 300°F (150°C, or gas mark 2). Put the butter or coconut oil in a shallow roasting pan and put it in the oven as it warms.

2. When the butter or oil is melted, add the pecans to the pan and stir until they're all coated.

3. Roast for 15 minutes, and then remove from the oven and stir in the soy sauce. Sprinkle the ginger evenly over the nuts and stir that in as well.

4. Roast for another 10 minutes.

YIELD: 8 servings, each with: 235 Calories; 24 g Fat (86.9% calories from fat); 3 g Protein; 6 g Carbohydrate; 2 g Dietary Fiber; 4 g net carbs

WORCESTERSHIRE NUTS

I like to use this combination of nuts, but feel free to use just one or the other or to experiment with your own proportions. If you're dairy-free, be sure to use coconut oil.

4 tablespoons (55 g) butter or coconut oil

1 cup (100 g) shelled pecans

1 cup (100 g) shelled walnuts

3 tablespoons (45 ml) Worcestershire sauce

1. Preheat the oven to 300°F (150°C, or gas mark 2). Put the butter or coconut oil in a shallow baking pan and slide it into the oven as it warms.

2. When the butter or oil is melted, add the nuts to the pan and stir until they're all evenly coated.

3. Roast for 15 minutes and then remove from the oven and stir in the Worcestershire sauce.

4. Roast for another 10 minutes.

YIELD: 8 servings, each with: 240 Calories; 24 g Fat (83.7% calories from fat); 5 g Protein; 5 g Carbohydrate; 2 g Dietary Fiber; 3 g net carbs

CURRIED PECANS

When I first came up with this combination of seasonings, I intended to use it on chicken, but I've discovered that it's also delicious on pecans. Be sure to use coconut oil if you're dairy-free.

4 tablespoons (55 g) butter or coconut oil

2 cups (200 g) shelled pecans

1 tablespoon (9 g) Chicken Seasoning (page 275)

1. Preheat the oven to 300°F (150°C, or gas mark 2). Put the butter or coconut oil in a shallow roasting pan and put it in the oven as it warms.

2. When the butter or oil is melted, add the pecans and stir until they're evenly coated.

3. Roast for 20 to 25 minutes.

4. Remove from the oven, sprinkle the Chicken Seasoning over the nuts, and stir to coat.

YIELD: 8 servings, each with: 232 Calories; 24 g Fat (88.1% calories from fat); 2 g Protein; 5 g Carbohydrate; 2 g Dietary Fiber; 3 g net carbs

DANA'S SNACK MIX

You can buy shelled sunflower seeds and pumpkin seeds in bulk at most health food stores, and you should be able to get raw cashew pieces there, too. (You can also get pumpkin seeds at Latino markets under the name "pepitas.") This makes a lot! It's certainly enough for a party. If you're making it just for you and the family, consider freezing it in several small zipper-lock bags to prevent spoilage.

The wild card here is the seasoned salt. If you can find one that is gluten-free and grain-free, the recipe will be. The popular Lawry's brand includes cornstarch. It does not include any obvious gluten-bearing ingredients, but is not labeled "gluten-free." If you're avoiding gluten on principle, it should be fine. If you're a celiac disease sufferer, you'll want to be wary.

6 tablespoons (85 g) butter

3 tablespoons (45 ml) Worcestershire sauce

1½ teaspoons garlic powder

2½ teaspoons (10 g) seasoned salt

1 teaspoon onion powder

2½ (363 g) cups raw, shelled sunflower seeds

2½ cups (345 g) raw, shelled pumpkin seeds

1 cup (145 g) almonds

1 cup (100 g) pecans

1 cup (100 g) walnuts

1 cup (140 g) raw cashew pieces

3½ ounces (100 g) pork rinds, broken up into nut-sized bits

1. Preheat the oven to 250°F (120°C, or gas mark ½).

2. In a small pan, melt the butter and stir in the Worcestershire sauce, garlic powder, seasoned salt, and onion powder.

3. In a large bowl, combine the seeds, nuts, and pork rinds. Pour the melted butter mixture over them and mix very well.

4. Put the mixture in large roasting pan and bake for 2 hours, stirring occasionally.

5. Allow the mixture to cool and store in an airtight container.

YIELD: 22 servings, each with: 423 Calories; 36 g Fat (72.5% calories from fat); 19 g Protein; 12 g Carbohydrate; 4 g Dietary Fiber; 8 g net carbs

RANCH SNACK MIX

You've had ranch dressing and ranch dip, but how about that great ranch flavor cooked right into the snack? Hidden Valley Ranch brand dressing mix is gluten-free. I cannot vouch for other brands.

2 cups (276 g) raw, shelled pumpkin seeds

2 cups (290 g) raw, shelled sunflower seeds

2 cups (290 g) dry-roasted peanuts

1 cup (145 g) raw almonds

1 cup (140 g) raw cashew pieces

2 tablespoons (28 ml) MCT or bland coconut oil, melted

1 packet (1 ounce, or 28 g) of dry ranch salad dressing mix

1 teaspoon lemon pepper

1 teaspoon dried dill weed

½ teaspoon garlic powder

1. Preheat the oven to 350°F (180°C, or gas mark 4).

2. In a large mixing bowl, combine the pumpkin seeds, sunflower seeds, peanuts, almonds, and cashews. Add the oil and stir to coat. Add the dressing mix, lemon pepper, dill, and garlic powder and stir until well distributed.

3. Put the seasoned nuts in a shallow roasting pan and roast for 45 to 60 minutes, stirring occasionally, until the almonds are crisp through.

YIELD: 16 servings, each with: 473 Calories; 40 g Fat (71.3% calories from fat); 21 g Protein; 15 g Carbohydrate; 6 g Dietary Fiber; 9 g net carbs

ASIAN PUNKS

Pumpkin seeds are terrific for you—they're a great source of both magnesium and zinc. And they taste great, too. I can buy them in the bulk section of my local health food stores; they're also a staple at Latino markets, under the name "pepitas."

2 cups (276 g) raw, shelled pumpkin seeds

2 tablespoons (28 ml) soy sauce (Use San-J brand if you're gluten-free.)

½ teaspoon powdered ginger

Liquid stevia, monkfruit, or sucralose to equal 2 teaspoons of sugar in sweetness

1. Preheat the oven to 350°F (180°C, or gas mark 4).

2. In a mixing bowl, combine the pumpkin seeds, soy sauce, ginger, and sweetener, mixing well.

3. Spread the pumpkin seeds in a shallow roasting pan. Roast for about 45 minutes or until the seeds are dry, stirring two or three times during roasting.

YIELD: 6 servings, each with: 399 Calories; 32 g Fat (66.6% calories from fat); 25 g Protein; 11 g Carbohydrate; 3 g Dietary Fiber; 8 net carbs

INDIAN PUNKS

You can buy curry-flavored pumpkin seeds, but these are better tasting and better for you.

In addition to all the minerals found in the pumpkin seeds, you get the turmeric in the curry powder, which is believed to help prevent cancer and reduce inflammation. Be sure to use coconut oil if you're dairy-free.

4 tablespoons (55 g) butter or coconut oil

2½ tablespoons (16 g) curry powder, hot or mild as you prefer

2 cloves of garlic, crushed

2 cups (276 g) raw, shelled pumpkin seeds

Salt

1. Preheat the oven to 300°F (150°C, or gas mark 2).
2. Melt the butter or coconut oil in a small skillet over medium heat. Add the curry powder and garlic and stir for 2 to 3 minutes.
3. In a mixing bowl, add the seasoned butter to the pumpkin seeds and stir until well coated.
4. Spread the pumpkin seeds in a shallow roasting pan and roast for 30 minutes. Sprinkle lightly with salt.

YIELD: 6 servings, each with: 473 Calories; 40 g Fat (70.6% calories from fat); 25 g Protein; 12 g Carbohydrate; 4 g Dietary Fiber; 8 g net carbs

PUNKS ON THE RANGE

These are spicy-chili-crunchy. If you miss barbecue-flavored potato chips, try snacking on these.

2 cups (276 g) raw, shelled pumpkin seeds

1 tablespoon (15 ml) oil (I'd use MCT, but olive or bland coconut oil, melted, will work, too.)

1 tablespoon (8 g) chili powder

1 teaspoon salt

1. Preheat the oven to 350°F (180°C, or gas mark 4).
2. In a mixing bowl, combine the pumpkin seeds and oil and stir until well coated. Add the chili powder and salt and stir again.
3. Spread the seeds in a shallow roasting pan and roast for about 30 minutes.

YIELD: 6 servings, each with: 419 Calories; 34 g Fat (68.3% calories from fat); 25 g Protein; 11 g Carbohydrate; 3 g Dietary Fiber; 8 g net carbs

BARBECUED PEANUTS

Put these out at a party and watch them evaporate!
Read the label on your liquid smoke seasoning—
some have sugar and some do not. Some brands
of dry-roasted peanuts are gluten-free, some are
not, so pay attention to labels if gluten concerns you.

1 tablespoon (15 ml) liquid smoke

1 teaspoon Worcestershire sauce

Dash of Tabasco

½ cup (120 ml) water

1½ cups (218 g) dry-roasted peanuts

3 tablespoons (45 g) butter

Garlic salt

1. Preheat the oven to 250°F (120°C, or gas mark ½).

2. In a saucepan, combine the liquid smoke, Worcestershire sauce, Tabasco, and water. Bring to a simmer.

3. Turn off the heat and stir in the peanuts. Let the peanuts sit in the liquid for 30 minutes, stirring occasionally.

4. Drain off the liquid and spread the peanuts in a shallow roasting pan. Bake for at least 1 hour, stirring occasionally, until they're good and dry.

5. When the peanuts are thoroughly dry, melt the butter and stir it into the peanuts to coat. Sprinkle lightly with garlic salt.

YIELD: 6 servings, each with: 266 Calories; 24 g Fat (76.2% calories from fat); 9 g Protein; 8 g Carbohydrate; 3 g Dietary Fiber; 5 g net carbs

ANTIPASTO

This easy dish makes a nice light summer supper. Use some or all of the ingredients listed here, adjusting quantities as necessary.

Wedges of cantaloupe

Salami

Boiled ham

Pepperoncini (mildly hot salad peppers, available in jars near the pickles and olives)

Halved or quartered hard-boiled eggs

Marinated mushrooms

Black and green olives (Get the good ones.)

Jarred roasted red peppers

Tuna canned in olive oil

Sardines canned in olive oil

Marinated artichoke hearts (available in jars)

Simply arrange some or all of these things decoratively on a platter, put out a stack of small plates and some forks, and dinner is served.

YIELD: Yield varies with your taste and needs, but here are the basic nutritional breakdowns for the items on your antipasto platter:

Cantaloupe, ⅛ of a small melon: 24 Calories; trace Fat (6.4% calories from fat); 1 g Protein; 6 g Carbohydrate; 1 g Dietary Fiber; 5 g net carbs

Salami, 1 average slice: 58 Calories; 5 g Fat (73.7% calories from fat); 3 g Protein; 1 g Carbohydrate; 0 g Dietary Fiber; 1 g net carbs

Ham, 1 ounce (28 g): 52 Calories; 3 g Fat (53.5% calories from fat); 5 g Protein; 1 g Carbohydrate; 0 g Dietary Fiber; 1 g net carbs

Pepperoncini, 1 average piece: 3 Calories; 0 g Fat (0.0% calories from fat); 0 g Protein; 1 g Carbohydrate; trace Dietary Fiber; 1 g net carbs

Hard-boiled egg, ½: 33 Calories; 2 g Fat (62.2% calories from fat); 3 g Protein; trace Carbohydrate; 0 g Dietary Fiber; trace net carbs

Marinated mushrooms, 1 average piece: trace Protein; 1 g Carbohydrate; trace Dietary Fiber; 1 g net carbs (The fat numbers are omitted because we cannot determine how much is drained off with the marinade.)

Black olives, 1 large: 5 Calories; trace Fat (77.5% calories from fat); trace Protein; trace Carbohydrate; trace Dietary Fiber; 0 g net carbs

Green olives, 1 large: 5 Calories; trace Fat (77.5% calories from fat); trace Protein; trace Carbohydrate; trace Dietary Fiber; 0 g net carbs

Jarred roasted red pepper, 1 slice: 14 Calories; trace Fat (5.3% calories from fat); trace Protein; 3 g Carbohydrate; 1 g Dietary Fiber; 2 g net carbs

Tuna canned in olive oil, 3 ounces (85 g): 168 Calories; 7 g Fat (38.8% calories from fat); 25 g Protein; 0 g Carbohydrate; 0 g Dietary Fiber; 0 g net carbs

Sardines canned in olive oil, 2 average: 50 Calories; 3 g Fat (51.1% calories from fat); 6 g Protein; 0 g Carbohydrate; 0 g Dietary Fiber; 0 g net carbs (plus 92 mg of calcium!)

Marinated artichoke hearts, 1: 24 Calories; 1 g Fat (52.9% calories from fat); 1 g Protein; 2 g Carbohydrate; 1 g Dietary Fiber; 1 g net carbs

MAGGIE'S MUSHROOMS

Reader Maggie Cosey sent this recipe. It's so easy, so good! Use gluten-free Worcestershire sauce if you need to.

1½ pounds (680 g) large mushrooms

20 stuffed green olives

2 packages (8 ounces, or 225 g each) of cream cheese, softened

2 tablespoons (28 ml) Worcestershire sauce–or as much as ¼ cup (60 ml), but remember it adds carbs

1. Preheat the oven to 350°F (180°C, or gas mark 4).
2. Wipe the mushrooms clean with a damp cloth and remove their stems.
3. Chop the olives by hand or in a food processor.
4. In a mixing bowl, combine the olives, cream cheese, and Worcestershire sauce. (Be careful with the Worcestershire; there's a fine line between not enough and too much, it's better to err on the side of not enough.)
5. Spoon the mixture into the mushroom caps and place them in a broiler pan.
6. Bake for 15 to 20 minutes or until the cream cheese is slightly browned.

YIELD: About 45 pieces, each with: 42 Calories; 4 g Fat (78.9% calories from fat); 1 g Protein; 1 g Carbohydrate; trace Dietary Fiber; 1 g net carbs

SIMPLE LOW-CARB STUFFED MUSHROOMS

Reader Kayann Kretschmar says, "My Christmas Eve guests raved about them!" Don't forget to save the stems to sauté for omelets or steaks. If you're gluten-free, be sure to read the label on your sausage.

1 pound (455 g) medium mushrooms

1 pound (455 g) bulk breakfast sausage, hot, mild, or sage, as you prefer

1 package (8 ounces, or 225 g) of cream cheese

1. Preheat the oven to 350°F (180°C, or gas mark 4).
2. Wipe the mushrooms clean with a damp cloth. Remove their stems and use a paring knife to make the hole for stuffing larger.
3. Brown and drain the sausage and stir in the cream cheese. Spoon the mixture into the mushroom caps.
4. Bake for 20 minutes or until the sausage is cooked through.

YIELD: About 30 pieces, each with: 93 Calories; 9 g Fat (84.4% calories from fat); 3 g Protein; 1 g Carbohydrate; trace Dietary Fiber; 1 g net carbs

KAY'S CRAB-STUFFED MUSHROOMS

These are for my cyberpal Kay, who repeatedly begged me to come up with a low-carb recipe for crab puffs. I tried and tried, but all my attempts were relatively pathetic. So I made crab-stuffed mushrooms instead, and they were a big hit. Warning: You may be tempted to make these with "fake crab" to save money. Don't. That stuff has a ton of carbohydrates added. Spend the extra couple of bucks and use real crab. Or, come to think of it, try 'em with tuna instead.

1 pound (455 g) fresh mushrooms	¼ cup (33 g) grated Parmesan cheese
1 can (6½ ounces, or 180 g) of flaked crab	10–12 scallions, including the crisp part of the green shoot, finely sliced
2 ounces (55 g) cream cheese, softened	Dash of Tabasco
¼ cup (60 g) mayonnaise	¼ teaspoon pepper

1. Preheat the oven to 325°F (170°C, or gas mark 3).

2. Wipe the mushrooms clean with a damp cloth and remove their stems.

3. In a good-sized bowl, combine the crabmeat, cream cheese, mayonnaise, Parmesan cheese, scallions, Tabasco, and pepper, mixing well.

4. Spoon the mixture into the mushroom caps and arrange them in a large, flat roasting pan.

5. Bake for 45 minutes to 1 hour or until the mushrooms are done through. Serve hot (although folks will still scarf 'em down after they cool off).

YIELD: About 30 pieces, each with: 34 Calories; 3 g Fat (64.7% calories from fat); 2 g Protein; 1 g Carbohydrate; trace Dietary Fiber; 1 g net carbs

VICKI'S CRAB-STUFFED MUSHROOMS

This recipe is from Vicki Cash's 2002 book *Low Carb Success Calendar*, and it's quite different from my version. I didn't alter this recipe because it's Vicki's. Still, I don't eat Wasa crackers anymore. I'd probably use ¼ cup (20 g) or so of pork rind crumbs. Suit yourself. The pork rinds will drop the carb count, of course.

10 ounces (280 g) medium portobello mushrooms	1 tablespoon (3 g) dried dill weed
2 Wasa Fiber Rye crackers	1 teaspoon dehydrated onion flakes
1 can (6 ounces, or 170 g) of crabmeat	½ cup (50 g) grated Parmesan cheese
1 egg	
2 tablespoons (28 ml) lemon juice	

1. Preheat the oven to 400°F (200°C, or gas mark 6).

2. Wipe the mushrooms clean with a damp cloth and remove their stems. Set aside ½ cup (35 g) of stems. Place the caps on an ungreased rimmed baking sheet.

3. Use a food processor with the S-blade attached to grind the crackers into coarse crumbs. Add the ½ cup (35 g) of mushroom stems, processing until coarsely chopped. Add the crabmeat, egg, lemon juice, dill, onion flakes, and Parmesan cheese. Mix thoroughly.

4. Spoon the mixture into the mushroom caps and bake for 12 to 15 minutes or until the top of the stuffing is slightly browned. Serve hot.

YIELD: Serves 6 as an appetizer, each serving with:
94 Calories; 3 g Fat (31.8% calories from fat); 11 g Protein; 6 g Carbohydrate; 1 g Dietary Fiber; 5 g net carbs

TWO-CHEESE TUNA-STUFFED MUSHROOMS

Of all the stuffed mushrooms I've cooked or sampled, these are my absolute favorites. Again, save the stems for sautéing!

½ pound (225 g) fresh mushrooms

5 ounces (140 g) tuna canned in olive oil

½ cup (60 g) shredded smoked Gouda

2 tablespoons (10 g) grated Parmesan cheese

3 tablespoons (42 g) mayonnaise

1 scallion, finely minced

1. Preheat the oven to 350°F (180°C, or gas mark 4).

2. Wipe the mushrooms clean with a damp cloth and remove their stems.

3. Combine the tuna, Gouda cheese, Parmesan cheese, mayonnaise, and minced scallion and mix well.

4. Spoon the mixture into the mushroom caps and arrange them in a shallow roasting pan. Add just enough water to cover the bottom of the pan. Bake for 15 minutes and serve hot.

YIELD: About 15 pieces, each with: 59 Calories; 4 g Fat (65.7% calories from fat); 4 g Protein; 1 g Carbohydrate; trace Dietary Fiber; 1 g net carbs

TURKEY-PARMESAN STUFFED MUSHROOMS

Use the stuff labeled simply "ground turkey," rather than "ground turkey breast." It's less expensive, more flavorful, and has more fat.

1 pound (455 g) ground turkey

¾ cup (75 g) grated Parmesan cheese

½ cup (115 g) mayonnaise

1 teaspoon dried oregano

1 teaspoon dried basil

2 cloves of garlic, crushed

1 teaspoon salt or Vege-Sal

¼ teaspoon pepper

1½ pounds (680 g) mushrooms

1. Preheat the oven to 350°F (180°C, or gas mark 4).

2. Combine the ground turkey, Parmesan cheese, mayonnaise, oregano, basil, garlic, salt, and pepper, mixing very well.

3. Wipe the mushrooms clean with a damp cloth and remove their stems.

4. Spoon the mixture into the mushroom caps and place them in a shallow roasting pan. Add just enough water to cover the bottom of the pan. Bake for 20 minutes or until the turkey is cooked through and serve hot.

YIELD: About 45 pieces, each with: 43 Calories; 3 g Fat (68.6% calories from fat); 3 g Protein; 1 g Carbohydrate; trace Dietary Fiber; 1 g net carbs

HORS D'OEUVRES, SNACKS, AND PARTY NIBBLES

RUMAKI

A mid-century cocktail party classic, but there's no need to wait for a party. Think you can't get the family to eat liver? Make these.

½ cup (120 ml) soy sauce

¼ cup (60 ml) dry sherry

1 clove of garlic, crushed

1 slice of fresh ginger, about ¼ inch (6 mm) thick, finely minced

12 slices of bacon

12 chicken livers

24 canned whole water chestnuts

1. Mix together the soy sauce, sherry, garlic, and ginger to make the marinade.

2. Cut the bacon strips and chicken livers in half. (You'll find that the livers sort of have two halves naturally.)

3. Wrap each chicken liver half around a water chestnut and then wrap a half-strip of bacon around each chicken liver. Spear the whole thing with a large toothpick or bamboo skewer, making sure you pierce the water chestnut on the way through.

4. Submerge your speared bundles in the marinade and let them marinate in the fridge for at least an hour. (You can let them marinate overnight, if you want to prepare this dish well in advance of your company arriving.)

5. When you're ready to eat, take the bundles out of the marinade. Broil or grill them for 5 to 7 minutes on each side until the bacon is crisp.

YIELD: 24 pieces, each with: 80 Calories; 2 g Fat (25.3% calories from fat); 5 g Protein; 10 g Carbohydrate; 2 g Dietary Fiber, 8 g net carbs. MasterCook is assuming you'll consume all of the marinade and of course, you won't. I cannot find a carb count for individual water chestnuts, but they're the main source of carbs, here. If you like, you may leave the water chestnuts out of these, and the carb count will drop to a mere trace.

COUNTRY-STYLE PÂTÉ

This is really good. Plus, as pâté goes, it's easy to make. And how fancy will you feel, telling your friends, "Oh, the pâté'? Yes, I made that . . . ."

6 slices of bacon

2 tablespoons (28 g) butter

1 cup (70 g) sliced mushrooms

½ cup (80 g) chopped onion

1 cup (225 g) chicken livers

½ teaspoon Worcestershire sauce

2 tablespoons (28 g) mayonnaise

Scant ½ teaspoon salt or Vege-Sal

¼ teaspoon pepper

Celery sticks, bell pepper strips, or low-carb crackers (for serving)

1. In a heavy skillet over medium heat, fry the bacon until it just starts to get crisp. Remove the bacon and drain and reserve the grease.

2. Turn the burner down to low and melt the butter and a little of the bacon grease in the skillet. Sauté the mushrooms and onion in the skillet until they're quite limp (about 15 minutes).

3. While they're sautéing, fill a medium saucepan with water and bring it to a boil. Put the chicken livers in the water (make sure you keep stirring those sautéing vegetables) and bring the water back to a boil. Cover the pan, turn off the burner, and let it sit for 15 minutes.

4. Drain the chicken livers. Put them in a food processor with the S-blade in place and pulse two or three times to grind the chicken livers. Crumble and add the bacon and the mushroom-and-onion mixture. Pulse to combine. Add the Worcestershire sauce, mayonnaise, salt, and pepper and pulse again until well combined. Serve with celery sticks, pepper strips, or low-carb crackers.

YIELD: 12 servings, each with: 81 Calories; 6 g Fat (68.8% calories from fat); 5 g Protein; 2 g Carbohydrate; trace Dietary Fiber; 2 g net carbs (plus a ridiculous supply of vitamins from the liver!)

CHRISTMAS LIVER PÂTÉ

Reader Elizabeth Czilok sent this recipe and said, "It's cute, Christmassy, yummy, and low-carb." Save it for Christmas if you like, but my recipe tester insists it's good any time and on nearly anything.

8 ounces (225 g) liverwurst (Oscar Meyer is the lowest carb I've found.)

1 package (8 ounces, or 225 g) of cream cheese, softened

⅓ cup (53 g) finely chopped onion

2-3 tablespoons (30–45 g) sour cream

½ teaspoon Worcestershire sauce

¼ teaspoon hot pepper sauce (optional)

Stuffed olives (for garnish)

Low-carb crackers and cut-up vegetables (for serving)

1. Mix the liverwurst, half of the cream cheese, the onion, sour cream, Worcestershire sauce, and hot pepper sauce, combining well.

2. Form a mound of pâté in the center of a serving dish. Place the dish and pâté in the freezer for about 15 minutes.

3. Frost with the remaining softened cream cheese.

4. Slice a few green olives stuffed with pimentos so the green is a circle on the outside with the red pimento on the inside. Arrange them on the outside of the mound as a garnish and serve with low-carb crackers and veggies.

YIELD: 16 servings, each with: 101 Calories; 9 g Fat (83.2% calories from fat); 3 g Protein; 1 g Carbohydrate; trace Dietary Fiber; 1 g net carbs

CELERY STUFFED WITH BLUE CHEESE AND CREAM CHEESE

Reader Jeannette Regas sent this easy low-carb crowd-pleaser. I might add a dash or two of Tabasco to this, but then then I'm a chili-head.

5 or 6 large ribs of celery

¼ cup (30 g) crumbled blue cheese, at room temperature

1 package (8 ounces, or 225 g) of cream cheese, at room temperature

Heavy cream (optional)

Salt and pepper

1. Clean the ribs of celery and cut them into 3- to 4-inch (7.5 to 10 cm) pieces.

2. Mix the crumbled blue cheese with the cream cheese, adding a little heavy cream to make it smooth, if necessary. Add a little salt and pepper to taste.

3. Stuff into the celery and serve.

YIELD: 18 pieces, each with: 53 Calories; 5 g Fat (82.8% calories from fat); 1 g Protein; 1 g Carbohydrate; trace Dietary Fiber; 1 g net carbs

FRIED CHEESE

This is the sort of decadence I never would have considered in my low-fat days! If you miss cheese crackers, try this! The measurements here are just for the sake of analysis. You can eyeball this—just heat some oil or bacon grease and throw in a handful or two of shredded cheese. It is best to use freshly-shredded cheese, though. The cellulose used to prevent clumping in packaged shredded cheese changes the texture.

2 or 3 tablespoons (28 or 45 ml) olive, MCT, or melted bland coconut oil– or bacon grease!

½–¾ cup (58–90 g) shredded Cheddar, Monterey Jack, or jalapeño Jack cheese

1. Spray a small, heavy-bottomed, nonstick skillet with nonstick cooking spray and place over medium-high heat.
2. Add the oil and then the cheese. The cheese will melt and bubble and spread to fill the bottom of the skillet.
3. Let the cheese fry until it's crisp and brown around the edges. Use a spatula to lift up an edge and check whether the cheese is brown all over the bottom; if it isn't, let it go another minute or so.
4. When the fried cheese is good and brown, carefully flip it and fry the other side until it, too, is brown.
5. Remove the cheese from the skillet, drain, and lie it flat to cool. Break into pieces and eat.

YIELD: 1 serving with: 233 Calories; 23 g Fat (87.4% calories from fat); 7 g Protein; trace Carbohydrate; 0 g Dietary Fiber; trace net carbs

Cheesy Bowls and Taco Shells

For a tasty, cheesy, tortilla-like bowl, follow the directions for Fried Cheese, until you get to step 5. Then, remove and drain the cheese, but drape it over the bottom of a bowl to cool. When it cools and hardens, you'll have a cheesy, edible bowl to eat a taco salad out of.

You can also make a taco shell by folding the cheese disc in half and propping it partway open. Be careful when handling it, though; hot cheese can burn you pretty seriously.

SAGANAKI

If you've never tried the Greek cheese Kasseri, you're in for a treat. This dish is fantastically delicious and has a dramatic, fiery presentation to boot. I've tried this with or without the rice protein—it's a little crisper with, but there's not a huge difference. Do make sure your cheese is a good ½ inch (1.3 cm) thick, or it's liable to just melt away on you.

Olive oil

¼ pound (115 g) Kasseri, in a slab ½ inch (1.3 cm) thick

2 tablespoons (10 g) rice protein powder (optional)

1 shot of brandy

¼ of a lemon

1. Heat ¼ inch (6 mm) of olive oil in a heavy skillet over medium heat. When the oil is hot, add the cheese.
2. If using the rice protein powder, spread it on a plate and dust it all over the slab of cheese.
3. Fry until golden and crisp on both sides, turning only once. Remove from the pan and put on a fireproof plate.

4. Pour the brandy evenly over the hot cheese, strike a match, and light the brandy on fire. It is traditional to shout "Opa!" at this moment.

5. Squeeze the lemon over the flaming cheese, putting out the fire. Divide in half and scarf it down!

YIELD: 2 servings, each with: 311 Calories; 19 g Fat (58.2% calories from fat); 26 g Protein; 5 g Carbohydrate; trace Dietary Fiber; 5 g net carbs. The nutritional stats don't include the oil because I don't know how much you need to measure ¼ inch (6mm) in your skillet, and anyway, most of it gets left behind.

SOUTHWESTERN SAGANAKI

This is a yummy twist on the traditional Saganaki and a perfect starter for a fiery Mexican dinner for two.

Olive oil

¼ pound (115 g) pepper Jack cheese, in a slab ½ inch (1.3 cm) thick

2 tablespoons (10 g) rice protein powder (optional)

1 shot of tequila

¼ of a lime

---

1. Heat ¼ inch (6 mm) of olive oil in a heavy skillet over medium heat. When the oil is hot, add the cheese.

2. If using the rice protein powder, put it on a plate and dust the cheese all over with it.

3. Fry until golden and crisp on both sides, turning only once. Remove from the pan and put on a fireproof plate.

4. Pour the tequila evenly over the hot cheese, strike a match, and light on fire. I suppose for this version you should shout "Olé!"

5. Squeeze the lime over the flaming cheese, putting out the fire.

YIELD: 2 servings, each with: 275 Calories; 18 g Fat (64.2% calories from fat); 20 g Protein; 2 g Carbohydrate; trace Dietary Fiber; 2 g net carbs

PICKLED SHRIMP

This recipe will feed a crowd, so make it when you have plenty of people to share with. The statistics on this are high because I have no way to calculate for the marinade that is poured off. Just figure it's lower in carbs, calories, fat—everything but protein—than the numbers suggest.

6 cups (1.4 L) water

¼ cup (60 ml) dry sherry

½ teaspoon peppercorns

1 bay leaf

6 teaspoons (36 g) salt, divided

3 pounds (1.4 kg) raw shrimp, medium-sized, shelled and deveined

1 cup (235 ml) olive or MCT oil

⅔ cup (160 ml) lemon juice

½ cup (120 ml) white vinegar

3 tablespoons (19 g) mixed pickling spice

Liquid stevia, monkfruit, or sucralose to equal 2 teaspoons of sugar in sweetness

2 sprigs of fresh dill, coarsely chopped

---

1. In a large saucepan over high heat, bring the water, sherry, peppercorns, bay leaf, and 2 teaspoons of salt to a boil.

2. Add the shrimp and bring back to a boil. Cook 1 minute longer and drain.

3. In a large bowl, combine the oil, lemon juice, vinegar, pickling spice, sweetener, dill, and the remaining 4 teaspoons (24 g) of salt. Add the shrimp and toss with this pickling mixture.

4. Cover the bowl and chill it and the platter you will serve the shrimp on in the refrigerator overnight.

5. To serve, drain off and discard the marinade and arrange the shrimp on the platter. Garnish with additional dill, if desired.

If it's going to be a long party, it's a good idea to set the platter or bowl on a bed of crushed ice in another container, to keep the shrimp cold.

YIELD: This should feed 24. Each person will get: 150 Calories; 10 g Fat (62.9% calories from fat); 12 g Protein; 2 g Carbohydrate; trace Dietary Fiber; 2 g net carbs

CRAB AND BACON BUNDLES

This quick, hot hors d'oeuvre will impress your guests. The bundles themselves are pretty much carb-free. Just keep an eye on your intake of the duck sauce. Oh, and don't use fake crab! That stuff almost always has a bunch of added carbs.

1 can (6 ounces, or 170 g) of crab, drained

1 scallion, finely minced

½ pound (225 g) bacon

Duck Sauce (page 284)

1. Flake the crab, removing any bits of shell or cartilage. Stir in the minced scallion and set aside.

2. Cut all your bacon strips in half crosswise, to make two shorter strips. Place a rounded ½ teaspoon or so of the crab mixture on the end of a bacon strip and roll the strip up around it, stretching the bacon slightly as you go. Pierce the bundle with a toothpick, to hold. Repeat until all the crab and bacon strips are used up.

3. Broil about 8 inches (20 cm) from heat, turning once or twice, until the bacon is crisp—no more than 10 minutes. Serve with Duck Sauce for dipping.

YIELD: About 24 bundles, each with: 62 Calories; 5 g Fat (70.7% calories from fat); 4 g Protein; trace Carbohydrate; trace Dietary Fiber; 0 g net carbs. These numbers do not include the Duck Sauce.

LOW-CARB MARGARITA MIX

Okay, this is neither a snack nor a nibble, but it sure is good for parties! And although it's not super low in carbs, it's considerably less sugary than the commercial stuff. Our tester C. Robertson says she used ReaLemon and ReaLime bottled juice and gives the recipe a 10. She liked it so much she made it a second time—the first time she used liquid sucralose and orange extract, the second time she used Valencia orange liquid stevia. She liked both, but gives the edge to the Valencia orange stevia. She also says to use it up when it's fresh. Guess you'll just have to invite a few friends over!

1½ cups (355 ml) lime juice

½ cup (120 ml) lemon juice

1½ teaspoons Valencia orange flavor liquid stevia OR liquid stevia, monk fruit, or sucralose to equal 1½ cups (300 g) of sugar in sweetness, PLUS ½ teaspoon orange extract

2 cups (475 ml) water

1. Combine all the ingredients in a blender for 1 minute and pour into a clean bottle. Refrigerate until ready to use.

2. To make a margarita, combine 2 ounces (60 ml) of tequila with 6 ounces (175 ml) of margarita mix and either put it through the blender with lots of ice or simply serve it on the rocks. Salted rim is optional!

YIELD: 6 servings, each with: 22 Calories; trace Fat (1.7% calories from fat); trace Protein; 7 g Carbohydrate; trace Dietary Fiber; 7 g net carbs. The analysis does not include tequila!

CHAPTER 3

Eggs and Dairy

efore I get to the recipes, I'd like to urge you to stop thinking of eggs solely as a breakfast food. Eggs are wildly nutritious, infinitely versatile, they cook in a flash, and they're inexpensive, to boot. If you want a fast meal at any time of day, think eggs.

If you can afford them, locally raised, pastured eggs are worth the extra money (says the girl with twenty-some chickens in her yard). Don't be fooled by a carton that says, "Free Range"—that just means there is, somewhere, a small opening that allows the chickens out into a fenced area, often paved. Don't pay extra for eggs from "chickens fed vegetarian feed," either—chickens are definitely not natural vegetarians. They're dinosaurs. Allowed to run, they will it almost anything small enough that comes across their path. This results in superior eggs.

That said, grocery store eggs are still plenty nutritious! Now, for some things to do with 'em.

Omelets 101

There's this big mystique about omelets, maybe because they're a part of classical French cookery. People think that omelets are magically difficult and that only a true gourmet chef can get them right. But I say: Bah. Omelets are easy. Believe it or not, I've been known to turn out omelets for twenty on a propane camp stove. (This is when my friends started referring to my pop-up trailer as "Dana's House of Omelets.")

You can learn to do this quickly. Really—you can.

Before you begin, you'll need a good pan. What's a "good pan"? I prefer a 7-inch (18 cm; medium-sized) skillet with a heavy bottom, sloping sides, and a nonstick surface. If your skillet is not-so-nonstick, give it a good shot of cooking spray.

Here's the really important thing to know about making omelets: The word "omelet" comes from a word meaning "to laminate," or to build up layers. And that's exactly what you do; you let a layer of beaten egg cook and then you lift up the edges and tip the pan so the raw egg runs under the cooked part. You do this all around the edges, of course, so you build it up evenly. The point is, you don't just let the beaten egg lie there in the skillet and wait for it to cook through. If you try this, the bottom will be hopelessly overdone before the top is set.

DANA'S EASY OMELET METHOD

1. First, have your filling ready. If you're using vegetables, you'll want to sauté them first. If you're using cheese, have it grated or sliced and ready to go. If you're making an omelet to use up leftovers—a great idea, by the way—warm them through in the microwave and have them standing by.

2. Coat your omelet pan well with cooking spray if it doesn't have a good nonstick surface and set it over medium-high heat.

3. While the skillet is heating, grab your eggs (two is the perfect number for this size pan, but one or three will work, too) and a bowl, crack the eggs, and beat them with a fork. Don't add water or milk or anything; just mix them up.

4. Test your pan to see if it's hot enough: A drop of water thrown in the pan should sizzle right away. Add a tablespoon (15 ml) of oil or butter, slosh it around to cover the bottom, and then pour in the eggs, all at once. They should sizzle, too, and immediately start to set.

5. When the bottom layer of egg is set around the edges—and this should happen quite quickly—lift the edge using a spatula or fork and tip the pan to let the raw egg flow underneath. Do this all around the edges until there's not enough raw egg to run.

6. Turn your burner to the lowest heat if you have a gas stove. (If you have an electric stove, you'll need a "warm" burner standing by; electric elements don't cool off fast enough for this job.) Put your filling on one-half of the omelet, lid the pan, and let it sit over very low heat for a minute or two—no more. Peek and see if the raw, shiny egg is gone from the top surface (although you can serve it that way if you like; that's how the French prefer their omelets) and the cheese, if you've used any, is melted. If not, re-cover the pan and let it go another minute or two.

7. When your omelet is done, slip a spatula under the half without the filling, fold it over, and then lift the whole thing onto a plate. Or, you can get fancy and tip the pan, letting the filling side of the omelet slide onto the plate and folding the top over as you go, but that takes some practice.

This makes a single-serving omelet. I think it's a lot easier to make several individual omelets than one big one, and omelets are so fast to make that it's not that big a deal. Anyway, that way you can customize your omelets to each individual's taste. If you're making more than two or three omelets, just set your oven to its very lowest heat and keep them warm in there.

Now, here are some ideas for what to put in your omelets.

CHEESE OMELET

This is pretty obvious, but you can't ignore a classic!

1 tablespoon (14 g) butter

2 eggs, beaten

2–3 ounces (55–85 g) sliced or shredded cheese (Cheddar, Monterey Jack, Colby, American, Swiss, Gruyère, Muenster, or whatever you prefer)

1. Make your omelet according to Dana's Easy Omelet Method (page 66), placing the cheese over half of your omelet when you get to step 6.
2. Cover, turn the burner to low, and cook until the cheese is melted (2 to 3 minutes).
3. Follow the directions to finish making the omelet.

YIELD: 1 serving with: 233 Calories; 20 g Fat (79.0% calories from fat); 11 g Protein; 1 g Carbohydrate; 0 g Dietary Fiber; 1 g net carbs

MACRO CHEESE OMELET

This is my husband's favorite! With all that cheese, this is mighty filling. Originally, this called for processed Swiss, which comes in "singles" like American cheese, and you may use them if you prefer. This combination of cheeses is not definitive. What do you have kicking around that needs to be used up? The point is to have maximum cheese!

1 tablespoon (14 g) butter

2 eggs, beaten

1–2 ounces (30–55 g) Cheddar, sliced or shredded

1–2 ounces (28–55 g) Monterey Jack, sliced or shredded

1 slice of Swiss

1. Make your omelet according to Dana's Easy Omelet Method (page 66), placing the cheese over half of your omelet when you get to step 6.
2. Cover, turn the burner to low, and cook until the cheese is melted (3 to 4 minutes).
3. Follow the directions to finish making the omelet.

YIELD: 1 immense serving—or 2, if you're in a sharing mood. Assuming 1, it will have: 779 Calories; 64 g Fat (74.1% calories from fat); 47 g Protein; 3 g Carbohydrate; 0 g Dietary Fiber; 3 g net carbs

VEGGIE CHEESE OMELET

You might not want to do this on a busy weekday morning, but it's an awesome Sunday brunch or quick supper. Heck, grab the vegetables and cheese from the grocery store salad bar and you can be eating ten minutes after you get home.

Olive oil or butter

2 eggs, beaten

¼ of green pepper, sliced in small strips, sautéed

¼ of medium onion, sliced and sautéed

2 or 3 mushrooms, sliced and sautéed

2 ounces (55 g) sliced or shredded Cheddar, Monterey Jack, Swiss, or Gruyère cheese

1. Make your omelet according to Dana's Easy Omelet Method (page 66), placing the filling over half of your omelet when you get to step 6.
2. Cover, turn the burner to low, and cook until the cheese is melted (3 to 4 minutes).
3. Follow the directions to finish making the omelet.

YIELD: 1 serving with: 362 Calories; 32 g Fat (78.7% calories from fat); 13 g Protein; 7 g Carbohydrate; 1 g Dietary Fiber; 6 g net carbs

MEXICAN OMELET

This will open your eyes in the morning! It's one of my favorites—I enjoy breathing fire. Should you have a ripe avocado on hand, a few slices wouldn't come amiss. And I don't have to remind you to read the label on your salsa, right?

1 tablespoon (14 g) butter

2 eggs, beaten

2 ounces (55 g) jalapeño Jack cheese, shredded or sliced

2 tablespoons (32 g) salsa

Hot sauce (optional)

1. Make your omelet according to Dana's Easy Omelet Method (page 66), placing the filling over half of your omelet when you get to step 6.
2. Cover, turn the burner to low, and cook until the cheese is melted (3 to 4 minutes).
3. Follow the directions to finish making the omelet. Top with salsa and hot sauce (if using).

YIELD: 1 serving with: 453 Calories; 38 g Fat (74.5% calories from fat); 25 g Protein; 3 g Carbohydrate; 1 g Dietary Fiber; 2 g net carbs

TACO OMELET

This is a great way to use up leftover taco filling. Heck, it's a good reason to make taco filling in the first place. You can, if you like, jazz up this omelet with a little diced onion, olives, or whatever else you like on a taco.

1 tablespoon (14 g) butter

2 eggs, beaten

¼ cup (50 g) beef, turkey, or chicken taco filling, warmed

2 tablespoons (14 g) shredded Cheddar cheese or Mexican Blend

2 tablespoons (32 g) salsa

1 tablespoon (15 g) sour cream

1. Make your omelet according to Dana's Easy Omelet Method (page 66), placing the taco filling over half of your omelet when you get to step 6.
2. Cover, turn the burner to low, and cook until the cheese is melted (3 to 4 minutes).
3. Follow the directions to finish making the omelet. Sprinkle with the cheese and top with salsa and sour cream.

YIELD: 1 serving. Using beef taco filling, it will have: 487 Calories; 40 g Fat (74.4% calories from fat); 26 g Protein; 5 g Carbohydrate; 1 g Dietary Fiber; 4 g net carbs. The analysis includes the salsa and sour cream, but not any garnishes you may add.

DENVER OMELET

This diner favorite is a snap! This is the classic Denver Omelet, but mushrooms are a nice addition.

1 tablespoon (14 g) butter

2 eggs

1 ounce (28 g) Cheddar cheese, shredded or sliced

¼ cup (38 g) diced cooked ham

¼ of a green pepper, cut in small strips, sautéed

¼ of a small onion, sliced and sautéed

1. Make your omelet according to Dana's Easy Omelet Method (page 66), placing the cheese and the sautéed ham and vegetables over half of your omelet when you get to step 6.
2. Cover, turn the burner to low, and cook until the cheese is melted (3 to 4 minutes).
3. Follow the directions to finish making the omelet.

YIELD: 1 serving with: 427 Calories; 33 g Fat (70.5% calories from fat); 25 g Protein; 7 g Carbohydrate; 1 g Dietary Fiber; 6 g net carbs

ARTICHOKE PARMESAN OMELET

This is a terrific combination. Your carb count will vary some, depending on the size of your artichoke heart, but it's going to be low carb, regardless.

1 tablespoon (14 g) butter

2 eggs, beaten

1–2 tablespoons (14–28 g) mayonnaise

1 canned artichoke heart, drained and sliced or chopped

2 tablespoons (10 g) grated Parmesan cheese

1. Make your omelet according to Dana's Easy Omelet Method (page 66), spreading the mayonnaise over half of your omelet and topping it with the artichoke heart and Parmesan cheese when you get to step 6.

2. Cover, turn the burner to low, and cook until the cheese is melted (3 to 4 minutes).

3. Follow the directions to finish making the omelet.

YIELD: 1 serving with: 387 Calories; 35 g Fat (80.4% calories from fat); 16 g Protein; 3 g Carbohydrate; 0 g Dietary Fiber; 3 g net carbs

"MY DAY TO CRAB" OMELET

My grandmother, Philippa, never got to go crabbing when the family was at the shore because she was too busy keeping house. Finally, feeling crabby, she declared, "It's my day to crab!" If it's your day to crab, this omelet will cheer you up. Be sure to use coconut oil if you're dairy-free.

¼ cup (34 g) canned crabmeat, flaked and picked over for shells and cartilage

2 scallions, sliced, including the crisp part of the green

1 tablespoon (14 g) butter or (15 ml) olive oil

2 eggs, beaten

1–2 tablespoons (14–28 g) mayonnaise

1. Mix the crabmeat with the scallions and have the mixture standing by. Make your omelet according to Dana's Easy Omelet Method (page 66), spreading the mayonnaise over half the omelet and topping it with the crab and scallion mixture when you get to step 6.

2. Cover, turn the burner to low, and cook about 3–4 minutes or until the egg is set and the crab warmed through.

3. Follow the directions to finish making the omelet.

YIELD: 1 serving with: 473 Calories; 44 g Fat (81.8% calories from fat); 19 g Protein; 3 g Carbohydrate; 1 g Dietary Fiber; 2 g net carbs

LEFTOVER LAMBLET

I adore roast lamb, and the leftovers are way too good to waste! This is very hearty and would make a great quick supper.

¼ pound (115 g) leftover roast lamb, cut into small chunks

½ of a small onion

2 tablespoons (10 g) grated Parmesan cheese

3 tablespoons (42 g) mayonnaise

½ teaspoon prepared horseradish

1 tablespoon (14 g) butter

2 eggs, beaten

1. In a food processor with the S-blade in place, grind the lamb and the onion together. When you have a pretty uniform consistency, add the Parmesan cheese, mayonnaise, and horseradish and pulse until everything is combined.

2. Place in a microwave-safe bowl and microwave on 50 percent power for just 1 minute or so, to warm through.

3. Make your omelet according to Dana's Easy Omelet Method (page 66), placing the lamb mixture evenly over half of your omelet when you get to step 6.

4. Cover, turn the burner to low, and cook until the eggs are set (60 to 90 seconds).

5. Follow the directions to finish making the omelet.

YIELD: 1 huge serving with: 845 Calories; 76 g Fat (79.5% calories from fat); 38 g Protein; 6 g Carbohydrate; 1 g Dietary Fiber; 5 g net carbs

CALIFORNIA OMELET

I've had breakfast down near the waterfront in San Diego. This is what it tastes like.

1 tablespoon (15 ml) olive oil

2 eggs, beaten

2 ounces (55 g) Monterey Jack cheese, shredded

3 or 4 slices of ripe avocado

¼ cup (8 g) alfalfa sprouts

1. Make your omelet according to Dana's Easy Omelet Method (page 66), placing the Monterey Jack cheese over half of your omelet when you get to step 6.

2. Cover, turn the burner to low, and cook until the cheese is melted (2 to 3 minutes).

3. Arrange the avocado and sprouts over the cheese and follow the directions to finish making the omelet.

Note: Alfalfa sprouts have become harder to find. Sprouts of varying kinds have been the source of outbreaks of food poisoning, as has a variety of raw produce. Omit them if you prefer. If you're a fan, be sure of your source and look for absolute freshness. Rinsing them well before use reduces but does not eliminate risk. For the record, I've never gotten sick from sprouts, but your risks are your own to take.

YIELD: 1 serving with: 545 Calories; 47 g Fat (77.1% calories from fat); 26 g Protein; 5 g Carbohydrate; 1 g Dietary Fiber; 4 g net carbs (and as much potassium as a banana!)

NEW YORK SUNDAY BRUNCH OMELET

My husband was absolutely blown away by this. It's unbelievably filling, by the way.

1 tablespoon (14 g) butter

2 eggs, beaten

2 ounces (55 g) cream cheese, thinly sliced

¼ cup (34 g) flaked smoked salmon

2 scallions, sliced

1. Make your omelet according to Dana's Easy Omelet Method (page 66), placing the cream cheese over half of your omelet when you get to step 6. (Don't try to spread the cream cheese—it won't work!)

2. Top with the salmon, cover, turn the burner to low, and cook until hot all the way through (2 to 3 minutes).

3. Scatter the scallions over salmon and follow the directions to finish making the omelet.

YIELD: 1 serving with: 480 Calories; 42 g Fat (77.7% calories from fat); 22 g Protein; 5 g Carbohydrate; 1 g Dietary Fiber; 4 g net carbs

OMELET CORDON BLEU

Canned asparagus is fine for this, but you may cook some up if you prefer or use leftover asparagus, should you have any. It shouldn't take more than a minute or two in the microwave to cook three asparagus spears!

1 tablespoon (14 g) butter

2 eggs

¼ cup (30 g) shredded Gruyère cheese

1 ounce (28 g) boiled or baked deli ham (or sliced leftover ham)

3 asparagus spears, cooked

1. Make your omelet according to Dana's Easy Omelet Method (page 66), placing the Gruyère cheese, ham, and asparagus over half of your omelet when you get to step 6.

2. Cover, turn the burner to low, and cook until the cheese is melted (2 to 3 minutes).

3. Follow the directions to finish making the omelet.

YIELD: 1 serving with: 426 Calories; 34 g Fat (72.9% calories from fat); 25 g Protein; 3 g Carbohydrate; 1 g Dietary Fiber; 2 g net carbs

BRAUNSCHWEIGER OMELET

Hey, don't look like that! Some of us love liverwurst! In the years since I invented this, I've come to like topping it with mayonnaise and grated Parmesan cheese. Gild that lily! Or not. It's up to you.

1 tablespoon (14 g) butter

2 eggs, beaten

2 ounces (55 g) braunschweiger (liverwurst), mashed a bit with a fork

2 or 3 slices of ripe tomato

1. Make your omelet according to Dana's Easy Omelet Method (page 66), spooning the mashed braunschweiger over half of your omelet and topping with the tomato slices when you get to step 6.

2. Cover, turn the burner to low, and cook until heated through (2 to 3 minutes).

3. Follow the directions to finish making the omelet.

YIELD: 1 serving with: 443 Calories; 39 g Fat (78.9% calories from fat); 19 g Protein; 4 g Carbohydrate; trace Dietary Fiber; 4 g net carbs

PIZZA OMELET

Remember that the pizza sauce is where the carbs lurk in this omelet, so govern yourself accordingly. I like Pastorelli's best. Muir Glen is good, too. Ragú makes two—Ragú Homemade Style Pizza Sauce has no sugar, but Ragú Pizza Quick Traditional Sauce does. Be choosy!

1 tablespoon (15 ml) olive oil

2 eggs, beaten

2 ounces (55 g) mozzarella cheese

2 tablespoons (31 g) jarred no-sugar-added pizza sauce, warmed

1 teaspoon grated Parmesan cheese

1. Make your omelet according to Dana's Easy Omelet Method (page 66), placing the mozzarella cheese over half of your omelet when you get to step 6.

2. Cover, turn the burner to low, and cook until the cheese is melted (2 to 3 minutes).

3. Follow the directions to finish making the omelet and top with the pizza sauce and Parmesan cheese.

YIELD: 1 serving with: 453 Calories; 37 g Fat (74.4% calories from fat); 24 g Protein; 4 g Carbohydrate; trace Dietary Fiber; 4 g net carbs

TUNA MELT OMELET

It's worth making extra tuna salad just to make this omelet. This is a great lunch.

½ cup (103 g) leftover tuna salad

1 tablespoon (14 g) butter

2 eggs, beaten

1 ounce (28 g) Swiss cheese or processed Swiss-style singles

1. Bring your tuna salad to room temperature, either by letting it sit on the counter for a short time or by microwaving it briefly.

2. Make your omelet according to Dana's Easy Omelet Method (page 66), placing the Swiss cheese over half of your omelet when you get to step 6.

3. Spread the tuna salad over the cheese, cover, turn the burner to low, and cook until hot through (3 to 4 minutes).

4. Follow the directions to finish making the omelet.

YIELD: 1 serving. The total nutrition counts will depend on your tuna salad recipe. The eggs, butter, and cheese come to: 339 Calories; 28 g Fat (74.9% calories from fat); 19 g Protein; 2 g Carbohydrate; 0 g Dietary Fiber; 2 g net carbs.

FAJITA OMELET

Again, this is a great way to use up leftovers! A slice or two of avocado or a scoop of guacamole would not come amiss here, should you have some on hand.

1 tablespoon (15 ml) olive oil

2 eggs

Leftover steak or chicken fajitas, warmed

1 tablespoon (15 g) sour cream

1. Make your omelet according to Dana's Easy Omelet Method (page 66), placing the fajitas over half of your omelet when you get to step 6.

2. Cover, turn the burner to low, and cook for 2 to 3 minutes.

3. Follow the directions to finish making the omelet and top with the sour cream.

YIELD: 1 serving with: 434 Calories; 41 g Fat (84.5% calories from fat); 12 g Protein; 5 g Carbohydrate; 1 g Dietary Fiber; 4 g net carbs. Analyzed for ⅛ of the Beef Fajita recipe on page 219 in the filling.

CHILI OMELET

Beef chili or turkey chili, it doesn't matter—they both make a great omelet. This analysis is based on using one-sixteenth of the All-Meat Chili recipe on page 215 as filling.

1 tablespoon (15 ml) olive oil

2 eggs, beaten

½ cup (100 g) All-Meat Chili, warmed

2 tablespoons (14 g) shredded Cheddar cheese

1 tablespoon (15 g) sour cream

1. Make your omelet according to Dana's Easy Omelet Method (page 66), placing the chili over half of your omelet when you get to step 6.

2. Top with the Cheddar cheese, cover, turn the burner to low, and cook until the cheese is melted (2 to 3 minutes).

3. Follow the directions to finish making the omelet and top with the sour cream.

YIELD: 1 serving with: 530 Calories; 45 g Fat (77.0% calories from fat); 25 g Protein; 5 g Carbohydrate; 1 g Dietary Fiber; 4 g net carbs

GUACOMELET

This omelet has become a cinch now that prepackaged single-serving cups of good-quality guacamole are available in grocery stores. Wholly Guacamole is perfect for this, and Aldi has a house brand, too.

1 tablespoon (15 ml) MCT oil, bland coconut oil, or olive oil

2 eggs, beaten

2 ounces (55 g) Monterey Jack cheese, sliced or shredded

¼ cup (56 g) guacamole

1. Make your omelet according to Dana's Easy Omelet Method (page 66), placing the Montery Jack cheese over half of your omelet when you get to step 6.

2. Spread the guacamole over the cheese, cover, turn the burner to low, and cook until the cheese is melted (3 to 4 minutes).

3. Follow the directions to finish making the omelet.

YIELD: 1 serving with: 553 Calories; 48 g Fat (77.4% calories from fat); 26 g Protein; 6 g Carbohydrate; 1 g Dietary Fiber; 5 g net fiber (plus almost 500 mg of potassium!)

AVOCADO CHEESE DIP OMELET

This is perhaps the most decadently delicious omelet I know how to make, and it's certainly a good enough reason to hide some of the Avocado Cheese Dip at your next party.

1 tablespoon (15 ml) olive oil

Avocado Cheese Dip (page 47)

2 eggs, beaten

1. Make your omelet according to Dana's Easy Omelet Method (page 66), placing the Avocado Cheese Dip over half of your omelet when you get to step 6.
2. Cover, turn the burner to low, and cook until hot all the way through (3 to 4 minutes).
3. Follow the directions to finish making the omelet.

YIELD: Assuming you use about ⅛ of a batch of Avocado Cheese Dip, your omelet will have: 583 Calories; 53 g Fat (80.9% calories from fat); 21 g Protein; 7 g Carbohydrate; 1 g Dietary Fiber; 6 g net carbs

Frittatas

The frittata is the Italian version of the omelet, and it involves no folding! If you're still intimidated by omelets, try a frittata.

CONFETTI FRITTATA

Hmm. Looking over this recipe fifteen years later, I'm wondering why I chose Mrs. Dash instead of salt and pepper. It's good this way, but feel free to add salt and pepper to taste if you like. Mrs. Dash has no gluten-bearing ingredients, but is not manufactured in a gluten-free facility. I'm okay with it, but if you're a celiac disease sufferer, caution may be warranted.

¼ pound (115 g) bulk pork sausage

¼ cup (38 g) diced green pepper

¼ cup (38 g) diced sweet red pepper

¼ cup (40 g) diced sweet red onion

¼ cup (25 g) grated Parmesan cheese

1 teaspoon Mrs. Dash, original flavor

8 eggs, beaten

1. In a large, ovenproof skillet, start browning and crumbling the sausage over medium heat. As some fat starts to cook out of it, add the green pepper, red pepper, and onion to the skillet. Cook the sausage and veggies until there's no pink left in the sausage. Spread the sausage and veggie mixture into an even layer in the bottom of the skillet.
2. Beat the Parmesan cheese and Mrs. Dash into the eggs and pour the mixture over the sausage and veggies in the skillet.
3. Turn the burner to low and cover the skillet. (If your skillet doesn't have a cover, use foil.) Let the frittata cook until the eggs are mostly set. This will take 25 to 30 minutes, but the size of your skillet will affect the speed of cooking, so check periodically.
4. When all but the very top of the frittata is set, slide it under the broiler for about 5 minutes or until the top is golden. Cut into wedges and serve.

YIELD: 4 servings, each with: 281 Calories; 22 g Fat (70.8% calories from fat); 17 g Protein; 4 g Carbohydrate; 1 g Dietary Fiber; 3 g net carbs

FAJITA FRITTATA

This makes a good supper for a family that is taco- and burrito-oriented. Feel free to substitute ground beef or turkey for the chicken if you like.

3 tablespoons (45 ml) MCT oil, bland coconut oil, or olive oil

½ of a green pepper, cut into small strips

1 small onion, sliced

1 boneless, skinless chicken breast, cut into thin strips

½ teaspoon chili powder

½ teaspoon cumin

1 teaspoon lime juice

½ teaspoon salt

8 eggs, beaten

6 ounces (170 g) shredded Monterey Jack or jalapeño Jack cheese

Salsa

Sour cream

1. Heat the oil in a large, heavy, ovenproof skillet and sauté the green pepper, onion, and chicken until the chicken has turned white and is done through. Stir in the chili powder, cumin, lime juice, and salt.

2. Spread the fajita mixture in an even layer in the bottom of the skillet and pour the beaten eggs over it.

3. Turn the burner to low and cover the skillet. (If your skillet doesn't have a cover, use foil.) Let the frittata cook until the eggs are mostly set, but still soft on top (7 to 10 minutes).

4. Scatter the cheese evenly over the top and slide the skillet under the broiler, about 4 inches (10 cm) from the heat, for 2 to 3 minutes or until the eggs are set and the cheese is just turning golden.

5. Cut in wedges, top each serving with a tablespoon (16 g) of salsa and a couple of teaspoons of sour cream and serve.

YIELD: 4 servings, each with: 498 Calories; 37 g Fat (66.2% calories from fat); 35 g Protein; 7 g Carbohydrate; 1 g Dietary Fiber; 6 g net carbs

ARTICHOKE FRITTATA

With those artichokes, this stands alone as a one-dish meal and is higher carb than some other dishes. But if you can afford another gram or two, a simple green salad with vinaigrette would make a nice contrast.

2 tablespoons (28 g) butter

1 can (13½ ounces, or 380 g) of quartered artichoke hearts, drained

1 small onion, sliced

1 clove of garlic

8 eggs, beaten

⅓ cup (33 g) grated Parmesan cheese

6 ounces (170 g) shredded Gruyère cheese

1. In a large, heavy skillet sprayed with nonstick cooking spray, melt the butter and begin sautéing the artichoke hearts, onion, and garlic over medium-low heat.

2. While sautéing, stir the eggs and Parmesan cheese together.

3. When the onions are limp, spread the vegetables evenly over the bottom of the skillet and pour the egg mixture over them.

4. Turn the burner to low and cover the skillet. (If your skillet doesn't have a cover, use foil.) Let the frittata cook until the eggs are mostly set (7 to 10 minutes).

5. Top with the shredded Gruyère cheese and slide the skillet under the broiler, about 4 inches (10 cm) from the heat. Broil for 2 to 3 minutes or until the eggs are set on top and the cheese is lightly golden. Cut into wedges and serve.

YIELD: 4 servings, each with: 435 Calories; 30 g Fat (63.5% calories from fat); 29 g Protein; 10 g Carbohydrate; 1 g Dietary Fiber; 9 g net carbs

ARTICHOKE-MUSHROOM FRITTATA

This is similar to the Artichoke Frittata on the opposite page, but adding mushrooms and leaving out the Parmesan cheese gives a whole new flavor. It's a little lower carb, too!

3 tablespoons (45 g) butter

1 cup (300 g) canned, quartered artichoke hearts, drained

4 ounces (115 g) fresh mushrooms, sliced

½ of a small onion, sliced

8 eggs, beaten

6 ounces (170 g) shredded Gruyère cheese

1. In a heavy skillet, melt the butter and sauté the artichoke hearts, mushrooms, and onion over medium-low heat until the mushrooms are limp.

2. Spread the vegetables evenly over the bottom of the skillet and pour the eggs over them.

3. Turn the burner to low and cover the skillet. (If your skillet doesn't have a cover, use foil.) Let the frittata cook until mostly set (7 to 10 minutes).

4. Top with the Gruyère cheese and slide the skillet under the broiler, about 4 inches (10 cm) from the heat. Broil for 2 to 3 minutes or until the eggs are set on top and the cheese is lightly golden. Cut into wedges and serve.

YIELD: 4 servings, each with: 417 Calories; 31 g Fat (67.9% calories from fat); 26 g Protein; 7 g Carbohydrate; 1 g Dietary Fiber; 6 g net carbs

CHORIZO FRITTATA

This frittata is very South of the Border. If you like chorizo (Mexican sausage), you might cook some up, drain it well, and keep it in a container in the freezer so you can whip up this frittata on short notice. A little cilantro would be good on this, unless you're a cilantro-hater.

1 tablespoon (15 ml) MCT oil, bland coconut oil, or olive oil

½ of a green pepper, diced

1 small onion, sliced

⅔ cup (150 g) cooked, crumbled, drained chorizo

⅔ cup (173 g) salsa

8 eggs, beaten

6 ounces (170 g) shredded Cheddar or Monterey Jack or Mexican cheese blend

1. In a large, heavy skillet over medium heat, heat the oil and sauté the green pepper and onion for a few minutes until tender-crisp. Add the chorizo and the salsa, stir well, and heat through.

2. Spread the mixture into an even layer on the bottom of the skillet and pour in the eggs.

3. Turn the burner to low and cover the skillet. (If your skillet doesn't have a cover, use foil.) Let the frittata cook until the eggs are mostly set (7 to 10 minutes).

4. Uncover, top with the shredded cheese, and slide the skillet under the broiler, about 4 inches (10 cm) from the heat. Broil for 2 to 3 minutes or until the eggs are set and the cheese is melted. Cut into wedges and serve.

YIELD: 4 servings, each with: 538 Calories; 42 g Fat (69.8% calories from fat); 32 g Protein; 8 g Carbohydrate; 1 g Dietary Fiber; 7 g net carbs

Scrambles

When both omelets and frittatas are too much trouble, just make a scramble. The ways of varying scrambled eggs are endless, so you could have them several times a week and never get bored. These have been analyzed assuming a three-egg serving, but if you want a lighter meal, leave out one egg and subtract 0.5 gram of carbohydrates and 6 grams of protein from my analysis. Don't look at the number of servings and assume you can't feed a hungry family with a scramble—these recipes are a snap to double or triple, as long as you have a skillet large enough to scramble in.

COUNTRY SCRAMBLE

This fast-and-filling family-pleaser is a great way to use up leftover ham. Consider it the week after Easter, when you have leftover ham and eggs are cheap. It's great for breakfast, but consider this for a quick supper, too. These instructions are for 1 large serving, but would serve two small children—and, of course, this is easy to double, triple—how big is your skillet? If you're dairy-free, avoid butter.

1 tablespoon (14 g) butter, lard, bacon grease or (15 ml) olive oil

¼ cup (38 g) diced cooked ham

¼ cup (38 g) diced green pepper

2 tablespoons (20 g) diced onion

3 eggs, beaten

Salt and pepper

1. Melt the butter in a skillet over medium heat. Add the ham, green pepper, and onion and sauté for a few minutes until the onion is softened.

2. Pour in the eggs and scramble until the eggs are set.

3. Add salt and pepper to taste and serve.

YIELD: 1 serving with: 375 Calories; 28 g Fat (68.5% calories from fat); 23 g Protein; 6 g Carbohydrate; 1 g Dietary Fiber; 5 g net carbs

CURRY SCRAMBLE

Okay, I admit it: I'd probably eat dog food if you curried it. But with a green salad, this makes a great light supper whether you're a devoted curry lover or not. If you're dairy-free substitute coconut oil for the butter and canned coconut milk for the heavy cream.

1 tablespoon (14 g) butter	**3 eggs**
¼ teaspoon curry powder	**1 tablespoon (15 ml) heavy cream**
½ of a clove of garlic, crushed	**3 slices of bacon, cooked until crisp**

1. Melt the butter in a heavy skillet and sauté the curry powder and garlic over medium-low heat for a minute or two.
2. Beat the eggs and heavy cream together, pour into the skillet, and scramble until the eggs are set.
3. Crumble the bacon over the top.

YIELD: 1 serving with: 463 Calories; 40 g Fat (77.6% calories from fat); 23 g Protein; 3 g Carbohydrate; trace Dietary Fiber; 3 g net carbs

PIPERADE

Say "PEEP-er-ahd." This Basque peasant dish has so many vegetables in it that it's a whole meal in itself. If you'd like more protein and fewer carbs per serving, there's no law against doubling the eggs and calling it two servings, you know.

2 tablespoons (28 g) bacon grease	**⅓ cup diced tomato ([60 g] very ripe fresh or [80 g] canned)**
¼ cup (40 g) diced onion	
½ cup (75 g) diced green pepper	**3 eggs, beaten**
	Salt and pepper

1. Heat the bacon grease in a heavy skillet over the lowest heat. Add the onion and sauté for 5 to 7 minutes or until the onion is soft.
2. Add the green pepper and the tomato. Stir, cover, and cook at lowest heat for 15 minutes, stirring once or twice. (You want the vegetables to be quite soft.)
3. Pour in the eggs and scramble slowly until the eggs are just set.
4. Add salt and pepper to taste and serve.

YIELD: 1 serving with: 481 Calories; 40 g Fat (74.5% calories from fat); 18 g Protein; 13 g Carbohydrate; 3 g Dietary Fiber; 10 g net carbs

Hearty Piperade

Make just as you would regular Piperade, but add ¼ cup (38 g) diced ham for each serving. (This is a great time to use up any leftovers you've been saving.) Sauté the ham with the vegetables and then add the eggs and scramble as usual.

YIELD: 1 serving with: 481 Calories; 40 g Fat (74.5% calories from fat); 18 g Protein; 13 g Carbohydrate; 3 g Dietary Fiber; 10 g net carbs

ITALIAN SCRAMBLE

This recipe is easy to double or triple! It makes a good quick supper. Serve it with a green salad and maybe garlic bread
for the carbivores.

2 tablespoons (28 ml) olive oil

¼ cup (38 g) diced green pepper

¼ cup (40 g) chopped onion

1 clove of garlic, crushed

3 eggs

1 tablespoon (5 g) grated Parmesan cheese

1. Heat the olive oil in a heavy skillet over medium heat and sauté the green pepper, onion, and garlic for 5 to 7 minutes or until the onion is translucent.
2. Beat the eggs with the Parmesan cheese and pour into the skillet.
3. Scramble until the eggs are set and serve.

YIELD: 1 serving with: 489 Calories; 42 g Fat (76.8% calories from fat); 20 g Protein; 9 g Carbohydrate; 2 g Dietary Fiber; 7 g net carbs

MUSHROOM SCRAMBLE

Mushrooms are one of my favorite ingredients. Button and crimini mushrooms are super-low carb. (Some others are higher.) They absorb fat to increase the fat percentage of your recipe, and they're also a great source of umami—making anything you cook with them tastier! Use olive oil if you're dairy-free.

1 tablespoon (14 g) butter or (15 ml) olive oil

1 tablespoon (10 g) minced onion

¼ cup (18 g) sliced mushrooms

3 eggs, beaten

1. Melt the butter in a heavy skillet over medium heat and sauté the onion and mushrooms for 4 to 5 minutes or until the mushrooms are tender.
2. Add the eggs, scramble until set, and serve.

YIELD: 1 serving with: 306 Calories; 25 g Fat (73.3% calories from fat); 17 g Protein; 3 g Carbohydrate; trace Dietary Fiber; 3 g net carbs

GREEK SCRAMBLE

Since I first invented this scramble, my grocery store has installed a Mediterranean bar. One of the items on it is ¼-inch (6 mm) cubes of feta cheese and mixed kalamata and green olives marinated in seasoned olive oil. How perfect would that be for this dish?

2 tablespoons (28 ml) olive oil

1 tablespoon (10 g) minced onion

6 kalamata olives, chopped

3 eggs, beaten

¼ cup (38 g) crumbled feta cheese

1. Heat the olive oil in heavy skillet over medium heat. Sauté the onion for a minute or two and then add the olives and sauté for a minute more.

2. Pour in the eggs and add the feta cheese. Scramble until set and serve.

YIELD: 1 serving with: 597 Calories; 54 g Fat (81.7% calories from fat); 22 g Protein; 5 g Carbohydrate; trace Dietary Fiber; 5 g net carbs

CHICKEN LIVER SCRAMBLE

If you have traumatic childhood memories of strong, grainy, overcooked liver, try this. It's delicious, crazy-nutritious, and filling as all get-out. If you're super-hungry, add a second liver! If you're dairy-free, be sure to use olive oil.

1 tablespoon (14 g) butter or (15 ml) olive oil

¼ of a small onion, sliced

1 chicken liver, cut into bite-size pieces

3 eggs, beaten

Salt and pepper

1. Melt the butter in a heavy skillet over low heat. Sauté the onion for 2 to 3 minutes and then add the cut-up chicken liver.

2. Sauté, stirring frequently, until the chicken livers are no longer red but are still pinkish. Keep the heat very low and don't overcook! You want the insides still be pink and creamy when you eat them.

3. When the chicken liver pieces stop running red, pour in the eggs and scramble until they're set.

4. Add salt and pepper to taste and serve.

YIELD: 1 serving with: 349 Calories; 26 g Fat (67.8% calories from fat); 23 g Protein; 5 g Carbohydrate; trace Dietary Fiber; 5 g net carbs

HOT DOG SCRAMBLE

Okay, it's not haute cuisine, but I'll bet your kids will eat it without complaining. Hot dogs vary quite a lot in carb count, so read the labels! You may also want to check regarding gluten and/or grain. Again, this is one serving for an adult, but should serve two kids, unless one of them is sixteen and on the high school football team. If you're gluten-free, be sure to check the ingredients on your hot dogs.

1 tablespoon (14 g) butter

1 hot dog, sliced into rounds

½ of a small onion, chopped

3 eggs, beaten

¼ cup (30 g) shredded Cheddar cheese

1. Melt the butter in a heavy skillet over medium heat. Add the hot dog slices and onion, and sauté until the onion is limp and the hot dog slices are starting to brown.
2. Add the eggs and scramble until half-set. Add the cheese and continue to scramble until the eggs are set and the cheese is melted. Serve.

YIELD: 1 serving with: 602 Calories; 51 g Fat (76.3% calories from fat); 30 g Protein; 5 g Carbohydrate; trace Dietary Fiber; 5 g net carbs

Fried Eggs

Tired of all that scrambling? These next few recipes are, in one form or another, good old fried eggs.

FRIED EGGS NOT OVER REALLY EASY

If you're like me, you like your eggs over-easy, so that the whites are entirely set, but the yolks are still soft, but you find it maddeningly difficult to flip a fried egg without breaking the yolk. Here's the solution! For the easiest eggs, use a skillet that just fits the number of eggs you're frying. A 7- to 8-inch (18 to 20 cm) skillet is just right for a single serving of three eggs, but if you're doing two servings, 10 inches (25 cm) should do nicely.

3 eggs

1 tablespoon (14 g) butter, bacon grease, lard, bland coconut oil or (15 ml) MCT oil

1 teaspoon water

1. Spray your skillet with nonstick cooking spray and place it over medium-high heat. When the skillet is hot, add the fat and coat the bottom of the pan with it. Crack your eggs into the skillet—careful not to break the yolks!—and immediately cover them.
2. Wait about 2 minutes and check your eggs. They should be well set on the bottom, but still a bit slimy on top. Add a teaspoon of water (you can approximate this; the quantity isn't vital), turn the burner to low, and cover the pan again.
3. Check after a minute; the steam will have cooked the tops of the eggs. If there's still a bit of uncooked white, give it another 30 seconds to 1 minute. Lift out and serve.

YIELD: 1 serving with: 298 Calories; 25 g Fat (75.3% calories from fat); 17 g Protein; 2 g Carbohydrate; 0 g Dietary Fiber; 2 g net carbs

HUEVOS RANCHEROS

Traditionally served on corn tortillas, these are just as tasty without them. Surely you have a fork in the house? And be choosy about your salsa, of course. Sugar tends to sneak in.

1 tablespoon (14 g) butter, bacon grease, or (15 ml) oil, lard

2 eggs

3 tablespoons (49 g) salsa (hot or mild, as you prefer)

2 ounces (55 g) Monterey Jack cheese, shredded

1. Spray a heavy skillet with nonstick cooking spray and set it over medium heat. Add the fat, slosh it around to coat, and crack the eggs into the skillet. Turn down the burner and cover. Let the eggs fry for 4 to 5 minutes.

2. While the eggs are frying, warm the salsa in a saucepan or in the microwave.

3. When your fried eggs are set on the bottom but still a little underdone on top, scatter the cheese evenly over the fried eggs, add a teaspoon or two of water to the skillet, and cover it again. In a minute or two, the tops of the eggs should be set (but the yolks still soft) and the cheese melted.

4. Transfer the eggs to a plate with a spatula, top with the warmed salsa, and serve.

YIELD: 1 serving with: 356 Calories; 26 g Fat (66.2% calories from fat); 25 g Protein; 4 g Carbohydrate; 1 g Dietary Fiber; 3 g net carbs

RODEO EGGS

The was originally a sandwich recipe in the *I Hate To Cook Book*, but it works just as well without the bread, as do so many sandwiches. Bread is just an edible napkin.

4 slices of bacon, chopped into 1-inch (2.5 cm) pieces

4 thin slices of onion

4 eggs

4 thin slices of Cheddar cheese

1. Begin frying the bacon in a large, heavy skillet over medium heat. When some fat has cooked out of it, push the bacon aside and put the onion slices in, too. Fry the onion on each side, turning carefully to keep the slices together, until it starts to look translucent. Remove the onion from the skillet and set aside.

2. Continue frying the bacon until it's crisp. Pour off most of the grease, and distribute the bacon bits evenly over the bottom of the skillet. Break in the eggs and fry for a minute or two until the bottoms are set but the tops are still soft. (If you like your yolks hard, break them with a fork; if you like them soft, leave them unbroken.)

3. Place a slice of onion over each yolk then cover the onion with a slice of cheese. Add a teaspoon of water to the skillet, cover, and cook for 2 to 3 minutes or until the cheese is thoroughly melted.

4. Cut into four separate eggs with the edge of a spatula and serve.

YIELD: 2 servings, each with: 443 Calories; 34 g Fat (69.5% calories from fat); 29 g Protein; 4 g Carbohydrate; 1 g Dietary Fiber; 3 g net carbs

GRUYÈRE EGGS

I love this with Gruyère cheese, but Swiss will do nicely if you're on a budget. Any mild-ish nutty cheese will work well.

1 tablespoon (14 g) butter

2 eggs

¼ cup (30 g) shredded Gruyère cheese

1 scallion, sliced

1. Spray a heavy skillet with nonstick cooking spray and melt the butter in it over medium-high heat. Crack the eggs into the skillet and fry them until the bottoms are done, but the tops are still a little soft.

2. Scatter the Gruyère cheese over the eggs. Add a couple of teaspoons of water to the skillet, cover, and let cook another couple of minutes until the cheese is melted and the whites are set.

3. Move the eggs to a serving plate, scatter the sliced scallion on top, and serve.

YIELD: 1 serving with: 344 Calories; 28 g Fat (73.7% calories from fat); 19 g Protein; 3 g Carbohydrate; trace Dietary Fiber; 3 g net carbs

OEUFS AVEC LE BEURRE NOIRE

This just might be the easiest French cooking you'll ever do, and it lends new interest to good old fried eggs. With a lettuce and tomato salad and a glass of dry white wine, this would make a great quick supper.

1 tablespoon (14 g) butter

3 eggs

½ teaspoon lemon juice

1. Coat a skillet with cooking spray, put it over medium heat, and melt half of the butter in it. Crack the eggs into the skillet and fry as desired. Remove the eggs to a plate and keep them warm.

2. Add the rest of the butter to the skillet and let it cook until the foam on the butter shows a few flecks of brown. Stir in the lemon juice, pour the mixture over the eggs, and serve.

YIELD: 1 serving with: 299 Calories; 25 g Fat (75.1% calories from fat); 17 g Protein; 2 g Carbohydrate; trace Dietary Fiber; 2 g net carbs

CHILI EGG PUFF

Serve this versatile dish for brunch or supper. And don't be afraid of those chilies: The mild ones aren't hot, they're just very flavorful. (And if you like hot foods, feel free to use jalapeños instead of the green chilies.)

6 eggs

½ teaspoon salt or Vege-Sal

½ teaspoon baking powder

1 cup (225 g) small-curd cottage cheese

8 ounces (225 g) Monterey Jack cheese, grated or Mexican cheese blend

3 tablespoons (45 ml) melted butter

1 can (4 ounces, or 115 g) of diced green chilies, drained

1. Preheat the oven to 350°F (180°C, or gas mark 4). Coat an 8- × 8-inch (20 × 20 cm) Pyrex pan with cooking spray or butter it generously.

2. Break the eggs into a bowl and beat them with a whisk. Whisk in the salt and baking powder, mixing very well.

3. Whisk in the cottage cheese, Monterey Jack cheese, melted butter, and chilies. Pour the whole thing into the prepared casserole, put it in the oven, and bake for about 35 minutes. (It's okay if it's a little runny in the very center when you spoon into it; that part acts as a sauce for the rest.)

YIELD: 4 servings, each with: 449 Calories; 35 g Fat (69.8% calories from fat); 29 g Protein; 5 g Carbohydrate; trace Dietary Fiber; 5 g net carbs

HAM AND CHEESE PUFF

Buy extra eggs when they're on sale before Easter and make this with the leftover ham come Monday or Tuesday. You're reading the labels to find the lowest-carb ham, right? If you like, you can use fresh mushrooms, sautéed a bit in butter or leftover ham drippings, instead of the canned mushrooms. I just wanted to make this super easy.

¼ pound (115 g) ham in chunks (unless it's already sliced)

¼ pound (115 g) Cheddar cheese in chunks

1 green pepper

1 can (4 ounces, or 115 g) of mushrooms, well drained

6 eggs

½ teaspoon baking powder

½ teaspoon salt or Vege-Sal

1 cup (225 g) small-curd cottage cheese

2 tablespoons (30 g) grated horseradish

1. Preheat the oven to 350°F (180°C, or gas mark 4). Coat an 8- × 8-inch (20 × 20 cm) Pyrex baking dish with cooking spray or butter it generously.

2. Use a food processor with the S-blade in place and pulsing, grind the ham, Cheddar cheese, green pepper, and mushrooms together until finely chopped. (There should be no chunks of pepper or ham bigger than, say, a ½-inch [1.3 cm] cube.)

3. In a large bowl, whisk up the eggs with the baking powder and salt.

4. Whisk in the cottage cheese and horseradish and then add the chopped ham mixture.

5. Pour the egg mixture into the casserole. Bake for about 40 minutes or until it is puffy and golden and set but still jiggles a bit in the middle when you shake it.

YIELD: 4 servings, each with: 337 Calories; 22 g Fat (57.9% calories from fat); 28 g Protein; 8 g Carbohydrate; 1 g Dietary Fiber; 7 g net carbs

TURKEY CLUB PUFF

Disguise your Thanksgiving leftovers! This is a great Thanksgiving weekend brunch dish. Don't have leftovers? There's no law against buying deli turkey, you know.

6 eggs

½ teaspoon salt

½ teaspoon baking powder

1 cup (225 g) cottage cheese

½ pound (225 g) Swiss cheese, cubed

¼ cup (60 ml) melted butter

¾ cup (105 g) cubed turkey

6 slices of bacon, cooked until crisp and crumbled

1. Preheat the oven to 350°F (180°C, or gas mark 4). Coat a 6-cup (1.4 L) casserole with cooking spray or butter generously.

2. Break the eggs into a bowl and whisk them with the salt and baking powder, mixing very well.

3. Beat in the cottage cheese, Swiss cheese, melted butter, turkey, and crumbled bacon. Pour the whole thing into the greased casserole. Bake for 35 to 40 minutes or until set.

YIELD: 4 servings, each with: 418 Calories; 33 g Fat (70.6% calories from fat); 27 g Protein; 3 g Carbohydrate; 0 g Dietary Fiber; 3 g net carbs

SAUSAGE, EGG, AND CHEESE BAKE

This is a great choice for a family breakfast on a Sunday or holiday. Or, for that matter, it makes a satisfying family supper on a weeknight—just be sure to check the ingredients on your sausage if you're gluten-free.

1 pound (455 g) pork sausage (hot or mild, as you prefer)

½ cup (75 g) diced green pepper

½ cup (80 g) diced onion

8 eggs

¼ teaspoon pepper

1 cup (115 g) shredded Cheddar cheese

1 cup (110 g) shredded Swiss cheese

1. Preheat the oven to 350°F (180°C, or gas mark 4).

2. In a large, heavy, ovenproof skillet, start browning and crumbling the sausage over medium heat.

3. When some grease has cooked out of the sausage, add the green pepper and the onion and continue cooking, stirring frequently, until the sausage is no longer pink.

4. In a large bowl, beat the eggs and pepper together and stir in the Cheddar and Swiss cheeses.

5. Spread the sausage and vegetables evenly on the bottom of the skillet and pour the egg-and-cheese mixture over it.

6. Bake, uncovered, for 25 to 30 minutes, or until mostly firm but still just a little soft in the center.

YIELD: 6 servings, each with: 558 Calories; 48 g Fat (77.7% calories from fat); 26 g Protein; 4 g Carbohydrate; trace Dietary Fiber; 4 g net carbs

EGGS FLORENTINE

This is a great quick-and-simple supper for a tired night. You don't need a thing with it except maybe a glass of white wine. Or red. Who am I to quarrel?

1 batch of Creamed Spinach (page 136)

4 eggs

1. Make the Creamed Spinach according to the directions. After you've stirred in the cream and cheese, spread the spinach on the bottom of your skillet in an even layer.

2. Using the back of a spoon, make four evenly spaced hollows in the spinach and break an egg into each one. Turn the burner to low and cover the skillet.

3. Cook until the eggs are done (about 5 minutes). Divide into four sections with a spatula to make serving easier.

YIELD: 2 servings, each with: 316 Calories; 23 g Fat (64.8% calories from fat); 20 g Protein; 8 g Carbohydrate; 4 g Dietary Fiber; 4 g net carbs

FRIED MUSH

This idea would never have occurred to me, but it did occur to my friend Diana Lee: Ricotta cheese has a texture that's remarkably similar to that of cooked cornmeal. Based on that, she came up with this breakfast recipe, which she's allowed me to reprint from her book *Bread and Breakfast: Baking Low Carb II.*

4 large eggs

½ cup (125 g) ricotta cheese

¼ cup (60 ml) heavy cream

1 tablespoon (15 g) erythritol/monkfruit or erythritol/stevia sweetener, OR liquid stevia, monkfruit, or sucralose to equal 2 tablespoons (26 g) of sugar in sweetness

½ teaspoon cinnamon

¼ teaspoon nutmeg

1 tablespoon (15 ml) oil (I'd use MCT or bland coconut oil.)

1. Preheat the oven to 350°F (180°C, or gas mark 4). Coat an 8- × 8-inch (20 × 20 cm) baking dish with nonstick cooking spray.

2. Mix all the ingredients together and pour the mixture into the prepared baking dish.

3. Bake for 20 to 30 minutes until a knife inserted in the middle comes out clean. Cut into quarters.

4. Heat the oil in a skillet and fry the four pieces until they're brown on both sides. Serve with your favorite topping.

YIELD: 4 servings, each with: 202 Calories; 17 g Fat (77.3% calories from fat); 9 g Protein; 2 g Carbohydrate; trace Dietary Fiber; 2 g net carbs

YOGURT

When I tell people I make my own yogurt, they react as if I'd said I could transmute base metals into gold. But as you'll see, it's easy to make and considerably cheaper than buying the commercial stuff. "Officially," plain yogurt has 12 grams of carbohydrates per cup (230 g), but Dr. Goldberg and Dr. O'Mara point out in *The GO-Diet* that most of the lactose (milk sugar) is converted to lactic acid, leaving only about 4 grams per cup (230 g). So if you like yogurt, enjoy!

1 tablespoon (15 g) plain yogurt OR 1 envelope yogurt starter OR the contents of a pull-apart probiotic capsule (I have had luck with all of these.)

1½–2 cups (192–256 g) instant dry milk, or a 1-quart (946 ml) envelope

1. Fill a clean, 1-quart (946 ml), snap-top container half full with water.

2. Add the plain yogurt and stir. Add the powdered milk and whisk until the lumps are gone.

   For your first batch, you'll use store-bought plain yogurt or yogurt starter, but after that, you can use a spoonful from the previous batch. Every so often it's good to start over with fresh, store-bought cultures, though. Random bacteria may creep after several batches.

3. Fill the container to the top with water, whisk it one last time, and lid it.

4. Put your yogurt-to-be in a warm place. I use a bowl lined with an old electric heating pad set on low, but any warm spot will do. I've made yogurt by placing the container over a heating duct and putting a large bowl over it to prevent drafts. If you have an old-fashioned gas stove with pilot lights, inside the oven or over a stovetop pilot light works, too.

5. Let your yogurt sit for 12 hours or so. It should be thick and creamy by then, but if it's still a little thin, give it a few more hours—up to 24 isn't excessive.

6. When your yogurt has "yogged," stick it in the refrigerator and use it just like store-bought plain yogurt. Or flavor it with vanilla or lemon extract and some Splenda or stevia/FOS blend. You can also stir in a spoonful of sugar-free preserves or mash a few berries with a fork and stir them in.

7. Want Greek yogurt? Once your yogurt has finished incubating, put a strainer over a bowl, line it with a coffee filter, and dump in your yogurt. Stash in the fridge overnight. In the morning, you'll find that much of the whey—the liquid part of the yogurt—has drained off into the bowl. What's left in your strainer is Greek-style yogurt.

Regarding those two different amounts of dry milk: Using the full 2 cups (256 g) will give you richer, creamier yogurt, with more protein and more calcium, but with a couple extra grams of carbohydrates, as well. It's up to you. If you'd like, you can add ¼ cup (60 ml) or more of heavy cream in place of some of the water, to make a higher-fat "whole milk" yogurt. Or, you can stir a dollop of sour cream into each serving.

You can also, if you prefer, make your yogurt from fluid milk. You have to scald the milk first and then cool it again before adding the "starter" yogurt, which seems like a lot of bother to me.

One last useful tidbit: If you use a lot of buttermilk, you can make your own buttermilk exactly the same way you'd make yogurt. Simply substitute a couple of tablespoons (28 ml) of commercial buttermilk for a "starter" instead of the yogurt.

If you're dairy-free, you can culture canned coconut milk the same way. I call this "cocoyo."

CHAPTER 4

Breads, Muffins, Cereals, and Other Grainy Things

O h, boy. This is the chapter that needed the most reworking.

Baked goods and other grain products, such as bread, cereal, pancakes, waffles, and so on, are among the foods that new low-carb dieters miss most. They are also among the foods that sell best for the low-carb specialty merchants. Many of these products are quite good, but they're often pricey.

Accordingly, when I went low-carb, I started working on recipes for these things. And I was successful!

But things have changed. I no longer eat gluten—I do not have celiac disease, I just feel better when I avoid it—so I don't make my own yeast-raised bread recipes. Yet, many people do still eat gluten-bearing low-carb baked goods—breads, tortillas, etc. I have, accordingly, left in a few wheat- and gluten-containing recipes, while replacing others.

The original edition of this book had several recipes for yeast-raised breads. Vital wheat gluten—extracted wheat protein—was a major, and essential, ingredient in them all. I haven't made any of those recipes in years.

Too, while all of those recipes worked beautifully for me when I created them, or I wouldn't have published them, they were by far the most problematic recipes I have ever published. Some people raved about them, while others could not get them to rise for love nor money.

I picked out a couple of favorites and tried making them again—in, it should be noted, a different bread machine than I had originally used. They didn't rise. I have no idea why; maybe my old bread machine was magical. (Although I heard from a pal that my recipe for oatmeal molasses bread nearly "blew the top off her bread machine" it rose so well.)

So I am flummoxed. Accordingly, I have scratched all of the yeast bread recipes from this book. In their place, I have added several bread recipes I have come up with or discovered since.

COCONUT-FLAX BREAD

This is grain-free, gluten-free, and delicious! Buttered toast is a staple again in my house. Once again, this recipe, which originally appeared in *The Fat Fast Cookbook*, appears by the kind permission of my friend Andrew DiMino of CarbSmart.com. This slices beautifully and can be sliced thick or thin. I get about twenty slices per loaf, so that's what I calculated on. Oh, and just so you know: Someone once wrote and asked, "I don't like the flavor of vinegar, I can leave it out, right?" No, no you can't! It reacts with the baking soda and makes the bread rise. Your bread won't taste vinegar-y, I promise. Butter this well, and it will hit ketogenic macros.

4 cups (320 g) shredded coconut meat

¾ cup (78 g) flaxseed meal

1 tablespoon (9 g) guar or xanthan

1 teaspoon erythritol (It's not essential, but I think it improves the flavor.)

1½ teaspoons baking soda

½ teaspoon salt

½ cup (120 ml) water

2 tablespoons (28 ml) cider vinegar

4 eggs

1. Preheat the oven to 350°F (180°C, or gas mark 4). Grease a loaf pan—standard, not super-huge; the opening on mine is 8½ × 4½ inches (21 × 11 cm). Now, line it with nonstick aluminum foil or baking parchment.

2. In your food processor, with the S-blade in place, combine the coconut, flaxseed meal, guar, erythritol, baking soda, and salt. Run the processor till everything is ground to a fine meal. Scrape down the sides and run the processor some more.

3. While that's happening, in a glass measuring cup, combine the water and the vinegar. Have this standing by the food processor.

4. While the food processor is running, add the eggs, one at a time, through the feed tube.

5. Finally, pour the water-and-vinegar mixture in through the feed tube. Run just another 30 seconds or so.

6. Pour/scrape the batter into the prepared loaf pan. Bake for 1 hour and 15 minutes. Turn out on a wire rack to cool.

YIELD: 20 slices, each with: 111 Calories; 9 g Fat (69.9% calories from fat); 4 g Protein; 5 g Carbohydrate; 4 g Dietary Fiber; 1 g net carbs

COCONUT-ALMOND FLAX BREAD

This, too, originally appeared in *The Fat Fast Cookbook* and appears by permission of Andrew DiMino of CarbSmart.com. This has a slightly firmer, finer grain than the Coconut-Flax Bread. Try cubing it and frying in garlicky olive oil for croutons!

2 cups (160 g) shredded coconut meat

½ cup (52 g) flaxseed meal

½ cup (56 g) almond meal

½ cup (65 g) vanilla whey protein powder

1 tablespoon (9 g) guar or xanthan

1½ teaspoons baking soda

½ teaspoon salt

½ cup (120 ml) water

2 tablespoons (28 ml) cider vinegar

6 drops of liquid stevia–English toffee

4 eggs

1. Preheat the oven to 350°F (180°C, or gas mark 4). Grease a loaf pan—standard, not super-huge; the opening on mine is 8½ × 4½ inches (21 × 11 cm). Now, line it with nonstick aluminum foil or baking parchment.

2. In your food processor, with the S-blade in place, combine the coconut, flaxseed meal, almond meal, protein powder, guar, erythritol, baking soda, and salt. Run the processor till everything is ground to a fine meal. Scrape down the sides and run the processor some more.

3. While that's happening, combine the water, vinegar, and liquidstevia in a glass measuring cup. Have this standing by the food processor.

4. While the food processor is running, add the eggs, one at a time, through the feed tube.

5. Finally, pour the water-and-vinegar mixture in through the feed tube. Run just another 30 seconds or so.

6. Pour/scrape the batter into the prepared loaf pan. Bake for 1 hour and 15 minutes. Turn out on a wire rack to cool.

YIELD: 20 slices, each with: 105 Calories; 7 g Fat (53.1% calories from fat); 8 g Protein; 5 g Carbohydrate; 3 g Dietary Fiber; 2 g net carbs

SOUL BREAD

This recipe, originated by someone who goes by the moniker "Soul Song," has made the rounds of the online low-carb community. I've changed it only a little—using MCT oil instead of olive oil, increasing the baking soda just a tad. It's remarkably, well, bread-like. With butter, this will be ketogenic!

12 ounces (340 g) cream cheese at room temperature

¼ cup (55 g) butter

¼ cup (60 ml) MCT oil

4 eggs

3 drops of liquid stevia–plain

¼ cup (60 ml) heavy cream

1⅔ (133 g) cups unflavored whey protein powder

2½ teaspoons (12 g) baking powder

1 teaspoon guar or xanthan

½ teaspoon salt

½ teaspoon baking soda

¼ teaspoon cream of tartar

(continued)

1. Preheat the oven to 325°F (170°C, or gas mark 3). Coat a 9- × 5-inch (23 × 13 cm) loaf pan with nonstick cooking spray or line with nonstick foil (my preference).

2. Put the cream cheese and butter in a microwaveable bowl and nuke for 1 minute on High.

3. Add the MCT oil to the cream cheese and butter and use your electric mixer to beat them until well blended, scraping down the sides of the bowl as needed.

4. Now, beat in the eggs, 1 at a time, incorporating one thoroughly before adding the next.

5. Beat in the liquid stevia and heavy cream.

6. Measure all the dry ingredients—everything from the protein powder through the cream of tartar—into another bowl. Stir them together until everything is evenly distributed.

7. Using a spoon rather than your mixer, stir the dry ingredients into the cream cheese–egg mixture, adding about ⅓ cup (120 ml) at a time and stirring each addition in before adding more.

8. Pour/scrape the batter into the prepared loaf pan. Bake for 45 minutes or until golden brown.

9. Turn out onto a wire rack to cool. Store in a plastic bag in the refrigerator. Or, if you're not likely to eat it up quickly, slice it all, wrap it in a plastic bag, and freeze. You can remove and thaw just a slice or two at a time.

YIELD: 20 slices, each with: 201 Calories; 14 g Fat (62.3% calories from fat); 17 g Protein; 2 g Carbohydrate; trace Dietary Fiber; 2 g net carbs

WHOLE-GRAIN SOUL BREAD

Long before I went low carb, I became a health food freak. I have long preferred whole-grain bread to white. The addition of oat bran and flaxseed meal add a whole-grain flavor and texture. Oats are not a gluten grain, but are sometimes processed in the same facilities as gluten grains and can be contaminated. I don't worry about it, but if you're seriously sensitive, look for oat bran marked "gluten-free."

12 ounces (340 g) cream cheese at room temperature

¼ cup (55 g) butter

¼ cup (60 ml) MCT oil

4 eggs

36 drops of liquid stevia–English toffee

¼ cup (60 ml) heavy cream

1 cup (80 g) unflavored whey protein powder

⅓ cup (40 g) oat bran

⅓ cup (35 g) flaxseed meal

1 tablespoon (14 g) baking powder

1 teaspoon guar or xanthan

½ teaspoon salt

¾ teaspoon baking soda

½ teaspoon cream of tartar

1. Preheat the oven to 325°F (170°C, or gas mark 3). Coat a 9- × 5-inch (23 × 13 cm) loaf pan with nonstick cooking spray or line with nonstick foil (my preference).

2. Put the cream cheese and butter in a microwaveable bowl and nuke for 1 minute on High.

3. Add the MCT oil to the cream cheese and butter and use your electric mixer to beat them until well blended, scraping down the sides of the bowl as needed.

4. Now, beat in the eggs, 1 at a time, incorporating one thoroughly before adding the next.

5. Beat in the liquid stevia and heavy cream.

6. Measure all the dry ingredients—everything from the protein powder through the cream of tartar—into another bowl. Stir them together until everything is evenly distributed.

7. Using a spoon rather than your mixer, stir the dry ingredients into the cream cheese–egg mixture, adding about ⅓ cup (120 ml) at a time and stirring each addition in before adding more.

8. Pour/scrape the batter into the prepared loaf pan. Bake for 1 hour or until golden brown.

9. Turn out onto a wire rack to cool. Store in a plastic bag in the refrigerator. Or, if you're not likely to eat it up quickly, slice it all, wrap it in a plastic bag, and freeze. You can remove and thaw just a slice or two at a time.

YIELD: 20 slices, each with: 194 Calories; 15 g Fat (67.6% calories from fat); 12 g Protein; 4 g Carbohydrate; 2 g Dietary Fiber; 2 g net carbs

WALNUT BREAD

A recipe in an English cookbook called for "walnut bread," obviously assuming it was something one could buy. Well, I can't here, and even if I could it would be full of things I won't eat. So, I made this! With a little butter, this will hit keto macros.

1½ cups (150 g) walnuts	½ cup (52 g) flaxseed meal
3 cups (240 g) shredded coconut meat	6 drops of liquid stevia–English Toffee
2 teaspoons erythritol	4 eggs
1½ teaspoons baking soda	½ cup (120 ml) water
1 teaspoon guar or xanthan	1 tablespoon (15 ml) cider vinegar
¾ teaspoon salt	

1. Preheat the oven to 350°F (180°C, or gas mark 4). Line an 8½- × 4½-inch (21 × 11 cm) loaf pan with nonstick foil.

2. Spread the walnuts on a shallow baking pan, put them in the oven, and set the timer for 6 minutes.

3. Meanwhile, put the coconut, erythritol, baking soda, guar, and salt in your food processor and start it running. Scrape down the sides every few minutes.

4. When the timer beeps, pull the walnuts out of the oven, add 1 cup (100 g) of them to the mixture in the food processor, and then run it again. You want to keep running the food processor until the mixture has the texture of a nut butter.

5. When the coconut-walnut mixture reaches a nut butter consistency, add the flaxseed meal and run the processor, scraping down the sides once or twice, until it's well blended in.

6. Add the liquid stevia, then the eggs, one by one, blending each in thoroughly before adding another. Don't forget to scrape down the sides when needed.

7. In a glass measuring cup, combine the water and the vinegar. With the food processor running, pour this through the feed tube in 3 additions, letting each get worked in before adding more. Do I have to repeat it? Scrape down the sides if needed.

8. Once the vinegar-water is in, you need to work quickly. Add the remaining walnuts and pulse a few times to chop them in—you want there to be chunks of walnut in your finished bread.

9. Scrape the dough into your prepared loaf pan, distributing it evenly, and smooth the top.

10. Bake for 75 minutes and then cool in the pan before turning out.

YIELD: 20 slices, each with: 140 Calories; 12 g Fat (73.2% calories from fat); 5 g Protein; 5 g Carbohydrate; 3 g Dietary Fiber; 2 g net carbs

PEANUT BUTTER BREAD

You have to try this! I found a recipe for Peanut Butter Bread in *The Boston Cooking School Cook Book*, originally published in 1896. Intrigued, I decarbed it. It worked out even better than I hoped—mildly sweet, distinctly peanutty, with a lovely texture.

The loaf rises steeply in the center, tapering at the end. This means the slices are of varying sizes, making exact per-slice statistics impossible. Still, you can count on this being quite low carb.

1 cup (112 g) almond meal

1 cup (129 g) vanilla whey protein powder

2 tablespoons (30 g) erythritol

1 teaspoon guar or xanthan

1 tablespoon (14 g) baking powder

1 teaspoon salt

¾ cup (195 g) natural peanut butter

1 cup (235 ml) unsweetened, pourable coconut milk

1 egg

¼ teaspoon liquid stevia–English toffee

1. Preheat the oven to 350°F (180°C, or gas mark 4). Coat a loaf pan generously with nonstick cooking spray.

2. In your food processor, with the S-blade in place, assemble the almond meal, protein powder, erythritol, guar, baking powder, and salt. Pulse 15 to 20 times, making sure everything is evenly mixed.

3. Add the peanut butter. Pulse 5 to 6 times and then run the processor for a minute or two, scraping down the sides at least once. Turn off the processor.

4. In a Pyrex measuring cup, measure your coconut milk. Add the egg and liquid stevia to it and use a fork or whisk to stir until they're all well blended.

5. With the food processor running, pour in the coconut milk–egg blend through the feed tube. When it's all in, scrape down the sides of the processor and process for another 30 seconds or so.

6. Scrape the batter into the prepared loaf pan, smoothing the top. Bake for 1 hour. Cool in the pan for 5 minutes before turning out on a rack to cool.

7. Serve warm or toasted, slathered with butter!

YIELD: 20 slices, each with about: 434 Calories; 7 g Fat (45.3% calories from fat); 14 g Protein; 5 g Carbohydrate; 1 g Dietary Fiber; 4 g net carbs

MUG BREAD TOAST

Recipes like this are going around the Internet, so I tried it. Turns out it's quick and good! Don't bother eating this without toasting it. It's uninteresting straight out of the mug. But fried in butter? Yum.

2 tablespoons (28 g) butter, divided

3 tablespoons (21 g) almond meal

½ teaspoon baking powder

1 pinch of salt

1 egg white

1. Coat a mug or a small ramekin with cooking spray. Put 1½ (21 g) tablespoons of the butter in the mug and microwave on High for 30 seconds or until melted.

2. Add the almond meal, baking powder and salt and then the egg white. Place a whisk down into the mug and roll the handle between your palms to mix. Make sure you have no pockets of dry stuff left.

3. Microwave on High for 90 seconds to 1 minute 45 seconds. (Microwaves vary in power.) When it's done, tip your bread it out of the mug onto a cutting board. It will be pale and flabby and unexciting. Fret not.

4. Slice your bread in half, into two rounds. Put a skillet over low heat, melt the rest of the butter, and fry the bread rounds until golden on both sides.

5. Feel free to melt cheese on this or spread it with liverwurst or any good, rich spread. You could put a poached egg on each round, too!

YIELD: 1 serving with: 327 Calories; 28 g Fat (73.6% calories from fat); 14 g Protein; 8 g Carbohydrate; 0 g Dietary Fiber; 8 g net carbs

MUG BREAD SUPREME TOAST

The little bit of guar or xanthan gives a texture closer to "real" bread, while the nutritional yeast lends it the yeasty flavor we all know and love.

2 tablespoons (28 g) butter, divided

3 tablespoons (21 g) almond meal

1 teaspoon nutritional yeast flakes

½ teaspoon baking powder

⅛ teaspoon guar or xanthan

1 pinch of salt

1 egg white

1. Coat a mug or small ramekin with cooking spray and add 1½ (21 g) tablespoons of the butter. Microwave for a minute to melt.

2. In a separate dish, stir together all the dry ingredients, from the almond meal through the salt. You want all the ingredients evenly distributed. Smash any lumps of baking powder!

3. When the butter is melted, remove from the microwave and let it cool for just a minute or two. Add the dry ingredient mixture and then the egg white. Use a fork or whisk to stir until you've got a smooth batter with no pockets of dry stuff at the bottom.

4. Microwave for 1 minute and 45 seconds. (Well, that's in my microwave. They vary a bit.)

5. Using pot holders, remove from the microwave and tip the bread out of the cup onto a cutting board. Let it cool a minute while you . . .

6. Put a skillet over medium-low heat. Melt the remaining butter.

7. Slice your bread into two rounds. Fry in the butter, tipping the pan occasionally to slosh any stray butter under the toast, until it's golden on both sides.

YIELD: 1 serving with: 341 Calories; 28 g Fat (70.5% calories from fat); 16 g Protein; 10 g Carbohydrate; 1 g Dietary Fiber; 9 g net carbs

FRENCH TOAST

Make this for breakfast some lazy weekend morning and the family will think you're cheating on your diet! I like this with a little erythritol and cinnamon sprinkled on top.

4 eggs

½ cup (120 ml) heavy cream

½ cup (120 ml) water or unsweetened pourable coconut milk

1 teaspoon vanilla extract (optional)

6 slices of low-carb bread of your choice

Butter

1. Beat together the eggs, heavy cream, water, and vanilla extract (if using) and place the mixture in a shallow dish, such as a pie plate.

2. Soak the slices of bread in the mixture until they're well saturated; you'll have to do them one or two at a time. Let each slice soak for at least 5 minutes, turning once.

3. Fry each soaked piece of bread in plenty of butter over medium heat in a heavy skillet or griddle. Brown well on each side.

4. Serve with sugar-free syrup, cinnamon and sweetener, or sugar-free preserves, as you choose.

YIELD: 6 servings: The carb count will vary with the type of bread you use, but the egg and cream add only 2 grams of carbs, no fiber, and 4 grams of protein per slice.

GINGERBREAD WAFFLES

This is a real special-occasion breakfast! How about making these on Christmas morning or for someone's birthday?

1 cup (112 g) almond meal

¾ cup (97 g) vanilla whey protein powder

2 tablespoons (30 g) erythritol/monkfruit or erythritol/stevia blend OR 2 tablespoons (30 g) erythritol PLUS liquid stevia, monkfruit, or sucralose to equal 2 tablespoons (26 g) of sugar in sweetness

1 tablespoon (14 g) baking powder

½ teaspoon salt

2 teaspoons ground ginger

¾ cup (175 ml) heavy cream

¾ cup (175 ml) unsweetened pourable coconut milk

2 eggs

4 tablespoons (60 ml) melted butter

Whipped Cream (page 303)

1. Start your waffle iron heating first.

2. In a mixing bowl, preferably one with a pouring lip, combine the dry ingredients, stirring them together until everything is equally distributed.

3. In another bowl or a large measuring cup, mix together the heavy cream, pourable coconut milk, and eggs and then stir the butter into them. Pour this into the dry ingredients and whisk it in with a few quick strokes.

4. Pour or ladle the batter into the waffle iron and bake until done—my waffle iron has a light that goes out when the waffle is ready, but follow the instructions for your unit.

5. Serve with Whipped Cream.

YIELD: In my waffle iron, this makes 6 waffles, each with: 452 Calories; 32 g Fat (61.6% calories from fat); 35 g Protein; 10 g Carbohydrate; 3 g Dietary Fiber; 7 g net carbs

KIM'S DUTCH BABY

A Dutch Baby is a big, puffy, eggy, baked pancake, and my sister Kim adores them, so I came up with this recipe for her. It's great for Sunday brunch. Your Dutch Baby will come out gloriously puffed, but it will quickly sink in the middle. That's okay—it's supposed to. It will be crunchy around the edges and soft in the middle.

The traditional accompaniment for a Dutch Baby is a sprinkle of lemon juice and confectioner's sugar, but lemon and Splenda works great. You could also try cinnamon and Splenda, plain Splenda, some thawed frozen berries, or sugar-free jam or jelly. Yummy!

2 tablespoons (28 g) butter

½ cup (56 g) almond meal

¼ cup (32 g) vanilla whey protein powder

2 tablespoons (30 g) erythritol/monkfruit or erythritol/stevia blend OR 2 tablespoons (30 g) erythritol PLUS liquid stevia, monkfruit, or sucralose to equal 2 tablespoons (26 g) of sugar in sweetness

½ teaspoon salt

½ teaspoon cinnamon

4 eggs

1 cup (240 ml) heavy cream

1 teaspoon vanilla extract

1. Preheat the oven to 425°F (220°C, or gas mark 7). It is essential that the oven be up to temperature before putting your Dutch Baby in, so don't combine the wet and dry ingredients until the oven is ready.

2. Spray a large, cast-iron skillet or a 10-inch (25 cm) pie pan with nonstick cooking spray and melt the butter in the bottom. Set aside.

3. In a bowl, combine the almond meal, protein powder, sweetener, salt, and cinnamon.

4. In a separate bowl, beat together the eggs, heavy cream, and vanilla extract and whisk it vigorously for a couple of minutes. (Beating air into it will make the Dutch Baby puff more.)

5. Beat in the dry ingredients just until well mixed and pour the batter into the prepared pan.

6. Bake for 20 minutes; reduce the temperature to 350°F (180°C, or gas mark 4) and bake for another 3 to 5 minutes. Cut in to wedges to serve.

YIELD: 4 servings, each with: 451 Calories; 36 g Fat (71.0% calories from fat); 24 g Protein; 9 g Carbohydrate; 1 g Dietary Fiber; 8 g net carbs

CINNAMON GRANOLA

This stuff is addictive. When I make a batch, That Nice Boy I Married eats little else until it's gone. I mean, seriously, the man will eat granola for supper.

2 cups (208 g) flaxseed meal

2 cups (160 g) shredded coconut meat

¾ cup (97 g) vanilla whey protein powder

2 tablespoons (30 g) erythritol/stevia or erythritol/monkfruit blend OR 2 tablespoons (30 g) erythritol PLUS liquid stevia, monkfruit, or sucralose to equal 2 tablespoons (26 g) of sugar in sweetness (I'd use English toffee stevia.)

1 teaspoon cinnamon

½ teaspoon salt

½ cup (120 ml) oil (I'd use MCT or melted coconut oil.)

½ cup (120 ml) water

1 cup (145 g) sunflower seeds

1 cup (144 g) sesame seeds

¾ cup (90 g) chopped walnuts

¾ cup (83 g) slivered almonds

1. Preheat the oven to 200°F (93°C, or gas mark ¼). Coat a large roasting pan with cooking spray or better yet, line the pan with nonstick foil.

2. In a large mixing bowl, combine the flaxseed meal, shredded coconut, protein powder, erythritol blend or erythritol, cinnamon, and salt. Stir together well.

3. Stir in the oil, then the water—if you're using a liquid sweetener, add it to the water first. Stir the whole mixture up.

4. Dump this mixture into the roasting pan and press it out firmly into an even layer with your hands. Slide into the oven and toast for an hour.

5. Use a spatula to cut the flax-coconut mixture into 1-inch (2.5 cm) squares and turn everything over. Stir in the sunflower seeds, sesame seeds, walnuts, and almonds.

6. Toast for another hour, stirring and turning everything over every 15 minutes or so and breaking those chunks of flax-coconut mixture a bit more.

7. When it's nicely toasted, pull it out of the oven, let it cool, and store in a tight-lidded container. Eat with cream, coconut milk, or stirred into yogurt—you know, like granola.

YIELD: 16 servings, each with: 452 Calories; 37 g Fat (68.0% calories from fat); 22 g Protein; 17 g Carbohydrate; 13 g Dietary Fiber; 4 g net carbs

EVELYN'S GRANOLA

From reader Evelyn Nordahl, here's a much lower-carbohydrate granola recipe. Evelyn eats this granola topped with about 2 tablespoons (28 ml) of water and 2 tablespoons (28 ml) of heavy cream, and she says it's "satisfying, crunchy and delicious." Textured Vegetable Protein (TVP) is a soy product, so if you're avoiding soy, this one is not for you.

I've left the Splenda because the light and fluffy texture helps it adhere to the TVP. Confectioner's-style Swerve (erythritol-based sweetener) would work, too.

1 cup (96 g) Textured Vegetable Protein granules (available at health food stores)

1 teaspoon cinnamon

2 tablespoons (3 g) Splenda

½ cup (30 g) unsweetened coconut flakes

½ cup (55 g) chopped pecans

½ cup (50 g) chopped, (46 g) sliced, or (55 g) slivered almonds

1. Combine the Textured Vegetable Protein granules, cinnamon, and Splenda in a plastic or glass container large enough to hold all the ingredients.

2. Spread the coconut, pecans, and almonds on a cookie sheet and toast under the broiler just until the coconut starts to brown. Remove from the oven and cool.

3. Add the toasted nuts to the granule mixture, attach the lid, and shake to mix.

YIELD: 10 servings of about ¼ cup (25 g), each with: 169 Calories; 9 g Fat (44.9% calories from fat); 17 g Protein; 8 g Carbohydrate; 6 g Dietary Fiber; 2 g net carbs

BUTTERMILK PANCAKE AND WAFFLE MIX

Look for dried buttermilk powder in the baking aisle of big grocery stores and online, of course. Heck, Walmart.com lists it, and, of course, Amazon has every darned thing.

1 cup (128 g) dried buttermilk powder

2 cups (224 g) almond meal

1½ cups (194 g) vanilla whey protein powder

½ cup (52 g) flaxseed meal

2 tablespoons (30 g) erythritol/stevia or erythritol/monkfruit blend

4 teaspoons (18 g) baking powder

2 teaspoons baking soda

1 teaspoon salt

1. Simply measure all the ingredients into a big mixing bowl and use your whisk to stir it up till everything is very evenly blended.

2. Store in a snap-top container in your fridge or freezer. (You could use a big zipper-lock bag, but it's far easier to scoop the mix out of a snap-top container.)

YIELD: 16 servings, each with: 217 Calories; 8 g Fat (29.6% calories from fat); 27 g Protein; 13 g Carbohydrate; 3 g Dietary Fiber; 9 g net carbs

PANCAKES FROM BUTTERMILK PANCAKE MIX

These are high enough carb that you won't want to eat them every day. But they're a great thing to make when you're serving people who are skeptical about low-carbing!

1½ cups (190 g) Buttermilk Pancake and Waffle Mix

1 egg

½ cup (120 ml) water

2 tablespoons (28 g) butter, lard, or bacon grease

Butter, sugar-free syrup, erythritol and cinnamon, or low-sugar preserves (for serving)

1. First, put a big skillet or griddle over medium heat. The temperature of your cooking surface is important; when I used too cool a pan, and the pancakes took a long time to brown, they became dry. You want your pan or griddle at a temperature where the first side of each pancake will brown in 4 or 5 minutes. A good guide is if one drop of water dripped on the cooking surface skitters around, rather than sitting there (too cool) or simply evaporating (too hot).

2. Measure your Buttermilk Pancake and Waffle Mix into a mixing bowl and add the egg and water. Stir with a whisk just until you're sure no pockets of dry stuff remain.

3. Melt the butter or other fat in the skillet or on the griddle and spread it around.

4. Scoop the batter with a ¼ cup (60 ml) measure and cook as for regular pancakes—flip when the edges look dry. Serve hot, with butter, and your choice of sugar-free pancake syrup, erythritol and cinnamon, or low-sugar preserves.

YIELD: Four 2-pancake servings, each with: 374 Calories; 17 g Fat (40.2% calories from fat); 40 g Protein; 19 g Carbohydrate; 4 g Dietary Fiber; 15 g net carbs

WAFFLES FROM BUTTERMILK PANCAKE AND WAFFLE MIX

If you have leftover waffles—I usually do, what with only two of us in the house—reheat them in the toaster, not the microwave. Flabby waffles are a tragedy.

1 cup (125 g) Buttermilk Pancake and Waffle Mix

½ cup (120 ml) water

1 egg

¼ cup (60 ml) melted butter

Toppings of your choice (for serving)

1. Preheat your waffle iron—don't even start mixing stuff up till you have it plugged in.

2. Measure your Buttermilk Pancake and Waffle Mix into a mixing bowl.

3. In a separate bowl, whisk together the water, egg, and melted butter. When your waffle iron is hot and ready to cook, dump this into the dry stuff and whisk it up—just till there are no pockets of dry stuff left.

4. Bake immediately, according to the directions that come with your waffle iron. Serve with butter and sugar-free pancake syrup, with cinnamon and sweetener, berries and whipped cream, low-sugar jam or jelly, or other topping of your choice.

Note: For super light and crispy waffles, separate the egg and whip the white stiff before you add the wet ingredients to the dry. Then, once you've stirred up your batter, fold the whipped egg white into the batter just before baking. This makes for great waffles, but I seldom want to do that much work before breakfast!

YIELD: The size of your waffles will depend on your waffle iron, of course. In mine, I get four 2-waffle servings, each with: 323 Calories; 20 g Fat (52.8% calories from fat); 27 g Protein; 12 g Carbohydrate; 3 g Dietary Fiber; 9 g net carbs

PERFECT PROTEIN PANCAKES

These taste just like mom used to make—you'd never guess they were low carb and grain-free. I'd call five of these tiny pancakes a "serving," so double or triple your batches accordingly. Even better, make extras to freeze, and you can warm them up in the toaster oven for a healthy breakfast on a hurried morning.

2 eggs

½ cup (125 g) ricotta cheese

¼ cup (32 g) vanilla whey protein powder

½ teaspoon baking powder

⅛ teaspoon salt

Butter, sugar-free syrup, sugar-free jelly, Splenda, cinnamon, or mashed berries (for serving)

1. Spray a heavy skillet or griddle with nonstick cooking spray and place it over medium heat.

2. In a mixing bowl, whisk together the eggs and ricotta cheese until quite smooth. Whisk in the protein powder, baking powder, and salt, only mixing until well combined.

3. Drop the batter onto the skillet or griddle by the tablespoonful (15 ml). When the bubbles on the surface of the pancakes are breaking and staying broken, flip them and cook the other side.

4. Serve with butter and sugar-free syrup, sugar-free jelly, Splenda and cinnamon, or a few mashed berries sweetened with Splenda.

YIELD: 5 servings of 5 little silver dollar pancakes, each with:
268 Calories; 16 g Fat (53.4% calories from fat); 27 g Protein; 4 g Carbohydrate; 1 g Dietary Fiber; 3 g net carbs

ZUCCHINI PANCAKES

Our tester, Tammera, when asked, "On a scale of one-to-ten, with one being, 'Oh, dear God, you expect me to eat this?' and ten being 'Wow, I'd be happy to pay big bucks for this in a restaurant,' where do you rate this recipe?" responded, "10, with 'big bucks' being the going rate for pancakes at IHOP or Denny's." She also said that the recipe is great as written and also good with sugar-free caramel coffee-flavoring syrup in place of the half-and-half.

3 eggs

2 tablespoons (28 ml) half-and-half

¼ cup (60 ml) oil (I'd use MCT or bland coconut, melted.)

⅓ cup (37 g) almond meal

⅓ cup (43 g) vanilla whey protein powder

1 tablespoon (15 g) erythritol/monkfruit or erythritol/stevia sweetener

1 teaspoon cinnamon

¾ teaspoon baking powder

½ teaspoon salt

½ teaspoon nutmeg

½ teaspoon guar or xanthan

1½ cups (180 g) shredded zucchini

Your choice of toppings (for serving)

1. In a mixing bowl, whisk together the eggs, half-and-half, and oil.

2. In another bowl, preferably with a pouring lip, combine the almond meal, protein powder, sweetener, cinnamon, baking powder, salt, nutmeg, and guar. Stir until it's all evenly distributed.

3. Pour the liquid ingredients into the dry ingredients and whisk until you're sure you have no pockets of dry stuff.

4. Stir in the zucchini. Now, let the whole thing rest for 5 minutes. While your batter is having a nap, coat your skillet or griddle with cooking spray and put it over medium heat so it's ready when your batter is.

5. Pour the batter onto the hot surface in 3-inch (7.5 cm) rounds. Flip when the edges are browning. Serve with butter and pureed berries or a little erythritol-stevia or erythritol-monkfruit sweetener and cinnamon—or, for that matter, with sugar-free pancake syrup.

YIELD: Eighteen 3-inch (7.5 cm) pancakes, each with:
69 Calories; 5 g Fat (60.2% calories from fat); 5 g Protein; 2 g Carbohydrate; trace Dietary Fiber; 2 g net carbs

CHEESE POPOVERS

These are from *Lo-Carb Cooking*, by Debra Rowland, and they are tasty! How about serving these with a ham?

1 cup (112 g) almond flour

½ teaspoon salt

1 cup (235 ml) heavy cream

2 eggs

1 tablespoon (15 ml) melted butter

¼ cup (30 g) shredded Cheddar cheese

1. Preheat the oven to at 425°F (220°C, or gas mark 7).
2. Beat the flour, salt, heavy cream, eggs, and butter until smooth. Stir in the Cheddar cheese.
3. Spoon the mixture into 8 muffin cups. Bake for 15 minutes, reduce heat to 350°F (180°C, or gas mark 4), and bake for 25 additional minutes or until golden brown. Serve immediately.

YIELD: 8 servings, each with: 216 Calories; 18 g Fat (71.9% calories from fat); 10 g Protein; 6 g Carbohydrate; 0 g Dietary Fiber; 6 g net carbs

BUTTERMILK BRAN MUFFINS

These are tender, moist, sweet, and perfumed with cinnamon. And, using the GO-Diet's figure of 4 grams of carbohydrates per cup (235 ml) of buttermilk, not a bad deal, carbohydrates-wise. This recipe is not grain- or gluten-free. If you take the bran out of a bran muffin, you don't have much left. So, these are for those who eat wheat. Try doubling this recipe and freezing the leftovers. Thaw the muffins a few at a time to grab on those mornings when you need a fast breakfast.

⅔ cup (40 g) wheat bran

¾ cup plus 2 tablespoons (113 g) vanilla whey protein powder

2 tablespoons (15 g) vital wheat gluten

¼ teaspoon salt

1 teaspoon baking soda

2 tablespoons (30 g) erythritol/stevia or erythritol/monkfruit blend

½ teaspoon cinnamon

½ cup (60 g) chopped walnuts or (55 g) pecans (optional)

1 cup (235 ml) buttermilk

1 egg

3 tablespoons (45 ml) MCT oil or melted coconut oil

1 tablespoon (20 g) molasses

1. Preheat the oven to 350°F (180°C, or gas mark 4).
2. In a mixing bowl, combine the wheat bran, protein powder, wheat gluten, salt, baking soda, sweetener, cinnamon, and nuts and stir until well combined.
3. In a measuring cup, stir together the buttermilk, egg, oil, and molasses.
4. Spray 10 cups of a muffin tin well with nonstick cooking spray.
5. Give the wet ingredients one last stir and pour them into the dry ingredients. With a spoon, stir just long enough to moisten all the dry ingredients. Do not overmix! The batter should look rough, and a few lumps are fine.
6. Spoon into the prepared muffin cups, dividing the mixture evenly. (The muffin cups should be about one-third full.)
7. Bake for 20 to 25 minutes and then turn out of the muffin cups onto a wire rack to cool.

YIELD: 10 muffins, each with: 194 Calories; 10 g Fat (44% calories from fat); 21 g protein; 2 g Carbohydrate; 3 g Dietary Fiber; 4 g net carbs

SOUR CREAM LEMON-POPPY SEED MUFFINS

Our tester, Rebecca Jaxson, said the level of lemon and sweetness in these was perfect. In answer to our question, " Comparing ease and quickness of preparation to taste, how do you rate this recipe?" she rated these a 10, saying, "It's very tasty and satisfies my need for something bread-like." These are a bit low in fat, so butter is in order!

1½ cups (168 g) almond meal

½ cup (65 g) vanilla whey protein powder

2 teaspoons baking powder

½ teaspoon salt

3 tablespoons (45 g) erythritol/monkfruit or erythritol/stevia sweetener OR ⅓ cup (80 g) plain erythritol

1½ teaspoons guar or xanthan

1 teaspoon baking soda

2 tablespoons (18 g) poppy seeds

1 cup (230 g) sour cream

2 eggs

2 tablespoons (28 ml) lemon extract

¼ teaspoon liquid stevia–lemon drop

2 lemons

1. Preheat the oven to 400°F (200°C, or gas mark 6). Line a 12-cup muffin tin with muffin cups.

2. In a mixing bowl, combine the almond meal, protein powder, baking powder, salt, sweetener, guar, baking soda, and poppy seeds. If you have lumps, sift!

3. In another bowl, combine the sour cream, eggs, lemon extract, and liquid stevia.

4. Grate the zest from your lemons and add it to the sour cream and eggs.

5. Warm the lemons briefly—I give them about 30 to 45 seconds in the microwave. This increases juice yield. Then, roll each lemon firmly under the heel of your hand; this, too, will increase the juice. Now, halve 'em, squeeze 'em, remove any pits, and pour the juice into the sour cream mixture. Whisk it all together.

6. Pour the wet stuff into the dry stuff and whisk just enough to be sure you have no pockets of dry stuff left. Don't overmix!

7. Portion the batter out into the muffin cups. I used my 2-tablespoon (28 ml) cookie scoop, and 2 scoops per muffin was just about perfect, so you might try scooping with a ¼ cup (60 ml) measure.

8. Bake for 18 to 20 minutes or until a toothpick inserted into the center of a muffin comes out clean.

YIELD: 12 muffins, each with: 172 Calories; 9 g Fat (46.1% calories from fat); 16 g Protein; 8 g Carbohydrate; trace Dietary Fiber, 8 g net carbs

SOUR CREAM COFFEE CAKE

Here's a coffee cake for you, from Diana Lee's invaluable *Baking Low-Carb*. Notice that this has enough protein to be a satisfying breakfast all by itself. Our tester, Verna Haas, asked whether she'd make this recipe again, said, "Yes. I served the cake with coffee and everyone loved it. When asked if they would like to have the cake again, there was a resounding yes!" She also says to tell you that some of the nuts will sink down into the batter.

1 cup (230 g) sour cream

⅔ cup (160 ml) oil (I'd use MCT or bland coconut oil, melted.)

½ cup (120 ml) water

3 eggs

1 tablespoon (15 ml) almond extract

1¼ cups (161 g) vanilla whey protein powder

¼ cup (30 g) oat flour (You can find gluten-free versions.)

1 tablespoon (14 g) baking powder

2 teaspoons cinnamon

1 teaspoon baking soda

½ teaspoon guar or xanthan

½ cup (120 g) erythritol/monkfruit or erythritol/stevia sweetener OR ½ cup (120 g) erythritol plus liquid stevia, monkfruit, or sucralose to equal ½ cup (100 g) of sugar in sweetness

TOPPING

½ cup chopped nuts (Walnuts [60 g] or pecans [55 g] are lowest carb.)

1 tablespoon (15 g) erythritol/monkfruit or erythritol/stevia sweetener OR 2 tablespoons (30 g) erythritol

¼ teaspoon cinnamon

1. Preheat the oven to 350°F (180°C, or gas mark 4). Grease an 8-inch (20 cm) springform pan or coat with cooking spray.

2. In a mixing bowl, combine the sour cream, oil, water, eggs, and almond extract. Whisk together well.

3. In another bowl, combine the protein powder, oat flour, baking powder, cinnamon, baking soda, guar, and sweetener. (If using straight erythritol plus liquid sweetener, whisk the liquid sweetener in with the sour cream.) Stir the dry ingredients together until everything is evenly distributed.

4. Combine the chopped nuts, sweetener, and cinnamon. Stir together to make your topping.

5. Now: Add the dry ingredients to the wet ingredients and whisk together, making sure you have no pockets of dry stuff. Pour into the prepared springform pan.

6. Sprinkle the cinnamon-nut topping evenly over the batter.

7. Bake for 30 to 35 minutes. Let cool a bit before opening the springform.

YIELD: **12 servings, each with:** 317 Calories; 23 g Fat (63.2% calories from fat); 22 g Protein; 8 g Carbohydrate; 2 g Dietary Fiber; 6 net carbs

103

"CORN BREAD"

I can purchase almond meal at any local grocery or health food store, but cannot purchase hazelnut meal. I simply grind shelled hazelnuts to the texture of cornmeal in my food processor. If you'd like to make this even more corn bread–like, consider purchasing Amoretti or LorAnn corn flavorings and adding a teaspoon or two along with the butter flavoring. But this is quite nice as is. Proper Southern cornbread is not sweetened, so leave out the sweetener if you wish.

1 cup (225 g) butter, softened

Liquid stevia, monkfruit or sucralose to equal 2 teaspoons of sugar in sweetness

5 eggs

1½ cups (168 g) almond meal

½ cup (38 g) ground hazelnuts

¼ teaspoon guar or xanthan

1 teaspoon baking powder

2 teaspoons butter extract

1. Preheat your oven to 350°F (180°C, or gas mark 4). Coat a 9-inch (23 cm) springform with cooking spray.

2. Cream the butter and sweetener well. Add the eggs one at a time, beating well after each.

3. Mix the almond and hazelnut flours with baking powder and guar. Add this dry mixture to the egg mixture a little at a time while continuously beating.

4. Mix in the butter extract and pour the batter into a 9-inch (23 cm) springform or cake pan.

5. Bake for 50 to 55 minutes.

YIELD: 8 servings, each with: 426 Calories; 31 g Fat (63.4% calories from fat); 32 g Protein; 8 g Carbohydrate; 1 g Dietary Fiber; 7 g net carbs

HOT CEREAL

This is great for those cold winter mornings. Add heavy cream or half-and-half, plus the sweetener of your choice. I loved brown sugar on oatmeal as a kid, so I'd probably use English toffee stevia.

½ cup (73 g) raw, shelled sunflower seeds

1 cup (80 g) shredded coconut meat

1 cup (112 g) almond meal

1 cup (104 g) golden flaxseed meal

1 cup (129 g) vanilla whey protein powder

¾ teaspoon salt

1. Preheat the oven to 325°F (170°C, or gas mark 3).

2. Use your food processor to chop your sunflower seeds a bit. You want them about the size of a grain of rice or a little smaller.

3. Spread the sunflower seeds, coconut, and almond meal on a rimmed baking sheet. Toast for 8 to 10 minutes or until just getting golden.

4. Dump this mixture in a big bowl and add the flaxseed meal, protein powder, and salt. Stir everything together well and then transfer to a snap-top container and store in the fridge.

5. To serve, put about ⅓ cup (120 ml) of your cereal in a bowl and stir in ½ cup (120 ml) of boiling water. Put a saucer on top of the bowl to hold in the heat and let it sit for 2 to 3 minutes.

6. Thin with a little more water to get the texture you prefer and then eat like any hot cereal.

YIELD: 12 servings, each with: 270 Calories; 15 g Fat (47.5% calories from fat); 25 g Protein; 13 g Carbohydrate; 8 g Dietary Fiber; 5 g net carbs. The analysis does not include the heavy cream, coconut milk, or half-and-half.

CINNAMON HOT CEREAL

This is for those of you who used to eat your oatmeal with cinnamon and sugar. Add heavy cream, coconut milk, or half-and-half, plus the sweetener of your choice to taste.

½ cup (73 g) raw, shelled sunflower seeds

1 cup (80 g) shredded coconut meat

1 cup (112 g) almond meal

1 cup (104 g) golden flaxseed meal

1 cup (129 g) vanilla whey protein powder

1–2 teaspoons cinnamon

¾ teaspoon salt

1. Preheat the oven to 325°F (170°C, or gas mark 3).
2. Use your food processor to chop your sunflower seeds a bit. You want them about the size of a grain of rice or a little smaller.
3. Spread the sunflower seeds, coconut, and almond meal on a rimmed baking sheet. Toast for 8 to 10 minutes or until just getting golden.
4. Dump this mixture in a big bowl and add the flaxseed meal, protein powder, cinnamon, and salt. Stir everything together well and then transfer to a snap-top container and store in the fridge.
5. To serve, put about ⅓ cup (80 ml) of your cereal in a bowl and stir in ½ cup (120 ml) of boiling water. Put a saucer on top of the bowl to hold in the heat and let it sit for 2 to 3 minutes.
6. Thin with a little more water to get the texture you prefer and then eat like any hot cereal.

YIELD: 12 servings, each with: 270 Calories; 15 g Fat (47.5% calories from fat); 25 g Protein; 13 g Carbohydrate; 8 g Dietary Fiber; 5 g net carbs. The analysis does not include heavy cream, coconut milk, or half-and-half.

CHOCOLATE "CEREAL"

Remember Coco Wheats? Here's a chocolate hot cereal for the kid in you. My tester, Roy St. George, altered my original suggestion of ¼ cup (20 g) cocoa powder and used ½ cup (40 g). He said he thought it was perfect, but that he loves strong chocolate flavors. Feel free to use less, if you prefer.

Roy said he used vanilla stevia in his, while his daughter used chocolate stevia. They both loved it. He also suggests you could add a drop or two of coconut or almond extract. Sounds good to me!

½ cup (73 g) raw, shelled sunflower seeds

1 cup (80 g) shredded coconut meat

1 cup (112 g) almond meal

1 cup (104 g) golden flaxseed meal

1 cup (129 g) vanilla whey protein powder

¼ cup (20 g) cocoa powder

¾ teaspoon salt

Liquid stevia–dark chocolate or vanilla flavor or both

1. Preheat the oven to 325°F (170°C, or gas mark 3).
2. Use your food processor to chop your sunflower seeds a bit. You want them about the size of a grain of rice or a little smaller.
3. Spread the sunflower seeds, coconut, and almond meal on a rimmed baking sheet. Toast for 8 to 10 minutes or until just getting golden.
4. Dump this mixture in a big bowl and add the flaxseed meal, protein powder, cocoa powder, and salt. Stir everything together well and then transfer to a snap-top container and store in the fridge.
5. To serve, put about ⅓ cup (80 ml) of your cereal in a bowl and stir in ½ cup (120 ml) boiling water. Put a saucer on top of the bowl to hold in the heat and let it sit for 2 to 3 minutes.
6. Thin with a little more water to get the texture you prefer and sweeten to taste with chocolate or vanilla liquid stevia. Add some heavy cream, coconut milk, or half-and-half if you like and eat like any hot cereal.

YIELD: 12 servings, each with: 278 Calories; 16 g Fat (46.6% calories from fat); 26 g Protein; 15 g Carbohydrate; 9 g Dietary Fiber; 6 g net carbs. The analysis does not include heavy cream, coconut milk, or half-and-half.

About Making Low-Carb Crackers

To make all these cracker recipes, you will need a roll of baking parchment, available at housewares and grocery stores everywhere, or Teflon pan liners, available at really good cookware stores. My roll of baking parchment cost me all of three dollars. Do not try to simply make these crackers on a cookie sheet, no matter how well greased: As you stand at your sink, endlessly, laboriously chipping your crackers off the cookie sheet, you will be very sorry.

Since writing the original edition of this book, I made a great discovery: rolling pin rings. These are silicone rings you slip on either end of your rolling pin. They let you roll dough into a completely even sheet. They come in a set of 4 to 5 thicknesses; I use the thinnest ones for crackers and they're perfect! Find them at housewares or cooking stores or online.

SUNFLOWER PARMESAN CRACKERS

These have a great, crunchy texture and a wonderful flavor. They're a good source of minerals, too.

1 cup (145 g) raw, shelled sunflower seeds

½ cup (50 g) grated Parmesan cheese

¼ cup (60 ml) water

Salt for sprinkling

1. Preheat the oven to 325°F (170°C, or gas mark 3).

2. Put the sunflower seeds and Parmesan cheese in a food processor with the S-blade in place and process until the sunflower seeds are a fine meal with almost a flour consistency. Add the water and pulse the processor until the dough is well blended, soft, and sticky.

3. Cover your cookie sheet with a piece of baking parchment. Turn the dough out onto the parchment, tear off another sheet of parchment, and put it on top of the dough.

4. Through the top sheet of parchment, use a rolling pin to roll the dough into as thin and even a sheet as you can. Take the time to get the dough quite thin—the thinner, the better, so long as there are no holes in the dough. Peel off the top layer of parchment and use a thin, sharp, straight-bladed knife or a pizza cutter to score the dough into squares or diamonds. Sprinkle lightly with salt.

5. Bake for about 30 minutes or until evenly browned. Peel off the parchment, break along the scored lines, and let the crackers cool. Store them in a container with a tight lid.

YIELD: Carb count will depend on how thin your roll your dough and what size you cut your crackers. I make mine about the size of Wheat Thins and get about 6 dozen. If your count is the same, each cracker will have: 14 Calories; 1 g Fat (70.7% calories from fat); 1 g Protein; trace Carbohydrate; trace Dietary Fiber; 0 net carbs. That said, obviously the whole batch will have a few carbs; that zero count is an artifact of the small serving size. The whole batch has 28 g carbs with 15 g fiber, for a net carb count of 13 g for the batch.

SUNFLOWER SESAME CRACKERS

Do you think of crackers as being particularly nutritious? These are a good source of several B vitamins, folacin, calcium, and zinc!

1 cup (145 g) raw, shelled sunflower seeds

½ cup (72 g) sesame seeds

½ teaspoon salt, plus extra for sprinkling

¼ cup (60 ml) water

1. Preheat the oven to 325°F (170°C, or gas mark 3).
2. In a food processor with the S-blade attached, grind the sunflower seeds to a fine meal.
3. Add the sesame seeds and salt and pulse the food processor just long enough to combine. (You want the sesame seeds to stay whole.) Add the water and pulse to make a dough.
4. Cover your cookie sheet with a piece of baking parchment. Turn the dough out onto the parchment, tear off another sheet of parchment, and put it on top of the dough.
5. Through the top sheet of parchment, use your rolling pin to roll the dough into as thin and even a sheet as you can. Take the time to get the dough quite thin—the thinner, the better, so long as there are no holes in the dough. Peel off the top layer of parchment and use a thin, sharp, straight-bladed knife or a pizza cutter to score the dough into squares or diamonds. If you like, you could sprinkle a little salt over the surface and gently press it into the dough before scoring the crackers.
6. Bake for about 30 minutes or until they're a light golden color. Peel off the parchment, break along the scored lines, and let the crackers cool. Store them in a container with a tight lid.

YIELD: Carb count will depend on how thin you roll your dough and what size you cut your crackers. I make mine about the size of Wheat Thins and get about 6 dozen. If your count is the same, each cracker will have: 17 Calories; 1 g Fat (72.9% calories from fat); 1 g Protein; 1 g Carbohydrate; trace Dietary Fiber; 1 g net carbs.

SUNFLOWER CHEDDAR CRACKERS

Do you miss Cheese Nips? Try these. Thanks to the cheese, these crackers come with a bonus: 21 milligrams of calcium apiece!

1½ cups (218 g) raw, shelled sunflower seeds

1½ cups (173 g) grated Cheddar cheese

½ teaspoon salt, plus extra for sprinkling

¼ cup (60 ml) water

1. Preheat the oven to 325°F (170°C, or gas mark 3).
2. In a food processor with the S-blade attached, grind the sunflower seeds to a fine meal.
3. Add the Cheddar cheese and salt and pulse the processor 6 to 8 times to blend. Add the water and pulse until a dough ball forms.
4. Cover your cookie sheet with a piece of baking parchment. Turn the dough out onto the parchment, tear off another sheet of parchment, and put it on top of the dough.
5. Through the top sheet of parchment, use your rolling pin to roll the dough into as thin and even a sheet as you can. Take the time to get the dough quite thin—the thinner, the better, so long as there are no holes in the dough. Peel off the top layer of parchment. Sprinkle a little salt over the surface and gently press it into place. Use a thin, sharp, straight-bladed knife or a pizza cutter to score the dough into squares or diamonds.
6. Bake for about 30 minutes. Peel off the parchment, break along the scored lines, and let the crackers cool. Store them in a container with a tight lid.

YIELD: 72 crackers, each with: 27 Calories; 2 g Fat (73.3% calories from fat); 1 g Protein; 1 g Carbohydrate; trace Dietary Fiber; 1 g net carbs

BRAN CRACKERS

When I started low-carbing, bran crackers, being largely fiber, were very popular. We used them to scoop tuna salad, topped them with cheese, ate them with dips, all your usually cracker-y purposes. These are similar to the ones you can buy, only cheaper and better. Sorry, gluten-free and grain-free folks. Take the bran out of a bran cracker and you don't have much left.

1½ cups (90 g) wheat bran

½ cup (60 g) rice protein powder

1 teaspoon salt

1½ cups (355 ml) water

1. Preheat the oven to 350°F (180°C, or gas mark 4).
2. Combine the wheat bran, rice protein powder, and salt, stirring them together well. Stir in the water, making sure everything is wet, and let the mixture sit for about 5 minutes.
3. Cover a cookie sheet with baking parchment and turn the dough out onto the parchment (the dough will be very soft). Using the back of a spoon, pat and smooth this out into a thin, even, unbroken sheet.
4. Bake for 10 minutes and use a pizza cutter or a knife with a thin, sharp blade to score the sheet of dough into crackers. Put the sheet back in the oven and bake for another 20 minutes.
5. Turn the oven to its lowest temperature and let the crackers sit in the warm oven for at least 3 hours until they're good and dry and crisp. Break apart and store in an airtight container.

YIELD: 36 crackers, each with: 18 Calories; trace Fat (10.4% calories from fat); 3 g Protein; 2 g Carbohydrate; 1 g Dietary Fiber; 1 g net carbs

Jen's Whey Pizza Crusts

A big thank you to Jennifer Eloff for this recipe from *Splendid Low-Carbing*! To make these pizza crusts, you first have to make her Almond Whey Bake Mix #1.

ALMOND WHEY BAKE MIX #1

1⅓ cups (149 g) almond meal

¾ cup (60 g) unflavored whey protein powder

½ cup (60 g) unbleached spelt flour or ½ cup (63 g) unbleached all-purpose flour

1 tablespoon (8 g) vital wheat gluten

1. In a medium bowl, combine all the ingredients and stir well.
2. Store in an airtight container at room temperature.

YIELD: 12 servings of ¼ cup (31 g), each with: 159 Calories; 4 g Fat (21.6% calories from fat); 19 g Protein; 13 g Carbohydrate; 2 g Dietary Fiber; 11 g net carbs

WHEY PIZZA CRUSTS

Now, use the bake mix to make your pizza crusts. We trust you can figure out the part about sauce, cheese, and toppings. If you don't have a bread machine and don't want to spend a bundle, take heart: I see them at the Goodwill all the time. Oh, and this recipe uses Splenda because Jen's cookbook, *Splendid Low Carbing*, was all about the Splenda. Feel free to swap for another sweetener if you like.

¾ cup water, less 1 tablespoon (160 ml)

2 tablespoons (28 ml) olive oil

1½ cups (190 g) Almond Whey Bake Mix #1 (page 108)

⅔ cup (80 g) vital wheat gluten

½ cup (30 g) wheat bran

⅓ cup (27 g) unflavored whey protein powder

2 tablespoons (3 g) Splenda

1 tablespoon (8 g) spelt flour or all-purpose flour

1 tablespoon (13 g) sugar

1 tablespoon (8 g) skim milk powder

1 tablespoon (6 g) bread machine yeast

1 teaspoon salt

1. Preheat the oven to 375°F (190°C, or gas mark 5) and warm the water in the microwave for 30 seconds.

2. Place the water, olive oil, Almond Whey Bake Mix #1, wheat gluten, wheat bran, protein powder, Splenda, flour, sugar, skim milk powder, yeast, and salt in the bread machine.

3. Program the bread machine for pizza dough or knead and first rise.

4. When the dough is ready, remove it from the machine and divide it in half. On a lightly floured surface, roll out each ball of dough as far as possible. Cover with a towel and allow to sit for 10 to 20 minutes. Grease two 12-inch (30 cm) pizza pans.

5. Roll the dough again. Place it on the pizza pans and roll it out to fit each pan, using a small rolling pin or another small cylindrical object.

6. Cover the crusts with pizza sauce, toppings, and grated cheese. Bake on lowest oven rack for 20 to 25 minutes or until the crusts are browned. A convection oven bakes pizza evenly and more quickly, so be sure to adjust your baking time accordingly.

YIELD: 2 pizzas with 12 slices each, or 24 servings: The carb count of your toppings will vary, depending on what you use, but each serving of crust will have: 99 Calories; 3 g Fat (25.9% calories from fat); 13 g Protein; 6 g Carbohydrate; 1 g Dietary Fiber; 5 g net carbs

Tortillas

Yet another great recipe from *Splendid Low-Carbing* by Jennifer Eloff. Again, you start this recipe by making a bake mix.

ALMOND WHEY BAKE MIX #2

Obviously, this is neither grain- nor gluten-free. I didn't feel it was my place to alter Jen's recipe. I kept it because I have been unable to create a tortilla that is both low-carb and gluten-free that I consider worth eating.

1⅓ cup (149 g) almond meal

¾ cup (90 g) spelt flour

½ cup (40 g) unflavored whey protein powder

¼ cup (30 g) vital wheat gluten

1. In a medium bowl, combine all the ingredients. Mix with a wooden spoon until well combined.

2. Store in an airtight container.

YIELD: About 11 servings of ¼ cup (31 g), each with: 189 Calories; 4 g Fat (20.1% calories from fat); 21 g Protein; 18 g Carbohydrate; 2 g Dietary Fiber; 16 g net carbs

WHEY TORTILLAS

Jen Eloff, author of *Splendid Low-Carbing* says, "These, in my humble opinion, taste better than the regular, almost tasteless white flour tortillas we used to buy." Again, I've left the Splenda that Jen specified, but feel free to swap sweeteners.

¾ cup (120 ml) warm water (105° to 115°F, or 41 to 46°C; this will feel warm, but not hot, on your wrist)

2 tablespoons (26 g) sugar, divided

1 tablespoon (12 g) yeast

2 tablespoons (28 ml) olive oil

1⅓ cups (165 g) Almond Whey Bake Mix #2 (page 109)

⅔ cup (80 g) vital wheat gluten

½ cup (30 g) wheat bran

⅓ cup (40 g) spelt flour or (42 g) all-purpose flour

2 tablespoons (3 g) Splenda

1 tablespoon (8 g) skim milk powder

1 teaspoon salt

(continued)

1. Preheat the oven to 200°F (93°C, or gas mark ¼).

2. Pour the warm water in a large electric mixer bowl. Dissolve 1 tablespoon (13 g) of sugar in the water and then sprinkle the yeast over the water's surface.

3. Allow the mixture to sit for 3 to 5 minutes and then stir to dissolve completely.

4. Add the olive oil, Almond Whey Bake Mix #2, wheat gluten, wheat bran, flour, Splenda, the remaining sugar, skim milk powder, and salt. Using a dough hook attachment on an electric mixer, mix, scraping the sides of the bowl occasionally, until the dough is moist and elastic. (If you don't have an electric mixer, you can do this by hand, with a wooden spoon.)

5. On a lightly floured surface, knead the dough briefly and then place it in a greased bowl. Cover loosely with foil and place it in the oven. Turn the oven off and allow the dough to double in size. This will take about 1 hour.

6. When the dough has risen, remove, punch down, and break into 20 small balls. Cover the dough balls with a clean dish towel to keep them from drying out.

7. Roll each dough ball into a paper-thin circle on a lightly floured surface.

8. In a dry, nonstick skillet, cook each dough round briefly on both sides until brown spots appear. Place your tortillas in a plastic bag to keep them supple or refrigerate or freeze for longer storage.

YIELD: 20 tortillas, each with: 121 Calories; 3 g Fat (23.8% calories from fat); 13 g Protein; 11 g Carbohydrate; 2 g Dietary Fiber; 9 g net carbs

FATHEAD PIZZA CRUST

My friend Tom Naughton, comedian, filmmaker, author, all-around smart and funny guy, and blogger at fathead-movie.com, first posted this recipe in 2013. It quickly took the low carb world by storm. Tom kindly granted me permission to use it here, provided I inform you that it's actually his oldest son's invention, not his. I will also urge you to watch Tom's movie *Fat Head*—it's the most fun you'll ever have getting smarter. And if despair of the children in your life ever moving past Pop Tarts and McNuggets, buy them *Fat Head Kids: Stuff About Diet and Health I Wish I Knew When I Was Your Age*, by Tom and his wife, Chareva.

1½ cups (175 g) shredded mozzarella

2 tablespoons (30 g) cream cheese in small cubes

¾ cup (84 g) almond flour

1 egg

Garlic salt

1. Preheat the oven to 425°F (220°C, or gas mark 7). Line a baking sheet with baking parchment.

2. Place the two cheeses in a microwaveable bowl. Microwave for 1 minute on full power. Stir, then microwave another 30 seconds, and stir again. The mixture will be very hot!

3. Stir in the almond flour and egg.

4. Wet hands and spread the "dough" thinly on the parchment paper. It should spread evenly with dough-like consistency (if "stringy" then your cheese has hardened too much—just put it back in the microwave for maybe another 20 seconds).

5. Dock (poke rows of holes) with a fork to prevent bubbling. Sprinkle with garlic salt.

6. Bake for 8 minutes and then check to see if it's bubbling up. If it is, poke the bubbles with a fork to deflate them. Slide your crust back into the oven.

7. Bake for another 4 to 6 minutes or until lightly golden.

8. Top with sauce, cheese, sausage, pepperoni—whatever you please.

YIELD: Tom says the pizza made with this crust fed "five hungry adults." This analysis does not include toppings, but each share of the crust will have: 226 Calories; 15 g Fat (58.4% calories from fat); 17 g Protein; 7 g Carbohydrate; 0 g Dietary Fiber; 7 g net carbs

CHAPTER 5

Hot Vegetable Dishes

When folks first go low-carb, they suddenly don't know what to serve for side dishes. The answer is vegetables. If you're used to thinking of vegetables as something that sits between the meat and the potato, usually being ignored, read this chapter and think again!

You'll notice a certain reliance on frozen vegetables in this chapter. I confess, I use them often, especially green beans and broccoli. The convenience is worth it to me, and I think the quality is good. Feel free to use fresh, if you like, remembering that they'll take a few more minutes to cook.

Here, right up front, are four recipes that every low-carber needs:

CAULIFLOWER PURÉE (A.K.A. "FAUXTATOES")

This is a wonderful substitute for mashed potatoes if you want something to put a fabulous sour cream gravy on! Feel free, by the way, to use frozen cauliflower instead; it works quite well here. This is a basic recipe; play with it! Add shredded cheese, crumbled bacon, sour cream and chives—anything you might add to mashed potatoes.

1 head of fresh or 1½ pounds (680 g) frozen cauliflower

4 tablespoons (55 g) butter

Salt and pepper

1. Steam or microwave the cauliflower until it's soft.
2. Drain it thoroughly and put it through the blender or food processor until it's well pureed. Or, you can put it in a deep, narrow bowl and use your stick blender.
3. Add the butter and season with salt and pepper to taste.

YIELD: 6 servings, each with: 79 Calories; 8 g Fat (84.2% calories from fat); 1 g Protein; 2 g Carbohydrate; 1 g Dietary Fiber; 1 g net carbs

FAUXTATOES DELUXE

This extra-rich Fauxtatoes recipe comes from Adele Hite of Eathropology.com, and it is the basis for the "grits" part of her Low-Carb Shrimp and "Grits" recipe (page 204). Adele suggests, "Give your Fauxtatoes a little zing by adding a few cloves of sliced garlic to the cooking water or some roasted garlic to the food processor when blending the cauliflower with the other ingredients. Each clove of garlic added will add just 1 gram of carbohydrates to the carb count for the batch."

1 large head of cauliflower

⅓ cup (80 ml) cream (Adele does not specify heavy cream or half-and-half, but since it's drained off, it shouldn't matter to the nutrition count.)

4 ounces (115 g) sour cream

1 tablespoon (14 g) butter

Salt and pepper

1. Simmer the cauliflower in water with the heavy cream added to it. (This keeps the cauliflower sweet and prevents it from turning an unappetizing gray color.) When the cauliflower is very soft, drain thoroughly.
2. Put the still-warm cauliflower in a food processor with the sour cream, butter, and salt and pepper to taste and process until smooth. (You may have to do this in more than one batch.)

YIELD: 6 servings, each with: 140 Calories; 13 g Fat (84.0% calories from fat); 3 g Protein; 3 g Carbohydrate; 1 g Dietary Fiber; 2 g net carbs

CAULIFLOWER RICE

Many thanks to Fran McCullough! I got this idea from her book *Living Low-Carb*, and it's served me very well. This is great if you're serving a main dish with a rich sauce or gravy, but I've found so many other ways to use it! Stir in some bouillon concentrate, some snipped herbs, a little onion or scallion, some chopped nuts or crumbled bacon, and you've got an endlessly variable side dish. This also works in place of cracked wheat or couscous in salads. It's really amazing stuff.

½ of a head of cauliflower

Simply put the cauliflower through your food processor using the shredding blade. This gives the cauliflower a texture that's remarkably similar to rice. You can steam, microwave, or even sauté it in butter. Whatever you do, though, don't overcook it!

YIELD: 3 servings, each with: 24 Calories; trace Fat (6.1% calories from fat); 2 g Protein; 5 g Carbohydrate; 2 g Dietary Fiber; 3 net carbs

CAULIFLOWER RICE DELUXE

This is higher carb than plain cauliflower rice, but the wild rice adds a grain flavor that makes it quite convincing. Plus, wild rice has about 25 percent less carbohydrates than most other kinds of rice. I only use this for special occasions, but it's wonderful.

¼ cup (40 g) wild rice

¾ cup (175 ml) water

3 cups (300 g) Cauliflower Rice (page 113)

1. Put the wild rice and water in a saucepan, cover it, and set it on a burner on lowest heat until all the water is gone (at least 30 minutes, maybe a bit more).
2. Cook your cauliflower rice as desired, taking care not to overcook it to mushiness, but just until it's tender. (I steam mine in the microwave.)
3. Toss together the cooked cauliflower rice and wild rice and season as desired.

YIELD: 8 servings, each with: 27 Calories; trace Fat (3.9% calories from fat); 1 g Protein; 6 g Carbohydrate; 1 g Dietary Fiber; 5 g net carbs

COMPANY DINNER "RICE"

This is my favorite way to season the Cauliflower Rice Deluxe. It's a big hit at dinner parties!

1 small onion, chopped

1 stick of butter, melted

4 cups (400 g) Cauliflower Rice Deluxe (page 113)

6 slices of bacon, cooked until crisp, and crumbled

¼ teaspoon salt or Vege-Sal

¼ teaspoon pepper

½ cup (50 g) grated Parmesan cheese

1. Sauté the onion in the butter until it's golden and limp.
2. Toss the Cauliflower Rice Deluxe with the sautéed onion and the bacon, salt, pepper, and Parmesan cheese. Serve.

YIELD: 8 servings, each with: 184 Calories; 15 g Fat (73.9% calories from fat); 5 g Protein; 7 g Carbohydrate; 1 g Dietary Fiber; 6 g net carbs

SAUTÉED MUSHROOMS

What could be better with a steak? Feel free to play with this recipe—use all butter or all olive oil or throw in a clove of garlic; try a few variations until you find what you like. Try this recipe with mushrooms other than the familiar "button" 'shrooms. Criminis and portobellos are both delicious prepared this way, for instance. Avoid shitakes, however; they are much higher in carbohydrates.

2 tablespoons (28 g) butter

2 tablespoons (28 ml) olive oil

8 ounces (225 g) mushrooms, thickly sliced

Salt and pepper

1. Melt the butter and heat the olive oil over medium-high heat in a heavy skillet.
2. Add the mushrooms and sauté, stirring frequently, for 5 to 7 minutes or until the mushrooms are limp and brown and most of the liquid has evaporated. Salt and pepper lightly and serve.

YIELD: 3 servings, each with: 166 Calories; 17 g Fat (88.1% calories from fat); 2 g Protein; 4 g Carbohydrate; 1 g Dietary Fiber; 3 g net carbs

MUSHROOMS IN SHERRY CREAM

This is rich and flavorful and best served with a simple roast or the like. If you have a simmer burner on your stove, this is a good place to use it. If not, a heat diffuser or double boiler will reduce the risk of the sour cream "cracking."

8 ounces (225 g) small, very fresh mushrooms

¼ cup (60 ml) dry sherry

¼ teaspoon salt or Vege-Sal, divided

½ cup (115 g) sour cream

1 clove of garlic

⅛ teaspoon pepper

1. Wipe the mushrooms clean with a damp cloth and trim the woody ends off the stems.
2. Place the mushrooms in a small saucepan with the sherry and sprinkle with ⅛ teaspoon of salt.
3. Bring the sherry to a boil, turn the burner to low, cover the pan, and let the mushrooms simmer for just 3 to 4 minutes, shaking the pan once or twice while they're cooking.
4. In another saucepan over very low heat, stir together the remaining ⅛ teaspoon of salt, sour cream, garlic, and pepper. You want to heat the sour cream through, but don't let it boil or it will separate.
5. When the mushrooms are done, pour off the liquid into a small bowl. As soon as the sour cream is heated through, spoon it over the mushrooms and stir everything around over medium-low heat. If it seems a bit thick, add a teaspoon or two of the reserved liquid.
6. Stir the mushrooms and sour cream together over very low heat for 2 to 3 minutes, again making sure that the sour cream does not boil, and serve.

YIELD: 3 servings, each with: 125 Calories; 8 g Fat (68.8% calories from fat); 3 g Protein; 6 g Carbohydrate; 1 g Dietary Fiber; 5 g net carbs

SLICE OF MUSHROOM HEAVEN

This is rich enough to give Dean Ornish fits and oh-so-good. Thanks to my friend Kay for the name! This dish is good hot, but I actually like it better cold—plus, when it's cold, it cuts in nice, neat squares. It's a great breakfast or lunch, and it's definitely a fine side dish. It would even make a good vegetarian main course.

4 tablespoons (55 g) butter

1 pound (455 g) mushrooms, sliced

½ of a medium onion, finely chopped

1 clove of garlic, crushed

¼ cup (60 ml) dry white wine

1 teaspoon lemon juice

1½ cups (355 ml) half-and-half

3 eggs

1 teaspoon salt or Vege-Sal

¼ teaspoon pepper

3 cups (360 g) shredded Gruyère cheese, divided

1. Preheat the oven to 350°F (180°C, or gas mark 4).
2. Melt the butter in a heavy skillet over medium heat and begin frying the mushrooms, onion, and garlic. When the mushrooms are limp, turn the heat up a bit and boil off the liquid. Stir in the white wine and cook until that's boiled away, too.
3. Stir in the lemon juice and turn off the heat. Transfer the mixture to a large mixing bowl and stir in the half-and-half, eggs, salt, pepper, and 2 cups (240 g) of the Gruyère cheese.
4. Spray an 8- × 8-inch (20 × 20 cm) baking pan with nonstick cooking spray and spread the mixture from step 3 evenly over the bottom. Sprinkle the rest of the cheese on top and bake for 50 minutes or until the cheese is golden.

YIELD: 9 generous servings, each with: 283 Calories; 22 g Fat (69.5% calories from fat); 15 g Protein; 7 g Carbohydrate; 1 g Dietary Fiber; 6 g net carbs

KOLOKYTHIA KROKETTES

These are rapidly becoming one of our favorite side dishes. They're Greek and very, very tasty. They make a terrific side dish with roast lamb or Greek roasted chicken. Shave some time preparing the ingredients for this dish by running the zucchini and the onion through a food processor.

3 medium zucchini, grated

1 teaspoon salt
or Vege-Sal

3 eggs

1 cup (150 g) crumbled
feta cheese

1 teaspoon dried oregano

½ of a medium onion,
finely diced

⅛ teaspoon pepper

3 tablespoons (21 g)
almond meal

⅛ teaspoon guar
or xanthan

Butter

1. Mix the zucchini with the salt in a bowl and let it sit for an hour or so. Squeeze out and drain the liquid.

2. Mix in the eggs, feta cheese, oregano, onion, pepper, almond meal, and guar and combine well.

3. Spray a heavy skillet with nonstick cooking spray, add a healthy tablespoon (14 g) of butter, and melt over medium heat. Fry the batter by the tablespoonful (15 ml), turning once. Add more butter between batches, as needed, and keep the cooked krokettes warm. The trick to these is to let them get quite brown on the bottom before trying to turn them, or they tend to fall apart. If a few do fall apart, don't sweat it; the pieces will still taste incredible.

YIELD: 6 servings, each with: 134 Calories; 8g Fat (55.0% calories from fat); 9g Protein; 6g Carbohydrate; 1g Dietary Fiber; 5g net carbs. The analysis does not include butter for frying.

ZUCCHINI WITH SOUR CREAM FOR PEOPLE WHO DON'T LOVE ZUCCHINI

Marilee Wellersdick sends this recipe. My sister, who tested it, says the name is no joke—it went over well with non-zucchini-loving in-laws.

4 tablespoons (55 g) butter

1 medium onion, chopped

8 small zucchini, sliced
about ⅛ inch (3 mm) thick

Salt and pepper

1 cup (230 g) sour cream

1. Melt the butter in a large, preferably nonstick skillet. Add the onion and zucchini and salt and pepper to taste.

2. Cover and cook on medium heat, stirring occasionally, until the zucchini is translucent (15 to 20 minutes).

3. Remove from the heat and stir in the sour cream. Serve.

YIELD: 6 servings, each with: 193 Calories; 16 g Fat (70.3% calories from fat); 5 g Protein; 11 g Carbohydrate; 3 g Dietary Fiber; 8 g net carbs

ZUCCHINI CASSEROLE

Jodee Rushton, who contributed this recipe, says, "Since each serving has protein as well as vegetable, it's great as part of a lunch with some other veggies. It's also a great snack."

2 tablespoons (28 g) butter

1½ pounds (680 g) zucchini

2 eggs, beaten

½ teaspoon dry mustard

½ teaspoon ground nutmeg

½ teaspoon salt

Pepper

Liquid stevia, monkfruit, or sucralose to equal 2 teaspoons of sugar in sweetness

1 cup (235 ml) heavy cream

¼ teaspoon guar or xanthan

6 ounces (170 g) shredded sharp Cheddar cheese

1. Preheat the oven to 325°F (170°C, or gas mark 3) and coat a large casserole with cooking spray.

2. Melt the butter in a large, heavy skillet. Add the sliced zucchini and sauté over medium-high heat until tender, stirring frequently. When done, remove from the heat and let cool until lukewarm. Place in the prepared casserole.

3. Combine the eggs, dry mustard, nutmeg, salt, pepper to taste, and sweetener in a large mixing bowl. Whisk together well.

4. Add the heavy cream. Then, whisking constantly, sprinkle the guar over the mixture and whisk it in.

5. Add the Cheddar cheese to the eggs and cream and mix well.

6. Combine the egg-and-cheese mixture with the cooled zucchini in the casserole. Place in the oven and bake for 30 minutes or until set. Cool and serve.

YIELD: 6 servings, each with: 323 Calories; 30 g Fat (80.7% calories from fat); 11 g Protein; 5 g Carbohydrate; 1 g Dietary Fiber; 4 g net carbs

ZUCCHINI-CRUSTED PIZZA

This is like a somewhat-more-substantial quiche on the bottom and pizza on top. Our tester, Christina Robertson, calls this "Super easy and really really good!" adding, "plus, I could feel self-righteous since I was eating a totally wholesome pizza."

3½ cups (420 g) shredded zucchini

3 eggs

⅓ cup (27 g) unflavored whey protein powder

1½ cups (175 g) shredded mozzarella, divided

½ cup (50 g) grated Parmesan cheese

A pinch or two of dried basil

½ teaspoon salt

¼ teaspoon pepper

Oil

1 cup (245 g) sugar-free pizza sauce

Toppings as desired (sausage, pepperoni, peppers, mushrooms, or whatever you like)

1. Preheat the oven to 350°F (180°C, or gas mark 4).

2. Sprinkle the zucchini with a little salt and let it sit for 15 to 30 minutes. Put it in a strainer and press out the excess moisture.

3. Beat together the strained zucchini, eggs, protein powder, ½ cup (60 g) of mozzarella cheese, Parmesan cheese, basil, salt, and pepper.

4. Spray a 9- × 13-inch (23 x 33 cm) baking pan with nonstick cooking spray and spread the zucchini mixture in it.

5. Bake for about 25 minutes or until firm. Brush it with a little oil and broil it for about 5 minutes until it's golden.

6. Next, spread on the pizza sauce and then add the remaining 1 cup (115 g) of mozzarella cheese and other toppings. If you're using vegetables as toppings, you may want to sauté them a bit first.

7. Bake for another 25 minutes and then cut into squares and serve.

YIELD: 4 servings, each with: 348 Calories; 19 g Fat (49.1% calories from fat); 34 g Protein; 11 g Carbohydrate; 3 g Dietary Fiber; 8 g net carbs

HOT VEGETABLE DISHES

EGGPLANT PARMESAN SQUARED

When you put Parmesan cheese in the "breading," it becomes Eggplant Parmesan Squared. Two testers tried this! Cheryl Readio says that while this is time-consuming, it's a good family meal. Christina Robertson rates it a 10, and says she'd be willing to pay big bucks for this in a restaurant! How many eggs and how much pork rind–Parmesan mixture you will need will depend on how big your eggplant is.

1 large eggplant

Salt

3¼ ounces (92 g) pork rinds (There are bags just this size, but 3 oz or 3½ oz should be fine.)

1¾ cups (175 g) Parmesan cheese, divided

1 teaspoon Italian seasoning

3 eggs

¾ cup (175 ml) olive oil

1 clove of garlic, cut in half

1½ cups (375 g) no-sugar-added spaghetti sauce, divided

8 ounces (225 g) shredded mozzarella cheese or Italian Blend

1. Preheat the oven to 350°F (180°C, or gas mark 4).

2. Slice your eggplant into ¼-inch (6 mm)-thick rounds. Lay the slices on paper toweling and sprinkle them with salt on both sides. Let them sit for at least 30 minutes.

3. Put the pork rinds in your food processor along with 1½ cups (150 g) of the Parmesan cheese and the Italian seasoning. Run until the pork rinds are crumbs and the two are well-incorporated.

4. Put the pork rind–Parmesan mixture in a pie plate. Break the eggs into a shallow bowl or a second pie plate and beat well.

5. Blot each eggplant slice on paper towels, then dip each slice in the egg, and then in the pork rind–Parmesan mixture so each side is well coated. Lay the coated slices out on plates or cookie sheets and refrigerate for at least half an hour or up to an hour or two.

5. Pour ½ inch (1.3 cm) of olive oil in the bottom of a heavy skillet over medium heat. Add the garlic, letting it sizzle for a minute or two before removing it. (Our tester says to make sure you remove it all, or you'll get burnt garlic!) Now, fry the refrigerated eggplant slices until they're golden brown and crisp on both sides. (You'll have to add more olive oil as you go along.)

6. Spread ½ cup (125 g) of spaghetti sauce in the bottom of a 9- × 11-inch (23 × 33 cm) Pyrex roasting pan. Arrange half of the eggplant slices to cover the bottom of the pan. Cover with the mozzarella cheese and top with the remaining eggplant slices.

7. Pour the rest of the spaghetti sauce on and sprinkle the remaining ¼ cup (25 g) of Parmesan on top.

8. Bake for 30 minutes.

YIELD: 6 servings, each with roughly: 592 Calories; 49 g Fat (73.8% calories from fat); 28 g Protein; 11 g Carbohydrate; 3 g Dietary Fiber; 8 g net carbs

CAULIFLOWER-GREEN BEAN CASSEROLE

Reader Honey Ashton says her family loves this. How about serving this at Thanksgiving dinner?

2 bags (1 pound, or 455 g each) of frozen cauliflower

1 cup (100 g) crosscut green beans

1 cup (225 g) mayonnaise

1 cup (225 g) butter

¼ of a small yellow or white onion, finely sliced

1 cup (80 g) freshly cooked, crumbled bacon

1 cup (115 g) shredded mixture Mozzarella and Cheddar cheeses

1. Preheat the oven to 300°F (150°C, or gas mark 2).

2. Follow the package directions to cook the cauliflower; add the green beans to cook with the cauliflower. Drain after cooking. (These are Honey's instructions. Me, I'd steam those vegetables in my microwave according to, as she says, package directions.)

3. Place the cooked veggies in a large casserole and stir in the mayonnaise, butter, onion, and bacon. Mix thoroughly.

4. Top the casserole with the cheese mixture. Bake for 20 minutes or until the cheese has melted and serve immediately.

YIELD: 8 servings, each with: 538 Calories; 54 g Fat (84.9% calories from fat); 11 g Protein; 10 g Carbohydrate; 4 g Dietary Fiber; 6 g net carbs

CAULIFLOWER KUGEL

A kugel is a traditional Jewish casserole that comes in both sweet and savory varieties. This savory kugel makes a nice side dish with a simple meat course. It could also be served as a vegetarian main dish.

2 packages (12 ounces, or 340 g each) of frozen cauliflower, thawed

1 medium onion, chopped

1 cup (225 g) cottage cheese

1 cup (115 g) shredded Cheddar cheese

4 eggs

½ teaspoon salt or Vege-Sal

¼ teaspoon pepper

Paprika

1. Preheat the oven to 350°F (180°C, or gas mark 4).

2. Chop the cauliflower into ½-inch (1.3 cm) pieces. Combine with the onion, cottage cheese, Cheddar cheese, eggs, salt, and pepper in a large mixing bowl and mix very well.

3. Spray an 8- × 8-inch (20 × 20 cm) baking pan with nonstick cooking spray and spread the cauliflower mixture evenly on the bottom. Sprinkle paprika lightly over the top and bake for 50 to 60 minutes or until the kugel is set and lightly browned.

YIELD: 9 servings, each with: 125 Calories; 7 g Fat (48.0% calories from fat); 11 g Protein; 6 g Carbohydrate; 2 g Dietary Fiber; 4 g net carbs

SMOKY CAULIFLOWER AND SAUSAGE

Holly Holder, who sent this recipe, says, "My kids, who wouldn't touch cauliflower, loved this recipe. They had no idea what it was—and my lips are sealed!" She adds, "Don't be fooled into overcooking your casserole: smoked Gruyère will not look melted, but it will be very creamy when dished out."

1 medium head of cauliflower or 1 bag (1 pound, or 455 g) of frozen cauliflower

1 package (8 ounces, or 225 g) of cream cheese, softened

½ pound (225 g) bulk sausage, cooked and crumbled

4 ounces (115 g) smoked Gruyère, Swiss, Provolone, or any other smoked cheese, cut into thin slices

Salt and pepper

1. Preheat the oven to 350°F (180°C, or gas mark 4).

2. Cut up the cauliflower and steam or microwave it until tender. Mash with a potato masher and mix in the cream cheese and sausage.

3. Spread half of the cauliflower mixture in a 2-quart (1.9 L) casserole. Top with half of the cheese slices.

4. Add the remaining cauliflower and top with the remaining cheese. Bake until bubbly (about 30 minutes).

YIELD: 6 servings, each with: 375 Calories; 35 g Fat (82.5% calories from fat); 13 g Protein; 3 g Carbohydrate; 1 g Dietary Fiber; 2 g net carbs

GREEN BEANS ALMONDINE A.K.A. GREEN ALMOND BEANS

My girlfriend Tonya always though that this was a terribly complicated dish because it's elegant and delicious. As if! It's child's play. This was a feature of all the holiday meals of my childhood, but it's too good to save for just holidays!

1 bag (1 pound, or 455 g) of frozen French-cut green beans (You can use crosscut if you prefer, but French-cut are dressier.)

½ cup (55 g) slivered or (46 g) sliced almonds

4 tablespoons (55 g) butter

1. Steam or microwave the green beans according to the package directions.

2. While the beans are cooking, sauté the almonds in the butter over medium heat, stirring frequently.

3. When the beans are done and the almonds are golden, drain the water off of the beans and pour the almonds and butter over them; use a scraper to get all the butter. Toss the mixture and serve.

YIELD: 4 servings, each with: 245 Calories; 21 g Fat (72.9% calories from fat); 6 g Protein; 12 g Carbohydrate; 4 g Dietary Fiber; 8 g net carbs

Green Beans Pecandine

Make this exactly as you would Green Beans Almondine, only substitute ½ cup (55 g) of chopped pecans for the slivered almonds. It's just as good!

YIELD: 4 servings, each with: 238 Calories; 22 g Fat (77.0% calories from fat); 3 g Protein; 11 g Carbohydrate; 4 g Dietary Fiber; 7 g net carbs

Cashew Green Beans

This tasty twist comes from a reader known only as Starrc—thanks, whoever you are! Make as you would Green Beans Almondine, but substitute ½ cup (70 g) of raw cashew pieces for the almonds. (Or to skip the sautéing step, chop roasted, salted cashews and toss with the green beans and butter. But all my local health food stores carry raw cashew pieces in bulk, which are considerably cheaper than whole, roasted cashews.)

YIELD: 4 servings, each with: 233 Calories; 20 g Fat (71.0% calories from fat); 5 g Protein; 13 g Carbohydrate; 4 g Dietary Fiber; 9 g net carbs

LEMON-PEPPER BEANS

I think this makes a particularly good side dish with chicken or fish. Use fresh green beans if you prefer; I just enjoy the ease of frozen. Anyway, they're what Mom used. If you do use fresh, get a little more than a pound (455 g) to compensate for trimming.

1 bag (1 pound, or 455 g) of frozen green beans, French-cut or crosscut, thawed

¼ cup (60 ml) olive oil

1 clove of garlic, crushed

1 tablespoon (15 ml) lemon juice

¼ teaspoon pepper

1. Over high heat, stir-fry the green beans in the olive oil until they're tender-crisp, about 7 to 10 minutes.

2. Stir in the garlic, lemon juice, and pepper.

3. Cook just another minute and serve.

YIELD: 4 servings, each with: 159 Calories; 14 g Fat (73.1% calories from fat); 2 g Protein; 9 g Carbohydrate; 3 g Dietary Fiber; 6 g net carbs

HOT VEGETABLE DISHES

HERBED GREEN BEANS

Again, feel free to use fresh green beans, if you like, and fresh herbs, too, if you have them on hand. If you do, use at least a couple of teaspoons of each, minced. (I really need to plant an herb garden.)

3 tablespoons (45 g) butter

1 bag (1 pound, or 455 g) of frozen, crosscut green beans, thawed

¼ cup (30 g) finely diced celery

¼ cup (40 g) finely diced onion

1 clove of garlic, crushed

½ teaspoon dried rosemary, slightly crushed

½ teaspoon dried basil, slightly crushed

Salt

1. Melt the butter in a heavy skillet over medium heat. Add the green beans, celery, onion, and garlic to the skillet and sauté until the beans are tender-crisp.

2. Stir in the rosemary and basil and sauté another minute or so.

3. Salt to taste and serve.

YIELD: 4 servings, each with: 121 Calories; 9 g Fat (61.5% calories from fat); 2 g Protein; 10 g Carbohydrate; 4 g Dietary Fiber; 6 g net carbs

ITALIAN BEAN BAKE

If you're having a roast, simplify your life by serving this dish—it can cook right alongside the meat. Find Italian green beans with the other frozen vegetables in big grocery stores with particularly complete frozen vegetable sections. They're wider than regular green beans and flat, though the flavor is similar. If you can't find them, go ahead and use crosscut green beans. If you're not serving a roast and you'd like to slice 30 minutes off the baking time for this dish, microwave the beans until they're tender-crisp before you combine them with the sauce.

1 bag (1 pound, or 455 g) of frozen Italian green beans, thawed

1 can (8 ounces, or 225 g) of tomato sauce

¼ of a small onion, minced

1 clove of garlic, crushed

1 teaspoon spicy brown or Dijon mustard

¼ teaspoon pepper

½ cup (58 g) shredded mozzarella

1. Preheat the oven to 350°F (180°C, or gas mark 4).

2. Put the green beans in an 8-cup (1.9 L) casserole.

3. Combine the tomato sauce, onion, garlic, mustard, and a dash of pepper in a mixing bowl. Stir the sauce into the beans.

4. Bake for 1 hour or until the beans are tender. Then, top with the mozzarella cheese and bake for another 3 to 5 minutes or until the cheese is melted. Serve.

YIELD: 4 servings, each with: 106 Calories; 4 g Fat (30.3% calories from fat); 6 g Protein; 14 g Carbohydrate; 4 g Dietary Fiber; 10 g net carbs

GREEK BEANS

I love Greek food! I find green beans cooked much like this at nearly every Greek restaurant I visit.

2 tablespoons (28 ml) olive oil, plus more if needed

½ of a small onion, finely minced

1 clove of garlic, crushed

1 bag (1 pound, or 455 g) of frozen, cut green beans, thawed

½ cup (121 g) diced canned tomatoes

¼ cup (60 ml) beef broth or bouillon

¼ cup (60 ml) dry white wine

1. Heat the olive oil in a large, heavy skillet over medium heat. Add the onion and garlic and sauté for a minute or two.

2. Drain the green beans and add them to the skillet, stirring to coat. Sauté the beans for 6 to 7 minutes, adding another tablespoon (15 ml) of oil if the skillet starts to get dry.

3. Stir in the tomatoes, beef broth, and wine. Turn up the heat to medium-high and let everything simmer until the beans are just tender-crisp and most of the liquid has cooked off (about 5 minutes).

YIELD: 4 servings, each with: 126 Calories; 7 g Fat (50.5% calories from fat); 3 g Protein; 12 g Carbohydrate; 3 g Dietary Fiber; 9 g net carbs

GREEN BEANS VINAIGRETTE

This is easy-peasy if you have the dressing in the fridge! Feel free to add a sprinkle of Parmesan cheese if you like and if you're dairy-free, be sure to use olive oil.

1 bag (1 pound, or 455 g) of frozen, cut green beans, thawed

4 tablespoons (55 g) butter or (60 ml) olive oil

4 tablespoons (60 ml) Italian Vinaigrette Dressing (page 163, or use bottled)

1. Sauté the green beans in the butter in a large, heavy skillet set over medium-high heat.

2. When they're not quite tender-crisp, maybe 6 to 7 minutes, stir in the Italian Vinaigrette Dressing and simmer for another 4 to 5 minutes.

YIELD: 4 servings, each with: 209 Calories; 20 g Fat (79.8% calories from fat); 2 g Protein; 9 g Carbohydrate; 3 g Dietary Fiber; 6 g net carbs

GREEN BEANS A LA CARBONARA

Bacon, cheese, and garlic—if these three things won't get your family to eat green beans, nothing will. Another great recipe from the *Low Carb Success Calender* by Vicki Cash, this has enough protein to be a main dish.

7 to 10 thick slices of bacon	**6 eggs**
1 teaspoon olive oil	**3 tablespoons (45 ml) cream**
½ of a small onion, chopped	**½ teaspoon red pepper flakes**
1 clove of garlic, minced	**¼ teaspoon nutmeg**
1 bag (1 pound, or 455 g) of frozen French-cut green beans	**Salt and pepper**
	¾ cup (75 g) grated Parmesan cheese

1. Fry the bacon slices in a large, nonstick skillet over medium heat until they're not quite crisp. Drain on paper towels, add the olive oil to the pan, and sauté the onion and garlic in the remaining bacon grease until brown.

2. Place the green beans in a 2-quart (1.9 L) microwave-safe bowl with 1 tablespoon (15 ml) of water. Cover and microwave on High for 10 minutes, stirring halfway through cooking.

3. While the beans are cooking, dice the bacon and add it to the onion and garlic. Keep the skillet over a warm burner. Beat together the eggs, cream, red pepper flakes, nutmeg, and salt and pepper to taste, as if you were preparing scrambled eggs.

4. Turn the heat under the skillet up to medium. Add the hot green beans, egg mixture, and Parmesan cheese to the skillet, stirring until the eggs are cooked. Serve immediately.

YIELD: 4 servings, each with: 324 Calories; 22 g Fat (60.8% calories from fat); 20 g Protein; 12 g Carbohydrate; 3 g Dietary Fiber; 9 g net carbs

In Defense of Brussels Sprouts

I know of few vegetables that draw such a reflexive negative reaction as Brussels sprouts. I sympathize; I, too, once considered myself a Brussels sprout–hater. Thinking of them as Barbie cabbages, I had tried them simply boiled and buttered. I found them nasty and bitter, tasting like I'd imagine nail polish remover does. I was so disappointed, I didn't try them again for years.

Then, dear friends served them to us fried, as described as follows, and both my husband—another Brussels-phobe—and I loved them! My mind reopened, I tried new ways of cooking them, only to discover that the only way we *don't* like Brussels sprouts is boiled and butter. If you "hate" Brussels sprouts because of traumatic childhood memories, do give them another try with one of these recipes. Properly cooked, they're divine.

FRIED BRUSSELS SPROUTS

We've served these to company many times, and they're always a hit, even with people who think they don't like Brussels sprouts. We didn't think we liked Brussels sprouts, either, until our dear friends John and Judy Horwitz served them to us this way—and suddenly we were addicted.

1 pound (455 g) Brussels sprouts (Fresh is best, but frozen will do.)	**Olive oil** **3 or 4 cloves of garlic, crushed**

1. If you're using fresh Brussels sprouts, remove any bruised, wilted, or discolored outer leaves and trim the stems. If you're using frozen Brussels sprouts, just thaw them.

2. In a heavy-bottomed pot or skillet, heat ½ inch (1.3 cm) of olive oil over a medium flame. Add the Brussels sprouts and fry them, stirring occasionally, until they are dark brown all over—you really want them just about burned.

3. For the last minute or so, add the garlic and stir it around well. Remove the skillet from the heat and serve the sprouts before the garlic burns. They're unbelievable!

YIELD: 4 servings, each with: 4 g Protein; 10 g Carbohydrate; 4 g Dietary Fiber; 6 g net carbs. I can't possibly get the calorie and fat numbers here, but certainly these are good and oily!

SIMPLE SPROUTS

Slicing Brussels sprouts makes them a whole new vegetable! Some of my local grocery stores have started carrying them presliced, making this Super-Simple Sprouts.

1 pound (455 g) Brussels sprouts	**3–4 tablespoons (45–55 g) butter**

1. Trim the stems of your Brussels sprouts and remove any wilted or yellowed leaves. Run your sprouts through the slicing blade of your food processor.

2. Melt the butter in a heavy skillet and sauté the Brussels sprouts over medium-high heat until they're tender but not mushy (about 7 to 10 minutes). They should be getting a few brown spots around the edges. Serve.

YIELD: 4 servings, each with: 146 Calories; 12 g Fat (67.6% calories from fat); 4 g Protein; 9 g Carbohydrate; 4 g Dietary Fiber; 5 g net carbs

HOT VEGETABLE DISHES

NUTTY BRUSSELS SPROUTS

I am very fond of Brussels Sprouts, but it is a rare food that cannot be improved with hazelnuts and bacon. This would be a great holiday side dish.

1 pound (455 g) Brussels sprouts	4 slices of bacon
½ cup (68 g) hazelnuts	¼ teaspoon salt or Vege-Sal
6 tablespoons (85 g) butter, divided	⅛ teaspoon pepper

1. Trim the stems of your Brussels sprouts and remove any wilted or yellowed leaves. Thinly slice your Brussels sprouts using the slicing blade of a food processor.

2. Chop the hazelnuts to a medium texture in a food processor.

3. Melt 2 tablespoons (28 g) of the butter in a heavy skillet over medium heat and add the hazelnuts. Sauté, stirring frequently, for about 7 minutes or until golden. Remove from the skillet and set aside.

4. Cook the bacon, either using a separate skillet or the microwave. While the bacon is cooking, melt the remaining 4 tablespoons (55 g) of butter over medium-high heat in the same skillet you used for the hazelnuts. Add the sliced Brussels sprouts and sauté, stirring frequently, for 7 to 10 minutes or until tender.

5. Stir in the toasted hazelnuts and the seasonings and transfer to a serving dish. Drain the bacon, crumble it over the top, and serve.

YIELD: 4 servings, each with: 344 Calories; 32 g Fat (78.3% calories from fat); 8 g Protein; 12 g Carbohydrate; 5 g Dietary Fiber; 7 g net carbs

'BAGA FRIES

I'll bet you've never tried a rutabaga, and you're just guessing you're not going to like them. Well, everyone who tries these likes them.

2 pounds (910 g) rutabaga (1 large)	3–4 tablespoons (45–55 g) butter
	Salt

1. Peel your rutabaga and cut it into strips the size of big steak fries, using a good, big, heavy knife with a sharp blade.

2. Steam the "fries" over boiling water in a pan with a tight lid until they're easily pierced with a fork but not mushy (about 10 to 15 minutes). You want them still to be al dente.

3. Melt the butter in a heavy-bottomed skillet over medium-high heat and fry the strips of rutabaga until they're browned on all sides—you'll need to do this in batches. Salt and serve.

YIELD: 6 servings, each with: 122 Calories; 8 g Fat (55.8% calories from fat); 2 g Protein; 12 g Carbohydrate; 4 g Dietary Fiber; 8 g net carbs

GLAZED TURNIPS

These make a wonderful substitute for potatoes with a roast. Try them for a holiday meal!

3 cups (450 g) chopped turnips, cut into small chunks

2 tablespoons (28 g) butter

½ of a small onion

2 teaspoons erythritol

½ teaspoon beef bouillon concentrate

½ teaspoon paprika

1. Steam or microwave the turnip chunks until tender and then drain. (I steam mine in the microwave for about 7 minutes on High.)

2. Melt the butter in a heavy skillet over medium heat. Add the turnips and onion and sauté until the onion is limp.

3. Stir in the erythritol, bouillon concentrate, and paprika, coating all the turnips, and sauté for just another minute or two.

YIELD: 6 servings, each with: 55 Calories; 4 g Fat (61.7% calories from fat); 1 g Protein; 5 g Carbohydrate; 1 g Dietary Fiber; 4 g net carbs

MASHED GARLIC TURNIPS

Are you growing restive with Fauxtatoes? Try this. It's great with a steak, a roast, or chops.

2 pounds (910 g) turnips, peeled and cut into chunks

8 cloves of garlic, peeled and sliced

2 tablespoons (28 g) butter

2 tablespoons (30 g) prepared horseradish

1 teaspoon salt or Vege-Sal

½ teaspoon pepper

⅛ teaspoon ground nutmeg

3 tablespoons (9 g) chopped fresh chives

1. Place the turnips and the garlic in a saucepan with a tight-fitting lid. Add water to fill about halfway, cover, and place over medium-high heat. Bring to a boil, turn down the burner, and simmer until quite soft (about 15 minutes). Drain the turnips and garlic very well.

2. Using a potato masher, mash the turnips and garlic together. Stir in the butter, horseradish, salt, pepper, and nutmeg and mix well. Just before serving, stir in the chives.

YIELD: 6 servings, each with: 76 Calories; 4 g Fat (44.7% calories from fat); 2 g Protein; 10 g Carbohydrate; 3 g Dietary Fiber; 7 g net carbs

TURNIPS AU GRATIN

This is sublime with top-quality Vermont Cheddar cheese, but you can make it with any good, sharp Cheddar. It makes great side dish with ham.

2 pounds (910 g) turnips, peeled and thinly sliced

1 cup (235 ml) heavy cream

1 cup (235 ml) half-and-half

3 cups (345 g) shredded sharp Cheddar cheese, divided

2 teaspoons prepared horseradish

¼ teaspoon ground nutmeg

½ of a medium onion, sliced

Salt and pepper

1. Preheat the oven to 350°F (180°C, or gas mark 4).

2. Steam the turnips until they're just tender. (I steam mine in the microwave for 7 minutes on High.)

3. While the turnips are cooking, combine the heavy cream and half-and-half in a saucepan over very low heat. Bring to a simmer.

4. When the cream is up to temperature, whisk in 2⅔ cups (307 g) of the Cheddar cheese, a couple of tablespoons (14 g) at a time. Stir each addition until it's completely melted before adding more. When all of the cheese is melted into the sauce, whisk in the horseradish and nutmeg. Turn off the burner.

5. Spray an 8- × 8-inch (20 × 20 cm) glass baking dish with nonstick cooking spray. Put about one-third of the turnips in the dish and scatter half of the sliced onion over it. Add another layer of one-third of the turnips, half of the onions, and the final third of the turnips on top. Pour the cheese sauce over the whole thing and scatter the last ⅓ cup (38 g) of cheese over the top.

6. Bake for 30 to 40 minutes or until golden.

YIELD: 6 servings, each with: 455 Calories; 38 g Fat (74.4% calories from fat); 17 g Protein; 12 g Carbohydrate; 2 g Dietary Fiber; 10 g net carbs

INDIAN CABBAGE

This is good with anything curried. The combination of seasonings works well with green beans, too. If you're dairy-free, use oil instead of butter.

Extra virgin coconut oil or butter

1 teaspoon black mustard seed

1 teaspoon turmeric

4 cups (280 g) shredded cabbage

1 teaspoon salt or Vege-Sal

1. Put a heavy skillet over medium heat. Add a few tablespoons of (45 to 60 ml) oil or (45 to 55 g) butter (I like to use coconut oil). Then, add the mustard seed and the turmeric. Sauté together for just a minute.

2. Stir in the cabbage, add the salt, and stir-fry for a few minutes, combining the cabbage well with the spices.

3. Add a couple of tablespoons (28 ml) of water, cover, and let the cabbage steam for a couple more minutes until it is tender-crisp.

YIELD: 4 servings, each with: 112 Calories; 11 g Fat (80.7% calories from fat); 1 g Protein; 4 g Carbohydrate; 2 g Dietary Fiber; 2 g net carbs

SWEET-AND-SOUR CABBAGE

This dish is old-timey and kinda country. I think it would be great with simple pan-broiled pork chops.

3 slices of bacon

4 cups (280 g) shredded cabbage

2 tablespoons (28 ml) cider vinegar

Liquid stevia, monkfruit, or sucralose to equal 2 teaspoons of sugar in sweetness

1. In a heavy skillet, cook the bacon until crisp. Remove and drain.
2. Add the cabbage to the bacon grease and sauté it until tender-crisp.
3. Stir in the vinegar and sweetener, crumble in the bacon, and serve.

YIELD: 4 servings, each with: 46 Calories; 3 g Fat (45.7% calories from fat); 2 g Protein; 4 g Carbohydrate; 2 g Dietary Fiber; 2 g net carbs

THAI STIR-FRIED CABBAGE

This exotic and tasty dish cooks lightening-fast, so make sure you have everything cut up, mixed up, and ready to go before you start stir-frying. Add shrimp for a main dish!

2 tablespoons (28 ml) lime juice

2 tablespoons (28 ml) Thai fish sauce (nam pla)

⅔ teaspoon red pepper flakes

3 tablespoons (45 ml) peanut or coconut oil

6 cups (450 g) finely shredded napa cabbage

6 scallions, sliced

2 cloves of garlic, crushed

⅓ cup (20 g) unsweetened, flaked coconut

¼ cup (36 g) chopped, dry-roasted peanuts

1. Mix together the lime juice, fish sauce, and red pepper flakes. Set aside.
2. In a wok or heavy-bottomed skillet, heat the oil over high heat. Add the cabbage, scallions, and garlic and stir-fry for no more than 5 minutes or just until the cabbage is hot through.
3. Add the lime juice mixture to the cabbage and stir to coat. Let it cook just another minute and stir in the coconut. Serve topped with chopped peanuts.

YIELD: 4 servings, each with: 252 Calories; 18 g Fat (78.4% calories from fat); 4 g Protein; 7 g Carbohydrate; 2 g Dietary Fiber; 5 g net carbs

RATATOUILLE

You pronounce this oh-so-French dish "rat-a-TOO-ee." You want to use your largest skillet for this dish—possibly even your wok, if you have one. This quantity of veggies will nearly overwhelm even a 10-inch (25 cm) skillet. And don't be afraid to toss in a little more olive oil if you need it while sautéing. Try this with a simple fish dish—it would be nice to make a bed of the vegetables and serve the fish on top!

¾ cup (175 ml) olive oil, plus more if needed

3 cups (246 g) chopped eggplant, cut into 1-inch (2.5 cm) cubes

3 cups (360 g) sliced zucchini

1 medium onion, sliced

2 green peppers, cut into strips

3 cloves of garlic

1 can (14½ ounces, or 410 g) of sliced tomatoes

1 can (4 ounces, or 115 g) of sliced black olives, drained

1½ teaspoons dried oregano

½ teaspoon salt

¼ teaspoon pepper

1. Heat the olive oil in a heavy skillet over medium heat. Add the eggplant, zucchini, onion, green peppers, and garlic.

2. Sauté for 15 to 20 minutes, turning with a spatula from time to time so it all comes in contact with the olive oil. Once the vegetables are all starting to look about half-cooked, add the tomatoes (including the liquid), olives, oregano, salt, and pepper.

3. Stir it all together, cover, turn the burner to low, and let the whole thing simmer for 40 minutes or so.

YIELD: 8 servings, each with: 238 Calories; 22 g Fat (79.6% calories from fat); 2 g Protein; 11 g Carbohydrate; 3 g Dietary Fiber; 8 g net carbs

ZUCCHINI-MUSHROOM SKILLET

Consider this as a side toward the end of July, when every home gardener is frantically giving away zucchini! Add grilled chicken or steak, and you're done! For that matter, you could turn this into a veggie packet in foil and cook it on the grill.

1 large or 2 medium zucchini

8 ounces (225 g) mushrooms

1 medium onion

½ cup (120 ml) olive oil

2 cloves of garlic, crushed

½ teaspoon oregano

Salt

1. Halve the zucchini lengthways and then cut into 1-inch (2.5 cm) half-rounds. Wipe the mushrooms clean with a damp cloth and then quarter them vertically. Halve the onion and cut it into slices about ¼ inch (6 mm) thick.

2. Heat the olive oil in a heavy skillet over medium-high heat. Add the zucchini, mushrooms, onion, and garlic and stir-fry until the zucchini and mushrooms are just barely tender and the onion is tender-crisp (about 10 minutes).

3. Stir in the oregano, salt to taste, and serve.

YIELD: 4 servings, each with: 273 Calories; 27 g Fat (87.1% calories from fat); 2 g Protein; 7 g Carbohydrate; 2 g Dietary Fiber; 5 g net carbs

SNOW PEAS, MUSHROOMS, AND BEAN SPROUTS

The combination of flavors here is magical, somehow. These three vegetables seem to be made for each other.

3 tablespoons (45 ml) peanut oil

4 ounces (115 g) fresh mushrooms, sliced

4 ounces (115 g) fresh snow peas, ends pinched off and any strings removed

4 ounces (115 g) fresh bean sprouts

1 teaspoon soy sauce

1. Heat the oil in a wok or heavy skillet over high heat. Add the snow peas and mushrooms and stir-fry until the snow peas are almost tender-crisp (3 to 4 minutes).

2. Add the bean sprouts and stir-fry for just another 30 seconds to 1 minute.

3. Stir in the soy sauce and serve.

YIELD: **3 servings, each with:** 157 Calories; 14 g Fat (75.6% calories from fat); 3 g Protein; 7 g Carbohydrate; 2 g Dietary Fiber; 5 g net carbs

BUTTERED SNOW PEAS

If you've only had snow peas in Chinese food, try them this way. They're really wonderful.

4 tablespoons (55 g) butter

12 ounces (340 g) fresh snow peas

1. Melt the butter in a heavy skillet over medium-high heat.

2. Add the snow peas and sauté just until tender-crisp.

YIELD: **3 servings, each with:** 183 Calories; 16 g Fat (74.6% calories from fat); 3 g Protein; 9 g Carbohydrate; 3 g Dietary Fiber; 6 g net carbs

About Cooking Asparagus

Asparagus is divine if cooked correctly and mushy and nasty if overcooked—and it's way too easy to overcook. If you're cooking it on the stove top, the best way, believe it or not, is standing up in an old stove top coffee perker with the guts removed. This lets the tougher ends boil while the tender tips steam. I put my asparagus in the coffee pot, add about 3 inches (7.5 cm) of water, and put on the lid. Set it over a medium-high burner and bring the water to a boil. Once it's boiling, 5 minutes is plenty!

If you don't have a coffee perker (or an asparagus pot, for that matter, which lets you do the same thing), I'd recommend that you microwave your asparagus. Place the stems in a microwave-safe casserole or glass pie plate. If you're using a pie plate or a round casserole, arrange the asparagus with the tips toward the center. (I've microwaved asparagus in a rectangular casserole, and it's come out fine.) Add a tablespoon or two (15 to 28 ml) of water and cover with plastic wrap or a lid, if your casserole has one. Microwave it on High for 5 to 6 minutes and then remove the plastic wrap or lid immediately, or the trapped steam will keep cooking your asparagus. These directions work well for 1 pound (450 g) of asparagus—you may need to play around with timing if you're using a different amount.

One more asparagus note: Believe it or not, the proper way to eat asparagus is with your fingers, dipping it in whatever sauce may be provided. This is according to Miss Manners, Amy Vanderbilt, and all other etiquette authorities. It's definitely more fun than using a fork, and it's amusing to see people look at you, thinking, "With her fingers?" knowing all along that you are the one who is correct.

ASPARAGUS WITH LEMON BUTTER

To me, this is the taste of springtime. With roast lamb, it's Easter Dinner!

1 pound (455 g) asparagus

¼ cup (55 g) butter

1 tablespoon (15 ml) lemon juice

1. Break the ends off the asparagus where they snap naturally. Steam or microwave the asparagus until just barely tender-crisp.

2. While the asparagus is cooking, melt the butter and stir in the lemon juice. Put the lemon butter in a pretty little pitcher and let each diner pour a pool of it onto his or her plate for dipping.

YIELD: 4 servings, each with: 116 Calories; 12 g Fat (85.2% calories from fat); 1 g Protein; 3 g Carbohydrate; 1 g Dietary Fiber; 2 g net carbs

ASPARAGUS WITH AIOLI AND PARMESAN

Yes, it's cold asparagus, dipped in garlic sauce and cheese. Yum!

2 pounds (910 g) asparagus

Aioli (page 278)

½ cup (50 g) grated Parmesan cheese

1. Break the ends off the asparagus where they snap naturally. Steam or microwave the asparagus for a bare 3 to 4 minutes or just until the color brightens. (You want these even less done than tender-crisp.) Chill the asparagus.

2. At dinnertime, give each diner a couple of tablespoons (28 g) of aioli and a little hill of Parmesan cheese. Dip each asparagus stalk in the Aioli, then in the Parmesan, and eat.

YIELD: 6 servings, each with: 223 Calories; 21 g Fat (81.5% calories from fat); 6 g Protein; 5 g Carbohydrate; 2 g Dietary Fiber; 3 g net carbs

ASPARAGUS PECANDINE

I never thought anything could be as good with asparagus as lemon butter. Then I tried this.

5 tablespoons (70 g) butter

½ cup (55 g) chopped pecans

1½ teaspoons tarragon vinegar

1 pound (455 g) asparagus, steamed just until tender-crisp

1. Melt the butter in a heavy skillet over medium-high heat. Stir in the pecans and sauté, stirring frequently, for 5 to 7 minutes or until the pecans are golden and crisp through. Stir in the tarragon vinegar.

2. Place the asparagus on serving plates and spoon the sauce over it. Serve immediately.

YIELD: 4 servings, each with): 240 Calories; 25 g Fat (87.1% calories from fat); 3 g Protein; 6 g Carbohydrate; 2 g Dietary Fiber; 4 g net carbs

GARLIC ASPARAGUS

This dish you don't eat with your fingers. It's quick, easy, and good, especially with fish or chicken.

1 pound (455 g) fresh asparagus

¼ cup (60 ml) olive oil

2 cloves of garlic, crushed

1. Break the ends off the asparagus where they snap naturally. Cut asparagus on the diagonal into 1-inch (2.5 cm) lengths.

2. Heat the olive oil in a heavy skillet over medium-high heat. Add the asparagus and sauté, stirring occasionally, until it is tender-crisp (6 to 8 minutes).

3. Stir in the garlic, sauté 1 minute more, and serve.

YIELD: 4 servings, each with: 148 Calories; 14 g Fat (78.8% calories from fat); 3 g Protein; 6 g Carbohydrate; 2 g Dietary Fiber; 4 g net carbs

FRIED ARTICHOKES

This is one of the fastest ways I know to cook artichokes. If you've never encountered a fresh artichoke, you may be surprised to find that they're sort of fun to eat: You peel off the leaves, one by one, and drag the base of each one between your teeth, scraping off the little bit of edible stuff and the bottom of each leaf. When you've finished doing that and you have a big pile of artichoke leaves on your plate, use a fork and knife to eat the delectable heart.

2 large artichoke

Olive oil

Lemon wedges

Salt

1. Cut about 1 inch (2.5 cm) off the top of your artichoke, trim the stem, and pull off the bottom few rows of leaves. Now, slice it vertically down the center. You'll see the "choke"—the fuzzy, inedible part at the center. Using the tip of a spoon, scrape every last bit of this out. (It pulls off of the yummy bottom part of the artichoke quite easily.)

2. In a large, heavy skillet, heat 1 inch (2.5 cm) of olive oil over medium-high heat. When the oil is hot, add your cleaned artichoke, flat-side down. Fry for about 10 minutes, turning over halfway through. It should be tender and just starting to brown a bit. Drain on paper towels or a brown paper bag.

3. Serve the artichoke halves with lemon wedges to squeeze over them and with salt to sprinkle on them to taste.

YIELD: 2 servings, each with: 60 Calories; trace Fat (2.4% calories from fat); 4 g Protein; 13 g Carbohydrate; 7 g Dietary Fiber; 6 g net carbs. The carb and protein counts are accurate, but without a way to determine how much olive oil clings to each artichoke, it's impossible to get an accurate calorie or fat count. It's higher than this, though!

ARTICHOKES WITH AIOLI

Here we have artichokes with a rich, garlicky sauce. What's not to like?

6 artichokes　　　　　　**1 batch of Aioli (page 278)**

Salt

1. Cut about 1 inch (2.5 cm) off the top of each artichoke, trim the stems, and pull off the bottom few rows of leaves.

2. Put enough water to cover the artichokes in a good-size kettle and bring it to a boil. Add a couple of teaspoons of salt and drop in your artichokes.

3. Turn the burner down and let the artichokes simmer until they're tender. Depending on how big they are, this could take anywhere from 15 to 45 minutes. When the artichokes are done, drain them well.

4. Divide the Aioli between 6 small dishes and put a dish of Aioli and an artichoke on each serving plate.

5. Peel off the leaves, one by one, and dip the tender, edible bottom ends in the Aioli. Then, scrape them between your teeth. Each diner will need to cut or scrape off the fuzzy "choke" after eating all the leaves. They can then use a knife and fork to cut up the artichoke's heart and dip it in the remaining Aioli.

YIELD: 6 servings, each with: 234 Calories; 19 g Fat (68.2% calories from fat); 5 g Protein; 15 g Carbohydrate; 7 g Dietary Fiber; 8 g net carbs

STIR-FRIED SPINACH

Spinach originated in Asia, so stir-frying it is a very traditional way of preparing it. Bagged baby spinach works fine here.

¼ cup (60 ml) peanut oil　　**2 cloves of garlic, crushed**

2 pounds (910 g) fresh spinach, washed and dried

1. Heat the oil in a heavy skillet or wok over high heat.

2. Add the spinach and garlic, stir-fry for only a minute or two, and then serve.

YIELD: 6 servings, each with: 114 Calories; 10 g Fat (68.2% calories from fat); 4 g Protein; 6 g Carbohydrate; 4 g Dietary Fiber; 2 g net carbs

SICILIAN SPINACH

See those anchovies? If you're not a fan, you can skip them. But they don't make this dish so much fishy as savory.

3 tablespoons (45 g) butter　　**1 clove of garlic, crushed**

2 pounds (910 g) fresh spinach, washed and dried, or bagged baby spinach　　**1 or 2 anchovy fillets, minced**

1. Heat the butter in a heavy skillet. Add the spinach and garlic and sauté until the spinach is just limp.

2. Stir in the anchovies and serve.

YIELD: 6 servings, each with: 88 Calories; 6 g Fat (58.4% calories from fat); 5 g Protein; 5 g Carbohydrate; 4 g Dietary Fiber; 1 g net carbs

CREAMED SPINACH

This perennial favorite is quick, easy, and delicious. My husband has been known to eat a whole batch by himself and call it supper.

1 package (10 ounces, or 280 g) of frozen, chopped spinach, thawed

¼ cup (60 ml) heavy cream

¼ cup (25 g) grated Parmesan cheese

1 clove of garlic, crushed

1. Put all the ingredients in a heavy-bottomed saucepan over medium-low heat.
2. Simmer for 7 to 8 minutes.

YIELD: 3 servings, each with: 123 Calories; 10 g Fat (66.6% calories from fat); 6 g Protein; 5 g Carbohydrate; 3 g Dietary Fiber; 2 g net carbs

GREEK SPINACH

This is so cheesy and yummy! It's great with roasted chicken or broiled fish.

1 tablespoon (14 g) butter

¼ of a small onion, minced

1 package (10 ounces, or 280 g) of frozen, chopped spinach, thawed

¼ cup (35 g) crumbled feta cheese

¼ cup (60 g) cottage cheese

1. Melt the butter in a heavy skillet over medium heat. Add the onion and let it sizzle for just a minute. Add the spinach and sauté, stirring now and then, for 5 to 7 minutes.
2. Add in the cheeses and stir until they start to melt. Let the spinach cook for another minute or so and then serve.

YIELD: 3 servings, each with: 108 Calories; 7 g Fat (56.4% calories from fat); 7 g Protein; 5 g Carbohydrate; 3 g Dietary Fiber; 2 g net carbs

SAG PANEER

With cottage cheese, this isn't totally authentic, but it's mighty tasty. And cottage cheese is available in every grocery store, while paneer is a bit harder to find.

2 tablespoons (28 g) butter

1 teaspoon curry powder

1 package (10 ounces, or 280 g) of frozen, chopped spinach, thawed and drained

1 teaspoon salt or Vege-Sal

⅓ cup (75 g) small-curd cottage cheese, 4% fat

2 teaspoons sour cream

1. Melt the butter in a heavy skillet over low heat and stir in the curry powder. Let the curry powder cook in the butter for 3 to 4 minutes.
2. Stir in the spinach and the salt. Cover the skillet and let the spinach cook for 4 to 5 minutes or until heated through.
3. Stir in the cottage cheese and sour cream and cook, stirring, until the cheese has completely melted.

YIELD: 3 servings, each with: 124 Calories; 10 g Fat (66.9% calories from fat); 6 g Protein; 5 g Carbohydrate; 3 g Dietary Fiber; 2 g net carbs

About Cooking Broccoli

Broccoli is another vegetable that's great when it's cooked just barely enough, but revolting when it's overcooked. I often think that the reason there are so many broccoli-haters in the world is because they've only been exposed to mushy, sulfurous, gray, overcooked broccoli. So above all, don't overcook your broccoli!

You can steam broccoli on the stove top or in the microwave. On the stove top, start timing after the water comes to a boil. Fresh broccoli needs about 7 minutes, and frozen broccoli (assuming you start with it still frozen) needs 10 or 11 minutes. If you're microwaving your broccoli (my favorite way to cook it), put it in a microwave-safe casserole, add a tablespoon or two (15 to 28 ml) of water, and cover with a plate, plastic wrap, or a lid. Microwave on High for about 5 minutes for fresh broccoli or closer to 10 minutes for frozen, stirring halfway through to make sure it cooks evenly. However you steam your broccoli, uncover it as soon as it reaches the degree of doneness you prefer, or it will continue to cook and end up mushy.

If you're using fresh broccoli, cut it up and peel the stems. If you've been discarding the stems, you'll be startled to discover that they're the best part of the broccoli once you've peeled off the tough skin.

BROCCOLI WITH LEMON BUTTER

I'm always bemused when I see frozen broccoli with lemon butter at the grocery store. I mean, how hard is it to add butter and lemon juice to your broccoli?

1 pound (455 g) frozen broccoli or 1 large head of fresh broccoli	4 tablespoons (55 g) butter
	1 tablespoon (15 ml) lemon juice

1. Steam or microwave your broccoli.
2. When it's cooked, drain off the water and toss the broccoli with the butter and lemon juice until the butter is melted. That's it!

YIELD: 4 servings, each with: 132 Calories; 12 g Fat (74.5% calories from fat); 3 g Protein; 6 g Carbohydrate; 3 g Dietary Fiber; 3 g net carbs

BROCCOLI PIQUANT

This is a country-style dish that's good with pork chops. I'd used this sort of preparation with cabbage, then thought, "Wait, broccoli is related to cabbage . . . ."

1 bag (1 pound, or 455 g) of frozen broccoli "cuts" or fresh broccoli cut in bite-sized pieces	4 slices of bacon
	1 clove of garlic, crushed
	3 tablespoons (45 ml) cider vinegar

(continued)

1. Steam or microwave the broccoli until just tender-crisp.

2. While the broccoli is cooking, fry the bacon until crisp, remove from the pan, and drain. Pour off all but a couple of tablespoons (28 ml) of the fat.

3. When the broccoli is cooked, drain and add it to the bacon fat in the skillet. Add the garlic and vinegar and stir over medium heat for a minute or two.

4. Crumble the bacon over the broccoli, stir for another minute or so, and serve.

YIELD: 4 servings, each with: 69 Calories; 3 g Fat (40.2% calories from fat); 5 g Protein; 6 g Carbohydrate; 3 g Dietary Fiber; 3 g net carbs

GINGER STIR-FRY BROCCOLI

Are you missing Chinese take-out? Try this. You could add a handful of shrimp or diced chicken and call it a meal, for that matter.

2–3 tablespoons (28– 45 ml) peanut oil or other bland oil

2 cloves of garlic, crushed

1 bag (1 pound, or 455 g) of frozen broccoli "cuts," thawed

1 tablespoon (8 g) grated fresh ginger

1 tablespoon (15 ml) soy sauce

1. Heat the peanut oil in a wok or heavy skillet over high heat. Add the garlic and the broccoli and stir-fry for 7 to 10 minutes or until the broccoli is tender-crisp.

2. Stir in the ginger and soy sauce, stir-fry for just another minute, and serve.

YIELD: 4 servings, each with: 125 Calories; 10 g Fat (70.0% calories from fat); 4 g Protein; 7 g Carbohydrate; 4 g Dietary Fiber; 3 g net carbs

About Cooking Spaghetti Squash

If you've never cooked a spaghetti squash, you may be puzzled as to how to go about it. It's really easy: Just stab it several times (to keep it from exploding) and put it in your microwave on High for 12 to 15 minutes. When it's softish when you squeeze it (wearing an oven mitt, of course!), slice it open and scoop out and discard the seeds. Now, take a fork and start scraping at the "meat" of the squash. You will be surprised and charmed to discover that it separates into strands very much like spaghetti, only yellow-orange in color.

Spaghetti squash is not a terribly low-carb vegetable, but it's much lower carb than spaghetti, so it's a useful substitute in many recipes, especially casseroles. If you only need half of your cooked spaghetti squash right away, the rest will live happily in a zipper-lock bag or snap-top container in your fridge for 3 to 4 days until you do something else with it.

Since writing the original edition of this book, I have discovered tofu shirataki (page 22). All of these recipes will work with tofu shirataki as well as with spaghetti squash. Tofu shirataki has fewer carbs, while spaghetti squash is easier to get and has more vitamins. Take your pick.

SPAGHETTI SQUASH ALFREDO

We love this! My husband is an Alfredo fiend, so by using spaghetti squash instead of pasta, he gets his fix without all those additional carbs.

2 cups (510 g) cooked spaghetti squash

3 tablespoons (45 g) butter

3 tablespoons (45 ml) heavy cream

1 clove of garlic, crushed

¼ cup (25 g) grated or (20 g) shredded Parmesan cheese

1. Simply heat up your squash and stir in everything else.
2. Stir until the butter is melted and serve!

YIELD: 4 servings, each with: 160 Calories; 14 g Fat (78.9% calories from fat); 3 g Protein; 6 g Carbohydrate; 1 g Dietary Fiber; 5 g net carbs

SPAGHETTI SQUASH CARBONARA

This makes a very filling side dish. You can make this dish higher in protein by using a cup or two (150 to 300 g) of diced, leftover ham in place of the bacon. Brown the ham in olive oil, remove from the pan, cook the squash mixture in the oil, and then toss in the ham just before serving.

8 slices of bacon

4 eggs

¾ cup (75 g) grated Parmesan cheese

3 cups (765 g) cooked spaghetti squash

1 clove of garlic, crushed

1. Fry the bacon until it's crisp. Remove from the pan and pour off all but a couple tablespoons (28 ml) of grease.
2. Beat the eggs with the cheese and toss with the spaghetti squash. Pour the squash mixture into the hot fat in the skillet and add the garlic. Toss for 2 to 3 minutes.
3. Crumble in the bacon, toss, and serve.

YIELD: 6 servings, each with: 160 Calories; 10 g Fat (57.9% calories from fat); 11 g Protein; 6 g Carbohydrate; 1 g Dietary Fiber; 5 g net carbs

HOT VEGETABLE DISHES

SPICY SESAME "NOODLES" WITH VEGETABLES

This isn't terribly low-carb, but it sure can pull you out of the hole when you've got vegetarians coming to dinner. This is a great dish to make for guests because so much of it can be done ahead of time: You can prepare the spaghetti squash (step 2) and the garnish (step 3) before your company arrives and then just warm the squash, stir-fry the veggies, and garnish the plates when it's time to eat.

3 cups (765 g) cooked spaghetti squash

¼ cup (60 ml) water

3 tablespoons (45 ml) soy sauce

5 tablespoons (75 g) tahini

1½ tablespoons (23 ml) rice vinegar

½ teaspoon red pepper flakes

1 tablespoon (8 g) sesame seeds

2–3 tablespoons (28–45 ml) peanut oil or other bland oil

1½ cups (105 g) mushrooms, thickly sliced

⅔ cup (100 g) diced green pepper

½ cup (60 g) diced celery

½ cup (80 g) chopped onion

¼ pound (115 g) snow peas, cut into 1-inch (2.5 cm) lengths

2 tablespoons (16 g) grated fresh ginger

2 cloves of garlic, crushed

½ cup cooked shrimp or diced leftover chicken, pork, or ham per serving (optional; weight will vary)

1. Place the spaghetti squash in a large mixing bowl.

2. In a separate bowl, combine the water, soy sauce, tahini, rice vinegar, and red pepper flakes, mixing well. Pour over the spaghetti squash and set aside.

3. Place your sesame seeds in a small, heavy skillet over high heat and shake the skillet constantly until the seeds start to "pop." They won't pop like popcorn, but they will make little popping sounds and jump in the skillet. When that happens, immediately turn off the heat and shake the seeds out onto a small plate to cool. Set aside.

4. Just before you're ready to serve the dish, heat the oil in a large skillet or wok. Add the mushrooms, green pepper, celery, onion, snow peas, ginger, and garlic and stir-fry over high heat for 7 to 10 minutes or until tender-crisp.

5. When the vegetables are done, add them to the large mixing bowl with the spaghetti squash mixture and toss until well combined.

6. Pile the veggies and "noodles" on serving plates. Top the meat-eaters' servings with the shrimp, chicken, pork, or ham (if using) and scatter sesame seeds over each serving.

Note: If you swap 3 packets of shirataki noodles, drained and rinsed according to the instructions on page 23, for the spaghetti squash, this drops to 19 grams total carbohydrate with 7 grams of fiber, for a net carb count of 12 grams.

YIELD: 4 servings, each with: 314 Calories; 22 g Fat (60.8% calories from fat); 13 g Protein; 19 g Carbohydrate; 4 g Dietary Fiber; 15 g net carbs

CHAPTER 6

Side Dish Salads

I'm hard-pressed to think of a food that is more ill-done-by than salad. Way too many people dump some "iceberg mix" in a bowl, throw in some pink, mealy winter tomatoes, slosh some gooey bottled dressing on top, and then wail that their families show no enthusiasm for salad.

Made with just a little attention, salad is one of the most delicious, exciting foods imaginable. It is, of course, one of the most nutritious, as well, so learn to pay attention to your salads.

First of all, ditch the iceberg lettuce; not only is it the least-nutritious lettuce on the market, it's also the blandest. Try all sorts of other green and leafy things, such as romaine, Boston lettuce, butterhead, radicchio, frisée, fresh spinach, or whatever else you can find. Try making some fresh dressings, too. And unless all the members of your family have violently opposing opinions on salad dressing, try actually tossing your salad with the dressing, instead of just sloshing it on top. I think you'll be surprised at the difference it makes in the end product.

The dressings, by the way, are at the end of this chapter. But let's get to the salads themselves right now.

GREEK SALAD

This is a wonderful, filling, fresh-tasting salad we never tire of. With lamb kabobs or Greek roasted chicken, there's supper!

1 large head of romaine lettuce	**¼ of a sweet red onion, thinly sliced into rings**
1 cup (60 g) chopped fresh parsley	**12 to 15 Greek olives**
½ of a cucumber, sliced	**2 ripe tomatoes, cut into wedges**
1 green pepper, sliced	**4–6 ounces (115–170 g) feta cheese, crumbled**
Greek Lemon Dressing (page 163)	**Anchovy fillets packed in olive oil (if desired)**

1. Wash and dry your romaine and break or cut it into bite-size pieces. Cut up and add the parsley, cucumber, and green pepper.

   TIP: You can do step 1 ahead of time, if you like, which makes this salad very doable on a weeknight.

2. Just before serving, pour on the Greek Lemon Dressing, and toss the salad like crazy.

3. Arrange the onion, olives, and tomatoes artistically on top and sprinkle the crumbled feta in the middle. You can also add the anchovies at this point, if you know that everybody likes them, but I prefer to make them available for those who like them to put on their individual serving.

YIELD: 4 servings, each with: 177 Calories; 11 g Fat (51.1% calories from fat); 9 g Protein; 14 g Carbohydrate; 6 g Dietary Fiber; 8 g net carbs

AUTUMN SALAD

The flavor contrasts in this salad are lovely, and the texture contrasts are too. I've kept the pear to a quantity that won't add too many carbs.

2 tablespoons (28 g) butter	**2 teaspoons wine vinegar**
½ cup (60 g) chopped walnuts	**2 teaspoons lemon juice**
10 cups (550 g) loosely packed assorted greens (such as romaine, red leaf lettuce, and fresh spinach)	**¼ teaspoon spicy brown or Dijon mustard**
	⅛ teaspoon salt
	⅛ teaspoon pepper
¼ of a sweet red onion, thinly sliced	**½ of a ripe pear, chopped**
¼ cup (60 ml) olive oil	**⅓ cup (40 g) crumbled blue cheese**

1. Melt the butter in a small, heavy skillet over medium heat. Add the walnuts and let them toast in the butter, stirring occasionally, for about 5 minutes.

2. While the walnuts are toasting—and make sure you keep an eye on them and don't burn them—wash and dry your greens and put them in salad bowl with the onion. Toss with the olive oil first and then combine the vinegar, lemon juice, mustard, salt, and pepper and add that to the salad bowl. Toss until everything is well covered.

3. Top the salad with the pear, the warm toasted walnuts, and the crumbled blue cheese. Serve.

YIELD: 6 servings, each with: 236 Calories; 21 g Fat (76.0% calories from fat); 7 g Protein; 8 g Carbohydrate; 4 g Dietary Fiber; 4 g net carbs

ARUGULA-PEAR SALAD

This is an extraordinary combination of flavors. If you've never tried arugula, you'll be surprised: It tastes almost as if it's been roasted. You could use grated or shredded Parmesan cheese, but I think the bigger pieces of thinly sliced Parmesan make a difference in the salad's flavor and texture.

3½–4 cups (70–80 g) washed, dried, torn-up arugula

½ of a ripe pear, cut in small chunks or slices

3 tablespoons (45 ml) extra-virgin olive oil

Juice of 1 lemon

Salt and pepper

2 tablespoons (10 g) very thinly sliced bits of Parmesan cheese

1. Combine the arugula and pear in a salad bowl. Add the olive oil and toss well.

2. Add the lemon juice, salt, and pepper and lightly toss again.

3. Top with Parmesan cheese and serve.

YIELD: 2 servings, each with: 238 Calories; 22 g Fat (80.7% calories from fat); 3 g Protein; 9 g Carbohydrate; 2 g Dietary Fiber; 7 g net carbs

SPINACH PECAN SALAD

This salad is very simple and quite wonderful. It could not be more different from the standard spinach salad! The dark spinach looks particularly pretty next to a light-colored main dish of fish or poultry.

2 pounds (910 g) bagged baby spinach

Salt or Vege-Sal

10 scallions, thinly sliced, including about 2 inches (5 cm) of the green sprout

¼ cup (60 ml) extra-virgin olive oil

¼ cup (60 ml) lemon juice

¼ pound (115 g) toasted, salted pecans, chopped

1. Put the spinach in a salad bowl and sprinkle it with a little salt—maybe a teaspoonful—and squeeze the leaves gently with your hands. You'll find that the spinach "deflates," or sort of gets a bit limp and reduces in volume. Add the scallions to the bowl.

2. Pour on the olive oil and toss the salad thoroughly. Add the lemon juice and toss again.

3. Top with the pecans and serve.

YIELD: 6 servings, each with: 250 Calories; 22 g Fat (74.0% calories from fat); 6 g Protein; 11 g Carbohydrate; 6 g Dietary Fiber; 5 g net carbs

CLASSIC SPINACH SALAD

This dish is a mid-twentieth-century classic! It's great with grilled steak or burgers—pretty, too.

4 cups (120 g) fresh spinach

⅛ of a large, sweet red onion, thinly sliced

3 tablespoons (45 ml) light olive oil or MCT oil

2 tablespoons (28 ml) apple cider vinegar

2 teaspoons tomato paste

Liquid stevia, monkfruit, or sucralose to equal 1½ teaspoons of sugar in sweetness

¼ of a small onion, grated

⅛ teaspoon dry mustard

Salt and pepper

2 slices of bacon, cooked until crisp, and crumbled

1 hard-boiled egg, chopped

1. Wash the spinach very well and dry. Tear up the larger leaves. Combine with the onion in a salad bowl.
2. In a separate bowl, mix up the oil, vinegar, tomato paste, sweetener, onion, dry mustard, and salt and pepper to taste. Pour the mixture over the spinach and onion and toss.
3. Top the salad with the bacon and egg and serve.

YIELD: 2 servings, each with: 285 Calories; 26 g Fat (81.3% calories from fat); 7 g Protein; 6 g Carbohydrate; 2 g Dietary Fiber; 4 g net carbs

SUMMER TREAT SPINACH SALAD

Are you worried about where you'll get your potassium now that you're not eating bananas? Each serving of this salad has more potassium than three bananas!

Be aware: Despite being highly nutritious, sprouts have taken a hit in the past decade. Turns out that the environment needed to grow them also is ideal for some germs, and they've been the source of some outbreaks of food poisoning. Buy yours from a store with a brisk turnover, and if they look less than supremely fresh, skip it. The Centers for Disease Control say that children, the elderly, and pregnant women shouldn't eat them at all. But then, they also say I shouldn't eat fried eggs with runny yolks, and I do that all the time and have never gotten ill. Your risks are your own to take.

2 pounds (910 g) raw spinach

1 ripe avocado

¼ of a cantaloupe

½ cup (17 g) alfalfa sprouts

2 scallions, sliced

French Vinaigrette Dressing (page 162)

1. Wash the spinach very well and dry. Tear up the larger leaves.
2. Cut the avocado in half, remove the pit and the peel, and cut into chunks.
3. Peel and chunk the cantaloupe or if you want to be fancy, use a melon baller.
4. Add the avocado and cantaloupe to the spinach, along with the alfalfa sprouts and scallions.
5. Toss with the French Vinaigrette Dressing right before serving.

YIELD: 6 servings, each with: 98 Calories; 6 g Fat (45.4% calories from fat); 5 g Protein; 10 g Carbohydrate; 5 g Dietary Fiber; 5 g net carbs

MIXED GREENS WITH WARM BRIE DRESSING

This elegant dinner-party fare is a carbohydrate bargain with lots of flavor. I wouldn't spring for expensive imported Brie for the dressing. The grocery store stuff serves fine.

6 cups (330 g) torn romaine lettuce, washed and dried

6 cups (330 g) torn red leaf lettuce, washed and dried

2 cups (80 g) torn radicchio, washed and dried

1 cup (60 g) chopped fresh parsley

4 scallions, thinly sliced, including the crisp part of the green shoot

½ cup (120 ml) extra-virgin olive oil

½ of a small onion, minced

3 cloves of garlic, crushed

6 ounces (170 g) Brie, rind removed, cut into small chunks

¼ cup (60 ml) sherry vinegar

1 tablespoon (15 ml) lemon juice

1½ teaspoons Dijon mustard

1. Put the lettuce, radicchio, parsley, and scallions in a large salad bowl and keep cold.

2. Put the olive oil in a heavy-bottomed saucepan over medium-low heat. Add the onion and garlic and let them cook for 2 to 3 minutes.

3. Melt in the Brie, one chunk at a time, continuously stirring with a whisk. (It'll look dreadful at first, but don't sweat it.)

4. When all the cheese is melted in, whisk in the sherry vinegar, lemon juice, and Dijon mustard. Let it cook for a few minutes, stirring all the while, until your dressing is smooth and thick. Pour over the salad and toss.

YIELD: 6 servings, each with: 285 Calories; 26 g Fat (80.5% calories from fat); 8 g Protein; 6 g Carbohydrate; 2 g Dietary Fiber; 4 g net carbs

BAYSIDE SALAD

This is my version of a fantastic salad I had at a restaurant called Bayside Grill, down near the Gulf Coast. The combination of greens isn't vital—you can change it some, as long as you make sure to include some bitter greens, such as endive.

2 tablespoons (28 g) butter

¼ cup (28 g) chopped pecans

2 cups (94 g) torn romaine

1 cup (40 g) torn radicchio

1 cup (50 g) torn frisée

1 cup (55 g) torn Boston lettuce

1 cup (50 g) torn curly endive

¼ of a sweet red onion, thinly sliced

Raspberry Vinaigrette (page 167)

¼ cup (30 g) crumbled blue cheese

4 slices of bacon, cooked until crisp

1. Melt the butter in a heavy skillet. Add the pecans and toast them over medium heat, stirring for 5 minutes or so, until brown and crisp.

2. Toss the romaine, radicchio, frisée, Boston lettuce, curly endive, and onion with the Raspberry Vinaigrette.

3. Pile the salad on 4 serving plates and top each with one-quarter of the pecans, one-quarter of the blue cheese, and 1 crumbled slice of bacon.

YIELD: 4 servings, each with: 182 Calories; 16 g Fat (78.8% calories from fat); 5 g Protein; 5 g Carbohydrate; 2 g Dietary Fiber; 3 g net carbs

CAESAR SALAD

This is the salad that made Tijuana restaurateur Caesar Cardini famous. If you've only had that wilted stuff that passes for Caesar salad on salad bars and buffets, you have to try this—and make your own dressing, fresh! Surely, I don't have to remind you that grilled chicken is nice on this, but you might also consider a handful of cooked shrimp.

1 large head of romaine lettuce	**Caesar Dressing (page 169)**

1. Wash, dry, and tear up an entire head of romaine lettuce.
2. Toss it with the Caesar Dressing. That's it!

YIELD: 6 servings, each with: 149 Calories; 12 g Fat (70.6% calories from fat); 6 g Protein; 5 g Carbohydrate; 2 g Dietary Fiber; 3 g net carbs

OUR FAVORITE SALAD

We've served this salad over and over, and we never tire of it. This dressing tastes a bit like Caesar, but it's less trouble, and there's no blender to wash afterwards.

1 clove of garlic	**¼ of a sweet red onion**
½ cup (120 ml) extra-virgin olive oil	**2–3 tablespoons (28–45 ml) lemon juice**
1 head of romaine	**2–3 teaspoons (28–45 ml) Worcestershire sauce**
½ cup (30 g) chopped fresh parsley	**¼ cup (20 g) shredded Parmesan cheese**
½ of a green pepper, diced	**1 medium ripe tomato, cut into thin wedges**
¼ of a cucumber, quartered and sliced	

1. Crush the clove of garlic in a small bowl, cover it with the olive oil, and set it aside.
2. Wash and dry your romaine, break it up into a bowl, and add the parsley, green pepper, cucumber, and onion. Pour the garlic-flavored oil over the salad and toss until every leaf is covered.
3. Sprinkle on the lemon juice and toss again. Then, sprinkle on the Worcestershire sauce and toss again. Finally, sprinkle on the Parmesan cheese and toss one last time.
4. Top with the tomatoe wedges and serve.

YIELD: 6 servings, each with: 208 Calories; 19 g Fat (79.8% calories from fat); 4 g Protein; 7 g Carbohydrate; 3 g Dietary Fiber; 4 g net carbs

UPDATE SALAD

This recipe went around in the 1960s, using curly endive instead of this mixture of bitter greens and of course, using sugar in the dressing. I like to think I've brought it into the twenty-first century—hence the name. Unlike most salads, this one has no oil. Feel free to drizzle it with some olive oil if you like.

SALAD

2 medium green peppers, cut in smallish strips

1 large bunch of parsley, chopped

⅔ cup (27 g) torn radicchio

⅔ cup (33 g) chopped curly endive

⅔ cup (33 g) chopped frisée

3 tomatoes, each cut in 8 lengthwise wedges

⅛ of a large, sweet red onion, thinly sliced

2 tablespoons (13 g) chopped black olives

DRESSING

¼ cup (60 ml) water

½ cup (120 ml) tarragon vinegar

½ teaspoon salt or Vege-Sal

1½ tablespoons (3 ml) lemon juice

Liquid stevia, monkfruit, or sucralose to equal 1 tablespoon (13 g) of sugar in sweetness

⅛ teaspoon molasses

TOPPING

6 tablespoons (90 g) sour cream

1. Put the green peppers, parsley, radicchio, endive, frisée, tomatoes, onion, and olives in a big bowl and set aside.

2. In a separate bowl, combine the water, vinegar, salt, lemon juice, sweetener, and molasses. Pour it all over the salad and toss.

3. Stick the whole thing in the refrigerator and let it sit there for a few hours, stirring it now and then if you think of it.

4. To serve, put a 1-tablespoon (15 g) dollop of sour cream on each of the 6 servings.

YIELD: 6 servings, each with: 70 Calories; 4 g Fat (42.6% calories from fat); 2 g Protein; 9 g Carbohydrate; 2 g Dietary Fiber; 7 g net carbs

PARSLEY SALAD

This is similar to a salad I used to love at a Turkish restaurant in Chicago. If you've always thought of parsley as a garnish, it's time to start thinking of it as a food. It's delicious and very, very nutritious. Use flat-leaf or curly parsley, as you prefer.

3 tomatoes, diced

1 cucumber, peeled (if desired) and diced

3 scallions, sliced

1 bunch of parsley, stems removed, leaves chopped

¼ cup (60 ml) fresh lemon juice

½ cup (120 ml) extra-virgin olive oil

Salt and pepper

1 small can (2¼ ounces, or 64 g) of sliced ripe olives, drained

1. Combine the tomatoes, cucumber, scallions, and parsley; chill.

2. Combine the lemon juice, olive oil, and salt and pepper to taste and toss with the vegetables.

3. Top with the olives and serve.

YIELD: 4 servings, each with: 299 Calories; 29 g Fat (84.0% calories from fat); 2 g Protein; 10 g Carbohydrate; 3 g Dietary Fiber; 7 g net carbs

CALIFORNIA SALAD

This salad is super-simple. Simple is good! As discussed on page 70, alfalfa sprouts (and all raw sprouts) can pose a risk of foodborne illness. Be careful about your source or skip 'em. That said, I've never gotten sick from sprouts. If you're thinking about substituting a green avocado for the black one called for, remember that the little black avocados are substantially lower in carbs.

4 cups (188 g) torn romaine lettuce	2 tablespoons (28 ml) lemon juice
4 cups (112 g) torn red leaf lettuce	Salt and pepper
1 ripe, black avocado	½ cup (17 g) alfalfa sprouts
3 tablespoons (45 ml) extra-virgin olive oil	

1. Combine the romaine and red leaf lettuces in a salad bowl. Then, peel the avocado and cut it into small chunks. (It's easiest just to scoop out bits with a spoon.) Add the avocado to the bowl.
2. Toss the salad first with the olive oil, then the lemon juice, and then finally with salt and pepper to taste.
3. Top with the alfalfa sprouts and serve.

YIELD: 4 servings, each with: 186 Calories; 18 g Fat (82.0% calories from fat); 2 g Protein; 7 g Carbohydrate; 3 g Dietary Fiber; 4 g net carbs

TOMATOES BASILICO

This is a simple, elegant summer classic, but you shouldn't even bother trying it with second-rate tomatoes. Hit the farmers' market in the morning and serve this with a grilled steak for supper.

4 medium-sized, ripe tomatoes	Olive oil, salt, and pepper (for serving)
½ cup (20 g) fresh, coarsely chopped basil	

1. Slice the tomatoes and arrange them on a platter.
2. Sprinkle the basil over them and let the salad sit for 30 minutes or so before serving.
3. Pass olive oil for drizzling and serve with salt and pepper to taste.

YIELD: 4 generous servings, each with: 27 Calories; trace Fat (12.0% calories from fat); 1 g Protein; 6 g Carbohydrate; 2 g Dietary Fiber; 4 g net carbs

TOMATO-MOZZARELLA PLATE A.K.A. CAPRESE SALAD

It's hard to know whether this is a salad or an appetizer—That Nice Boy I Married and I have been known to eat this as a cool, light supper on a stifling August night. All that really matters is that it's good and remarkably easy. The tomatoes you use must be superb, and you must use fresh mozzarella, not the cheap kind sold for pizza. Look for it in a tub of water in the fancy-cheese case.

½ cup (20 g) fresh, finely chopped basil

¼ cup (60 ml) extra-virgin olive oil

1 pound (455 g) fresh mozzarella

3 ripe tomatoes, sliced

Fresh ground or coarsely ground pepper

1. Mix the basil with the olive oil and set aside.
2. Cut 18 slices of mozzarella and tomatoes (6 slices from each tomato). Arrange 3 slices of tomato and 3 slices of mozzarella on each serving plate.
3. Spoon a couple of teaspoons of the basil and olive oil over each plate.
4. Scatter just a tiny bit of pepper over each plate and serve.

YIELD: 6 servings, each with: 334 Calories; 28 g Fat (74.2% calories from fat); 17 g Protein; 5 g Carbohydrate; 1 g Dietary Fiber; 4 g net carbs

MELON WITH PROSCIUTTO

Another dish that's hard to classify, this one is an Italian classic. This makes a nice finger food for a cookout or an elegant first course.

1 ripe cantaloupe

12 very thin slices of prosciutto (6 to 8 ounces, or 170 to 225 g)

1. Cut your melon into 12 wedges, removing seeds and rind.
2. Wrap each melon wedge in a slice of prosciutto. Serve and enjoy!

YIELD: 12 servings, each with: 53 Calories; 2 g Fat (28.6% calories from fat); 6 g Protein; 4 g Carbohydrate; trace Dietary Fiber; 4 g net carbs

MELON PROSCIUTTO SALAD

This dish is similar to the previous recipe, but with a different presentation. The orange-and-green melon pieces make this very pretty, too. It's worth looking for half-melons. My grocery store carries them; maybe yours does, too.

½ of a ripe cantaloupe

½ of a ripe honeydew

8 ounces (225 g) prosciutto

1. Seed and peel the melons and cut them into 1-inch (2.5 cm) chunks (or use a melon baller).
2. Chop the prosciutto, toss everything together, and you're done.

YIELD: 10 servings, each with: 76 Calories; 2 g Fat (23.2% calories from fat); 7 g Protein; 8 g Carbohydrate; 1 g Dietary Fiber; 7 g net carbs

Make-Ahead Salads

I just love deli-style salads—you know, the kind you can make ahead and just pull out of the refrigerator when you want them. There are so many varieties and they are so, so convenient. I like to make them in big batches. That way, I have fast, easy vegetables for a few days. Our first several make-ahead salads feature cucumbers—not only because cucumbers are delicious, but also because they're about the lowest-carb vegetable around!

SOUR CREAM AND CUKE SALAD

This is a great choice for a summer potluck. Use the fresh dill if you have it on hand, but the dried is good and doesn't require a grocery store run. You can eat this right away and it will be great, but it improves overnight.

1 green pepper

2 cucumbers, scrubbed but not peeled

½ of a large, sweet red onion

½ of a head of cauliflower

2 teaspoons salt or Vege-Sal

1 cup (230 g) sour cream

2 tablespoons (28 ml) vinegar (Cider vinegar is best, but wine vinegar will do.)

2 rounded teaspoons dried dill weed or 2 tablespoons (8 g) snipped fresh dill weed

1. Slice the green pepper, cucumbers, onion, and cauliflower as thinly as you possibly can. The slicing blade on a food processor works nicely, and it saves you mucho time, but I've also done it with a good, sharp knife.

2. Toss the vegetables well with the salt and chill them in the refrigerator for an hour or two.

3. In a separate bowl, mix the sour cream, vinegar, and dill, combining well.

4. Remove the veggies from the fridge, drain off any water that has collected at the bottom of the bowl, and stir in the sour cream mixture.

YIELD: 10 servings, each with: 64 Calories; 5 g Fat (65.8% calories from fat); 2 g Protein; 4 g Carbohydrate; 1 g Dietary Fiber; 3 g net carbs

MONICA'S IN-LAWS' CUCUMBER SALAD

Monica is a reader who didn't send me her last name, but she did send me this great salad recipe. Thanks, Monica!

3 medium cucumbers, thinly sliced

3 teaspoons (18 g) salt

Liquid stevia, monkfruit, or sucralose to equal ¼ cup (50 g) of sugar in sweetness

¼ cup (60 ml) vinegar (Monica didn't specify, but I'd use cider vinegar.)

1 cup (230 g) sour cream

½ cup (80 g) finely chopped onion (Again, Monica didn't specify, but red, Bermuda, or Vidalia onion would be good here.)

1 teaspoon chopped fresh dill weed

Salt and pepper

1. Put the cukes in a large bowl and sprinkle with the salt. Refrigerate for 1 to 2 hours.

2. Drain off any water that has collected at the bottom of the bowl, rinse, and drain again.

3. Combine the sweetener with the vinegar, whisk in the sour cream, onion, and dill, and fold the mixture into the cukes.

4. Season with salt and pepper to taste and serve.

YIELD: 8 servings, each with: 143 Calories; 12 g Fat (74.2% calories from fat); 3 g Protein; 7 g Carbohydrate; 1 g Dietary Fiber; 6 g net carbs

GORKENSALAD

This recipe is from reader Heather Firth, who says this is "a really amazing cucumber salad. The cucumbers are limp but still crunchy."

4 peeled cucumbers, thinly sliced

1½ tablespoons (27 g) salt, plus more for seasoning

¼ cup (60 ml) water

3 tablespoons (45 ml) cider vinegar

3 tablespoons (45 ml) MCT oil or light olive oil

Liquid stevia, monkfruit, or sucralose to equal 2 tablespoons (26 g) of sugar in sweetness

Pepper

1. Peel and slice the cucumbers. Put them in a large bowl and sprinkle the salt over them. Stir the salt into the cucumbers, cover, and refrigerate overnight.

2. An hour or so before serving, remove the cucumbers from the refrigerator and squeeze the water out of them, using your hands and working in small batches. The slices will go from kind of stiff and opaque to limp and almost translucent. Pour off the resulting water.

3. Mix together the water, vinegar, oil, and sweetener, and salt and pepper to taste. This is the "dressing"— it should be light, tangy, and just slightly sweet. Pour this over the cucumbers and mix them up.

4. Chill until ready to serve.

YIELD: 10 servings, each with: 52 Calories; 4 g Fat (68.4% calories from fat); 1 g Protein; 4 g Carbohydrate; 1 g Dietary Fiber; 3 g net carbs

THAI CUCUMBER SALAD

Here's a salad that's sweet and hot and so good! This, by the way, is one of those magnificent recipes that is low carb, low fat, low calorie, okay for vegetarians, and tastes great, which means even in a group with diverse dietary restrictions, everyone can eat it. Don't forget to wash your hands thoroughly with soap and water after handling that jalapeño!

½ of a small red onion

1 small, fresh jalapeño, seeds removed

3 medium cucumbers

2 or 3 cloves of fresh garlic, crushed

2 tablespoons (16 g) grated fresh ginger

½ cup (120 ml) rice vinegar

½ teaspoon salt

¼ teaspoon pepper

Liquid stevia, monkfruit, or sucralose to equal 2 tablespoons (26 g) of sugar in sweetness

1. Using a food processor with the S-blade in place, put the onion and jalapeño in the food processor and pulse until they are both finely chopped.

2. Remove the S-blade and put on the slicing disk. Quarter the cucumbers lengthwise and then run them through the processor. If you're not using a food processor, you'll want to dice the onion and mince the jalapeño and then slice the cucumber as thin as you can.

3. Put the onion, jalapeño, and cucumbers in a big bowl.

4. In a separate bowl, thoroughly combine the garlic, ginger, vinegar, salt, pepper, and sweetener. Pour over the vegetables and mix well.

5. Chill for a few hours before serving, for the best flavor.

YIELD: 8 generous servings, each with: 23 Calories; trace Fat (6.1% calories from fat); 1 g Protein; 5 g Carbohydrate; 1 g Dietary Fiber; 4 g net carbs

BROCCOLI SALAD

Of course, if you prefer, you can use fresh broccoli to make this salad. You'll have to peel the stems, cut it up, and steam it for about 5 minutes first. And at that point, it will be very much like thawed frozen broccoli! Personally, I take the easy route.

½ cup (120 ml) olive oil

¼ cup (60 ml) vinegar

1 clove of garlic, crushed

½ teaspoon Italian seasoning herb blend

½ teaspoon salt or Vege-Sal

⅛ teaspoon pepper

4 cups (300 g) frozen broccoli "cuts"

1. Whisk the olive oil, vinegar, garlic, herbs, salt, and pepper together.

2. Don't even bother to thaw the broccoli—just put it in a bowl and pour the olive oil mixture on top of it.

3. Mix well and let it sit for several hours in the fridge. Stir it now and then if you think of it and serve as is or on greens.

YIELD: 6 servings, each with: 189 Calories; 18 g Fat (82.4% calories from fat); 3 g Protein; 6 g Carbohydrate; 3 g Dietary Fiber; 3 g net carbs

THE NEW 500 LOW-CARB RECIPES

PARMESAN BEAN SALAD

This salad is filling enough to make a nice light lunch. You can use fresh green beans if you prefer, of course.

1 pound (455 g) bag of frozen, crosscut green beans

½ cup (80 g) minced red onion

4 tablespoons (60 ml) extra-virgin olive oil

5 tablespoons (75 ml) cider vinegar

½ teaspoon salt or Vege-Sal

½ teaspoon paprika

¼ teaspoon dried ginger

¾ cup (75 g) grated Parmesan cheese

1. Steam or microwave the green beans according to package directions until they're tender-crisp.
2. Let the beans cool a bit and then stir in the onion, olive oil, vinegar, salt, paprika, ginger, and finally the Parmesan cheese.
3. Chill well before serving.

YIELD: 4 servings, each with: 237 Calories; 18 g Fat (66.5% calories from fat); 9 g Protein; 12 g Carbohydrate; 4 g Dietary Fiber; 8 g net carbs

LOW-CARB ROSY RADISH SALAD

This recipe, adapted from one in Peg Bracken's *I Hate To Cook Book*, is surprisingly mild and looks very pretty on the plate. Once again, use fresh green beans if you prefer.

1 bag (1 pound, or 455 g) of frozen crosscut green beans

4 slices of bacon, cooked until crisp, and crumbled

1 small onion, chopped

1 cup (116 g) sliced radishes

3 tablespoons (45 ml) cider vinegar

Liquid stevia, monkfruit, or sucralose to equal 1½ tablespoons (20 g) of sugar in sweetness

¾ teaspoon salt or Vege-Sal

¼ teaspoon pepper

1. Steam or microwave the green beans according to package directions until they're tender-crisp.
2. Combine the beans, bacon, onion, and radishes in a mixing bowl. In a separate bowl, combine the vinegar, sweetener, salt, and pepper.
3. Pour the mixture over the salad, toss, and serve.

YIELD: 5 servings, each with: 74 Calories; 3 g Fat (31.6% calories from fat); 4 g Protein; 10 g Carbohydrate; 3 g Dietary Fiber; 7 g net carbs

COLORFUL BEAN SALAD

This sweet-tart bean salad is a throw-back to the mid-twentieth century—minus the starchy kidney beans. It is quite sweet, so feel free to cut back on the sweetener if you like.

I originally made this with canned beans because fresh and frozen wax beans were hard to find. Now I can get frozen mixed green-and-wax beans! Two 1-pound (455 g) bags, thawed and snipped to 1½- to 2-inch (3.5 to 5 cm) lengths, then steamed tender-crisp, would be great here. Or, if you're lucky enough to have a local farmers' market or a home garden, use fresh!

1 can (14½ ounces, or 410 g) of cut green beans	**1 teaspoon salt**
	½ teaspoon pepper
1 can (14½ ounces, or 410 g) of cut wax beans	**½ cup (120 ml) MCT or light olive oil**
½ cup (80 g) chopped sweet red onion	**⅔ cup (160 ml) cider vinegar**
Liquid stevia, monkfruit, or sucralose to equal ¾ cup (150 g) of sugar in sweetness	

1. Drain the green beans and wax beans and combine them in a bowl with the onion.
2. In a separate bowl, combine the sweetener, salt, pepper, oil, and vinegar; pour the mixture over the vegetables.
3. Let it marinate for several hours at least; overnight won't hurt.
4. Drain off the marinade and serve.

YIELD: 4 servings, each with: 291 Calories; 27 g Fat (80.8% calories from fat); 2 g Protein; 12 g Carbohydrate; 4 g Dietary Fiber; 8 g net carbs

DILLED BEANS

It's hard to say if this is a salad or a pickle, but whatever you call it, it's tasty. This would be a nice addition to a cold-cut or relish platter.

1 bag (1 pound, or 455 g) of frozen crosscut green beans	**1 clove of garlic**
	2 teaspoons salt
½ cup (120 ml) wine vinegar	**2 teaspoons red pepper flakes**
½ cup (120 ml) water	**3 tablespoons (9 g) dried dill weed**

1. Steam or microwave the green beans until they're tender-crisp.
2. While the beans are cooking, combine the vinegar, water, garlic, salt, red pepper flakes, and dill in a small saucepan and bring to a boil.
3. Drain the beans and put them in a jar with a tight-fitting lid. Pour the vinegar mixture over the beans and cover. Refrigerate for a day or two, shaking the jar whenever you think of it. Serve cold.

YIELD: 8 servings, each with: 24 Calories; trace Fat (5.0% calories from fat); 1 g Protein; 6 g Carbohydrate; 2 g Dietary Fiber; 4 g net carbs

SESAME ASPARAGUS SALAD

This is from Jennifer Eloff's wonderful cookbook *Splendid Low-Carbing*. Jen points out that it's simple, yet it has an eye-catching presentation.

1 pound (455 g) fresh asparagus

5 cups (1.2 L) water

4 teaspoons (20 ml) soy sauce

2 teaspoons sesame or olive oil

1 tablespoon (8 g) sesame seeds

1. Break off the tough ends of the asparagus by bending each stalk back until it snaps.

2. Bring the water to a boil in a large saucepan and drop the asparagus stalks into the rapidly boiling water. Parboil for 5 minutes, drain immediately, and rinse in cold water. Pat dry with paper towels.

3. Combine the soy sauce and oil in a small bowl. Lay the asparagus stalks in a casserole and toss with the soy sauce mixture.

4. Sprinkle with the sesame seeds and chill in for an hour or two before serving.

YIELD: 6 servings, each with: 42 Calories; 2 g Fat (46.2% calories from fat); 2 g Protein; 4 g Carbohydrate; 2 g Dietary Fiber; 2 g net carbs

COLESLAW

Have you just got invited to a picnic and you're short on time for making something that'll feed a crowd? This recipe makes a veritable bucketful, and it's a wonderful side dish to almost any plain meat, including chops and chicken. If you like, you could even use bagged coleslaw from the grocery store and just add a little minced onion, plus my dressing; I promise not to tell!

By the way, if you make the dressing with mayonnaise you've made yourself with MCT oil, this is super-ketogenic.

1 head of green cabbage

¼ of a sweet red onion

Coleslaw Dressing (page 169)

1. This is super-simple: Shred the cabbage, mince the onion, and put 'em both in a big mixing bowl.

2. Add the Coleslaw Dressing and stir to coat.

3. It's great right away or refrigerated overnight.

YIELD: 10 servings, each with: 234 Calories; 24 g Fat (85.2% calories from fat); 2 g Protein; 7 g Carbohydrate; 2 g Dietary Fiber; 5 g net carbs

COLESLAW FOR COMPANY

The colors in this slaw are so intense, it's almost too beautiful to eat.

1 head of red cabbage

1 small carrot, shredded

¼ of a sweet red onion, finely minced

Coleslaw Dressing (page 169)

1. Using a food processor's slicing blade or a sharp knife, shred your cabbage and put it in a big bowl.
2. Add the carrot and onion and toss with the Coleslaw Dressing. Admire and enjoy.

YIELD: 10 servings, each with: 133 Calories; 12 g Fat (74.8% calories from fat); 2 g Protein; 7 g Carbohydrate; 2 g Dietary Fiber; 5 g net carbs

COLESLAW ITALIANO

When we were little, my sister and I didn't like creamy coleslaw dressing. So our mom would toss the cabbage with Italian vinaigrette, and we'd yum it down. Give it a try!

4 cups (280 g) shredded cabbage

½ cup (120 ml) Italian Vinaigrette Dressing (page 163)

Toss the cabbage with the Italian Vinaigrette Dressing and serve.

YIELD: 8 servings, each with: 90 Calories; 9 g Fat (87.6% calories from fat); 1 g Protein; 2 g Carbohydrate; 1 g Dietary Fiber; 1 g net carbs

ASIAN GINGER SLAW

Even my slaw-hating husband likes this! It has a very different texture and flavor than your standard slaw.

4 cups (300 g) finely shredded napa cabbage

¼ cup (28 g) shredded carrot

2 scallions, thinly sliced

¼ cup (25 g) thinly sliced pale, inner celery stalk

¼ cup (60 g) mayonnaise

1 teaspoon grated fresh ginger

2 tablespoons (28 ml) rice vinegar

1 teaspoon soy sauce

Liquid stevia, monk fruit, or sucralose to equal 1 teaspoon of sugar in sweetness

1. Combine the cabbage, carrot, scallions, and celery in a salad bowl.
2. In a separate bowl, combine the mayonnaise, ginger, vinegar, soy sauce, and sweetener. Beat together until smooth.
3. Pour the dressing over the vegetables, toss, and serve.

YIELD: 8 servings, each with: 62 Calories; 6 g Fat (78.5% calories from fat); 1 g Protein; 3 g Carbohydrate; 1 g Dietary Fiber; 2 g net carbs

CONFETTI UNSLAW

This may be a raw cabbage salad, but it's not much like coleslaw. Plus, it's utterly gorgeous on the plate.

2 cups (140 g) shredded green cabbage

2 cups (140 g) shredded red cabbage

½ of a sweet red pepper, chopped

½ of a green pepper, chopped

4 scallions, sliced, including the crisp part of the green

⅓ cup (37 g) grated carrot

1 small celery rib, thinly sliced

2 tablespoons (8 g) minced fresh parsley

Creamy Garlic Dressing (page 168)

Just cut up and combine all these vegetables and toss with the Creamy Garlic Dressing.

YIELD: 8 servings, each with: 152 Calories; 15 g Fat (83.8% calories from fat); 1 g Protein; 5 g Carbohydrate; 2 g Dietary Fiber; 3 g net carbs

CAULIFLOWER-OLIVE SALAD

Here's another salad with eye-catching color contrast! It's unusual and unusually good.

½ of a head of cauliflower, broken into small florets

½ cup (80 g) diced red onion

1 can (2¼ ounces, or 65 g) of sliced ripe olives, drained

½ cup (30 g) chopped fresh parsley

¼ cup (60 ml) lemon juice

¼ cup (60 ml) olive oil

¼ cup (60 g) mayonnaise

½ teaspoon salt or Vege-Sal

About a dozen cherry tomatoes

Lettuce (optional)

---

1. Combine the cauliflower, onion, olives, and parsley in a bowl.

2. Combine the lemon juice, olive oil, mayonnaise, and salt in a separate bowl. Pour over the veggies and toss well.

3. Chill for at least an hour—a whole day wouldn't hurt a bit.

4. When you're ready to serve the salad, cut the cherry tomatoes in half and add them to the salad. Serve on a bed of lettuce if you wish, but it's wonderful alone, too.

YIELD: 4 servings, each with: 186 Calories; 18 g Fat (82.3% calories from fat); 2 g Protein; 7 g Carbohydrate; 2 g Dietary Fiber; 5 g net carbs

UNPOTATO SALAD

You are going to be so surprised; this is amazingly like potato salad. I've had people take two or three bites before saying, "Wait, that's not potatoes . . . ."

1 large head of cauliflower, cut into small chunks

2 cups (240 g) diced celery

1 cup (120 g) diced red onion

2 cups (450 g) mayonnaise

¼ cup (60 ml) cider vinegar

2 teaspoons salt or Vege-Sal

Liquid stevia, monkfruit, or sucralose to equal 2 teaspoons of sugar in sweetness

½ teaspoon pepper

4 hard-boiled eggs, chopped

1. Put the cauliflower in a microwave-safe casserole, add just a tablespoon (15 ml) or so of water, and cover. Cook it on High for 8 minutes and let it sit, covered, for another 5 minutes. You want your cauliflower tender, but not mushy. (And you may steam it on the stovetop if you prefer.) Use the time while the cauliflower cooks to dice your celery and onions.

2. Drain the cooked cauliflower and combine it with the celery and onions. (You'll need a big bowl.)

3. Combine the mayonnaise, vinegar, salt, sweetener, and pepper. Pour the mixture over the vegetables and mix well.

4. Mix in the chopped eggs last and only stir lightly, to preserve some small hunks of yolk. Chill and serve.

YIELD: 12 servings, each with: 310 Calories; 33 g Fat (89.6% calories from fat); 4 g Protein; 5 g Carbohydrate; 2 g Dietary Fiber; 3 g net carbs

BACON, TOMATO, AND CAULIFLOWER SALAD

This recipe originally called for cooked rice, so I thought I'd try it with cauliflower "rice." I liked it so much, I ate it all up and made it again the very next day. This salad holds a molded shape well, so you can pack it into a custard cup and unmold it on a lettuce-lined plate. It looks quite pretty served this way.

½ of a head of cauliflower

½ pound (225 g) bacon, cooked until crisp, and crumbled

2 medium tomatoes, chopped

10 to 12 scallions, sliced, including all the crisp part of the green

½ cup (115 g) mayonnaise

Salt and pepper

Lettuce (optional)

1. Put the cauliflower through a food processor with the shredding disk. Steam or microwave it until it's tender-crisp, about 8 minutes or so. Undercooking is better than overcooking!

2. Combine the cooked cauliflower with the bacon, tomatoes, scallions, and mayonnaise in a big bowl. Salt and pepper to taste and mix.

YIELD: 5 servings, each with: 454 Calories; 41 g Fat (79.6% calories from fat); 16 g Protein; 8 g Carbohydrate; 3 g Dietary Fiber; 5 g net carbs

CAULIFLOWER-MOZZARELLA SALAD BASILICO

Just like the Bacon, Tomato, and Cauliflower Salad (page 158), this originally called for rice, but it works great with cauliflower. Make your own pesto or use store-bought, whichever you prefer.

½ of a head of cauliflower, run through the shredding blade of a food processor (about 4 cups, or 400 g)	**1 tablespoon (10 g) finely minced sweet red onion**
	2 tablespoons (28 ml) olive oil
15 cherry tomatoes, halved	**¼ cup (65 g) pesto (Tootsie's Pesto, page 284)**
15 strong black olives, pitted and coarsely chopped	**1 tablespoon (15 ml) wine vinegar**
⅓ pound (150 g) mozzarella, cut in ½-inch (1.3 cm) cubes	**½ teaspoon salt**
	¼ teaspoon pepper

1. Cook the cauliflower "rice" until tender-crisp (about 5 minutes on High in a microwave). Let it cool.

2. When the "rice" is cool, add the tomatoes, olives, mozzarella, and onion and toss well.

3. Whisk together the olive oil, pesto, vinegar, salt, and pepper. Pour the mixture over the salad and toss.

4. Let the salad sit for at least a half an hour for the flavors to blend; refrigerating overnight won't hurt.

YIELD: **5 servings, each with:** 247 Calories; 20 g Fat (71.2% calories from fat); 10 g Protein; 8 g Carbohydrate; 3 g Dietary Fiber; 5 g net carbs

AVOCADO-LIME SALAD

When avocados are in season, there is no easier or more nutritious salad than this. It's loaded with healthy, monounsaturated fats and potassium. And while this doesn't quite fit our parameters for "ketogenic," avocados are the HEAL Clinics diabetes treatment plan's only exception to the "no more than 5 grams of total carbs per meal" rule because they are so good for you.

2 big lettuce leaves	**2 teaspoons lime juice**
1 ripe, black avocado	**Salt**

1. Simply line two salad plates with the lettuce, slice the avocado, and arrange the avocado slices attractively on the lettuce.

2. Sprinkle a teaspoon of lime juice over each serving and salt lightly.

YIELD: **2 servings, each with:** 164 Calories; 15 g Fat (77.4% calories from fat); 2 g Protein; 8 g Carbohydrate; 3 g Dietary Fiber; 5 g net carbs

GUACAMATOES

This dish is so pretty and just wonderful served with a simple grilled steak. With over 1,000 mg of potassium in a serving, you're going to want to find a way to serve Guacamatoes often. Feel free to use purchased guacamole if you prefer. Single-serving packs of guac are widely available now, so you can make this just for yourself, if you like!

6 ripe, smallish tomatoes

Lettuce leaves or other greenery

1 batch of Guacamole (page 45)

1. Cut the cores out of the tomatoes and then slice each tomato into eight wedges, being careful not to cut through the tomato skin at the very bottom of the stem.

2. Place a lettuce leaf or some other greenery on each salad plate and put a tomato on top, spreading the wedges out to look like a flower.

3. Spoon 2 to 3 heaping tablespoons (14 to 42 g) of Guacamole into the middle of the tomato flower and serve.

YIELD: 6 servings, each with: 248 Calories; 21 g Fat (69.0% calories from fat); 4 g Protein; 17 g Carbohydrate; 5 g Dietary Fiber; 12 g net carbs

Mayonnaise Reconsidered

In the original edition of this book, I assured you it was fine to use commercially-made mayonnaise. I have since reassessed that opinion and make most of my own mayonnaise. Grocery store mayo is near-invariably made out of cheap, nasty oil, mostly soy oil. The stuff labeled "made with olive oil" is, indeed, made "with" olive oil—a little olive oil, mixed with plenty of cheap vegetable oil. It's hard to say which is worse for you, sugar or cheap vegetable oil.

MAYONNAISE BY THE QUART

I can use a lot of mayonnaise, especially in warm weather. This has become my go-to mayonnaise recipe–it fills a standard 1-quart (946 ml) mayonnaise jar. You'll need a big food processor–mine holds 14 cups (3.2 L).

Here's another reason to make your own mayo: if you use MCT oil to make your mayonnaise, every mayonnaise-dressed salad you make will catapult you deep into ketosis. (Unless you use it on a high-carb salad, of course.)

If you don't have MCT oil, light olive oil will serve and is better for you than soy or canola oil. But just making mayonnaise is enough of a reason to buy MCT oil!

Are you afraid of raw eggs? See the directions on page 22 for pasteurizing them.

2 eggs

3 egg yolks

1 tablespoon (15 ml) red wine vinegar

1 tablespoon (15 ml) lemon juice

1 teaspoon dry mustard OR 2–3 teaspoons (10–15 g) Dijon or spicy brown mustard

½ teaspoon salt

2 dashes of hot sauce (I use Frank's.)

Liquid stevia, monkfruit, or sucralose to equal ½ teaspoon of sugar in sweetness (optional)

1 teaspoon water

3 cups (700 ml) MCT oil

1. With the S-blade in place, put the eggs, egg yolks, vinegar, lemon juice, mustard, salt, and hot sauce in your food processor. Turn the processor on. While it's running, add the water.

2. Pour the oil into a glass measuring cup with a pouring lip. With the processor running, add the oil in a thin stream, about the diameter of a pencil lead. When it's all worked in, you're done! Transfer to a tight-lidded jar and stash in the fridge.

3. Theoretically, the shelf-life of this is about a week in the fridge, but I've used mine after 10 to 12 days with no ill-effects. Your risks are your own to take.

YIELD: 32 servings, each with: 191 Calories; 21 g Fat (98.4% calories from fat); 1 g Protein; trace Carbohydrate; trace Dietary Fiber; 0 net carbs

MAYONNAISE FOR A SMALLER JAR

If you won't use up a quart (946 ml) of mayonnaise before it goes bad, make this. It takes less time to do it than it does to write about it and certainly less time than it takes to run to the store for mayonnaise!

1 egg

1 egg yolk

1 tablespoon (15 ml) wine vinegar

1 tablespoon (15 ml) lemon juice

1 teaspoon dry mustard

2 drops of liquid stevia extract

½ teaspoon salt

2 dashes of hot sauce– Tabasco, Frank's, or Louisiana

1 cup (235 ml) MCT oil

1. I put everything but the oil in my little food processor. (Yes, I have a little and a big food processor; I find them both useful. You can use a blender instead if that's what you have.)

2. Have the oil standing by in a Pyrex measuring cup with a pouring lip.

3. Run the food processor for 20 seconds or so. Then, with the processor still running, slowly pour in the oils, in a stream about the diameter of a pencil lead. When all the oil is in, it's done!

4. Scrape it into a jar or snap-top container and stick it in the fridge.

YIELD: 12 servings, each with: 172 Calories; 19 g Fat (97.7% calories from fat); 1 g Protein; trace Carbohydrate; trace Dietary Fiber; 0 net carbs

Dressings

Again, my feelings about salad dressing have changed since the first edition of this book. I virtually never use bottled dressings anymore. The quality of the oils is just too bad, and when you're eating a high-fat diet, the quality of those fats counts even more than before. Anyway, salad dressing is easy to make.

These dressings are a great place to use home-made mayonnaise. Some of these recipes will give you leftovers that you should store in your refrigerator.

About yield: my general rule is that "6 servings" is about what I'd put on a large, family-size salad. So, if you see "12 servings," figure that you can get two salads out of it if you're a family of 6, more if you have a smaller family, or a dozen salads if you live alone!

We'll start with the basics. The French Vinaigrette and Italian Vinaigrette Dressing recipes make approximately enough for two big, family-size salads, but feel free to double them and keep them in the fridge. They make good marinades for chicken, fish, or seafood, too.

FRENCH VINAIGRETTE DRESSING

No, this is not that sweet, tomatoey stuff that somehow has gotten the name "French dressing." No Frenchman would eat that stuff on a bet! This is a classic vinaigrette dressing.

½ teaspoon salt

¼ teaspoon pepper

¼–⅓ cup (60–80 ml) wine vinegar

½ teaspoon Dijon mustard

¾ cup (175 ml) extra-virgin olive oil

1. Put all the ingredients in a container with a tight lid and shake well.

2. Shake again before pouring over a salad and tossing.

YIELD: 12 servings, each with: 120 Calories; 14 g Fat (98.9% calories from fat); trace Protein; trace Carbohydrate; trace Dietary Fiber; 0 g net carbs

ITALIAN VINAIGRETTE DRESSING

Add a little extra zip to French Vinaigrette, and you've got Italian vinaigrette.

⅓ cup (80 ml) wine vinegar

2 cloves of garlic, crushed

½ teaspoon oregano

¼ teaspoon basil

1 or 2 drops of Tabasco

⅔ cup (160 ml) extra-virgin olive oil

Put all the ingredients in a container with a tight-fitting lid and shake well.

YIELD: 12 servings, each with: 108 Calories; 12 g Fat (97.6% calories from fat); trace Protein; 1 g Carbohydrate; trace Dietary Fiber; 1 g net carbs

Creamy Italian Dressing

This is a simple variation on Italian Vinaigrette. Just add 2 tablespoons (28 g) of mayonnaise to the Italian Vinaigrette Dressing and whisk until smooth.

YIELD: 12 servings, each with: 124 Calories; 14 g Fat (97.9% calories from fat); trace Protein; 1 g Carbohydrate; trace Dietary Fiber; 1 g net carbs

GREEK LEMON DRESSING

The use of lemon juice in place of vinegar in salad dressings is distinctively Greek.

¾ cup (175 ml) extra-virgin olive oil

¼ cup (60 ml) lemon juice

2 tablespoons (6 g) dried oregano, crushed

1 clove of garlic, crushed

Salt and pepper

1. Put all the ingredients in a container with a tight-fitting lid and shake well.

2. This is best made at least a few hours in advance, but don't try to double the recipe and keep it around. Lemon juice just doesn't hold its freshness the way vinegar does.

YIELD: 12 servings, each with: 185 Calories; 20 g Fat (96.5% calories from fat); trace Protein; 2 g Carbohydrate; 1 g Dietary Fiber; 1 g net carbs

BLUE CHEESE DRESSING

That Nice Boy I Married adores blue cheese dressing! Not just on salads—he dips chicken and even pork rinds in it, too.

2 cups (450 g) mayonnaise

½ cup (120 ml) buttermilk

½ cup (115 g) small-curd cottage cheese

½ teaspoon Worcestershire sauce

1 clove of garlic, crushed

1 teaspoon salt or Vege-Sal

3 ounces (85 g) crumbled blue cheese

1. Whisk together the mayonnaise, buttermilk, cottage cheese, Worcestershire sauce, garlic, and salt, mixing well.
2. Gently stir in the blue cheese, to preserve some chunks.
3. Store in the fridge in a container with a tight-fitting lid.

YIELD: 24 servings, each with: 151 Calories; 17 g Fat (94.9% calories from fat); 2 g Protein; trace Carbohydrate; trace Dietary Fiber; 0 g net carbs

BALSAMIC-PARMESAN DRESSING

This rich, full flavor complements mixed greens with the ripest of tomatoes and a sprinkle of chopped olives. It makes an unusual chicken salad, too.

3 tablespoons (45 ml) balsamic vinegar

⅓ cup (80 ml) extra-virgin olive oil

1 tablespoon (14 g) mayonnaise

2 cloves of garlic, crushed

1 teaspoon grated onion

¼ teaspoon salt or Vege-Sal

¼ teaspoon pepper

1 teaspoon spicy brown or Dijon mustard

1 tablespoon (15 g) grated Parmesan cheese

1. Whisk all the ingredients together until smooth.
2. Store in the fridge in a container with a tight-fitting lid and shake or whisk again before tossing with a salad.

YIELD: 6 servings, each with: 130 Calories; 14 g Fat (95.5% calories from fat); trace Protein; 1 g Carbohydrate; trace Dietary Fiber; 1 g net carbs

DOREEN'S DRESSING

My friend Doreen Devitt made this up and told me about it when I first told her I was writing a cookbook. So I tried it, and I discovered that it's simple and wonderful. Serendipitously, I ran into Doreen a few days before sending this manuscript in. She says she's started adding a little dried basil to this dressing, and that you should try it!

½ cup (115 g) mayonnaise

3 tablespoons (45 ml) balsamic vinegar

1 clove of garlic, crushed

Simply combine all the ingredients and store in the fridge in a container with a tight-fitting lid.

YIELD: 6 servings, each with: 133 Calories; 16 g Fat (97.5% calories from fat); trace Protein; 1 g Carbohydrate; trace Dietary Fiber; 1 g net carbs

RANCH DRESSING

Here's America's favorite dressing, only fresher and better! Substitute sour cream for the buttermilk, and you'll have ranch dip.

1 cup (225 g) mayonnaise

1 cup (235 ml) buttermilk

2 tablespoons (12 g) finely chopped scallions

¼ teaspoon onion powder

2 tablespoons (8 g) minced fresh parsley

1 clove of garlic, crushed

¼ teaspoon paprika

⅛ teaspoon cayenne pepper or a few drops of Tabasco

¼ teaspoon salt

¼ teaspoon black pepper

1. Combine all the ingredients well, either whisking them together or running them through the food processor or blender.

2. Store in a tight-lidded container in the fridge.

YIELD: 24 servings, each with: 71 Calories; 8 g Fat (95.7% calories from fat); trace Protein; trace Carbohydrate; trace Dietary Fiber; 0 g net carbs

165

TANGY "HONEY" MUSTARD DRESSING

You know that honey, despite being "natural," is pure sugar, right? Make this instead. This makes a little over ½ cup (120 ml), or just enough for one big salad, but feel free to double, or even quadruple, this recipe. You can sub sugar-free imitation honey for the sweetener to good effect, but the results will be a bit higher carb.

¼ cup (60 ml) MCT oil or light olive oil

2 tablespoons (28 ml) cider vinegar

2 tablespoons (30 g) spicy brown or Dijon mustard

Liquid stevia, monkfruit, or sucralose to equal 5 teaspoons (1 tablespoon plus 2 teaspoons) of sugar in sweetness

⅛ teaspoon pepper

⅛ teaspoon salt

Combine all the ingredients and store in a container with a tight-fitting lid.

YIELD: 6 servings, each with: 86 Calories; 9 g Fat (95.2% calories from fat); trace Protein; 1 g Carbohydrate; trace Dietary Fiber; 1 g net carbs

MELLOW "HONEY" MUSTARD DRESSING

This is good on salads, of course, but also for those who like honey-mustard dip with chicken nuggets. It's good for basting pork or salmon, too. Again, you can use sugar-free imitation honey in this instead of the liquid sweetener, if you prefer, but the results will be carbier. That would be nice if you're using it for a baste, though—you'll get a glazed effect.

1¼ cups (285 g) mayonnaise

¼ cup (60 g) spicy brown mustard

Liquid stevia, monkfruit, or sucralose to equal ⅓ cup (67 g) of sugar in sweetness

4 tablespoons (60 ml) water

1 teaspoon salt

Combine all the ingredients and store in a tight-lidded container in the refrigerator.

YIELD: 12 servings, each with: 169 Calories; 20 g Fat (97.8% calories from fat); 1 g Protein; trace Carbohydrate; trace Dietary Fiber; 0 g net carbs

RASPBERRY VINEGAR

A lot of brands of raspberry vinegar have added sugar. If you can't find a sugar-free brand, this is a good substitute.

½ cup (120 ml) white vinegar

¼ teaspoon raspberry cake flavoring (This is a highly concentrated oil in a teeny little bottle.)

Liquid stevia, monkfruit, or sucralose to equal 3 tablespoons (39 g) of sugar in sweetness

Just combine all the ingredients and store in a container with a tight-fitting lid.

YIELD: 8 servings, each with: 2 Calories; 0 g Fat (0.0% calories from fat); 0 g Protein; 1 g Carbohydrate; 0 g Dietary Fiber; 1 g net carbs

RASPBERRY VINAIGRETTE DRESSING

Sweet-and-tangy, Raspberry Vinaigrette is a favorite you'll get to enjoy more often once you're making your own low-carb variety.

¼ cup (60 ml) Raspberry Vinegar, homemade or sugar-free store-bought

¼ cup (60 ml) MCT or light olive oil

3 tablespoons plus 1 teaspoon (47 g) mayonnaise

1 teaspoon spicy brown or Dijon mustard

Pinch each of salt and pepper

Blend all the ingredients and store in a tight-lidded container in the refrigerator.

YIELD: 6 servings, each with: 137 Calories; 16 g Fat (97.7% calories from fat); trace Protein; 1 g Carbohydrate; trace Dietary Fiber; 1 g net carbs

PARMESAN PEPPERCORN DRESSING

Here's another favorite that's easy to make at home. It's fresher and better tasting than store-bought, too.

2 tablespoons (28 ml) olive oil

3 tablespoons (42 g) mayonnaise

2 tablespoons (28 ml) wine vinegar

3 tablespoons (15 g) grated Parmesan cheese

1 teaspoon freshly ground black pepper (Coarse-cracked pepper will do, if you don't have a pepper mill.)

Blend all the ingredients and store in a tight-lidded container in the refrigerator.

YIELD: 6 servings, each with: 102 Calories; 11 g Fat (93.4% calories from fat); 1 g Protein; 1 g Carbohydrate; trace Dietary Fiber; 1 g net carbs

CREAMY GARLIC DRESSING

Look at all that garlic! If you plan to get kissed, make sure you share your salad with the object of your affections. This is only enough for one big salad, but I wouldn't double it; I'd make this one fresh so the garlic flavor will be better.

½ cup (115 g) mayonnaise

Pinch each of pepper and salt

8 cloves of garlic, crushed

2 tablespoons (28 ml) olive oil

2 tablespoons (28 ml) wine vinegar

Combine all the ingredients well and store in a tight-lidded container in the refrigerator.

YIELD: 8 servings, each with: 178 Calories; 20 g Fat (95.6% calories from fat); trace Protein; 2 g Carbohydrate; trace Dietary Fiber; 2 g net carbs

CAESAR DRESSING

If you're afraid of raw eggs, see the instructions for pasteurizing eggs on page 22. Me, I just use an egg. This is far better than any bottled Caesar dressing I've found, if it's not quite as wonderful as what I had on my honeymoon in Mexico—although I suspect that the atmosphere had something to do with that.

4 tablespoons (60 ml) lemon juice

¼ cup (60 ml) olive oil

1 teaspoon pepper

1½ teaspoons Worcestershire sauce

1 clove of garlic, peeled and smashed

½ teaspoon salt or Vege-Sal

1 raw egg

½ cup (50 g) grated Parmesan cheese

1–2 anchovy fillets (or a good squeeze of anchovy paste)

1. Put everything in a blender and run it for a minute. Toss with one really huge Caesar salad (dinner-party-sized) or with a couple of smaller salads.

2. Use it up pretty quickly and keep it refrigerated because of the raw egg.

Note: If you'd like this a little thicker, you could add ¼ teaspoon of guar to the mix.

YIELD: 8 servings, each with: 98 Calories; 9 g Fat (81.3% calories from fat); 3 g Protein; 1 g Carbohydrate; trace Dietary Fiber; 1 g net carbs

COLESLAW DRESSING

Virtually all commercial coleslaw dressing is simply full of sugar, which is a shame, because cabbage is a very low-carb vegetable. I just love coleslaw, so I came up with a sugar-free dressing. You may, of course, vary these proportions to taste. Also, a teaspoon or so of celery seed can be nice in this, for a little variety. I use this much dressing for a whole head of cabbage. If you're used to commercial coleslaw, which tends to be simply swimming in dressing, you may want to double this or use this recipe for half a head.

½ cup (115 g) mayonnaise

½ cup (115 g) sour cream

1–1½ tablespoons (15–23 ml) cider vinegar

1–1½ teaspoons prepared mustard

½–1 teaspoon salt or Vege-Sal

Liquid stevia, monk fruit, or sucralose to equal 1–2 teaspoons of sugar in sweetness

Combine all the ingredients well and toss with coleslaw. (See the recipes on pages 155–156.)

YIELD: 12 servings, each with: 87 Calories; 10 g Fat (95.9% calories from fat); trace Protein; 1 g Carbohydrate; trace Dietary Fiber; 1 g net carbs

CHAPTER 7

Chicken and Turkey

A round here we eat chicken no fewer than a couple of times a week, and many other families do the same. After all, chicken is inexpensive, and it's always tasty. It also lends itself to infinite variation, as this chapter will prove.

Until fairly recently, you could buy a cut-up broiler-fryer—a package with two breasts with wings attached and two leg-and-thigh quarters. This is what my mother always bought because some of us liked white meat and some of us—me included—preferred dark. Sadly, the cut-up broiler-fryer no longer appears in my grocery stores. Instead we have packages of just breasts, wings, thighs, drumsticks, etc. I feel this is a shame, but most people must prefer it, or it wouldn't have taken over the market.

So feel free to use the chicken parts you prefer. Me, I stock the freezer when thighs drop to sixty-nine cents per pound. If you would like to have a cut-up broiler-fryer, you could pick out a whole chicken and ask the nice meat guys to cut it up for you. They tend to be obliging folks.

Overwhelmingly, I prefer chicken with the skin on and the bones in. Chicken skin is not only delicious, it is also nutritious, being a great source of collagen. And the bones can be saved for bone broth. To me, the only real point in favor of the boneless, skinless chicken breast is that it is quick to cook.

Ground turkey is also good to have on hand, and it's a nice change from ground beef. You'll find some interesting ways to use it in this chapter.

RANCHHOUSE CHICKEN

This recipe is super-simple, and the family will like it. It's good with coleslaw.

3 pounds (1.4 kg) chicken–legs, thighs, breasts–whatever you like

¼ cup (60 ml) Ranch Dressing (page 165)

1. Preheat the oven to 375°F (190°C, or gas mark 5).
2. Arrange the chicken in a roasting pan and spoon the Ranch Dressing over it, smearing it a bit with the back of the spoon to cover each piece.
3. Roast for 75 to 90 minutes, depending on the size of your pieces of chicken. You want the juices to run clear when it's pierced to the bone.

YIELD: 6 servings, each with: 416 Calories; 33 g Fat (71.6% calories from fat); 29 g Protein; trace Carbohydrate; trace Dietary Fiber; 0 g net carbs

TARRAGON CHICKEN

Très 1960! Add a green salad with French Vinaigrette Dressing (page 162) and some crusty bread for the carbivores and you have a retro dinner party.

3 pounds (1.4 kg) chicken (legs, thighs, breasts whatever you like)

2 tablespoons (28 g) butter

1 teaspoon salt or Vege-Sal

Pepper

3 tablespoons (6 g) dried tarragon

1 clove of garlic, crushed

½ cup (120 ml) dry white wine

1. If your chicken is in quarters, cut the legs from the thighs and the wings from the breasts. (It will fit in your skillet more easily this way.)
2. Melt the butter in a heavy skillet over medium-high heat and brown the chicken, turning it once or twice, until it's golden all over.
3. Pour off most of the fat and sprinkle the chicken with the salt and just a dash of pepper. Scatter the tarragon over the chicken, crushing it a little between your fingers to release the flavor, and then add the garlic and the wine.
4. Cover the skillet, turn the burner to low, and simmer for 30 minutes, turning the chicken at least once. Spoon a little of the pan liquid over each piece of chicken when serving.

Note: If you don't have a skillet big enough to cook all the chicken at once, brown it all in your skillet and arrange it in a roasting pan that will hold it all. When it's all browned, rinse the skillet with the wine mixture to get all the nice brown bits and then pour it over the chicken in the roasting pan. Cover with a lid if you have one, or foil if you don't, and put it in the oven at 300°F (150°C, or gas mark 2) for 40 minutes or so, again, turning once or twice in that time.

YIELD: 6 servings, each with: 408 Calories; 30 g Fat (68.5% calories from fat); 29 g Protein; 2 g Carbohydrate; trace Dietary Fiber; 2 g net carbs

CURRIED CHICKEN

This was one of the first low-carb recipes I invented, and it's still one of my best. If you have some on hand, try subbing canned coconut milk for the heavy cream. Yum! Cauliflower Rice (page 113) is great with this, to soak up the sauce.

4 or 5 chicken quarters, white meat, dark meat, or both, cut up and skinned

1 medium onion

1 tablespoon (14 g) butter

1 rounded (about 16 g) tablespoon curry powder

1 cup (235 ml) heavy cream

3 or 4 cloves of garlic, crushed

½ cup (120 ml) water

1. Preheat the oven to 375°F (190°C, or gas mark 5).

2. Arrange the chicken in a shallow baking pan. Chop the onion and scatter it over the chicken.

3. Melt the butter in a small, heavy skillet and sauté the curry powder in it for a couple of minutes—just until it starts to smell good.

4. Mix together the heavy cream, garlic, water, and sautéed curry powder and pour this over the chicken. Bake it, uncovered, for 1 hour to 1 hour and 20 minutes, turning the chicken over every 20 to 30 minutes so that the sauce flavors both sides.

5. To serve, arrange the chicken on a platter. Take the sauce in the pan (it will look dreadful, sort of curdled up, but it will smell like heaven) and scrape it all into your blender. Blend it with a little more water or cream, if necessary, to get a nice, rich, golden sauce. Pour it over the chicken and serve.

Note: Ahem. Take a look at the first ingredient in the recipe above—the chicken is skinned, right? That's not because you can't have chicken skin on a low-carb diet, it's because cooking chicken with the skin on in a recipe like this only results in flabby, uninteresting chicken skin. Do you like crispy chicken skin? I sure do. Check out Chicken Chips (page 172) to find out what I do with the skin I pull off that chicken.

YIELD: 6 servings, each with: 519 Calories; 42 g Fat (74.0% calories from fat); 30 g Protein; 4 g Carbohydrate; 1 g Dietary Fiber; 3 g net carbs

CHICKEN CHIPS

Chicken skin has been a sad victim of the slurs of the anti-fat crew. It is highly nutritious stuff, loaded with collagen, great for your skin, joints, and all connective tissue. So eat the skin!

I have my local specialty butcher save skin for 3 to 4 days, and buy 10 to 12 pounds (4.6 to 5.5 kg) at a time. I freeze it in baggies, in quantities that will just about cover my broiler rack. Sometimes, we eat just these as a quick, light supper.

Chicken skin   **Salt**

1. Preheat the oven to 375°F (190°C, or gas mark 5).

2. Take any and all chicken skin you have on hand—chunks of chicken fat will work, too—and spread them out as flat as you can on the broiler rack.

3. Bake for 10 to 15 minutes or until the skin gets brown and crunchy (thicker pieces take longer than thinner ones). Sprinkle with salt and eat like chips—these are not to be believed!

4. Don't forget to pour off the fat from the broiler pan to save for cooking! That's schmaltz, revered in Jewish cuisine, and one of the most-used fats before the vegetable oil industry started spreading ugly rumors about animal fats. My grandma used it in brownies.

YIELD: Yield will totally depend on how much chicken skin you bake, but here's the info that really matters: There are no carbohydrates here at all. It may be ketogenic, but I have no way of knowing the fat percentage here.

PIZZA CHICKEN

This recipe is basically a skillet cacciatore, except for the mozzarella—that's what makes it Pizza Chicken. Serve this over tofu shirataki spaghetti, if you like.

3 chicken leg-and-thigh quarters

1–2 tablespoons (15–28 ml) olive oil

1 can (8 ounces, or 225 g) of plain tomato sauce

1 can (4 ounces, or 115 g) of mushrooms, drained

½ cup (120 ml) dry red wine

1 green pepper, chopped

1 small onion, chopped

1 or 2 cloves of garlic, crushed, or 1 to 2 teaspoons jarred chopped garlic in oil

1 to 1½ teaspoons dried oregano

3 ounces (85 g) shredded mozzarella cheese

Parmesan cheese (optional)

1. Strip the skin off the chicken (save the skin for Chicken Chips, page 172). Cut the leg-and-thigh quarters in two at the leg joint.

2. Over medium heat, warm the olive oil in a big, heavy skillet and brown the chicken all over.

3. Pour in the tomato sauce, mushrooms, and wine. Add the green pepper, onion, garlic, and oregano. Cover the whole thing, turn the burner to its lowest setting, and forget about it for 45 minutes to 1 hour.

4. When the chicken is cooked through, remove the pieces from the skillet and put them on the serving plates. If the sauce isn't good and thick by now, turn up the burner to medium-high and let the sauce boil down for a few minutes.

5. While the sauce is thickening, sprinkle the shredded mozzarella cheese over the chicken and warm each plate in the microwave for 20 to 30 seconds on 50 percent power to melt the cheese. (Your microwave may take a little more or a little less time.)

6. Spoon the sauce over each piece of chicken and serve. Sprinkle a little Parmesan cheese over your Pizza Chicken, if you like.

YIELD: 4 servings, each with: 578 Calories; 38 g Fat (61.8% calories from fat); 42 g Protein; 12 g Carbohydrate; 3 g Dietary Fiber; 9 g net carbs

LOOED CHICKEN

Traditionally, looing is done on the stove, but this makes a terrific slow-cooker recipe. Asian Ginger Slaw (page 156) would be good with this.

3 pounds (1.4 kg) chicken—legs, thighs, breasts, as you like, or 4–5 boneless, skinless breasts and/or thighs

1 batch of Looing Sauce (page 281)

Scallions, sliced

Toasted sesame oil

1. Put your chicken in your slow cooker and pour the Looing Sauce over it. Cover the slow cooker, set it to Low, and forget about it for 8 to 9 hours.

2. At dinnertime, remove the chicken from the looing sauce and put each piece on a serving plate. Scatter a few sliced scallions over each serving and top with a few drops of toasted sesame oil.

YIELD: 6 servings, each with: 353 Calories; 26 g Fat (66.9% calories from fat); 28 g Protein. There is no way to calculate what is absorbed from the sauce, but it cannot add more than 1–2 grams of carbohydrate, total.

CHICKEN AND TURKEY

ROAST CHICKEN WITH BALSAMIC VINEGAR

This recipe yields wonderfully crunchy skin, with a sweet-and-tangy sauce to dip bites of chicken in. Broccoli is nice with this.

Dried bay leaves

3 pounds (1.4 kg) chicken-legs, thighs, or breasts, as you prefer

Salt or Vege-Sal

Pepper

3–4 tablespoons (45–60 ml) olive oil

3–4 tablespoons (45–55 g) butter

½ cup (120 ml) dry white wine

3 tablespoons (45 ml) balsamic vinegar

1. Preheat the oven to 350°F (180°C, or gas mark 4).

2. Tuck a bay leaf or two under the skin of each piece of chicken. Sprinkle each piece with salt and pepper and arrange them in a roasting pan.

3. Drizzle the chicken with olive oil and dot them with the same amount of butter. Roast in the oven for 1½ hours, turning each piece every 20 to 30 minutes. (This makes for gloriously crunchy, tasty skin.)

4. When the chicken is done, put it on a platter and pour off the fat from the pan, saving it to cook with. Remove the bay leaves.

5. Put the pan over a burner set on medium and pour in the wine and balsamic vinegar. Stir this around, dissolving the tasty brown stuff stuck to the pan to make a sauce. Boil this for just a minute or two, pour into a sauceboat or a pitcher, and serve with the chicken.

YIELD: 6 servings, each with: 478 Calories; 38 g Fat (74.6% calories from fat); 28 g Protein; 1 g Carbohydrate; 0 g Dietary Fiber; 1 g net carbs

SPICY PEANUT CHICKEN

This takes ten minutes to put together and only another fifteen to cook. It's hot and spicy, quasi-Thai. Some like it hot, and some like it a little bit less so. So, when you're buying your ingredients, choose a little jalapeño or a big one, depending on how hot you like your food. I use a big one, and it made this dish pretty hot. And there's no law against using only half a jalapeño.

1 teaspoon ground cumin

½ teaspoon ground cinnamon

3 boneless, skinless chicken breasts

3 tablespoons (45 ml) olive or peanut oil for sautéing (I think peanut is better here.)

½ of a smallish onion, thinly sliced

1 can (14½ ounces, or 410 g) of diced tomatoes

2 tablespoons (32 g) natural peanut butter

1 tablespoon (15 ml) lemon juice

2 cloves of garlic, crushed

1 fresh jalapeño, cut in half and seeded

1. On a saucer or plate, stir the cumin and cinnamon together and then rub into both sides of chicken breasts.

2. Put the oil in a heavy skillet over medium heat and add the chicken and sliced onion. Brown the chicken a bit on both sides.

3. While that's happening, put all the liquid and half the tomatoes from the can of tomatoes in a blender or food processor, along with the peanut butter, lemon juice, garlic, and jalapeño. (Wash your hands well after handling that hot pepper, or you'll be sorry the next time you touch your nose or eyes!) Blend or process until smooth.

4. Pour this rather thick sauce over the chicken (which you've turned at least once by now, right?). Add the rest of the canned tomatoes, cover, and turn the burner to low.

5. Let it simmer for 10 to 15 minutes or until the chicken is cooked through.

YIELD: 3 servings, each with: 503 Calories; 25 g Fat (45.1% calories from fat); 56 g Protein; 12 g Carbohydrate; 3 g Dietary Fiber; 9 g net carbs

SKILLET CHICKEN FLORENTINE

My husband took one bite of this and said, "This is going to get you a lot of new readers!" I know of no other dish that's so quick and easy, yet so incredibly good.

Olive oil

3 boneless, skinless chicken breasts

1 package (10 ounces, or 280 g) of frozen chopped spinach, thawed and drained

2 cloves of garlic, crushed

¼ cup (60 ml) heavy cream

¼ cup (25 g) grated Parmesan cheese

1. Warm a little olive oil in a heavy skillet and brown the chicken breasts over medium heat to the point where they just have a touch of gold. Remove the chicken from the skillet.

2. Add a couple more tablespoons (28 ml) of olive oil, the spinach, and the garlic and stir for 2 to 3 minutes. Stir in the heavy cream and Parmesan cheese and spread the mixture evenly over the bottom of the skillet. Place the chicken breasts on top, cover, turn the burner to low, and let simmer for 15 minutes.

3. Serve chicken breasts on beds of the spinach.

YIELD: 3 servings, each with: 383 Calories; 23 g Fat (53.0% calories from fat); 40 g Protein; 5 g Carbohydrate; 3 g Dietary Fiber; 2 g net carbs

THOSE CHICKEN THINGS

Do you want to impress everyone at the cookout? Kate Sutherland sends this recipe and says this works best on a gas grill.

1 bunch of scallions (about 10)

1 package (8 ounces, or 225 g) of cream cheese, softened

8 boneless, skinless chicken breasts

16 to 24 slices of bacon

1. Clean, trim, and chop the scallions, including a generous portion of the green. Mix the scallions into the cream cheese and set aside.

2. Butterfly the chicken breasts from the thinnest edge in toward the thickest. (This thickest edge will be the middle of the breast once it is opened up.) Working one piece at a time, open the breast up and put it in a heavy zipper-lock bag. Seal the bag and with a rolling pin, hammer, dumbbell, or whatever else you can find, pound the chicken breast until it is ¼-inch (6 mm) thick all over. Repeat with the remaining chicken breasts.

3. Once all 8 breasts have been flattened, place an equal amount of the cream cheese and scallion mixture on each. Wrap the chicken meat around the cheese mix so that it is completely enclosed.

4. Wrap a strip of bacon around the ball of chicken, stretching it a bit to provide maximum overlap. Then, wrap a second piece of bacon around the still exposed portion of the chicken, again giving it a bit of a stretch. Secure with a few toothpicks. (Depending on the size of the chicken breasts, you may need a third piece of bacon. Most of the chicken should be covered by the bacon strips.)

5. Refrigerate for several hours or overnight. They should be well chilled before they go on the grill.

(continued)

6. Cover the barbecue rack with a sheet of aluminum foil and spray it with nonstick cooking spray. (The foil helps prevent flare-ups from the bacon fat and also helps the chicken cook evenly.) Preheat the grill to High.

7. Place the chicken on the covered rack, reduce the heat to Medium, and close the lid. Turn about every 5 minutes until all sides are nicely browned. When the cheese starts to ooze out in a few places, they are done. (Depending on the size of the pieces and the overall temperature of your barbecue, this should take 20 to 30 minutes.) Remove the toothpicks and serve.

YIELD: 8 servings, each with: 348 Calories; 22 g Fat (58.8% calories from fat); 34 g Protein; 1 g Carbohydrate; trace Dietary Fiber; 1 g net carbs

CHICKEN AND ARTICHOKE SKILLET

This is quick and easy enough for a weeknight, but elegant enough for company. By the way, feel free to use thighs, if you prefer. They're smaller, so 6 should be about right.

3 tablespoons (45 g) butter, divided	**1 medium onion, sliced**
4 boneless, skinless chicken breasts	**1 clove of garlic, crushed**
	¼ cup (60 ml) dry white wine
1 can (14 ounces, or 390 g) of quartered artichoke hearts, drained	**1 teaspoon dried thyme or 1 tablespoon (3 g) fresh thyme leaves**
½ of a red bell pepper, cut into strips	

1. Melt 2 tablespoons (28 g) of butter in a heavy skillet over medium heat and sauté the chicken breasts until they're golden (5 to 7 minutes per side). Remove from the skillet.

2. Melt the remaining tablespoon (14 g) of butter and toss the artichoke hearts, bell pepper, onion, and garlic into the skillet. Sauté for 3 minutes or so, stirring frequently.

3. Pour in the wine and sprinkle the thyme over the vegetables. Place the chicken breasts over the vegetables, turn the heat to medium-low, cover, and simmer for 10 minutes.

YIELD: 4 servings, each with: 279 Calories; 12 g Fat (40.2% calories from fat); 29 g Protein; 10 g Carbohydrate; 1 g Dietary Fiber; 9 g net carbs

TERIYAKI CHICKEN

This is a classic and a favorite! Sliced scallions or toasted sesame seeds—or, heck, both!—are a nice garnish, here. Consider stir-fried snow peas or Asian Ginger Slaw (page 156) on the side.

4 to 6 boneless, skinless chicken breasts or thighs	**1 batch of Teriyaki Sauce (page 280)**

1. Put your chicken in a large zipper-lock bag and pour the Teriyaki Sauce over it. Seal the bag, pressing out the air as you go, and turn a few times to coat. Stick the bag in the refrigerator and let the breasts marinate for at least 1 hour. (Longer won't hurt; if you do this in the morning, you can cook as soon as you come home at night.)

2. When you're ready to cook, pour off the marinade into a small saucepan. Grill or broil your chicken for 5 to 7 minutes per side, checking doneness by cutting into one piece—if it's still pink, toss it back on the grill or under the broiler. Don't overcook, or your chicken will be dry.

3. While your chicken is cooking, bring the marinade to a complete, rolling boil for a few minutes. Pour a little on each piece of chicken before serving.

YIELD: Assuming 6 servings, each will have: 167 Calories; 3 g Fat (18.5% calories from fat); 28 g Protein; 3 g Carbohydrate; trace Dietary Fiber; 3 g net carbs (This assumes you consume all the teriyaki sauce, which is unlikely.)

SATAY WITHOUT A STICK

Here's a recipe for boneless, skinless chicken breasts that reminds me of satay, the popular Asian kebabs.

1 tablespoon (15 ml) oil

1 clove of garlic, crushed

1 teaspoon curry powder

4 boneless, skinless chicken breasts

Not-Very-Authentic Peanut Sauce (page 274)

1. Put a heavy skillet over medium heat. Add the oil, garlic, and curry powder and stir for a few seconds to flavor the oil.
2. Add the chicken breasts and sauté for about 7 minutes on each side or until done through.
3. Serve with the Not-Very-Authentic Peanut Sauce, warming it first, if desired.

YIELD: 4 servings, each with: 422 Calories; 25 g Fat (54.2% calories from fat); 34 g Protein; 14 g Carbohydrate; 3 g Dietary Fiber; 11 g net carbs. The analysis includes a serving of sauce.

PICNIC CHICKEN

This marinade doesn't so much season the chicken as point up the flavor of the chicken itself. It makes it juicier, too. I've called for broiling here, but this is a great choice for your barbecue grill, as well. You know, when you're on a picnic!

⅔ cup (160 ml) cider vinegar

3 tablespoons (45 ml) oil

2 teaspoons salt

¼ teaspoon pepper

1 cut-up broiler-fryer

1. Combine the vinegar, oil, salt, and pepper and pour over the chicken in a large zipper-lock bag. Marinate in the fridge for at least an hour; longer wouldn't hurt.
2. Preheat the broiler to High. Pour the marinade off the chicken into a small saucepan and put it over a high burner. Arrange the chicken on your broiler rack and broil it about 8 inches (20 cm) from the flame.
3. Once the marinade has boiled at a complete, rolling boil for a few minutes, use it to baste the chicken every 10 to 15 minutes while cooking. Give it about 25 minutes per side or until done through. (Pierce it to the bone; the juices should run clear, not pink.) You may need to rearrange the chicken pieces on your broiler rack to get them to cook evenly, so they're all ready at the same time.

YIELD: 6 servings, each with: 417 Calories; 32 g Fat (70.8% calories from fat); 28 g Protein; 2 g Carbohydrate; trace Dietary Fiber; 2 g net carbs. (This assumes you consume all of the marinade, which you won't.)

MIDDLE EASTERN SKILLET CHICKEN

Don't let that list of ingredients scare you! You can have this on the table in 30 minutes or less.

3 boneless, skinless chicken breasts

3 tablespoons (45 ml) olive oil

1 medium onion, chopped

½ teaspoon ground coriander

1 teaspoon ground cumin

¼ teaspoon ground cinnamon

½ teaspoon turmeric

¼ teaspoon black pepper

1 tablespoon (8 g) freshly grated ginger

1 can (14½ ounces, or 410 g) of diced tomatoes

2 cloves of garlic, crushed

1 cup (235 ml) chicken broth

1. Cut the chicken breasts into cubes. Heat the olive oil over medium heat in a heavy skillet and add the chicken and onions.

2. Sauté for a couple of minutes and then stir in the coriander, cumin, cinnamon, turmeric, and pepper. Cook until the chicken is white all over.

3. Add the ginger, tomatoes, garlic, and chicken broth; stir. Cover, turn the burner to Low, and simmer for 15 minutes.

YIELD: 3 servings, each with: 312 Calories; 16 g Fat (45.8% calories from fat); 31 g Protein; 11 g Carbohydrate; 2 g Dietary Fiber; 9 g net carbs

CHICKEN PAPRIKASH

Making my paprikash with real sour cream is one of the great joys of low-carbing! Since this dish is all about the paprika, use the best quality sweet paprika you can find. Be sure to serve plenty of Cauliflower Purée (page 112) or Fauxtatoes Deluxe (page 113) with it, to smother in the extra gravy!

3 tablespoons (45 g) butter

3 pounds (1.4 kg) chicken– breasts, legs, and/or thighs, as you prefer

1 small onion

2 tablespoons (14 g) paprika

½ cup (120 ml) chicken broth

1 cup (230 g) sour cream

Salt or Vege-Sal and pepper

1. Melt the butter in a heavy skillet and brown the chicken and onion over medium-high heat.

2. In a separate bowl, stir the paprika into the chicken broth. Pour the mixture over the chicken.

3. Cover the skillet, turn the burner to low, and let it simmer for 30 to 45 minutes.

4. When the chicken is tender and cooked through, remove it from the skillet and put it on a serving platter.

5. Stir the sour cream into the liquid left in the pan and stir until smooth and well blended. Heat through, but do not let it boil, or it will curdle. Salt and pepper to taste and serve this gravy with the chicken.

YIELD: 6 servings, each with: 503 Calories; 40 g Fat (71.8% calories from fat); 31 g Protein; 5 g Carbohydrate; 1 g Dietary Fiber; 4 g net carbs

HOMESTYLE TURKEY LOAF

Turkey loaf makes a nice change from meatloaf made of ground beef. The vegetables and apple add both flavor and juiciness.

1 pound (455 g) ground turkey	1½ tablespoons (23 ml) Worcestershire sauce
½ cup (40 g) crushed pork rinds	2 teaspoons poultry seasoning
1 rib of celery, finely chopped	1 teaspoon salt or Vege-Sal
1 small onion, finely chopped	1 egg
½ cup (75 g) finely chopped apple	

1. Preheat the oven to 350°F (180°C, or gas mark 4).
2. Combine all the ingredients in a big bowl and—with clean hands—squeeze it together until it's very well combined.
3. Spray a loaf pan with nonstick cooking spray and pack the turkey mixture into the pan. Bake for 50 minutes or until cooked through.

YIELD: 4 servings, each with: 213 Calories; 11 g Fat (45.7% calories from fat); 22 g Protein; 7 g Carbohydrate; 1 g Dietary Fiber; 6 g net carbs

CURRIED TURKEY LOAF

This has a good, rich curry flavor. It's great with Cranberry Chutney (page 282).

2 pounds (910 g) ground turkey	1–2 tablespoons (6–12 g) curry powder
1 medium onion, chopped fairly fine	1 tablespoon (18 g) salt or (12 g) Vege-Sal
2 eggs	1 teaspoon pepper
2 cloves of garlic, crushed	

1. Preheat the oven to 350°F (180°C, or gas mark 4).
2. Combine all the ingredients in a big bowl and—with clean hands—squeeze it together until it's very well combined.
3. Spray a loaf pan with nonstick cooking spray and pack the turkey mixture into the pan. Bake for 60 to 75 minutes, until the juices run clear.

YIELD: 6 servings, each with: 260 Calories; 14 g Fat (50.2% calories from fat); 29 g Protein; 3 g Carbohydrate; 1 g Dietary Fiber; 2 g net carbs

LOW-CARB MICROWAVE PASTICCHIO

This has become my sister's standby recipe for potlucks and other casserole occasions. Feel free to substitute tofu shirataki, prepared according to the instructions on page 138, for the spaghetti squash.

PASTICCHIO

½ of a medium onion, chopped

1 clove of garlic, crushed

1 pound (455 g) ground turkey

¾ teaspoon ground cinnamon

⅛ teaspoon ground nutmeg

1 cup (250 g) ricotta cheese

¼ cup (15 g) chopped fresh parsley

¼ teaspoon salt or Vege-Sal

⅛ teaspoon pepper

SAUCE

2 tablespoons (28 g) butter

½ teaspoon salt or Vege-Sal

2 cups (510 g) cooked spaghetti squash

1½ cups (355 ml) heavy cream

½ cup grated (50 g) Parmesan cheese

1. In a microwave-safe casserole, combine the onion and garlic; place the turkey on top. Microwave this, uncovered, for 5 minutes at full power. Stir it up a bit, breaking up the ground turkey in the process. Microwave the turkey-and-onion mixture for another 3 minutes or until the turkey is done through.

2. Break up the turkey some more—you want it well crumbled—and drain off the fat. Stir in the cinnamon and nutmeg and microwave it for just another minute, to blend the flavors. Transfer the turkey mixture to a bowl.

3. In a separate bowl, combine the ricotta cheese, parsley, salt, and pepper.

4. In yet another bowl or a measuring cup (okay, you need both a microwave and a dishwasher for this to be a convenient recipe!), combine the butter, salt, heavy cream, and Parmesan cheese to make the sauce.

5. Spray your microwave-safe casserole with nonstick cooking spray. In the dish, layer half of the spaghetti squash, then half the turkey mixture, then half the ricotta mixture, and then half the sauce. Repeat the layers, ending with the sauce.

6. Microwave the pasticchio at full power for 6 to 8 minutes or until it's bubbly and hot clear through. Let it sit for 5 minutes or so and serve.

YIELD: 6 servings, each with: 474 Calories; 40 g Fat (74.6% calories from fat); 22 g Protein; 8 g Carbohydrate; 1 g Dietary Fiber; 7 g net carbs

ASIAN TURKEY BURGERS

Ground turkey is handy, but by itself it can be bland. Here's a good way to liven it up. These would be good served on a bed of Asian Ginger Slaw (page 156).

1 pound (455 g) ground turkey

¼ cup (40 g) minced onion

3 tablespoons (12 g) chopped fresh parsley

2 tablespoons (28 ml) Worcestershire sauce

2 tablespoons (19 g) minced green bell pepper

1 tablespoon (15 ml) soy sauce

1 tablespoon (15 ml) cold water

1 tablespoon (8 g) grated fresh ginger

¼ teaspoon pepper

2 cloves of garlic, crushed

1. Combine all the ingredients in a big bowl and—with clean hands—squeeze it together until it's very well combined.

2. Divide into three equal portions and form into burgers about ¾ inch (2 cm) thick.

3. Spray a skillet with nonstick cooking spray and place over medium-high heat. Cook the burgers for about 5 minutes per side, until done through.

YIELD: 3 servings, each with: 249 Calories; 13 g Fat (46.6% calories from fat); 27 g Protein; 5 g Carbohydrate; 1 g Dietary Fiber; 4 g net carbs

SALTIMBOCCA

Who says all Italian food involves pasta? I first read of this classic recipe in a book by Gayelord Hauser, an early health food advocate. It was one of his old books that started me low-carbing. A crisp green salad with Italian Vinaigrette Dressing (page 163) is all you need with this.

4 boneless, skinless chicken breasts

¼ pound (115 g) prosciutto or good boiled ham, thinly sliced

40 leaves fresh or dry sage (Fresh is preferable.)

2 tablespoons (28 g) butter

2 tablespoons (28 ml) olive oil

½ cup (120 ml) dry white wine

1. Place a chicken breast in a large, heavy, zipper-lock bag and using a hammer, meat tenderizer, or what-have-you, pound it until it's ¼ inch (6 mm) thick. Repeat with the remaining chicken breasts.

2. Once all your chicken breasts are pounded thin, place a layer of the prosciutto on each one, scatter about 10 sage leaves over each one, and roll each breast up. Fasten with toothpicks.

3. Melt the butter with the olive oil in a heavy skillet over medium heat. Add the chicken rolls and sauté, turning occasionally, until golden all over.

4. Add the wine to the skillet, turn the burner to low, cover the skillet, and simmer for 15 minutes.

5. Remove the chicken to a serving plate and cover to keep warm. Turn the burner up to High and boil the liquid in the skillet hard for 5 minutes, to reduce. Spoon over the chicken and serve.

YIELD: 4 servings, each with: 464 Calories; 21 g Fat (43.7% calories from fat); 60 g Protein; trace Carbohydrate; 0 g Dietary Fiber; trace net carbs

SALTIMBOCCA GRUYÈRE

This is a variation on the original. I couldn't decide which version I liked best, so I included both! Again, I think a green salad with Italian Vinaigrette Dressing (page 163) is the perfect accompaniment—well, and maybe a glass of prosecco.

4 boneless, skinless chicken breasts

¼ pound (115 g) prosciutto or good boiled ham, thinly sliced

1 cup (120 g) shredded Gruyère cheese

2 tablespoons (28 g) butter

2 tablespoons (28 ml) olive oil

½ cup (120 ml) dry white wine

1. Place a chicken breast in a large, heavy, zipper-lock bag and using a hammer, meat tenderizer, or what-have-you, pound it until it's ¼ inch (6 mm) thick. Repeat with the remaining chicken breasts.

2. Once all your chicken breasts are pounded thin, place a layer of the prosciutto followed by some shredded Gruyère cheese over each one and then roll each breast up. Fasten with toothpicks.

3. Melt the butter with the olive oil in a heavy skillet over medium heat. Add the chicken rolls and sauté, turning occasionally, until golden all over.

4. Add the wine to the skillet, turn the burner to low, cover the skillet, and simmer for 15 minutes.

5. Remove the chicken to a serving plate and cover to keep warm. Turn the burner up to high and boil the liquid in the skillet hard for 5 minutes, to reduce. Spoon over the chicken and serve.

YIELD: 4 servings, each with: 571 Calories; 29 g Fat (48.1% calories from fat); 69 g Protein; 1 g Carbohydrate; 0 g Dietary Fiber; 1 g net carbs

KEY LIME CHICKEN

This is an unusual—and good!—combination of flavors. It is good on the grill, too.

3 pounds (1.4 kg) chicken-breasts, thighs, legs, or a combo

½ cup (120 ml) lime juice

½ cup (120 ml) olive oil

1 tablespoon (10 g) grated onion

2 teaspoons tarragon

1 teaspoon seasoned salt

¼ teaspoon pepper

1. Arrange the chicken pieces on the broiler rack, skin-side down.

2. In a bowl, combine the lime juice, olive oil, onion, tarragon, salt, and pepper and brush the chicken well with the mixture. Let sit for 15 to 30 minutes.

3. Pour off the marinade into a saucepan and bring to a complete, rolling boil for a few minutes.

4. Broil the chicken about 8 inches (20 cm) from the flame for 45 to 50 minutes, turning the chicken and basting with more of the marinade every 10 minutes or so.

5. Boil the remaining marinade again for 4 to 5 minutes and serve as a sauce with the chicken.

YIELD: 6 servings, each with: 521 Calories; 44 g Fat (75.9% calories from fat); 29 g Protein; 3 g Carbohydrate; trace Dietary Fiber; 3 g net carbs

DEVILED CHICKEN

This is both sweet and spicy! Creamy coleslaw or cucumber salad would be a nice foil for this.

4 tablespoons (55 g) butter

¼ cup (60 g) erythritol/ stevia or erythritol/ monkfruit blend OR ¼ cup (60 g) erythritol PLUS Liquid stevia, monkfruit, or sucralose to equal ¼ cup (50 g) of sugar in sweetness

¼ cup (60 g) spicy brown mustard

1 teaspoon salt

1 teaspoon curry powder

3 pounds (1.4 kg) chicken– breasts, thighs, or legs, as you prefer.

1. Preheat the oven to 375°F (190°C, or gas mark 5).

2. Melt the butter in a shallow roasting pan. Add the sweetener, mustard, salt, and curry powder and stir until well combined.

3. Roll the chicken pieces in the butter mixture until coated and then arrange them skin-side up in the pan. Bake for 1 hour.

YIELD: 6 servings, each with: 431 Calories; 34 g Fat (71.7% calories from fat); 29 g Protein; 1 g Carbohydrate; trace Dietary Fiber; 1 g net carbs

JERK CHICKEN

This hot-and-sweet Jamaican chicken is great for a special barbecue, but you have to remember to begin marinating the chicken the day before. Serve with something cooling, like coleslaw or cucumber salad, to balance the heat.

1 batch of Jerk Marinade (page 280)

1 cut-up broiler-fryer

1. Smear the Jerk Marinade all over your chicken—even up under the skin. Coat it well and put the chicken in a zipper-lock bag.

2. Wash your hands very well! You don't want the habanero peppers to stay on them, not even a little bit.

3. Let the chicken sit in the refrigerator overnight. When dinnertime comes, preheat the oven to 375°F (190°C, or gas mark 5).

4. Pull your chicken out of the bag, but do not wipe the marinade off. Roast your chicken for about 40 minutes and then finish on the grill. (This prevents the chicken from drying out and scorching.)

YIELD: 6 servings, each with: 428 Calories; 33 g Fat (69.4% calories from fat); 29 g Protein; 4 g Carbohydrate; 1 g Dietary Fiber; 3 g net carbs

CHICKEN AND TURKEY

TASTY ROASTED CHICKEN

Whole chickens are often a bargain and offer both light and dark meat, should your family have opposing viewpoints on these things. If you like grocery store rotisserie chickens, you'll like this, though of course, it takes longer. Mayonnaise makes a remarkably good baste for chicken! I use it on turkeys, too.

1 whole chicken (about 5 pounds, or 2.3 kg)	Salt
	Pepper
1 heaping tablespoon (about 14 g) mayonnaise	Paprika
	Onion powder

1. Preheat the oven to 375°F (190°C, or gas mark 5).

2. If your chicken was frozen, make sure it's completely thawed. (If it's still a bit icy in the middle, run hot water inside it until it's not icy anymore.) Take out the giblets.

   TIP: If you've never cooked a whole chicken before and you're wondering where the heck the giblets are, you'll find them in the body cavity.

3. Dry your chicken and put it on a plate. Rub every inch of the chicken's skin with the mayonnaise.

4. Sprinkle the chicken liberally with equal parts salt, pepper, paprika, and onion powder, on all sides. Put the chicken on a rack in a shallow roasting pan and put it in the oven.

5. Roast for 1½ hours or until the juices run clear when you stick a fork in where the thigh joins the body or when a meat thermometer registers 165°F (74°C).

6. Remove the chicken from the oven and let it sit for 10 to 15 minutes before carving, to let the juices settle.

YIELD: 6 servings, each with: 572 Calories; 41 g Fat (65.5% calories from fat); 48 g Protein; trace Carbohydrate; 0 g Dietary Fiber; trace net carbs

CHICKEN TACO FILLING

This is easy, versatile, and likely to be popular with the family. Don't know what to do with your taco filling? See Cheesy Bowls and Taco Shells (page 62), Taco Salad (page 253), and Taco Omelet (page 68).

1½ pounds (680 g) boneless, skinless chicken breasts or thighs, or 2½ pounds (1.1 kg) chicken parts on the bone	1 cup (235 ml) chicken broth
	2 tablespoons (16 g) Taco Seasoning (page 275)

1. If you're using chicken parts (I like to make this with leg-and-thigh quarters), skin them first. Put your chicken in either a large, heavy-bottomed pot or in your slow cooker.

2. Mix together the chicken broth and the Taco Seasoning and pour the mixture over the chicken.

3. If you're cooking this on the stove top, simply cover the pot, put it over low heat, and let it simmer for about 1½ hours. If you're using a slow cooker, set the pot on Low and leave it for 6 to 8 hours.

4. With either method, when the chicken is done, use two forks to tear it into largish shreds. If you've used bone-in chicken parts, this is the time to remove the bones, as well. If you've cooked this on the stove top, most of the liquid will have cooked away, but if you've used a slow cooker, there will be quite a lot of liquid, so turn the pot up to High, leave the cover off, and let the liquid cook down. Stir the chicken back into the reduced seasoning liquid and it's ready to serve.

YIELD: 4 servings, each with: 215 Calories; 5 g Fat (21.0% calories from fat); 39 g Protein; 1 g Carbohydrate; trace Dietary Fiber; 1 g net carbs

CHICKEN PICCATA

Meat cooked "piccata" is traditionally floured first, but with all this flavor going on, who'll miss it? A simple green salad with an Italian vinaigrette is all you need with this.

4 boneless, skinless chicken breasts	**½ cup (120 ml) dry white wine**
¼ cup (60 ml) olive oil	**1 tablespoon (9 g) capers, chopped**
1 clove of garlic, crushed	**3 tablespoons (12 g) fresh parsley, chopped**
1 tablespoon (15 ml) lemon juice, or the juice of ½ of a lemon	

1. Place a chicken breast in a large, heavy, zipper-lock bag and using a hammer, meat tenderizer, or what-have-you, pound it until it's ¼ inch (6 mm) thick all across. Repeat with the remaining chicken breasts.

2. Heat the olive oil in a large, heavy skillet over medium-high heat. Add the chicken; if it doesn't all fit at the same time, cook it in two batches, keeping the first batch warm while the second batch is cooking. Cook the chicken until it's done through (3 to 4 minutes per side).

3. Remove the chicken from the pan. Add the garlic, lemon juice, white wine, and capers to the pan, stirring it all around to get the tasty little brown bits off the bottom of the pan. Boil the whole thing hard for about 1 minute, to reduce it a little.

4. Put the chicken back in the pan for another minute, sprinkle the parsley over it, and serve.

YIELD: 4 servings, each with: 344 Calories; 18 g Fat (50.9% calories from fat); 38 g Protein; 1 g Carbohydrate; trace Dietary Fiber; 1 g net carbs

Pork Piccata

Make this variation just like Chicken Piccatta, substituting 1½ pounds (680 g) of boneless pork shoulder or butt in four slices for the chicken breasts.

YIELD: 4 servings, each with: 444 Calories; 36 g Fat (78.1% calories from fat); 22 g Protein; 1 g Carbohydrate; trace Dietary Fiber; 1 g net carbs

CHICKEN-ALMOND STIR-FRY

Serve this tasty stir-fry over rice for the carb-eaters in your family and enjoy yours straight. There's one hard-and-fast rule with stir-fries: Make sure all your ingredients are chopped, sliced, and grated before you begin cooking. With all those vegetables, this is a one-dish meal.

2 tablespoons (28 ml) soy sauce	**1½ cups (95 g) snow peas, cut in half**
4 tablespoons (60 ml) dry sherry	**1½ cups (105 g) sliced mushrooms**
1 clove of garlic, smashed	**15 scallions, cut into pieces about 1 inch (2.5 cm) long**
1 inch (2.5 cm) or so fresh ginger, grated	**¼ cup (50 g) sliced water chestnuts (These are optional; they up the carb count, but they're tasty.)**
¼ teaspoon guar (optional)	
6 tablespoons (90 ml) peanut oil (MCT or bland coconut oil would work, too.), divided	**3 large boneless, skinless chicken breasts, cut into ½-inch (1.3 cm) cubes**
⅓ cup (37 g) slivered almonds	

(continued)

1. Stir together the soy sauce, sherry, garlic, and ginger. (If you're using the guar, put these seasonings through the blender with the guar.)

2. Heat a couple of teaspoons of the peanut oil in a wok or large, heavy skillet over high heat. Add the almonds and stir-fry them until they're light golden. Remove and set aside.

3. Heat another couple of tablespoons (28 ml) of oil in the pan and add the snow peas, mushrooms, scallions, and water chestnuts (if using). Stir-fry for about 5 minutes or until just barely tender-crisp. Remove from the pan and set aside.

4. Heat another couple of tablespoons (28 ml) of oil in the pan and add the chicken. Stir-fry for 5 to 7 minutes or until done; there should be no pink left.

5. Return the vegetables to the skillet and add the soy sauce–sherry mixture from step 1. Toss everything together well. Cover and simmer for 3 to 4 minutes. Top with the almonds and serve.

YIELD: 3 servings, each with: 608 Calories; 40 g Fat (60.0% calories from fat); 41 g Protein; 18 g Carbohydrate; 5 g Dietary Fiber; 13 g net carbs

LEMON-PEPPER CHICKEN AND GRAVY

Chicken takes to citrus of every kind. Serve this on a bed of Cauliflower Rice (page 113) to catch the flavorful gravy.

3 pounds (1.4 kg) chicken parts–breasts, legs, thighs, as you please

1¼ teaspoons lemon pepper, divided

1¼ teaspoons onion powder, divided

1 teaspoon salt

¼ cup (60 ml) chicken broth

½ cup (120 ml) heavy cream

1½ teaspoons spicy brown or Dijon mustard

1. Preheat the oven to 375°F (190°C, or gas mark 5).

2. Stir together 1 teaspoon of lemon pepper, 1 teaspoon of onion powder, and the salt and sprinkle this mixture all over the chicken parts. Arrange in a roasting pan and roast, basting once or twice, for about 1 hour or until the juices run clear when the chicken is pierced.

3. Remove the chicken from the roasting pan and skim off the excess fat, leaving just the brown drippings.

4. Place the roasting pan over a low burner, add the chicken broth to the pan, and stir, scraping up the tasty brown bits off the bottom of the pan. When the broth is simmering, add the heavy cream, the rest of the lemon pepper and onion powder, and the mustard. Stir well, heat through, and pour over the chicken.

YIELD: 6 servings, each with: 427 Calories; 33 g Fat (70.9% calories from fat); 29 g Protein; 1 g Carbohydrate; trace Dietary Fiber; 1 g net carbs

THAI-ISH CHICKEN BASIL STIR-FRY

If all you've had are Chinese stir-fries, you'll find this an interesting change. Basil in stir-fries is a distinctively Thai note. So is heat!

2 tablespoons (28 ml) Thai fish sauce (nam pla)

2 tablespoons (28 ml) soy sauce

Liquid stevia, monk fruit, or sucralose to equal 1 teaspoon of sugar in sweetness

¼ teaspoon guar or xanthan

2 tablespoons (5 g) minced fresh basil—Thai basil if you can get it!—or 2 teaspoons dried basil

1½ teaspoons red pepper flakes

Peanut, canola, or coconut oil

2 cloves of garlic, crushed

1½ pounds (680 g) boneless skinless chicken, breast or thighs, in ½-inch (1.3 cm) cubes

1 small onion, sliced

1½ cups (186 g) frozen, crosscut green beans, thawed and drained

1. Combine the fish sauce, soy sauce, sweetener, and guar in a blender. Blend for several seconds and then turn off the blender and add the basil and red pepper flakes. Set aside.

2. Heat a few tablespoons (45–60 ml) of oil in a wok or heavy skillet over high heat. When the oil is hot, add the garlic, chicken, and onion and stir-fry for 3 to 4 minutes. Add the green beans and continue to stir-fry until the chicken is done through.

3. Stir the blended seasoning mixture into the stir-fry. Turn the burner to medium, cover, and let it simmer for 2 to 3 minutes. (The beans should be tender-crisp.)

YIELD: 3 servings, each with: 326 Calories; 7 g Fat (19.3% calories from fat); 54 g Protein; 12 g Carbohydrate; 3 g Dietary Fiber; 9 g net carbs

SAUTÉED SESAME CHICKEN BREASTS

I originally recommended salad or broccoli with this, but asparagus sounds good, too! This is quick and easy.

1½ pounds (680 g) boneless, skinless chicken breasts

¼ cup (36 g) sesame seeds

Salt

3 tablespoons (45 ml) peanut oil

1. Place a chicken breast in a large, heavy, zipper-lock bag and using a hammer, meat tenderizing hammer, dumbbell, or what-have-you, pound it until it's ¼ inch (6 mm) thick. Repeat with the remaining chicken breasts.

2. Sprinkle each side of each breast evenly with ½ tablespoon of sesame seeds and lightly salt.

3. Heat the peanut oil in a heavy skillet over medium heat. Add the chicken breasts and sauté for about 5 minutes each side or until lightly golden. (You may have to do this in two batches; keep the first batch warm on an ovenproof plate in the oven, on its lowest temperature setting.) Serve.

YIELD: 4 servings, each with: 342 Calories; 19 g Fat (50.7% calories from fat); 39 g Protein; 2 g Carbohydrate; 1 g Dietary Fiber; 1 g net carbs

CHICKEN AND TURKEY

STEWED CHICKEN WITH MOROCCAN SEASONINGS

This is almost a Moroccan tagine, but all the recipes I've seen call for some sort of starch. So I ditched the starch and just kept the seasonings, which are exotic and delicious.

¼ cup (60 ml) olive oil

4 pounds (1.8 kg) chicken, cut up–breasts, legs, thighs

1 medium onion, thinly sliced

2 cloves of garlic, crushed

¾ cup (175 ml) chicken broth

½ teaspoon ground coriander

½ teaspoon ground cinnamon

½ teaspoon paprika

½ teaspoon ground cumin

1 teaspoon ground ginger

½ teaspoon pepper

¼ teaspoon cayenne

Liquid stevia, monk fruit, or sucralose to equal 1 tablespoon (13 g) of sugar in sweetness

1 tablespoon (16 g) tomato paste

1 teaspoon salt or Vege-Sal

1. Heat the olive oil in a Dutch oven over medium heat and brown the chicken in the oil.

2. When the chicken is golden all over, remove it from the Dutch oven and pour off the fat. Put the chicken back in the Dutch oven and scatter the onion over it.

3. Combine the garlic, chicken broth, coriander, cinnamon, paprika, cumin, ginger, pepper, cayenne, sweetener, tomato paste, and salt and whisk together well. Pour over the chicken, cover the Dutch oven, and turn the burner to low. Let the whole thing simmer for a good 45 minutes.

4. Uncover the chicken and let it simmer for another 15 minutes or so, to let the juices concentrate a bit.

5. Serve each piece of chicken with some of the onion and juices spooned over it.

YIELD: 4 servings, each with: 569 Calories; 44 g Fat (69.8% calories from fat); 39 g Protein; 4 g Carbohydrate; 1 g Dietary Fiber; 3 g net carbs

GREEK ROASTED CHICKEN

Many carry-out places do a brisk business in chickens roasted Greek-style, and it's no wonder why–they're terrific. But the best-kept secret about those roasters is that they're as easy as can be to make at home. If you have a rotisserie, this is a terrific dish to cook in it. Follow the instructions that come with your unit for cooking times.

¼ cup (60 ml) lemon juice

½ cup (120 ml) olive oil

½ teaspoon salt

¼ teaspoon pepper

3 pounds (1.4 kg) whole chicken

1. Combine the lemon juice, olive oil, salt, and pepper. Put your chicken in a 1 or 2 gallon (3.8 to 7.6 L) resealable bag sitting in a mixing bowl (for neatness) and pour the lemon juice–olive oil mixture over it. Pour some of it right into the body cavity. Seal the bag, carefully pressing out the air as you go. Turn the chicken this way and that, to coat. Stick 'er in the fridge.

2. Let your chicken marinate for several hours, and all day is great. Any time you're in the fridge, turn the bag. This helps the chicken marinate evenly.

3. A good 90 minutes before supper time, preheat the oven to 375°F (190°C, or gas mark 5). Pull your chicken out of the fridge and pour the marinade into a sauce pan. Arrange the chicken on a rack in a roasting pan. Bring the marinade to a complete, rolling boil for a few minutes.

4. Roast, basting now and then with the reserved marinade, for about 1 hour, or until the juices run clear when it's pierced to the bone. A meat thermometer stuck in the thickest part of the thigh should read 165°F (74°C). Stop basting about 15 minutes before it's done. Discard the rest of the marinade.

5. When your chicken is done, let it rest on a platter for 10 to 15 minutes before carving.

YIELD: 5 servings, each with: 595 Calories; 49 g Fat (75.6% calories from fat); 35 g Protein; 1 g Carbohydrate; trace Dietary Fiber; 1 g net carbs. The analysis assumes you'll eat all the marinade, so actually both the fat and carb counts are a bit lower than this.

CHICKEN LIVER AND "RICE" CASSEROLE

I'm a big fan of chicken livers, and they're highly nutritious. No, the liver is not the "filter of the body." It does not contain every toxin eaten by the animal during its life. The liver processes and removes this stuff, it doesn't just hold on to it forever. But do buy livers from organically raised chickens, if you prefer.

1 stick of butter

1 small onion, chopped

1 rib of celery, including leaves, diced

1 bay leaf, crumbled fine

½ teaspoon dried thyme

½ teaspoon salt
or Vege-Sal

½ teaspoon seasoned salt

1 pound (455 g) chicken livers, cut into bite-size pieces

4 cups (400 g) Cauliflower Rice Deluxe (page 113)

¼ cup (25 g) grated Parmesan cheese

1. Preheat the oven to 375°F (190°C, or gas mark 5).

2. Melt the butter in a heavy skillet over medium heat and sauté the onion, celery, bay leaf, thyme, salt, and seasoned salt.

3. When the onion is golden, add the chicken livers and cook for another 5 minutes, stirring frequently. Toss the vegetables and livers together with the Cauliflower Rice Deluxe.

4. Spray a good-sized casserole (10 cups [2.4 L] or so) with nonstick cooking spray and dump the liver and "rice" mixture into the casserole.

5. Sprinkle the top with the Parmesan cheese and bake the whole thing, uncovered, for 15 minutes.

YIELD: 5 servings, each with: 348 Calories; 23 g Fat (59.8% calories from fat); 21 g Protein; 15 g Carbohydrate; 3 g Dietary Fiber; 12 g net carbs. (Plus a truly ridiculous quantity of vitamins and minerals.)

CHICKEN WITH CAMEMBERT AND ALMONDS

This dish has it all—quick, simple, elegant, delicious. A few spears of asparagus and a glass of dry white wine would be perfect here.

If you're the type of person who likes to multitask, this recipe is for you. If you can slice and peel the cheese while the first side of the chicken cooks and get the almonds toasting while the second side cooks, you should be able to get the almonds done just in time to move hot almonds onto just-done chicken breasts.

4 boneless, skinless chicken breasts

6 tablespoons (85 g) butter, divided

8 ounces (225 g) Camembert

⅓ cup (37 g) slivered almonds

4 scallions, thinly sliced

1. Place a chicken breast in a large, heavy, zipper-lock bag and using a hammer, meat tenderizer, or what-have-you, pound it until it's ¼ inch (6 mm) thick. Repeat with the remaining chicken breasts.

2. Melt 4 tablespoons (55 g) of the butter in a heavy skillet over medium heat. Sauté the chicken until it's golden on the first side.

3. While the first side of the chicken is cooking, divide the cheese into four equal portions, peel off the white rind, and thinly slice each portion.

4. Flip the chicken and lay a portion of cheese over each chicken breast.

5. Melt the remaining 2 tablespoons (28 g) of butter in a small skillet and add the almonds. Stir until they're lightly golden.

6. When the second side of the chicken is golden and the cheese is melted, place each breast on a serving plate and divide the almonds evenly over them. Scatter a sliced scallion over each breast and serve.

YIELD: 4 servings, each with: 496 Calories; 30 g Fat (53.9% calories from fat); 53 g Protein; 3 g Carbohydrate; 1 g Dietary Fiber; 2 g net carbs

CHAPTER 8

Fish

Of all the good things that can be said about fish, this is the one that is likely to appeal to the greatest number of people: Fish is very quick to cook. Unlike the poultry, beef, and lamb and pork chapters, this is a chapter where the vast majority of the recipes take no more than fifteen minutes to get on the table. With today's jammed schedules, that's a good thing to keep in mind. The tighter your time is, the better the idea of eating fish becomes.

Of course, it's a good idea for another excellent reason: Fish is good for you, especially the fattier fish like salmon, with its heart-healthy EPA oils.

On the flip side, even fatty fish are low enough in fat that they don't get to ketogenic macros without oil, butter, or a rich sauce. You can, of course, serve them with a low-carb, high-fat vegetable dish.

You'll see it noted again and again in this chapter, and I'll say it here, too: Most mild, white fishes are interchangeable in recipes. They'll taste a bit different and have slightly different textures, but the same recipes that work for tilapia will work for sole; the same recipes that work for orange roughy will work for cod.

THE SIMPLEST FISH

Not only is this simple, it's lightening-quick, too. Try this with cod, sole, flounder–any mild white fish. Do I really have to tell you how to increase this to serve more people?

1 tablespoon (14 g) butter

1 fillet (about 6 ounces, or 170 g) mild white fish

1 tablespoon (4 g) minced fresh parsley

Wedge of lemon

1. Melt the butter in a heavy-bottomed skillet over low heat. Add the fish fillets and sauté for 5 minutes on each side or until the fish is opaque and flakes easily, turning carefully.

2. Transfer to serving plates, top with the minced parsley, and serve with a wedge of lemon.

YIELD: 1 serving with: 244 Calories; 13 g Fat (47.5% calories from fat); 31 g Protein; 1 g Carbohydrate; trace Dietary Fiber; 1 g net carbs

UNBELIEVABLY EASY SHRIMP

Do you want cold, cooked shrimp for dipping? Here's how to get them perfect, every time.

2 quarts (1.9 L) water

1 tablespoon (18 g) salt

1 pound (455 g) shelled, deveined raw shrimp

Dipping sauces (for serving)

1. Put the water in a large saucepan, put the salt in the water, and put the saucepan over high heat. When the water is boiling, dump in your shrimp.

2. Bring the water just back up to the boil and turn off the burner. Let the shrimp sit another minute if they're tiny or 2 to 3 minutes if they're big.

3. Drain them in a colander and run them under some cold water. Chill them and serve with Cocktail Sauce (page 277), Aioli (page 278), or Mellow "Honey" Mustard Dressing (page 166).

YIELD: 4 generous servings, each with: 120 Calories; 2 g Fat (15.2% calories from fat); 23 g Protein; 1 g Carbohydrate; 0 g Dietary Fiber; 1 g net carbs

SCAMPI!

Long a favorite at seafood restaurants, scampi is surprisingly quick and easy to make at home. It's much cheaper, too. Feel free to increase this recipe to however much your skillet can hold. This makes a great fast-and-easy company dinner; just add a salad and some crusty bread for the carb-eaters and call it a party.

½ cup (112 g) butter

¼ cup (60 ml) olive oil

3 cloves of garlic, crushed

1 pound (455 g) raw shrimp in the shell

¼ cup (60 ml) dry white wine

¼ cup (15 g) minced fresh parsley

1. Melt the butter with the olive oil in a heavy skillet over medium-low heat. Add the garlic and stir it around.

2. Add the shrimp to the skillet. If they're room temperature, they'll take 2 to 3 minutes per side; frozen shrimp will take 4 to 5 minutes per side. Be careful not to overcook them.

3. Add the wine and simmer for another 1 to 2 minutes. Serve garnished with the parsley and put out plenty of napkins!

YIELD: 4 servings, each with: 458 Calories; 38 g Fat (77.3% calories from fat); 23 g Protein; 2 g Carbohydrate; trace Dietary Fiber; 2 g net carbs

OBSCENELY RICH SHRIMP

This is a bit of trouble, and it's not cheap, so you'll probably only want to make it for company—but wow. Aren't you glad you're not afraid of fat?

2 packages (10 ounces, or 280 g each) of frozen chopped spinach or 20 ounces (560 g) bagged baby spinach

3 tablespoons (45 g) butter

1 pound (455 g) mushrooms, sliced

1 small onion, diced

1 bag (14 ounces, or 395 g) of frozen, cooked, shelled shrimp (The little ones are best.)

2 teaspoons liquid beef bouillon concentrate

1½ cups (355 ml) heavy cream

1 cup (230 g) sour cream

1 cup (100 g) grated Parmesan cheese

1 cup (60 g) unsweetened flaked coconut

1. Preheat the oven to 350°F (180°C, or gas mark 4).

2. Cook the spinach; I put mine in a glass casserole, cover it, and microwave it on High for 7 minutes.

3. Melt the butter in a heavy skillet over medium heat and start sautéing the mushrooms and onion. When they're starting to get limp, break up your frozen shrimp a bit and add them to the skillet.

4. When the shrimp are thawed and the onions are quite limp and translucent, scoop out the veggies and shrimp with a slotted spoon and put them aside in a bowl. Turn up the burner to medium-high. A fair amount of liquid will have accumulated in the bottom of the skillet; add the beef bouillon concentrate to it and boil the liquid until it's reduced to about one-third of its original volume.

5. Turn the burner back down to low, stir in the heavy cream, sour cream, and Parmesan cheese, and just heat it through (don't let it boil). Stir the shrimp and vegetables back into this sauce.

6. Rescue your spinach from the microwave and drain it well by putting it in a strainer and pressing it with the back of a spoon, to make sure all the liquid is removed.

7. Coat a 10-cup (2.4 L) casserole with cooking spray and spread half of the spinach in the bottom of it. Put half of the shrimp mixture over that. Repeat the layers with the rest of the spinach and the rest of the sauce.

8. Top with the coconut and bake for 1½ hours.

YIELD: 6 servings, each with: 562 Calories; 46 g Fat (71.1% calories from fat); 27 g Protein; 15 g Carbohydrate; 5 g Dietary Fiber; 10 g net carbs

SCALLOPS ON SPINACH WITH WALNUT SAUCE

This recipe is from the kitchen of Tanya Rachfal. She just said to "cook" the spinach; I was the one who decided sautéing would be good. You may steam it, if you prefer.

WALNUT SAUCE

2 cups (475 ml) water

¼ cup (40 g) chopped walnuts

2 tablespoons (28 ml) lemon juice

1 teaspoon grated lemon rind

4 tablespoons (60 ml) extra-virgin olive oil

½ teaspoon salt

½ teaspoon freshly ground black pepper

REMAINING INGREDIENTS

1 pound (455 g) turkey bacon (Use regular bacon if you prefer, but par-cook it for a few minutes first.)

12 ounces (340 g) large sea scallops (16 to 20)

3 tablespoons (45 ml) peanut oil, divided

1 pound (455 g) spinach

1. Bring the water to a boil in a small saucepan. Add the walnuts, boil for 30 seconds, and then drain. Put the walnuts in a bowl and combine with the lemon juice, lemon rind, olive oil, salt, and pepper. Mix well and set aside.

2. Cut the slices of turkey bacon in half. Wrap a piece of bacon around a scallop and slip onto a skewer. Baste the scallops with 1 tablespoon (15 ml) of the peanut oil.

3. Wash the spinach leaves thoroughly and sauté quickly in the rest of the peanut oil until just limp. Broil the scallops for 5 minutes, turn, baste, and broil the other side for 5 minutes. Serve the scallops over spinach and top with the sauce.

YIELD: 4 servings, each with: 636 Calories; 51 g Fat (71.1% calories from fat); 37 g Protein; 10 g Carbohydrate; 4 g Dietary Fiber; 6 g net carbs

BAKED ORANGE ROUGHY

Baking means no tending! Pour a glass of dry white wine and relax.

1½ pounds (680 g) orange roughy fillets, cut into serving-size pieces

1 teaspoon salt or Vege-Sal

Pepper

¼ of a medium onion, very thinly sliced

2 tablespoons (28 ml) lemon juice

¼ cup (60 g) butter, melted

Paprika

Minced fresh parsley (optional)

1. Preheat the oven to 325°F (170°C, or gas mark 3). Spray a shallow baking dish with nonstick cooking spray.

2. Arrange the fish in the prepared pan and sprinkle with salt and pepper to taste. Scatter the onion over the fish.

3. In a small bowl, combine the lemon juice and butter and pour over the fish and onions. Sprinkle with paprika.

4. Bake, uncovered, for 30 minutes. Sprinkle with parsley (if using) and serve.

YIELD: 4 servings, each with: 225 Calories; 13 g Fat (51.9% calories from fat); 25 g Protein; 1 g Carbohydrate; trace Dietary Fiber; 1 g net carbs

FISH BAKED IN A BED OF ROCK SALT

Maureen Bernardis sends this recipe all the way from Trieste, Italy, and says, "I have never been a fish eater, unless it was 'not fishy' fish. After discovering this recipe I am a total convert, and we now have fresh fish at least once a week." You can also put a lemon slice, a bay leaf, sage, or rosemary inside the fish before you cook it, for a different flavored dish every time you cook. Don't be afraid to experiment.

Fresh whole fish, about 2 pounds (910 g)

Rock salt (enough to cover the fish)

Salt and pepper

Olive oil

1. Preheat the oven to 350°F (180°C, or gas mark 4).

2. Clean the fish, leaving the scales and heads on. (Your fish market may do this for you, if you ask.)

3. Line the bottom of a pan with a layer of rock salt, place the fish on the salt, and cover it completely with more rock salt. Bake for 40 minutes.

4. Remove from the oven and break away the salt. Open the fish and season with salt, pepper, and olive oil to taste. Serve hot.

YIELD: 4 servings, each with: 336 Calories; 15 g Fat (41.7% calories from fat); 47 g Protein; 0 g Carbohydrate; 0 g Dietary Fiber; 0 g net carbs. MasterCook demanded that I specify a particular kind of fish before it would give me numbers, so I told it trout. But any whole, fresh fish cooked this way should be carb-free. The fat percentage will depend on how much olive oil you dress it with.

ORANGE ROUGHY BONNE FEMME ALMONDINE

This is my favorite fish recipe, and it's very simple to make. Kids will probably like it, too.

⅓ cup (37 g) almond meal

Pinch of salt or Vege-Sal

3–4 tablespoons (45–55 g) butter

1½ pounds (680 g) orange roughy fillets

Lemon juice (for serving; optional)

1. Mix the almond meal with the pinch of salt (about ¼ teaspoon). Dip the fillets in the almond meal, covering them lightly all over.

2. Melt the butter in a heavy skillet over medium heat. Sauté the "floured" fillets in the butter for 5 to 7 minutes per side or until golden brown. Serve just as it is or with a squeeze of lemon juice.

YIELD: 4 servings, each with: 268 Calories; 15 g Fat (50.2% calories from fat); 30 g Protein; 3 g Carbohydrate; 0 g Dietary Fiber; 3 g net carbs

WINE AND HERB TILAPIA PACKETS

When it's time to serve dinner, simply place a packet on each plate and let diners open their own. That way, no one loses a drop of the yummy butter, wine, and herb sauce the fish cooked in. You can substitute the white fish of your choice.

1½ pounds (680 g) tilapia fillets, cut into 4 portions

4 tablespoons (55 g) butter, divided

½ cup (120 ml) dry white wine

¼ cup minced fresh herbs (chives, basil, oregano, thyme, or a combination of these; weight will vary)

Salt

1. Preheat the oven to 350°F (180°C, or gas mark 4).

2. Tear a piece of aluminum foil about 18 inches (45 cm) square for each fillet. Place a fillet in the center of the foil square and curl the edges up a little. Put 1 tablespoon (14 g) of butter, 2 tablespoons (28 ml) of wine, a tablespoon (weight will vary) of minced herbs, and just a little salt on the fillet.

3. Fold the foil up around the fish, rolling the edges down in the middle and at the ends, so the packet won't leak in the oven. Repeat for all 4 servings.

4. Place the packets right on the oven shelf—there's no need for a pan if you've rolled the edges tightly—and bake for 35 minutes.

YIELD: 4 servings, each with: 261 Calories; 13 g Fat (48.1% calories from fat); 30 g Protein; trace Carbohydrate; 0 g Dietary Fiber; trace net carbs

TILAPIA ON A NEST OF VEGETABLES

This is quite beautiful to look at and a fast one-dish dinner. If your grocery store carries "stoplight peppers"—one each of green, yellow, and red bell peppers packaged together—use ⅔ cup (100 g) each for an even more colorful dish. Once again, feel free to substitute any mild white fish, here.

3 tablespoons (45 ml) olive oil

1 cup (150 g) red pepper, cut into thin strips

1 cup (150 g) yellow pepper, cut into thin strips

1½ cups (180 g) zucchini, cut in matchstick strips

1½ cups (180 g) yellow squash, cut in matchstick strips

1 cup (160 g) sweet red onion, thinly sliced

1 clove of garlic, crushed

1 pound (455 g) tilapia fillets

Salt and pepper

¼ teaspoon guar or xanthan

Lemon wedges (optional)

1. Heat the olive oil in a heavy skillet over medium-high heat and sauté the peppers, zucchini, yellow squash, onion, and garlic for just 2 to 3 minutes, stirring frequently.

2. Sprinkle the tilapia fillets lightly on either side with the salt and pepper and lay them over the vegetables in the skillet. Cover, turn the burner to medium-low, and let the fish steam in the moisture from the vegetables for 10 minutes or until it flakes easily.

3. With a spatula, carefully transfer the fish to a serving platter and use a slotted spoon to pile the vegetables on top of the fish. Pour the liquid that has accumulated in the skillet into a blender and add the guar. Run the blender for a few seconds and then pour the thickened juices over the fish and vegetables.

4. To serve, spoon a mound of the vegetables onto each diner's plate and place a piece of the fish on top. A few lemon wedges are nice with this, but hardly essential.

YIELD: 4 servings, each with: 281 Calories; 12 g Fat (37.2% calories from fat); 33 g Protein; 12 g Carbohydrate; 3 g Dietary Fiber; 9 g net carbs

RANCH FISH

Karen Andrews sends this easy and delicious recipe. Need I remind you to read the label on the ranch dressing mix? Hidden Valley Ranch brand, at least, is gluten-free.

2 pounds (910 g) white fish fillets

1 package (1 ounce, or 28 g) of dry ranch dressing mix

⅓ cup (80 ml) lemon juice

2 tablespoons (28 ml) olive oil

3 tablespoons (45 ml) white wine

1. Spray a rimmed sheet pan with nonstick cooking spray. Arrange the fillets on the sheet pan.

2. Combine the ranch dressing mix, lemon juice, olive oil, and wine and pour over the fish.

3. Broil for 9 to 12 minutes or until done.

YIELD: 4 servings, each with: 258 Calories; 8 g Fat (30.5% calories from fat); 41 g Protein; 2 g Carbohydrate; trace Dietary Fiber; 2 g net carbs

FISH

TUNA MELT CASSEROLE

Hey, we all grew up on tuna casserole. Here's one with no noodles, for the low-carb grownups we've become. It was sent in by a reader whose name I have, regrettably, lost. A problem has arisen since this recipe was originally written—tuna cans have shrunk. If you can't find a 6-ounce (170 g) can, you'll just have to decide whether to make due with a 5-ounce can or open a second can and use the leftovers for lunch tomorrow.

1 teaspoon MCT or olive oil	3 eggs
1 can (6 ounces, or 170 g) of tuna canned in olive oil, mashed	3 tablespoons (20 g) ground flaxseed meal
1 cup (115 g) shredded Cheddar cheese	1 teaspoon garlic powder
	½ to 1 teaspoon salt
3 slices (1½ ounces, or 42 g) of processed American cheese	

1. Preheat the oven to 400°F (200°C, or gas mark 6) and grease a 9-inch (23 cm) pie plate with the oil.
2. In a large bowl, combine the tuna, cheeses, eggs, flaxseed meal, garlic powder, and salt. Mix well.
3. Pour the tuna mixture into the prepared pie plate, pat down firmly, and bake for approximately 30 minutes or until browned and bubbly.

YIELD: 3 servings, each with: 467 Calories; 33 g Fat (62.2% calories from fat); 38 g Protein; 6 g Carbohydrate; 5 g Dietary Fiber; 1 g net carbs

CRISPY PARMESAN FISH

This comes from Dona Crawford, who says she first tried it on a retreat in Sun Valley, Idaho.

1 pound (455 g) cod fillets	1 tablespoon (10 g) minced onion
2½ tablespoons (35 g) mayonnaise	1 ounce (28 g) grated Parmesan cheese
1 teaspoon Dijon mustard	
1 teaspoon Worcestershire sauce	

1. Preheat the oven to 350°F (180°C, or gas mark 4) and spray a shallow baking dish with nonstick cooking spray. Place the fish in the prepared baking dish.
2. In a small bowl, combine the mayonnaise, mustard, Worcestershire sauce, and onion and spread evenly over the fillets.
3. Sprinkle the fillets with the Parmesan cheese and bake uncovered for 30 minutes or until crispy.

YIELD: 3 servings, each with: 253 Calories; 14 g Fat (48.9% calories from fat); 31 g Protein; 1 g Carbohydrate; trace Dietary Fiber; 1 g net carbs

BROILED MARINATED WHITING

With a big salad and some crusty bread for the carb-eaters, this makes a nice, simple supper. If you put the fish in to marinate in the morning, this is super-quick, too. If you're in a hurry or you just don't have all the ingredients to make this dish, use ¾ cup (175 ml) of whatever vinaigrette dressing you have on hand, instead.

½ cup (120 ml) olive oil

3 tablespoons (45 ml) wine vinegar

1 tablespoon (15 ml) lemon juice

1 teaspoon Dijon mustard

1 clove of garlic, crushed

½ teaspoon dried basil

¼ teaspoon salt

¼ teaspoon pepper

6 whiting fillets

1. Combine the olive oil, vinegar, lemon juice, mustard, garlic, basil, salt, and pepper and mix well.

2. Place the fillets in a large, zipper-lock bag and pour in the marinade. Refrigerate for several hours, turning the bag over from time to time.

3. Remove the fish from the marinade. Broil about 8 inches (20 cm) from the heat, for 4 to 5 minutes per side, or cook on a stove top grill.

4. While the fish is cooking, put the leftover marinade in a saucepan and boil it at a complete, rolling boil for a few minutes. Then, serve it as a sauce.

YIELD: 3 servings, each with: 253 Calories; 14 g Fat (48.9% calories from fat); 31 g Protein; 1 g Carbohydrate; trace Dietary Fiber; 1 g net carbs

SALSA FISH

Your family loves salsa, right? Why not on fish? These instructions are for a single portion, but it's dead simple to increase the recipe.

1 fillet (about 6 ounces, or 170 g) firm-fleshed white fish, such as cod or sole

2 tablespoons (32 g) salsa

1. Preheat the oven to 350°F (180°C, or gas mark 4).

2. Place the fish in a shallow baking pan, cover with the salsa, and bake for 30 to 40 minutes or until the fish flakes easily.

YIELD: 1 serving with: 149 Calories; 1 g Fat (7.7% calories from fat); 31 g Protein; 2 g Carbohydrate; 1 g Dietary Fiber; 1 g net carbs

SALMON WITH LEMON-DILL BUTTER

This is a classic flavor combination, and after you make this, you'll understand why. Do use fresh dill, if you can.

4 tablespoons (55 g) butter, softened

1 tablespoon (15 ml) lemon juice

1 tablespoon (4 g) snipped fresh dill or 1 teaspoon dry dill weed

4 salmon steaks, each 1 inch (2.5 cm) thick

Olive oil

1. Put the butter, lemon juice, and dill in a food processor with the S-blade in place. Pulse until well combined, scraping down the sides once or twice if necessary. (If you don't have a food processor, you can simply beat these things together by hand.) Chill.

2. About 15 minutes before dinner, rub each salmon steak on both sides with olive oil. Arrange the steaks on the broiler rack and broil 8 inches (20 cm) from high heat for 5 to 6 minutes per side or until the salmon flakes easily.

3. Place on the serving plates, top each steak with a tablespoon (14 g) of the lemon-dill butter, and serve.

YIELD: 4 very generous servings, each with: 300 Calories; 17 g Fat (53.2% calories from fat); 34 g Protein; trace Carbohydrate; trace Dietary Fiber; 0 g net carbs

FETA-SPINACH SALMON ROAST

I saw something like this being sold for an outrageous price in the fish case at the local grocery store, and I thought, "I can do that!" I was right! With the pink, green, and white layers, this looks gorgeous, too.

3 ounces (85 g) cream cheese, softened

¾ cup (113 g) crumbled feta

2 scallions, thinly sliced, including the crisp part of the green

½ cup (15 g) fresh spinach, chopped

2 skinless salmon fillets of roughly equal size and shape, totaling ¾ pound

Olive oil

1. Preheat the oven to 350°F (180°C, or gas mark 4).

2. Combine the cream cheese and feta cheese, mashing and stirring with a fork until well blended. Add the scallions and spinach and combine well.

3. Spread the mixture evenly over one salmon fillet. (The filling will be about ¾ inch [2 cm] thick.) Top with the second salmon fillet. Brush both sides with olive oil, turning the whole thing over carefully with a spatula.

4. Place the loaf on a shallow baking pan and bake for 20 minutes. Slice carefully with a sharp, serrated knife.

YIELD: 2 servings, each with: 501 Calories; 33 g Fat (59.3% calories from fat); 46 g Protein; 5 g Carbohydrate; 1 g Dietary Fiber; 4 g net carbs

ORANGE SALMON PACKETS

Everyone knows lemon goes with fish, but the orange flavor is great with salmon. You can put your salmon packets in a roasting pan if you're afraid they'll spring a leak, but I just put mine right on the oven rack.

¼ cup (60 g) plain full-fat yogurt

2 tablespoons (28 g) mayonnaise

¼ teaspoon orange extract

Liquid stevia, either orange or lemon drop flavor, to equal 1 tablespoon (13 g) of sugar in sweetness

1 tablespoon (15 ml) lemon juice

2 scallions, finely minced

1 tablespoon (4 g) parsley, finely minced

1 pound (455 g) salmon fillets

1. Preheat the oven to 425°F (220°C, or gas mark 7).

2. Combine the yogurt, mayonnaise, orange extract, sweetener, lemon juice, scallions, and parsley. Set aside.

3. If your salmon fillets have skin on them, remove it and cut the fish into 4 serving-size pieces.

4. Tear off 4 large squares of heavy-duty aluminum foil. Place each piece of salmon in the center of a square of foil and spoon 2 tablespoons (28 ml) of the sauce over it. Fold the foil up over the salmon, bringing the edges together, and roll the edges to make a tight seal. Roll up each end, as well.

5. When all your salmon fillets are snug in their own little packets, bake them for 15 minutes. You can put your salmon packets in a roasting pan, if you're afraid they'll spring a leak, but I just put mine right on the oven rack.

6. Place on individual serving plates, cut open, and serve. If you have a little sauce left over, serve it on the side.

YIELD: 4 servings, each with: 194 Calories; 10 g Fat (48.4% calories from fat); 23 g Protein; 1 g Carbohydrate; trace Dietary Fiber; 1 g net carbs

MUSTARD-GLAZED SALMON

Don't be squeamish about buying salmon with skin on it. It peels off quite easily and adds almost no time to the preparation process. Again, this makes one serving, but is easy to double, triple, whatever.

1 salmon fillet (5 ounces, or 140 g)

1 tablespoon (15 ml) Mellow "Honey" Mustard Dressing (page 116)

1 scallion, finely minced

½ teaspoon dried thyme

1. Preheat the oven to 350°F (180°C, or gas mark 4).

2. If there's skin on your salmon, remove it. Place the fillet on a baking tray.

3. In a small bowl, mix together the Mellow "Honey" Mustard Dressing, scallion, and thyme; spread it evenly over the fish.

4. Bake for 12 to 15 minutes or until the fish flakes easily.

YIELD: 1 serving with: 267 Calories; 13 g Fat (45.4% calories from fat); 34 g Protein; 2 g Carbohydrate; 1 g Dietary Fiber; 1 g net carbs

AIOLI FISH BAKE

The aioli not only flavors the fish, but keeps it moist, as well. If you don't have Aioli (page 278) in the house, spike mayonnaise with a clove of crushed garlic. Serve extra Aioli on the side to increase the fat percentage, if you like.

4 fillets (about 6 ounces, or 170 g each) of mild, white fish

½ cup (115 g) Aioli (page 278)

4 tablespoons (20 g) grated Parmesan cheese

1. Preheat the oven to 350°F (180°C, or gas mark 4).

2. Line a shallow baking dish with nonstick foil. Working right on the foil, spread a fillet with 1 tablespoon (14 g) of Aioli and sprinkle ½ tablespoon of Parmesan cheese over that. Turn carefully and spread Aioli and sprinkle Parmesan cheese on other side. Repeat with the rest of the fish, Aioli, and Parmesan cheese.

3. Bake for 20 minutes and serve.

YIELD: 4 servings, each with: 293 Calories; 17 g Fat (52.3% calories from fat); 33 g Protein; 1 g Carbohydrate; trace Dietary Fiber; 1 g net carbs

PANNED SWORDFISH STEAKS WITH GARLIC AND VERMOUTH

This is simple, fast, and elegant. And do you know how much you'd pay for this at a restaurant?

1 pound (455 g) swordfish steaks

Salt and pepper

1 tablespoon (15 ml) olive oil

¼ cup (60 ml) water

¼ cup (60 ml) dry vermouth

2 or 3 cloves of garlic, crushed

3–4 tablespoons (12–15 g) minced parsley

1. Sprinkle the swordfish steaks lightly on both sides with salt and pepper.

2. Place a heavy skillet over high heat and add the olive oil. When the oil is hot, add the swordfish and sear on both sides (about 1 to 1½ minutes per side). Then, add the water, vermouth, and garlic and turn down the heat to medium. Cover and let the fish simmer for 10 minutes.

3. Remove to a serving platter or individual serving plates and keep warm. Turn the heat under the skillet to high and boil the pan juices hard for a minute or two until they're reduced to ¼ cup (60 ml) or so. Pour over the fish and top with parsley.

YIELD: 3 servings, each with: 251 Calories; 11 g Fat (42.5% calories from fat); 30 g Protein; 2 g Carbohydrate; trace Dietary Fiber; 2 g net carbs

NOODLELESS SHRIMP PAD THAI

This isn't terribly low in carbs—it's a maintenance dish, really—but I know that there are a lot of Thai food fans out there and that Pad Thai is the most popular Thai dish. If this carb count sounds way too high to you, keep in mind that regular Pad Thai usually has over 60 grams of carbohydrates per serving, making this dish quite a bargain—plus, it's fast and incredibly tasty.

2 tablespoons (28 ml) Thai fish sauce (nam pla)

Liquid stevia, monkfruit, or sucralose to equal 1 tablespoon (13 g) of sugar in sweetness

2 tablespoons (28 ml) peanut oil or other bland oil

2 cloves of garlic, smashed

12 cooked, peeled shrimp

2 eggs, beaten slightly

3 cups (765 g) cooked spaghetti squash

1½ cups (156 g) bean sprouts

2 tablespoons (18 g) dry-roasted peanuts, chopped

4 scallions, sliced

2 tablespoons (2 g) cilantro, chopped

1 lime, cut into wedges

1. Mix the fish sauce and sweetener and set the mixture aside.

2. Put the oil in a heavy skillet over medium-high heat and sauté the garlic for a minute. Add the shrimp and sauté for another minute. Add the fish sauce mixture.

3. Pour the beaten eggs into the skillet, let them set for 15 to 30 seconds, and then scramble. Stir in the spaghetti squash and bean sprouts, mixing with the shrimp-and-egg mixture. Cook until just heated through.

4. Place on serving plates. Top each serving with peanuts, scallions, and cilantro and serve with a wedge of lime on the side.

YIELD: 3 servings, each with: 309 Calories; 17 g Fat (48.4% calories from fat); 24 g Protein; 18 g Carbohydrate; 2 g Dietary Fiber; 16 g net carbs

The spaghetti squash version is the original, but if you prefer, you can swap 2 packets of tofu shirataki spaghetti, prepared according to the instructions on page 23, for the spaghetti squash. If you do, the numbers work out to:

3 servings, each with: 278 Calories; 17 g Fat (52.6% calories from fat); 23 g Protein; 11 g Carbohydrate; 2 g Dietary Fiber; 9 g net carbs

SAUTÉED SEAFOOD AND RED PEPPER

This outstanding recipe comes from Alix Sudlow, who says that the leftovers are delicious for lunch the next day. But don't count on leftovers!

2 tablespoons (28 ml) olive oil

2 salmon fillets (about 6 ounces, or 170 g each)

1 red bell pepper, deseeded and thickly sliced

8 ounces (225 g) large fresh shrimp, shelled and deveined

8 ounces (225 g) sea scallops, rinsed and patted dry

4 cloves of garlic, peeled and chopped

1 tablespoon (15 ml) fresh lemon or lime juice (optional)

½ teaspoon ground red pepper or dried hot red pepper flakes, or a dash of hot pepper sauce

Salt and black pepper

2 tablespoons (2 g) fresh cilantro and/or (8 g) parsley, finely chopped

1. Heat the olive oil in a large skillet—do not crowd the ingredients—over medium heat. Put the salmon fillets in the skillet, skin-side down. Scatter the red pepper slices around. Cook for about 6 minutes on a medium heat, turning once halfway through.

2. Add the shrimp, scallops, garlic, lemon juice (if using), red pepper, salt, and pepper. Fry for 2 to 3 minutes more until the shrimp and scallops are opaque.

3. Move to serving dishes. Scatter the cilantro over it and serve.

YIELD: 4 servings, each with: 282 Calories; 11 g Fat (36.5% calories from fat); 38 g Protein; 5 g Carbohydrate; 1 g Dietary Fiber; 4 g net carbs

SHRIMP AND ANDOUILLE JAMBALAYA

If you can't find andouille, just substitute the lowest-carb smoked sausage you can find. They vary quite a lot, so read your labels! Feel free to make this with 4 packets of Miracle Rice, prepared according to the instructions on page 23, instead of the Cauliflower Rice, if you like. It will knock off about 4 grams of carbohydrate per serving.

12 ounces (340 g) andouille sausage, sliced ½ inch (1.3 cm) thick

¼ cup (60 ml) olive oil

1⅓ cups (240 g) chopped onion

2 cloves of garlic, crushed

1 large green pepper, diced

1 can (14½ ounces, or 410 g) of diced tomatoes, including liquid

1 cup (235 ml) chicken broth

1 teaspoon dried thyme

6 cups (600 g) Cauliflower Rice (about one good-size cauliflower; see page 113)

2 cups (128 g) shelled, deveined, medium-sized shrimp

Salt and pepper

Tabasco

1. In a Dutch oven, start browning the andouille in the olive oil. When it's lightly golden on both sides, add the onion, garlic, and green pepper. Sauté the vegetables until the onion is becoming translucent.

2. Add the tomatoes, chicken broth, and thyme and bring to a simmer. Let it simmer for 20 minutes or so, uncovered, to blend the flavors.

3. Add the Cauliflower Rice and simmer for another 15 minutes or until the cauliflower is starting to get tender.

4. Add the shrimp and simmer for another 5 minutes or so—just long enough to cook the shrimp. Add salt, pepper, and Tabasco to taste and serve.

YIELD: 6 servings, each with: 419 Calories; 28 g Fat (60.0% calories from fat); 28 g Protein; 15 g Carbohydrate; 4 g Dietary Fiber; 11 g net carbs

SALMON PATTIES

These are quick, easy, and from-the-pantry-shelf convenient. If you don't have scallions in the refrigerator, use a tablespoon (10 g) or so of finely minced onion. Not only do these patties have lots of healthy fish oils, they also contain half your day's requirement of calcium.

1 can (14¾ ounces, or 415 g) of salmon

¼ cup (20 g) pork rind crumbs

1 egg

2 scallions, minced

3 tablespoons (45 g) butter

1. Drain the salmon, place it in a mixing bowl, and mash it well. Don't worry about any skin that may be in there, just mash it right in.

2. Add the pork rind crumbs, egg, and scallions and mix everything well. Form into 4 patties.

3. Melt the butter in a heavy skillet over medium heat. Sauté the patties in the butter, turning carefully, until they're quite golden on both sides (7 to 10 minutes per side).

YIELD: 2 servings, each with: 533 Calories; 35 g Fat (60.4% calories from fat); 50 g Protein; 1 g Carbohydrate; trace Dietary Fiber; 1 g net carbs

TEQUILA LIME GRILLED SHRIMP

Are you tired of burgers and chicken at your cookouts? Try this, instead. How about California Salad (page 148) with it?

2 pounds (910 g) really large, raw shrimp in their shells (about 30 shrimp)

1 batch of Tequila Lime Marinade (page 279)

1. Put your shrimp in a big zipper-lock bag, pour the marinade over them, squeeze out the air, and seal the bag. Put the bag in the refrigerator and let the shrimp marinate for at least a few hours, turning the bag now and then.

2. When it's time for dinner, drain off the marinade into a saucepan and grill or broil your shrimp. (3 to 4 minutes per side should do it; you want them pink all the way through, of course.)

3. While the shrimp is cooking, boil the marinade at a complete, rolling boil for a few minutes. Then, serve it as a dipping sauce.

YIELD: 6 servings, each with: 183 Calories; 3 g Fat (14.4% calories from fat); 31 g Protein; 3 g Carbohydrate; trace Dietary Fiber; 3 g net carbs

Teriyaki Shrimp

Most people only use teriyaki on steak or chicken, but it's just as good on shrimp. Just follow the directions for the Tequila Lime Grilled Shrimp, but use Teriyaki Sauce (page 280) instead of Tequila Lime Marinade.

YIELD: 6 servings, each with: 163 Calories; 3 g Fat (14.9% calories from fat); 31 g Protein; 2 g Carbohydrate; trace Dietary Fiber; 2 g net carbs

INSTANT SHRIMP STIR-FRY

If you keep my Stir-Fry Sauce (page 273) in the fridge, this is dead simple. It's perfect for the end of a busy day. Serve over Miracle Rice prepared according to the instructions on page 23 if you like, but it's fine straight.

¼ cup (60 ml) peanut oil

15 medium-sized, frozen, cooked, peeled shrimp

1 cup (225 g) frozen "stir-fry blend" vegetables

1½ tablespoons (22 ml) Stir-Fry Sauce (page 273)

1. Heat the oil in a skillet or wok over high heat. Put the shrimp and vegetables, both still frozen, in the skillet. Stir-fry for 3 to 5 minutes or until the shrimp are hot through and the vegetables are tender-crisp.

2. Stir in the stir-fry sauce and serve. If you want to make 2 servings, double everything but the oil.

YIELD: 1 serving with: 635 Calories; 56 g Fat (77.8% calories from fat); 22 g Protein; 13 g Carbohydrate; 3 g Dietary Fiber; 10 g net carbs

CAJUN SKILLET SHRIMP

I threw this together when my husband brought a friend home for a quick lunch. This takes no more than ten minutes, and it was a big hit.

3 tablespoons (45 ml) olive oil

2 cups (128 g) shelled, deveined shrimp (cooked or uncooked)

1 clove of garlic, crushed

1 small onion, sliced

½ of a green pepper in strips

½ of a yellow pepper in strips

1 teaspoon Cajun Seasoning (page 276 or store-bought—I like Tony Chachere's More Spice Seasoning.)

1. Heat the olive oil in a heavy skillet over medium-high heat. If your shrimp are uncooked, throw them in now, along with the garlic, onion, and green and yellow peppers. Stir-fry the lot together until the shrimp are pink clear through and the vegetables are just tender-crisp. If you're using cooked shrimp, sauté the vegetables first and then add the shrimp and cook just long enough to heat them through. (I threw mine in still frozen, and they were thawed and hot in just 4 to 5 minutes.)
2. Sprinkle the Cajun Seasoning over everything. Stir it in and serve.

YIELD: 2 servings, each with: 473 Calories; 24 g Fat (47.4% calories from fat); 49 g Protein; 12 g Carbohydrate; 2 g Dietary Fiber; 10 g net carbs

SHRIMP ALFREDO

I invented this for my Alfredo-obsessed husband, and he loves it. Who doesn't love Alfredo sauce? Serve this over tofu shirataki fettuccini if you like.

2 cups (150 g) frozen broccoli "cuts"

3 tablespoons (45 g) butter

3 cloves of garlic, crushed

2 cups (128 g) thawed small, frozen shrimp, cooked, shelled, and deveined

¾ cup (175 ml) heavy cream

¼ teaspoon guar or xanthan

1 cup (100 g) grated Parmesan cheese

1. Steam or microwave the broccoli until tender-crisp.
2. Melt the butter in a heavy skillet over medium heat and stir in the garlic. Add the broccoli, drained, and the shrimp and stir to coat with garlic butter.
3. While the shrimp are heating through, put the heavy cream in the blender, turn it to a low speed, and add the guar. Turn the blender off quickly, so you don't make butter.
4. Pour the cream into the skillet and stir in the Parmesan cheese. Heat to a simmer and serve.

YIELD: 3 servings, each with: 580 Calories; 44 g Fat (67.2% calories from fat); 38 g Protein; 10 g Carbohydrate; 3 g Dietary Fiber; 7 g net carbs

PARMESAN SHRIMP

This recipe comes from reader Karen Nichols, who says: "This is a beautiful dish served with steamed asparagus alongside, and it's also good presented over baked fish fillets. The shrimp can go further this way and serve more people."

2 tablespoons (28 g) butter	3 tablespoons (15 g) grated Parmesan cheese
1 tablespoon (10 g) finely chopped onion	3 tablespoons (45 g) no-sugar-added ketchup
1 clove of garlic, crushed	1 pound (455 g) cooked shrimp, peeled and deveined
¼ teaspoon salt	
¼ teaspoon ground red pepper	Fresh chopped chives (for optional garnish)
¼ teaspoon white pepper	
1½ cups (355 ml) heavy cream	

1. Melt the butter in a medium saucepan and sauté the onion in it until tender, but not browned. Add the garlic, salt, and red and white pepper. Stir in the heavy cream, Parmesan cheese, and low-carb ketchup.

2. Bring to a boil and then reduce the heat and simmer, uncovered, stirring occasionally, until the sauce thickens (15 to 20 minutes).

3. Stir in the cooked shrimp. Move to a serving plate and garnish with chopped chives, if using.

YIELD: 4 servings, each with: 494 Calories; 41 g Fat (74.9% calories from fat); 27 g Protein; 4 g Carbohydrate; trace Dietary Fiber; 4 g net carbs

LOW-CARB SHRIMP AND "GRITS"

Here's one for you Southerners, from Adele Hite of Durham, North Carolina. (Since the original edition was published, Adele earned a master's in public health/registered dietician and has done advanced studies in nutritional epidemiology. All this, and she's a hilarious and fun person to know. Check out her blog at eathropology.com) My recipe tester—Kay, an Alabaman—loved this and said the "grits" were great all by themselves, too.

GRITS

1 recipe Fauxtatoes Deluxe (page 112)	1 cup (115 g) shredded white Cheddar cheese
4 ounces (115 g) sour cream	1 cup (100 g) grated Parmesan cheese
	1 teaspoon pepper

SHRIMP

2 tablespoons (28 g) butter	2 teaspoons lemon juice
2 ounces (55 g) chopped bacon	1 teaspoon minced garlic
1 cup (70 g) sliced mushrooms	½ cup (120 ml) dry white wine
2 ounces (55 g) very thinly sliced oil-packed sun-dried tomatoes (about 4 tomatoes)	½ pound (225 g) peeled, deveined shrimp
	½ cup (50 g) chopped scallions

1. Combine the Fauxtatoes Deluxe, cream cheese, Cheddar cheese, Parmesan cheese, and pepper in a saucepan. Stir over low heat until smooth.

2. Put the butter in a skillet and add the bacon. Brown the bacon slightly and add the mushrooms, tomatoes, lemon juice, garlic, and wine. Simmer until the mushrooms are cooked.

3. Add the shrimp and cook until they're just done. Toss with the scallions and serve over the grits.

YIELD: 5 servings, each with: 598 Calories; 49 g Fat (72.8% calories from fat); 31 g Protein; 10 g Carbohydrate; 3 g Dietary Fiber; 7 g net carbs

Cheese "Grits"

As Kay said, these "grits" are great even without the shrimp. Serve them as a side dish at dinner.

YIELD: 6 servings, each with: 343 Calories; 30 g Fat (78.3% calories from fat); 14 g Protein; 5 g Carbohydrate; 1 g Dietary Fiber; 4 g net carbs

FRIED CATFISH

I admit that without cornmeal this is somewhat inauthentic, but my catfish-loving spouse thought it was great. Catfish is among the least expensive fish, too, so this is a bargain to serve.

½ cup (56 g) almond meal	**1 tablespoon (15 ml) water**
¼ cup (20 g) pork rind crumbs	**1 pound (455 g) catfish fillets**
1½ teaspoons seasoned salt OR 1½ teaspoons Creole or Cajun seasoning plus ½ teaspoon salt	**Bacon grease, lard, bland coconut oil, or a combination (for frying)**
1 egg	**Lemon wedges**

1. On a plate, combine the almond meal, pork rind crumbs, and seasoning, stirring well.

2. In a shallow bowl, beat the egg with the water.

3. Wash and dry the catfish fillets. Dip each one in the egg, then in the almond meal–pork rind mixture, pressing it well into the fish.

4. Put your large, heavy skillet over medium heat. Add 1 inch (2.5 cm) of bacon grease. Let it heat for at least 5 minutes before cooking; you don't want to put your fish in until the oil is up to temperature. To test the oil, carefully put in one drop—no more—of water. It should sizzle, but not make the oil spit. If the oil spits, it's too hot. Turn the burner down and wait for it to cool a bit.

5. When the oil is hot, put in your fish and fry it until it's a deep gold in color. If the oil doesn't completely cover the fish, you'll have to carefully turn it after about 5 minutes. (Figure 7 to 10 minutes total frying time.) I have been known to do this when I didn't have sufficient bacon grease to cover the fish.

6. Serve with lemon wedges.

YIELD: Serves 3, unless one of them is my husband, in which case it may only serve 2. Assuming my husband isn't at your house (and if he is, I'd like to hear about it), each serving will have: 298 Calories; 12 g Fat (36.2% calories from fat); 40 g Protein; 8 g Carbohydrate; trace Dietary Fiber; 8 g net carbs. Once again, there is no way to calculate how much fat the catfish absorbs, but you can be sure it's higher fat than MasterCook says.

CHAPTER 9

Beef

There seems to be no end to the ways we can use beef—by itself, in casseroles, and in sandwiches, sauces, and pizzas, beef is a delicious way to get plenty of protein for no carbs at all.

Beef is also a source of good fats. Yes, I said good fats, especially grass-fed beef. But Peter Ballerstedt, Ph.D., a forage agronomist (studying crops for grazing animals) points out that even grain-finished beef is grass-fed for all but the last few weeks of its life and still has valuable fats.

This chapter gives you some low-carb editions of high-carb favorites, as well as showing you some ways to use beef that you may never have even considered before. So read on.

Hamburgers

Let's talk about hamburgers for a moment. There is much to be said in favor of the humble hamburger—it's cheap, it's quick, it's easy, and just about everybody likes it. Rarely will you hear the kids complain, "Oh, no. Hamburgers again?" Furthermore, it's a food that is easy to make for both the "normal" eaters and the low carbers: Just leave the bun off of yours!

On the other hand, plain hamburgers without a bun can become just a wee bit boring to the adult palate over time. What follows are some recipes to help you vary your burgers. All the carb and protein analyses are based on burgers that weigh 6 ounces (170 g) before cooking.

Cooking burgers: If, like me, you cook yours in a skillet, let me recommend that you make them ½ inch (1.3 cm) thick, no more. I used to make them thicker, having read in my youth that a 1-inch (2.5 cm) thick burger just looked more impressive or something. I then would curse when I couldn't get the center to the right degree of doneness without overcooking the outside. Now, I make them ½ inch (1.3 cm) thick, and they're just right on the outside when the center is still juicy and faintly pink. (Yes, I eat my burgers still a little pink in the center. Never has this made me ill. But, once again, your risks are up to you.)

By the way, if you're super-busy or just cooking-averse, sacks of premade, all-beef hamburgers are one of the most useful things you can keep in your freezer. I'm not cooking-averse, but I still grab a sack now and then at Costco. That Nice Boy I Married loves them and can fry one up himself—you cook them from frozen, in a hot skillet, 3 minutes per side. It's easy-peasy.

All of these burger toppings will work fine with store-bought burgers, though the numbers will be slightly different, since those patties are usually 4 ounces (115 g), not 6 ounces (170 g).

BLUE BURGER

This is completely different from your standard cheeseburger! It is one of my favorite burger toppings.

1 hamburger patty	**1 teaspoon finely minced sweet red onion**
1 tablespoon (8 g) crumbled blue cheese	

1. Cook your burger by your preferred method.
2. When it's almost done to your liking, top with the blue cheese and let it melt.
3. Remove from the heat, put it on plate, and top with the onion.

YIELD: 1 serving with: 500 Calories; 43 g Fat (77.7% calories from fat); 27 g Protein; trace Carbohydrate; trace Dietary Fiber; 0 g net carbs

SMOTHERED BURGERS

Mmmmushrooms and onions! Swiss cheese would be a nice addition to these, either over or under the mushrooms. Use olive oil if you're dairy-free.

4 hamburger patties	**½ cup (35 g) sliced mushrooms**
2 tablespoons (28 g) butter or (28 ml) olive oil	**Dash of Worcestershire sauce (Lea & Perrins is gluten-free.)**
½ cup (80 g) sliced onion	

(continued)

1. Cook your burgers by your preferred method.
2. While the burgers are cooking, melt the butter or heat the oil in a small, heavy skillet over medium-high heat. Add the onion and mushrooms and sauté until the onions are translucent.
3. Add a dash of Worcestershire sauce, stir, and spoon over the burgers.

YIELD: 4 servings, each with: 528 Calories; 46 g Fat (79.2% calories from fat); 26 g Protein; 2 g Carbohydrate; trace Dietary Fiber; 2 g net carbs

MEXIBURGERS

Are you a fan of Mexican food? Try this quick and easy cheeseburger. Read the labels to find salsa with no added sugar.

1 hamburger patty	**1 tablespoon (16 g) salsa**
1 ounce (28 g) jalapeño Jack or Monterey Jack cheese	

1. Cook your burger by your preferred method.
2. When it's almost done to your liking, melt the cheese over the burger.
3. Top with the salsa and serve.

YIELD: 1 serving with: 642 Calories; 54 g Fat (76.5% calories from fat); 35 g Protein; 2 g Carbohydrate; trace Dietary Fiber; 2 g net carbs

POOR MAN'S POIVRADE

This packs a real peppery bite—it's not for the timid! If you're using a store-bought hamburger patty, you'll need to thaw it first.

1 hamburger patty	**1 tablespoon (14 g) butter**
1 tablespoon (6 g) coarse-cracked pepper	**2 tablespoons (28 ml) dry white wine, dry sherry, or dry vermouth**

1. Roll your raw hamburger patty in the pepper until it's coated all over.
2. Fry the burger in the butter over medium heat until it's done to your liking.
3. Remove the burger to a plate. Add the wine to the skillet and stir it around for a minute or two until all the nice brown crusty bits are scraped up. Pour this over the hamburger and serve.

YIELD: 1 serving with between 4 and 6 grams of carbohydrates per serving (depending on whether you use wine, sherry, or vermouth—wine is lowest, vermouth is highest) and 2 grams of fiber, for a total of 2 to 4 g net carbs. **Full breakdown with dry white wine:** 665 Calories; 57 g Fat (79.3% calories from fat); 29 g Protein; 4 g Carbohydrate; 2 g Dietary Fiber; 2 g net carbs

PIZZA BURGER

Be careful buying pizza sauce! The carb counts vary a lot, and many have added sugar. I like Pastorelli's best, but it's not available everywhere. Ragú makes two—Pizza Quick has sugar, Homemade Style does not.

1 hamburger patty

1 tablespoon (16 g) sugar-free jarred pizza sauce

2 tablespoons (14 g) shredded mozzarella cheese

1. Cook the burger by your preferred method.
2. When it's almost done to your liking, top with the pizza sauce and then the mozzarella cheese. Cook until the cheese is melted and serve.

YIELD: 1 serving with: 579 Calories; 49 g Fat (77.0% calories from fat); 32 g Protein; 1 g Carbohydrate; trace Dietary Fiber; 1 g net carbs

ELLEN'S NOODLELESS LASAGNE

Ellen Radke sent this recipe for all you folks who miss lasagne! My dear friend Maria, who tested it on her husband and five kids, was asked if she would make this again. Her answer? An enthusiastic "Yes!" Ellen adds: "Next time, I'll try mixing in some Parmesan cheese with the ricotta, and maybe adding a layer of spinach." Sounds good!

Over the years I have heard from readers who have used thin slices of zucchini or sautéed eggplant as "noodles." Both are quite low carb, so go for it if you like.

1 pound (455 g) ground beef

1 cup (250 g) low-carb spaghetti sauce

1 can (4 ounces, or 115 g) of sliced mushrooms

1 cup (250 g) ricotta cheese

1 egg, beaten

1½ cups (175 g) shredded mozzarella cheese, divided

½ tablespoon (4 g) Italian seasoning

20 to 25 slices of pepperoni

1. Preheat the oven to 350°F (180°C, or gas mark 4).
2. Brown the ground beef in a frying pan and drain off the oil. Add the spaghetti sauce and mushrooms and simmer for 10 minutes.
3. In a small bowl, mix the ricotta cheese, egg, ½ cup (60 g) of mozzarella cheese, and Italian seasoning. Beat well with a fork.
4. Grease an 8- × 8-inch (20 × 20 cm) glass baking dish with nonstick cooking spray. Spread the beef mixture in the bottom of the dish. Spread the ricotta mixture on top of the beef mixture. Lay half the pepperoni slices on top of the ricotta mixture. Put remaining 1 cup (115 g) of the shredded mozzarella over the pepperoni slices and lay the remaining pepperoni on top of the cheese. Bake until bubbly (about 20 minutes).

YIELD: 4 servings, each with: 808 Calories; 65 g Fat (73.1% calories from fat); 45 g Protein; 9 g Carbohydrate; 2 g Dietary Fiber; 7 g net carbs

ULTRA MEAT SAUCE

This is spaghetti without the spaghetti, as it were. It is a good supper for the family because, again, it's easy to add carbs for those who want them—you eat your very meaty meat sauce with a good sprinkling of Parmesan cheese, and you let the carb-eaters have theirs over spaghetti. Serve a big salad with it, and there's dinner. Feel free to serve yours over tofu shirataki spaghetti, but it's quite good just like this. Skip the Parmesan if you're dairy-free.

1½ pounds (680 g) ground beef

1 small onion, diced

1 clove of garlic crushed

1 green pepper, diced

1 can (4 ounces, or 115 g) of mushrooms, drained

2 cups (500 g) low-carb spaghetti sauce

Parmesan cheese (for serving; optional)

1. Brown and crumble the ground beef in a large, heavy skillet. As the grease starts to collect in the skillet, add the onion, garlic, green pepper, and mushrooms. Continue cooking until the pepper and onion are soft.

2. Pour off the excess grease. Stir in the spaghetti sauce and serve. If you're not dairy-free, a sprinkle of Parmesan cheese is nice here.

YIELD: 5 servings, each with: 472 Calories; 37 g Fat (70.3% calories from fat); 25 g Protein; 10 g Carbohydrate; 3 g Dietary Fiber; 7 g net carbs

SKILLET STROGANOFF

I originally made this with canned mushrooms, and you can use them, but fresh are better. I've learned that if I take the plastic wrap off of mushrooms before putting them in the fridge, they keep longer and don't get slimy.

1 pound (455 g) ground beef

1 medium onion, diced

4 ounces (115 g) mushrooms–sliced (Buy 'em that way!) or canned mushrooms, drained

1 clove of garlic, crushed

1 teaspoon liquid beef-broth concentrate

2 tablespoons (28 ml) Worcestershire sauce

1 teaspoon paprika

¾ cup (173 g) sour cream

Salt or Vege-Sal and pepper

1. Brown and crumble the ground beef in a heavy skillet over medium heat. Add the onion, mushrooms if using fresh, and garlic as soon as there's a little grease in the bottom of the pan and cook until all pinkness is gone from the ground beef.

2. Drain the excess grease. Add the mushrooms now if you're using canned, plus the broth concentrate, Worcestershire sauce, and paprika. Stir in the sour cream and then add salt and pepper to taste. Heat through, but don't let it boil.

3. This is great as is, but you may certainly serve it over noodles for the non-low-carb set and over tofu shirataki fettuccini, prepared according to the instructions on page 23, for you.

YIELD: 3 servings, each with: 629 Calories; 53 g Fat (75.4% calories from fat); 29 g Protein; 10 g Carbohydrate; 1 g Dietary Fiber; 9 g net carbs

GROUND BEEF "HELPER"

When your family starts agitating for the "normal" food of yore, whip up this recipe. Originally, this recipe, sent in by a reader whose name I have lost, called simply for "low-carb pasta," but these days, shirataki are the only noodles I use.

1 pound (455 g) lean ground beef or ground turkey

½ cup (75 g) chopped green pepper

½ cup (80 g) chopped onion

½ cup (60 g) diced celery

2 cans (8 ounces, or 225 g each) of tomato sauce

2 cloves of garlic, crushed; 1 teaspoon minced garlic; or ½ teaspoon garlic powder

½ teaspoon Italian seasoning

2 cups (230 g) shredded Cheddar or Monterey Jack cheese

3 packages of tofu shirataki, prepared according to the directions on page 33 (I'd use fettuccini or macaroni-style.)

Salt and pepper

1. In a large, oven-safe skillet, brown the meat with the green pepper, onion, and celery. Drain off the grease.

2. Add the tomato sauce, garlic, seasoning, 1 cup (115 g) of the cheese, shirataki, and salt and pepper to taste. Cover and simmer over low heat for 10 minutes. Turn on the broiler to preheat during last the few minutes of cooking time.

3. Stir well. Spread the remaining 1 cup (115 g) of cheese over the top and broil until the cheese starts to brown.

YIELD: 6 servings, each with: 419 Calories; 33 g Fat (70.0% calories from fat); 23 g Protein; 8 g Carbohydrate; 2 g Dietary Fiber; 6 g net carbs

MEXICAN MEATBALLS

Or, as they say in Mexico, *albondigas*. Marilee Wellersdick sends this easy, South-of-the-Border skillet meal.

1 pound (455 g) ground beef or ground turkey

2 eggs

1 medium onion, finely chopped

3 cloves of garlic, minced

2 teaspoons ground coriander

½ teaspoon salt

2 tablespoons (28 g) lard or (28 ml) oil

1 can (14½ ounces, or 410 g) of cut or crushed tomatoes

1 can (8 ounces, or 225 g) of tomato sauce

1 tablespoon (8 g) chili powder

½ teaspoon ground cumin

1. Mix together the ground beef, eggs, half of the onion, and two-thirds of the garlic, coriander, and salt. Shape the mixture into 2-inch (5 cm) balls.

2. Heat the lard in a large skillet. Add the meatballs and brown them. Add the tomatoes, tomato sauce, the remaining half of the onion, and the remaining third of the garlic, chili powder, and cumin to the skillet.

3. Cover and simmer over medium-low heat for 45 minutes.

YIELD: 4 servings, each with: 504 Calories; 40 g Fat (70.5% calories from fat); 24 g Protein; 14 g Carbohydrate; 3 g Dietary Fiber; 11 g net carbs (made with beef)

GROUND BEEF STIR-FRY

This looks like a lot of instructions, but it actually goes together rather quickly. It's good when you're missing Chinese food, which is generally full of added sugar and starch. This is a good place to use Miracle Rice, though this is fine as is. This will have about 2 more grams of carb per serving if you use the green beans. Remember the Law of Stir-Frying: Have everything chopped, thawed, sliced, and prepped before you start cooking!

2 tablespoons (28 ml) soy sauce, divided	**½ cup (60 g) coarsely chopped walnuts**
3 tablespoons (45 ml) dry sherry, divided	**2 cups (450 g) frozen broccoli "cuts," thawed OR 2 cups (248 g) frozen crosscut green beans, thawed**
1 clove of garlic, crushed	
1 pound (455 g) ground beef	**1 medium onion, sliced**
¼ cup (60 ml) peanut oil or (56 g) bland coconut oil, divided	**1½ teaspoons grated fresh ginger**

1. In a bowl, combine 1 tablespoon (15 ml) of soy sauce, 4½ teaspoons (23 ml) of sherry, and the garlic. Add the ground beef and, with clean hands, mix the flavorings into the meat.

2. Heat 2 tablespoons (28 ml) of oil in a wok or large, heavy skillet over high heat. Put the walnuts in the skillet and fry for a few minutes until crispy. Drain and put aside.

3. Using the same oil, stir-fry bite-size chunks of the ground beef mixture until done through. Lift out the beef and drain.

4. Pour the oil and fat out of the skillet and put the rest of the oil in the pan. Heat it up over high heat and add the broccoli or green beans, onion, and ginger. Stir-fry until the vegetables are tender-crisp.

5. Add the beef back to the pan and stir everything up. Stir in the remaining soy sauce and sherry and another clove of crushed garlic if you like.

6. Serve without rice for you and on top of rice for the carb-eaters in the family. Sprinkle the toasted walnuts on top of each serving and pass the soy sauce at the table for those who like more.

YIELD: 4 servings, each with: 616 Calories; 53 g Fat (77.2% calories from fat); 26 g Protein; 9 g Carbohydrate; 4 g Dietary Fiber; 5 g net carbs

BURGER SCRAMBLE FLORENTINE

The only name I have to attribute this to is "Dottie," which is too bad because my sister, who tested this recipe, says it's great. Add crusty bread for the carbivores, and you're done.

1½ pounds (680 g) lean ground beef	**½ cup (120 ml) heavy cream**
½ cup (80 g) finely diced onion	**½ cup (50 g) shredded Parmesan cheese**
10 ounces (280 g) frozen spinach, thawed and drained	**Salt and pepper**
1 package (8 ounces, or 225 g) of cream cheese, softened	

1. Preheat the oven to 350°F (180°C, or gas mark 4). Coat a 2-quart (1.9 L) casserole with cooking spray.

2. In a large skillet, brown and crumble the ground beef with the onion. Add the spinach and cook until the pink is gone from the meat.

3. In a bowl, combine the cream cheese, heavy cream, Parmesan cheese, and salt and pepper to taste. Mix well.

4. Combine the cream cheese mixture and the meat mixture and spoon into the prepared casserole. Bake, uncovered, for 30 minutes or until bubbly and browned on top.

YIELD: 6 servings, each with: 596 Calories; 53 g Fat (79.3% calories from fat); 26 g Protein; 5 g Carbohydrate; 2 g Dietary Fiber; 3 net carbs

Garden Burger Scramble

Substitute a 10-ounce (280 g) package of frozen green beans for the spinach and use Garden Vegetable Cream Cheese—Kraft makes this—instead of plain.

YIELD: 6 servings, each with: 560 Calories; 47 g Fat (76.4% calories from fat); 25 g Protein; 8 g Carbohydrate; 2 g Dietary Fiber; 6 g net carbs. (I don't know for sure if this is gluten- or grain-free because Kraft's website does not include a customer service number. If you really need the info, I'm afraid you'll have to ask them yourself.)

GREEN BEAN SPAGHETTI

This recipe comes from reader Marcia McCance, who says it's a great dish if you're craving Italian food. If you use French-cut green beans, they'll remind you more of spaghetti. This is a clear demonstration of how even vegetable carbs can add up. You can slash the carb count to 8 grams, 2 of them fiber, by substituting 3 packets of tofu shirataki spaghetti, prepared according to the instructions on page 23, for the green beans. By the way—Marcia didn't include garlic, so I've left it out of the recipe, but I'd throw in a clove, crushed, while the vegetables are cooking.

1 package (12 ounces, or 340 g) of frozen green beans

2–3 tablespoons (28–45 ml) olive oil

1 small onion, chopped

1 green pepper, diced

4 or 5 medium mushrooms, sliced

1 pound (455 g) ground beef, turkey, or chicken

Salt

1 can (4 ounces, or 115 g) of plain tomato sauce

1 tablespoon (6 g) Italian seasoning

Parmesan cheese

1. Cook the green beans according to package directions. I'd steam mine in the microwave, but it's up to you.

2. While the beans are cooking, put the olive oil in a large, heavy skillet over medium heat and sauté the onion, green pepper, and mushrooms until the onion is translucent.

3. Add the ground beef, cook, and stir, crumbling the meat until all pinkness is gone. Salt to taste.

4. Add the tomato sauce and the Italian seasoning. Bring to a boil, reduce to a simmer, and cook for about 5 minutes. Do not overcook.

5. Drain your green beans and pour the meat sauce over them. Top with Parmesan cheese and serve.

YIELD: 4 servings, each with: 505 Calories; 41 g Fat (71.6% calories from fat); 22 g Protein; 14 g Carbohydrate; 4 g Dietary Fiber; 10 g net carbs

MEATZA!

Here's a dish for all you pizza-lovers, and I know you are legion. Just add a salad, and you have a supper that will please the whole family. Again, be careful about your pizza sauce!

¾ pound (340 g) ground chuck mixed with ¾ pound (340 g) Italian-style sausage OR 1½ pounds (680 g) ground chuck

1 small onion, finely chopped

1 clove of garlic, crushed

1 teaspoon dried oregano or Italian seasoning (optional)

8 ounces (225 g) sugar-free pizza sauce

8 ounces (225 g) shredded mozzarella

Parmesan or Romano cheese (optional)

Toppings (peppers, onions, mushrooms, or whatever you like)

Olive oil (optional)

1. Preheat the oven to 350°F (180°C, or gas mark 4).

2. In a large bowl and with clean hands, combine the meat with the onion and garlic and a teaspoon of oregano or Italian seasoning (if using). Mix well.

3. Pat the meat mixture out in an even layer in a 9- × 13-inch (23 × 33 cm) baking pan. Bake for 20 minutes.

4. When the meat comes out, it will have shrunk a fair amount because of the grease cooking off. Pour off the grease and spread the pizza sauce over the meat. Distribute the shredded mozzarella cheese evenly over the sauce and then sprinkle on the Parmesan cheese (if using).

5. Top with whatever you like: green peppers, banana peppers, mushrooms, olives, anchovies. You could also use meat toppings, such as sausage and pepperoni, but they seem a little redundant, since the whole bottom layer is meat.

6. Drizzle the whole thing with a little olive oil if you like, though it's not really necessary.

7. Put your Meatza! 4 inches (10 cm) below a broiler set on High. Broil for about 5 minutes or until the cheese is melted and starting to brown.

YIELD: 6 servings, each with: 510 Calories; 41 g Fat (72.9% calories from fat); 29 g Protein; 5 g Carbohydrate; 1 g Dietary Fiber; 4 g net carbs. (This is based on using sugar-free pizza sauce and only cheese, no veggies.)

JOE

This is our favorite one-dish skillet supper. It's flexible, too; don't worry if you use a little less or a little more ground beef, or one more or one fewer egg. It'll still come out great. This is how I originally made Joe. Over the years, I've started adding sliced mushrooms to the mix and have joined my sister in adding Parmesan cheese. It's a recipe you can play with!

1½ pounds (680 g) ground chuck

1 package (10 ounces, or 280 g) of frozen chopped spinach

1 medium onion, chopped

1 or 2 cloves of garlic, crushed

5 eggs

Salt and pepper

1. In a heavy skillet over a medium flame, begin browning the ground beef.

2. While the beef is cooking, cook the spinach according to the package directions (or 5 to 7 minutes on High in the microwave should do it).

3. When the ground beef is half done, add the onion and garlic and cook until the beef is completely done. Pour off the extra fat.

4. Drain the spinach well. I put mine in a strainer and press it with the back of a spoon. Stir it into the ground beef.

5. Mix up the eggs well with a fork and stir them in with the beef and spinach. Continue cooking and stirring over low heat for a few more minutes until the eggs are set. Salt and pepper to taste and serve.

YIELD: 6 servings, each with: 426 Calories; 34 g Fat (72.4% calories from fat); 25 g Protein; 4 g Carbohydrate; 2 g Dietary Fiber; 2 g net carbs

SLOPPY JOSÉ

This is so easy it's almost embarrassing, and the kids will probably like it. Different brands of salsa vary a lot in their carb contents, so read labels carefully. This is good with a salad or even on a salad. Of course, if you have carb-eaters around, they'll love the stuff on some corn tortillas.

1 pound (455 g) ground chuck

1 cup (115 g) shredded Mexican-style cheese

1 cup (260 g) salsa (mild, medium, or hot, as you prefer)

1. In a large skillet, crumble and brown the ground beef and drain off the fat.
2. Stir in the salsa and cheese and heat until the cheese is melted.

YIELD: 4 servings, each with: 475 Calories; 39 g Fat (73.9% calories from fat); 27 g Protein; 4 g Carbohydrate; 1 g Dietary Fiber; 3 g net carbs

Mega Sloppy José

Try adding another ½ cup (130 g) of salsa and another ½ cup (58 g) cheese.

YIELD: 4 servings, each with: 537 Calories; 43 g Fat (72.5% calories from fat); 30 g Protein; 6 g Carbohydrate; 2 g Dietary Fiber; 4 g net carbs

ALL-MEAT CHILI

Some folks consider tomatoes in chili to be anathema, but I like it this way. Don't look funny at that cocoa powder, by the way. It's the secret ingredient! It's easy to vary this recipe to the tastes of different family members. If some people like beans in their chili, just heat up a can of kidney or pinto beans, and let them spoon their beans into their own serving. If you like beans in your chili, buy a can of black soybeans at a health food store; there are only a couple of grams of usable carbs in a couple of tablespoons (33 g). And of course, if you like your chili hotter than this, just add crushed red pepper, cayenne, or hot sauce to take things up a notch. Skip the cheese and sour cream if you're dairy-free.

2 pounds (910 g) ground chuck

4 teaspoons (10 g) ground cumin

1 cup (160 g) chopped onion

2 teaspoons dried oregano

3 cloves of garlic, crushed

2 teaspoons unsweetened cocoa powder

1 can (14½ ounces, or 410 g) of tomatoes with green chilies

1 teaspoon paprika, sweet or hot

1 can (8 ounces, or 225 g) plain tomato sauce

Shredded cheese, sour cream chopped raw onion, or other low-carb toppings (for serving)

1. Brown and crumble the beef in a heavy skillet over medium-high heat. Pour off the grease and add the onion, garlic, tomatoes, tomato sauce, cumin, oregano, cocoa powder, and paprika. Stir to combine.
2. Turn the burner to low, cover, and simmer for 30 minutes. Uncover and simmer for another 15 to 20 minutes or until the chili thickens a bit.
3. Serve with shredded cheese, sour cream, raw onion, or other low-carb toppings.

YIELD: 6 servings, each with: 512 Calories; 41 g Fat (71.6% calories from fat); 27 g Protein; 9 g Carbohydrate; 2 g Dietary Fiber; 7 g net carbs

MEXICALI MEAT LOAF

Don't let the ingredient list scare you; this is just meat loaf with a Tex-Mex accent.

Do chop the onion quite fine for your meat loaves. If it's in pieces that are too big, it tends to make the loaf fall apart when you cut it. The Mexicali Meat Loaf may crumble a bit anyway because it's quite tender.

1 pound (455 g) ground chuck	**¾ cup (195 g) salsa (mild, medium, or hot, as desired)**
1 pound (455 g) mild pork sausage	**1 egg**
1 cup (80 g) pork rind crumbs	**2 or 3 cloves of garlic, crushed**
1 can (4½ ounces, or 130 g) diced mild green chilies	**2 teaspoons dried oregano**
	2 teaspoons ground cumin
1 medium onion, finely chopped	**1 teaspoon salt or Vege-Sal**
8 ounces (225 g) Monterey Jack cheese, cut into ¼- to ½-inch (6 mm to 1.3 cm) cubes or shredded	

1. Preheat the oven to 350°F (180°C, or gas mark 4).
2. Combine all these ingredients in a really big bowl and then, with clean hands, knead it all until it's thoroughly blended.
3. Dump it out on a clean broiler rack and form into a loaf—it'll be a big loaf—about 3 inches (7.5 cm) thick. Bake for 1½ hours or until cooked through. Let cool for 10 minutes before slicing.

YIELD: 8 servings, each with: 574 Calories; 47 g Fat (74.5% calories from fat); 31 g Protein; 5 g Carbohydrate; 1 g Dietary Fiber; 4 g net carbs

LOW-CARB SWISS LOAF

I adapted this from a recipe in Peg Bracken's 1960 classic, the *I Hate To Cook Book*. The original had a whole pile of bread crumbs and a cup (235 ml) of milk. I simply left them out, and I've never missed them.

2½ pounds (1.1 kg) ground chuck	**1 green pepper, chopped**
5 ounces (140 g) Swiss cheese, diced small or grated	**1 small rib of celery, chopped**
	1 teaspoon salt or Vege-Sal
2 eggs, beaten	**½ teaspoon pepper**
1 medium onion, chopped	**½ teaspoon paprika**

1. Preheat the oven to 350°F (180°C, or gas mark 4).
2. With clean hands, combine all the ingredients in a large bowl until the mixture is well blended.
3. Pack the meat into one large loaf pan or two small ones. Bake a large loaf for 1½ to 1¾ hours or until cooked through. Bake two small loaves for 1¼ hours.

Note: I turn the loaf out of the pan and onto the broiler rack, and I bake it there so the excess fat runs off—not because I'm afraid of fat, but because I like it better that way. If you like, though, you could bake yours right in the pan, and it would probably be a bit more tender.

YIELD: 8 servings, each with: 468 Calories; 35 g Fat (69.4% calories from fat); 32 g Protein; 3 g Carbohydrate; 1 g Dietary Fiber; 2 g net carbs

ZUCCHINI MEAT LOAF ITALIANO

The inspiration for this meat loaf was a recipe in an Italian cookbook. The original recipe was for a "zucchini mold," and it had only a tiny bit of meat in it. I thought to myself, "How could adding more ground beef be a problem here?" And I was right; it's very moist and flavorful.

3 tablespoons (45 ml) olive oil

2 medium zucchini, chopped (about 1½ cups [180 g])

1 medium onion, chopped

2 or 3 cloves garlic, crushed

1½ pounds (680 g) ground chuck

2 tablespoons (8 g) snipped fresh parsley

1 egg

¾ cup (75 g) grated Parmesan cheese

1 teaspoon salt

½ teaspoon pepper

1. Preheat the oven to 350°F (180°C, or gas mark 4).
2. Heat the olive oil in a skillet and sauté the zucchini, onion, and garlic in it for 7 to 8 minutes.
3. Let the veggies cool a bit and then put them in a big bowl with the ground beef, parsley, egg, Parmesan cheese, salt, and pepper. Using clean hands, mix thoroughly.
4. Take the rather soft meat mixture and put it in a big loaf pan, if you like, or form the loaf right on a broiler rack so the grease will drip off. (Keep in mind if you do it this way, your loaf won't stand very high, it'll be about 2 inches [5 cm] thick.)
5. Bake for 75 to 90 minutes or until the juices run clear but the loaf is not dried out.

YIELD: 5 servings, each with: 515 Calories; 41 g Fat (72.3% calories from fat); 31 g Protein; 4 g Carbohydrate; 1 g Dietary Fiber; 3 g net carbs

MY GRANDMA'S STANDBY CASSEROLE

This recipe is good for all casserole occasions. In the original edition I used 3 cups (765 g) of cooked spaghetti squash, not shirataki. Feel free to use it if you prefer! (Grandma used egg noodles.) If you do, you're looking at 15 grams of carbohydrate with 2 grams of fiber per serving.

1 pound (455 g) ground chuck

2 tablespoons (28 g) butter

1 clove of garlic, crushed

1 teaspoon salt

Dash of pepper

2 cans (8 ounces, or 225 g each) of plain tomato sauce

6 scallions

3 ounces (85 g) cream cheese

1 cup (230 g) sour cream

3 packages of tofu shirataki fettuccini, prepared according to the instructions on page 33

½ cup (58 g) shredded Cheddar cheese

1. Preheat the oven to 350°F (180°C, or gas mark 4).
2. Brown the ground beef in the butter. Pour off the grease and stir in the garlic, salt, pepper, and tomato sauce.
3. Cover, turn the burner to low, and simmer for 20 minutes.
4. While the meat is simmering, slice the scallions, including the crisp part of the green, and combine with the cream cheese and sour cream. Blend well.
5. In the bottom of a 6-cup (1.4 L) casserole, layer half the shirataki, half the scallion mixture, and half the tomato-beef mixture; repeat the layers. Top with the Cheddar cheese and bake for 20 minutes.

YIELD: 5 servings, each with: 518 Calories; 43 g Fat (74.0% calories from fat); 23 g Protein; 11 g Carbohydrate; 2 g Dietary Fiber; 9 g net carbs

BEEF TACO FILLING

What to do with taco filling in the absence of taco shells? Consider Taco Omelets (page 68) or Taco Salad (page 253)!

1 pound (455 g) ground chuck

2 tablespoons (16 g) Taco Seasoning (page 275)

¼ cup (60 ml) water

1. Brown and crumble the ground beef in a heavy skillet over medium-high heat.
2. When the meat is cooked through, drain the grease. Stir in the Taco Seasoning and water.
3. Let it simmer for about 5 minutes and serve.

YIELD: 4 servings, each with: 310 Calories; 24 g Fat (70.6% calories from fat); 21 g Protein; 2 g Carbohydrate; 1 g Dietary Fiber; 1 g net carbs

REUBEN CASSEROLE

Here's another great recipe from Vicki Cash. Thanks, Vicki! It's great reason to cook extra corned beef, or simply buy it thinly sliced at the deli counter.

4 small summer squash or zucchini

2 tablespoons (28 ml) water

1 can (27 ounces, or 765 g) of sauerkraut, drained

1 tablespoon (7 g) caraway seeds

2 tablespoons (30 g) Dijon mustard

8 ounces (225 g) shaved corned beef or pastrami

4 ounces (115 g) grated Swiss cheese

1. Slice the squash into bite-size pieces. Place the pieces in a 2-quart (1.9 L) microwave-safe casserole and add the water. Cover and microwave on High for 3 minutes.
2. Add the sauerkraut, caraway seeds, mustard, and meat, mixing well. Cover and microwave on High for 6 minutes, stirring halfway through.
3. Stir in the Swiss cheese and microwave for 3 to 5 more minutes or until the cheese is melted.

YIELD: 4 servings, each with: 304 Calories; 17 g Fat (49.4% calories from fat); 21 g Protein; 19 g Carbohydrate; 9 g Dietary Fiber; 10 g net carbs

BEEF FAJITAS

This is my take on a recipe sent to me by Carol Vandiver. You can serve these with low-carb tortillas, if you like, but I just pile mine on a plate, top them with salsa, sour cream, and guac, and eat 'em with a fork. Skip the sour cream if you're dairy-free.

½ cup (120 ml) lite beer (Miller Lite, Milwaukee's Best Light or Michelob Ultra all work here. Corona Lite, at 5 g carb per bottle, is gluten-free!)

½ cup (120 ml) MCT oil

2 tablespoons (28 ml) lime juice

½ of a small onion, thinly sliced

1 teaspoon red pepper flakes

¼ teaspoon ground cumin

¼ teaspoon pepper

1½ pounds (680 g) skirt steak

1 tablespoon (15 ml) MCT oil

1 medium onion, thickly sliced

1 green pepper, cut into strips

FOR SERVING (OPTIONAL)

Low-carb tortillas, store-bought or homemade (page 109)

Guacamole (page 45)

Salsa

Sour cream

1. Mix together the beer, oil, lime juice, onion, red pepper flakes, cumin, and pepper. This is your marinade.

2. Place the skirt steak in a large zipper-lock bag and pour all but a couple of tablespoons (28 ml) of the marinade over it. Seal the bag, pressing out the air, turn to coat, and put it in the fridge. Let your steak marinate for a minimum of several hours, turning the bag any time you look in the fridge. Store the reserved marinade in a small container in the fridge.

3. When you're ready to cook, remove your steak from the bag. Slice your steak quite thin, across the grain.

4. Add the oil to a large, heavy skillet over high heat and tilt to coat the bottom. When the skillet is good and hot, add the steak slices, onion, and green pepper. Stir-fry them until the meat is done through and the vegetables are crisp-tender.

5. Stir in the reserved marinade. Serve, with or without low-carb tortillas, topped with Guacamole, salsa, and sour cream (if using).

YIELD: 4 servings, each with: 606 Calories; 49 g Fat (73.0% calories from fat); 34 g Protein; 7 g Carbohydrate; 1 g Dietary Fiber; 6 g net carbs. The analysis does not include tortillas, guacamole, salsa, or sour cream.

STEAKHOUSE STEAK

Ever wonder why steak is better at a steakhouse than it is at home? Part of it is that the best grades of meat are reserved for the restaurants, but it's also the method: quick grilling, at very high heat, very close to the flame. Try it at home, with this recipe.

Olive oil

1½–2 pounds (680–910 g) well-marbled steak (sirloin, rib eye, or the like), 1 to 1½ inches (2.5 to 3.8 cm) thick

1. Rub a couple of teaspoons of olive oil on either side of the steak.

2. Arrange your broiler so you can get the steak so close that it's almost, but not quite, touching the broiling element. I have to put my broiler pan on top of a skillet turned upside down to do this. Turn the broiler to high and get that steak in there. Leave the oven door open—this is crucial. For a 1-inch (2.5 cm)-thick steak, set the oven timer for 5 to 5½ minutes; for a 1½-inch (3.8 cm)-thick steak, you can go up to 6 minutes.

3. When the timer beeps, quickly flip the steak and set the timer again. Check at this point to see if your time seems right. If you like your steak a lot rarer or more well-done than I do, or if you have a different brand of broiler, you may need to adjust how long you broil the second side for.

4. When the timer goes off again, get that steak out of there quickly, put it on a serving plate, and season it any way you like.

YIELD: The number of servings will depend on the size of your steak, but what you really need to know is that there are no carbs here at all.

SOUTHWESTERN STEAK

I adore steak, I adore guacamole, and the combination is fantastic.

Olive oil

1½–2 pounds (680–910 g) well-marbled steak (sirloin, rib eye, or the like), 1 to 1½ inches (2.5 to 3.8 cm) thick

Guacamole (page 45)

Salt and pepper

1. Prepare the Steakhouse Steak (page 220) to your preferred degree of doneness.

2. Spread each serving of steak with a heaping tablespoon (14 g) of Guacamole and salt and pepper to taste.

YIELD: The number of servings will depend on the size of your steak, but the guacamole will add: 4 grams of carbohydrates and 1 gram of fiber, for a total of 3 grams of net carbs. (You'll also get 275 milligrams of potassium.)

CAJUN STEAK

In the unlikely event that you tire of just plain steak, this is a fine way to vary it. You can make your own Cajun Seasoning (page 276) or use purchased seasoning. Penzeys is excellent.

2–3 teaspoons (8–12 g) Cajun Seasoning (page 276)	**1 pound (455 g) sirloin steak, 1 inch (2.5 cm) thick**
	Bacon grease

1. Put your large, heavy skillet over high heat. While it's heating, sprinkle both sides of the steak with the Cajun Seasoning.

2. When the skillet is good and hot, add the bacon grease and slosh it around as it melts.

3. Add the steak and cook for 5 to 8 minutes per side, depending on how well-done you like your steak!

YIELD: 3 servings, each with: 642 Calories; 53 g Fat (74.8% calories from fat); 38 g Protein; 1 g Carbohydrate; trace Dietary Fiber; 1 g net carbs

STEAK VINAIGRETTE

Want to turn a chuck roast into a grill-able steak? Add a spoonful of tenderizer to the vinaigrette, stab your chuck all over with a fork, and proceed with the recipe as written. Marinate for a couple-few hours.

Steak, in your preferred cut and quantity	**½ cup (120 ml) vinaigrette dressing for each pound of steak**

1. Put your steak in a 1-quart (946 ml) zipper-lock bag and pour the vinaigrette dressing over it. Let the steak marinate for at least 15 minutes or leave it all day, if you have the time.

2. When you're ready to cook your steak, remove it from the bag, discard the marinade, and broil or grill it, as you prefer.

YIELD: Consider a pound (455 g) to be 3 servings, each with: 519 Calories; 47 g Fat (82.5% calories from fat); 22 g Protein; 1 g Carbohydrate; 0 g Dietary Fiber; 1 g net carbs. This analysis assumes you consume the vinaigrette, which you won't, so both the carb and fat count will be a little lower than this.

BLUE CHEESE STEAK BUTTER

This is one of those recipes that would have horrified me back in my low-fat days—and it's so good! If you don't have a food processor, you can make this by hand; it will just take some vigorous mixing. If you have some steak-loving people on your Christmas list—and hey, who doesn't?—a ball of Blue Cheese Steak Butter wrapped in foil makes a nice present.

½ pound (225 g) blue cheese, crumbled

¾ cup (166 g) softened butter

1 or 2 cloves of garlic, crushed

1 tablespoon (15 g) spicy brown mustard

2 or 3 drops of Tabasco

1. Put all the ingredients in your food processor and run it until it's well blended and smooth. Taste it. Do you want a bit more mustard? A little salt and pepper? A dash more Tabasco? Go ahead and add it.

2. When it's so good you want to cry, put it in a pretty dish and chill it. Then pass it around and let each diner drop a good, rounded tablespoonful (15 g) over each serving of freshly grilled or broiled steak.

3. Optional: If you're fancier than me, you can put your steak butter on a piece of waxed paper, form it into a cylinder, wrap it up, and chill it. Then, you can cut neat pats to put on steaks. I'd only do that if I were really, really trying to impress somebody—really, the taste is impressive enough.

YIELD: 12 servings of roughly 1 tablespoon (15 ml), **each with:** 170 Calories; 17 g Fat (88.7% calories from fat); 4 g Protein; 1 g Carbohydrate; trace Dietary Fiber; 1 g net carbs

PLATTER SAUCE FOR STEAK

I like pan-broiling steak—I cook it in a little bacon grease or oil in a hot iron skillet. When it's done to your liking, put it on a platter and give it 5 minutes for the juices to settle, while you make this sauce! Not only does it taste great, but it adds healthy fats, increasing ketogenicity.

2 tablespoons (28 g) butter

1 teaspoon dry mustard

½ teaspoon Worcestershire sauce

½ teaspoon salt or Vege-Sal

½ teaspoon pepper

1. Melt the butter in the pan and then stir in the dry mustard, Worcestershire sauce, salt, and pepper, stirring it around so you scrape up the nice brown bits from the pan.

2. Let it bubble a minute, pour it over hot steak, and serve.

YIELD: 3 servings, each with: 72 Calories; 8 g Fat (95.8% calories from fat); trace Protein; trace Carbohydrate; trace Dietary Fiber; 0 net carbs

GARLIC BUTTER STEAK

And you thought garlic butter was only good on bread! Use rib eye, strip, T-bone, sirloin, whatever you favor. The fat percentage will vary a little, but not the carb count.

4 tablespoons (55 g) butter, softened

1½ pounds (680 g) steak

1 or 2 cloves of garlic, crushed

1. Blend the butter with the garlic. (A food processor is good for this, but not essential.)
2. Broil, grill, or pan-broil your steak. Melt a tablespoon (about 15 g) of garlic butter over each serving.

YIELD: 3 servings, each with: 476 Calories; 41 g Fat (79.0% calories from fat); 25 g Protein; trace Carbohydrate; trace Dietary Fiber; 0 g net carbs

MARINATED SIRLOIN

Since writing the original edition, I have become a fan of marinating chuck to make it tender and broil- or grill-able. The resulting steak has great flavor for a bargain price. Feel free to add a teaspoon of meat tenderizer to this marinade and use it to marinate a chuck steak. If you do this, pierce the chuck all over with a fork before putting it in the marinade.

1 cup (235 ml) water

½ tablespoon wine vinegar

½ cup (120 ml) soy sauce

1½ tablespoons (23 ml) lemon juice

3 tablespoons (45 ml) Worcestershire sauce

1 tablespoon (15 g) spicy brown or Dijon mustard

½ of a medium onion, finely minced

2 cloves of garlic, crushed

1½ tablespoons (23 ml) balsamic vinegar

2 pounds (910 g) sirloin steak, 1 inch (2.5 cm) thick

1. Combine the water, soy sauce, Worcestershire sauce, onion, balsamic vinegar, wine vinegar, lemon juice, mustard, and garlic in a large measuring cup or bowl with a pouring lip. This is your marinade.
2. Place the steak in a large, zipper-lock bag, pour in the marinade, and seal the bag. Place it in a flat pan (in case the bag springs a leak) and stick the whole thing in the fridge for at least several hours or overnight if you have the time.
3. About 15 minutes before you're ready to cook, remove your steak from the bag and then broil or grill it to your liking.

YIELD: 4 servings, each with: 501 Calories; 32 g Fat (57.5% calories from fat); 44 g Protein; 8 g Carbohydrate; 1 g Dietary Fiber; 7 g net carbs. Your steak will actually have considerably less carbohydrate than this, since you discard most of the marinade.

BEEF

TERIYAKI STEAK

This is tasty as is. It's also terrific served over a salad. What a great supper for a hot summer night!

2 pounds (910 g) thinly cut, lean, boneless steak, such as London broil or flank steak

1 batch of Teriyaki Sauce (page 280)

1. Put your steak in a large zipper-lock bag and pour the Teriyaki Sauce over it. Squeeze out the extra air, seal the bag, and let the steak marinate for at least a half an hour or overnight if you have the time.

2. When you're ready to cook the steak, pour the marinade into a small saucepan. Grill or broil (page 220) the steak quickly with high heat.

3. While the steak is cooking, boil the marinade at a complete, rolling boil for a few minutes.

4. When the steak is done, slice it thin, across the grain. Serve with the boiled marinade.

YIELD: 6 servings, each with: 467 Calories; 36 g Fat (71.9% calories from fat); 28 g Protein; 3 g Carbohydrate; trace Dietary Fiber; 3 g net carbs

STEAK AU POIVRE WITH BRANDY CREAM

This dish is for pepper lovers only! It is written for two because it struck me as a perfect stay-at-home date night dish.

¾ pound (340 g) tender, well-marbled steak (such as rib eye, NY strip, or T-bone), ½ to ¾ inch (1.3 to 2 cm) thick

4 teaspoons (8 g) coarse-cracked pepper

1 tablespoon (14 g) butter

1 tablespoon (15 ml) olive oil

2 tablespoons (28 ml) brandy

2 tablespoons (28 ml) heavy cream

Salt

1. Place your steak on a plate, and sprinkle 2 teaspoons of the pepper evenly over it. Using clean hands or the back of a spoon, press the pepper firmly into the steak's surface. Turn the steak over and do the same thing to the other side.

2. Add the butter and olive oil to a large, heavy skillet over high heat. When the skillet is hot, add your steak. For a ½-inch (1.3 cm)-thick steak, 4½ minutes per side is about right; go maybe 5½ minutes for a ¾-inch (2 cm)-thick steak.

3. When the steak is done on both sides, turn off the burner, pour the brandy over it, and light it on fire.

4. When the flames die down, remove the steak to a serving platter and pour the heavy cream into the skillet. Stir it around, dissolving the meat juices and brandy into it. Salt lightly and pour the sauce over the steak.

YIELD: 2 servings, each with: 496 Calories; 34 g Fat (66.1% calories from fat); 36 g Protein; 3 g Carbohydrate; 1 g Dietary Fiber; 2 g net carbs

BASIL BEEF STIR-FRY

Basil in stir-fries is a Thai touch, but this isn't hot, as most Thai food is. This would be good served over Miracle Rice, prepared according to the instructions on page 23, but it's fine as is.

1 pound (455 g) boneless chuck

½ cup (120 ml) peanut oil or other bland oil, divided

6 scallions, including the crisp part of the green, cut into 1-inch (2.5 cm) lengths

2 tablespoons (5 g) chopped fresh basil or 2 teaspoons dried basil

1 tablespoon (15 ml) soy sauce

1–2 drops of liquid stevia, monkfruit, or sucralose

Pepper

1. Thinly slice the beef across the grain. This is easiest if it's half-frozen.

2. Put the oil in a wok or heavy skillet over high heat. When it's hot, add the beef and stir-fry for a minute or two. Add the scallions and stir-fry for another 3 to 4 minutes or until all the pink is gone from the beef.

3. Add the basil, soy sauce, sweetener, and pepper to taste and toss with the beef, cooking just another minute or so.

YIELD: 3 servings, each with: 647 Calories; 60 g Fat (83.0% calories from fat); 25 g Protein; 3 g Carbohydrate; 1 g Dietary Fiber; 2 g net carbs

BEEF BURGUNDY

This is a handy one-dish company meal. Put it together on a Saturday morning, and it will cook happily by itself all afternoon. I'd pair this with a salad with French Vinaigrette Dressing (page 162), a baguette for the carb-eaters, and more wine! By the way, after five hours, there's not a lot of alcohol left in this. You can serve it to kids if you—and they—like.

¼ cup (60 ml) olive oil

2 pounds (910 g) boneless beef round or chuck, cut into 2-inch (5 cm) cubes

1 cup (235 ml) dry red wine (Pinot noir is from the same varietal as burgundy. Cabernet or Shiraz will also serve.)

¾ teaspoon guar or xanthan

1½ teaspoons salt or Vege-Sal

1 teaspoon paprika

1 teaspoon dried oregano

1 big onion, sliced

8 ounces (225 g) mushrooms, wiped clean with a damp cloth

2 green peppers, cut into chunks

1. Preheat the oven to 250°F (120°C, or gas mark ½).

2. Put the olive oil in a heavy skillet over medium-high heat and brown the beef in the oil.

3. Put the browned beef in a 10-cup (2.4 L) casserole with a lid.

4. Combine the wine and guar in the blender, blending for 10 seconds or so, and then pour the mixture over the beef.

5. Add the salt, paprika, oregano, onion, mushrooms, and green peppers to the casserole and give it a quick stir.

6. Cover and put it in the oven for 5 hours. When it comes out, you can boil down the liquid a bit in a saucepan to make it thicker, if you like, but it's quite nice just like this.

YIELD: 6 servings, each with: 452 Calories; 33 g Fat (69.7% calories from fat); 25 g Protein; 7 g Carbohydrate; 2 g Dietary Fiber; 5 g net carbs

Regarding Slow Cookers

Slow cookers are tremendously useful for folks who work all day, but it can be hard to find the time to assemble everything before you get out of the house in the morning. Here's the solution: Put together your slow-cooker recipe the night before. If your slow cooker is like mine, it has a removable crockery liner. Just plunk all of your ingredients into this, cover it, and stick it in the refrigerator. When you get up in the morning, slip that crockery liner into your microwave—I have to turn the lid upside down to make mine fit—and nuke it on half-power for about 10 minutes to take off the chill. Slip the crockery liner back into the base unit, set the slow cooker, and you're good to go.

If you can't fit your crockery liner in your microwave, figure an extra hour of slow cooking to make up for the chill. And you know not to take the lid off of your slow cooker while it's cooking, right? Every time you do this, you slow down the cooking by about 30 minutes! Just figure that your food hasn't disappeared or anything and leave it alone until dinnertime.

GOOD LOW-CARB SLOW-COOKED SHORT RIBS

Another recipe adapted from my professional idol, Peg Bracken. This recipe gives you tremendously tasty ribs in a thin but flavorful sauce—it's more like a broth. If you'd like, you could put about 1 cup (235 ml) of the sauce through the blender with ¾ teaspoon or so of guar or xanthan to thicken it, but I like it as is. Add another pound (455 g) of short ribs and you can serve 7. There's no need to up the rest of the ingredients.

1 can (8 ounces, or 225 g) of plain tomato sauce

¾ cup (175 ml) water

2 tablespoons (28 ml) wine or cider vinegar

4 tablespoons (60 ml) soy sauce

Liquid stevia, monkfruit, or sucralose to equal 2 teaspoons sugar in sweetness

3–4 pounds (1.4–1.8 kg) beef short ribs

1 large onion

1. In a bowl, mix together the tomato sauce, water, vinegar, soy sauce, and sweetener.

2. Put the ribs in the slow cooker. Slice the onion, and place it on top of the ribs. Pour the sauce over the onion and ribs.

3. Set the slow cooker on Low and cook for 7 to 8 hours.

YIELD: **5 servings, each with:** 594 Calories; 33 g Fat (51.1% calories from fat); 64 g Protein; 7 g Carbohydrate; 1 g Dietary Fiber; 6 g net carbs. Total carbs will vary with how much of the sauce you eat, since most of the carbs are in there.

NEW ENGLAND BOILED DINNER

This is our traditional Saint Patrick's Day dinner, but it's a simple, satisfying one-pot meal on any chilly night. If you have carb-eaters in the family, you can add a few little red boiling potatoes, still in their jackets, to this. Oh, and just recently I've learned how good cooked radishes are! A 1-pound (455 g) bag of radishes, halved, can substitute for the turnips. You'll be surprised!

6 small turnips (golf ball to tennis ball size)

2 big ribs of celery, cut into chunks

2 medium onions, cut into chunks

1 corned beef "for simmering" (about 3 pounds [1.4 kg])

½ of a head of cabbage

FOR SERVING

Spicy brown mustard

Horseradish

Butter

This is easy, but it takes a long time to cook. Do yourself a favor and assemble it ahead of time.

1. Peel the turnips and throw them into the slow cooker, along with the celery and the onions. Set your corned beef on top and add water to cover.

2. There will be a seasoning packet with your corned beef. Dump it into the slow cooker. Put the lid on the slow cooker, set it on Low, and leave it alone for 10 to 12 hours. (You can cut the cooking time down to 6 to 8 hours if you set the slow cooker on High, but the Low setting yields the most tender results.)

3. When you come home from work all those hours later, remove the corned beef from the cooker with a fork or some tongs, put the lid back on the slow cooker to retain heat, put the beef on a platter, and keep it someplace warm. Cut your cabbage into big wedges, and drop it into the slow cooker with the other vegetables.

4. Re-cover the slow cooker and turn it up to High. Have a green light beer while the cabbage cooks for 30 minutes.

5. With a slotted spoon, scoop out the vegetables and pile them around the corned beef on a platter. Serve with the mustard and horseradish as condiments for the beef and butter for the vegetables.

YIELD: 8 servings, each with: 385 Calories; 25 g Fat (59.8% calories from fat); 27 g Protein; 12 g Carbohydrate; 4 g Dietary Fiber; 8 g net carbs

BEEF IN BEER

The tea, the beer, and the long, slow cooking make this as tender as can be. To keep the carbs super low, use the lowest-carb light beer available: Michelob Ultra, Miller Lite, or Milwaukee's Best Light. To keep it gluten-free, use Corona Light. It's good served with Cauliflower Purèe (page 112) or Fauxtatoes Deluxe (page 112). Oh, and feel free to use fresh mushrooms if you prefer.

Salt and pepper

2 pounds (901 g) boneless beef round roast

Olive oil

1 medium onion, sliced

1 can (8 ounces, or 225 g) of plain tomato sauce

1 can (12 ounces, or 360 ml) of light beer

1 teaspoon instant tea powder

1 can (4 ounces, or 115 g) of mushrooms, drained

2 cloves of garlic, crushed

Guar or xanthan (optional)

1. Salt and pepper the beef on both sides.

2. Heat a few tablespoons (45–60 ml) of olive oil in a heavy skillet over medium-high heat and sear the meat until it's brown all over. Place the meat in a slow cooker.

3. In the oil left in the skillet, sauté the onion for a few minutes and add that to the slow cooker, too.

4. Now, pour the tomato sauce and beer over the beef. Sprinkle the instant tea over it and throw in the mushrooms and garlic.

5. Put the lid on the slow cooker, set it on Low, and let it cook for 8 to 9 hours. Thicken the sauce a little with your guar shaker if you feel it needs it.

YIELD: 6 servings, each with: 356 Calories; 24 g Fat (63.2% calories from fat); 25 g Protein; 6 g Carbohydrate; 1 g Dietary Fiber; 5 g net carbs

PEKING SLOW-COOKER POT ROAST

This sounds nuts, but tastes great! It takes starting ahead, but it's not a lot of work and makes enough for a crowd.

Warning: Do not try to make this with a tender cut of beef! This recipe will tenderize the toughest cut; a tender one will practically dissolve. Use inexpensive, tough cuts and prepare to be amazed at how fork-tender they get. (I have no idea why this is "Peking" roast; I see little that's Chinese about it. I adapted this from a recipe from the early 60s, and that's what they called it.)

5 pounds (2.3 kg) beef roast (round, chuck, or rump)

5 or 6 cloves of garlic

8 ounces (225 ml) cider vinegar

8 ounces (225 ml) water

1 small onion

1½ cups (355 ml) strong coffee (Instant mixed with water works fine.)

1 teaspoon guar or xanthan

Salt and pepper

1. At least 24 to 36 hours before you want to actually cook your roast, stick holes in the meat with a thin-bladed knife, cut your garlic cloves into slices, and insert a slice into each hole. Put your garlic-studded roast in a big, nonreactive bowl—stainless steel, ceramic, or glass—and pour the vinegar and water over it. Put it in the fridge and let it sit there for a day or so, turning it over when you think of it so the whole thing marinates.

2. On the morning of the day you want to serve your roast, pour off the marinade—it can go down the sink—and put your roast in your slow cooker. Thinly slice your onion and put it on top of the roast. Pour the coffee over the roast and onion, put on the lid, set the cooker on Low, and leave it alone for 8 hours for a smaller roast or up to 10 hours for a larger one.

3. When you're ready to eat, remove your roast from the cooker carefully because it will now be so tender it's likely to fall apart.

4. Scoop out 2 cups (475 ml) of the liquid and some of the onions and put them in the blender with the guar. Blend for few seconds and then pour into a saucepan set over high heat. Boil this sauce hard for about 5 minutes, to reduce it a bit. Salt and pepper the sauce to taste. (It's amazing the difference the salt and pepper make, here; I didn't like the flavor of this sauce until I added the salt and pepper, and then I liked it a lot.)

5. Slice and serve your roast with this sauce.

YIELD: 12 servings, each with: 403 Calories; 30 g Fat (67.1% calories from fat); 30 g Protein; 3 g Carbohydrate; trace Dietary Fiber; 3 g net carbs

REUBEN CORNED-BEEF CASSEROLE

This recipe comes from my pal Diana Lee, of *Baking Low-Carb* fame. It's great for using up leftover corned beef, or you could buy some from the deli.

8 ounces (225 g) fresh corned beef, shredded

2 eggs

½ cup (115 g) mayonnaise

½ cup (120 ml) heavy whipping cream

1 teaspoon dehydrated onion

½ teaspoon dry mustard

2 teaspoons caraway seeds

⅔ cup (95 g) sauerkraut

2 cups (220 g) shredded Swiss cheese

1. Preheat the oven to 375°F (190°C, or gas mark 5).

2. Grease a 6-cup (1.4 L) casserole and place the corned beef in the bottom of it.

3. In a bowl, combine the eggs, mayonnaise, whipping cream, dehydrated onion, dry mustard, and caraway seeds. Drain and rinse the sauerkraut and add it to the mayonnaise mixture.

4. Pour the mayo mixture over the corned beef and sprinkle the cheese on top. Bake covered for 30 minutes and then uncover and bake for an additional 15 minutes.

YIELD: 4 servings, each with: 670 Calories; 61 g Fat (79.9% calories from fat); 29 g Protein; 6 g Carbohydrate; 1 g Dietary Fiber; 5 g net carbs

Anglo-Saxon Soul Food, a.k.a. Roast Beef and Yorkshire Pudding

For those of us of English descent, this is the taste of the Sunday dinners of our childhood. These three recipes will impress the heck out of your family and friends.

THE NOBLE BEEF

From the price of prime rib these days, I suspect they're feeding the steers pure gold. Still, this will cost you just a little more than buying one slice of prime rib in a restaurant.

4 pounds (1.8 kg) beef standing rib roast	**¼ cup (60 ml) oil**

1. Preheat the oven to 550°F (288°C).

2. Have the beef at room temperature and rub it all over with the oil. Put it on a rack in a roasting pan, fatty-side up. Stick a meat thermometer in it, deep in the center, but not touching a bone.

3. Put the roast in the oven and immediately turn the heat down to 350°F (180°C, or gas mark 4). Beef generally takes about 20 minutes per pound (455 g) to come out medium-rare, so figure on about 1 hour and 20 minutes to cook this roast. Check that meat thermometer, though; I've had a roast surprise me more than once. When the thermometer reads between 140° (60°C; rare) and 160°F (71°C; almost well-done), take it out, put it on a platter in a warm place, and let it sit for a bit while you bake the Yorkshire pudding. (Keep in mind that that thermometer will continue to climb a bit as the roasts rests.)

YIELD: 8 servings, each with: 771 Calories; 68 g Fat (80.5% calories from fat); 37 g Protein; 0 g Carbohydrate; 0 g Dietary Fiber; 0 g net carbs

YORKSHIRE PUDDING

For the uninitiated, this is just a big popover flavored with beef drippings. Have the wet and dry ingredients assembled and ready to go when your beef comes out of the oven, or your roast will cool while you're making this.

My tester, Arleen, made individual puddings in a muffin tin (a popover tin would be even better!) instead of one big one in a skillet or pie plate. She greased it with olive oil and put it in the oven to heat as she made the batter. She also made the batter in her blender—just put every from the almond meal through the half-and-half in her blender and ran it. Having, like me, grown up on Yorkshire pudding, Arleen proclaimed these "really good."

¼ cup (60 ml) beef drippings (both the fat and the nice brown juice, mixed)

½ cup (56 g) almond meal

¼ cup (20 g) unflavored whey protein powder

1 teaspoon salt or Vege-Sal

4 eggs

2 teaspoons olive oil

1 cup (235 ml) half-and-half

1. Preheat the oven to 425°F (220°C, or gas mark 7). It is essential that the oven be all the way up to temperature before you put in your Yorkshire pudding or it won't puff up the way it should, so turn up the oven when you're taking out the roast.

2. Spray a large, cast-iron skillet or a 10-inch (25 cm) pie pan with nonstick cooking spray and then put the beef drippings in it and tilt the pan to cover the whole bottom. Set aside.

3. In a bowl, combine the almond meal, protein powder, and salt, stirring them together.

4. In a separate bowl, combine the eggs, olive oil, and half-and-half.

5. When the oven is up to temperature, whisk the liquid ingredients well for at least 1 minute; 2 wouldn't hurt. Add the dry ingredients and whisk just until everything is well combined.

6. Pour the mixture into the prepared pan and bake for 20 minutes. Turn the oven down to 350°F (180°C, or gas mark 4) and give it another 5 minutes or so. Cut into wedges and serve with Beef Gravy (page 231) or butter.

YIELD: 8 servings, each with: 145 Calories; 9 g Fat (53.8% calories from fat); 12 g Protein; 5 g Carbohydrate; trace Dietary Fiber; 5 g net carbs

BEEF GRAVY

Faced with leftover roast beef and no gravy I came up with this, and it's as good as any beef gravy I've ever had. If you have any nice, brown beef juices from your roast, they can only improve it further, but be sure to skim off the fat before adding them, as it will ruin the texture of your gravy.

The first ingredient in Gravy Master is sugar. It also includes soy and corn. Skip it if you wish. But this quantity adds <1 gram of carbohydrate to the entire recipe, so it should have exactly no effect on your blood sugar when you eat one serving of gravy. Gravy Master is gluten-free.

1 can (14½ ounces, or 410 g) of beef broth

2 tablespoons (28 ml) dry red wine

1 teaspoon beef bouillon concentrate

1 tablespoon (10 g) finely minced onion

1 small clove of garlic, crushed

¾ teaspoon guar or xanthan

⅓ cup (80 ml) heavy cream

¼ teaspoon Gravy Master or similar gravy seasoning/coloring liquid

Salt and pepper

1. In a heavy saucepan, combine the beef broth, wine, bouillon concentrate, onion, and garlic. Bring this to a boil over medium heat and let it boil until reduced to one-third the original volume. (This will take at least 15 to 20 minutes.)

2. When the mixture is reduced, pour it into a blender (if you're not sure your blender will take the heat, let it cool for 5 to 10 minutes first), turn it on, and add the guar. If you prefer, leave it in the pan and use your stick blender. Either way, blend for 15 to 30 seconds or so. If you've used a stand blender, pour the mixture back into the saucepan and turn the heat back on to low. Either way, whisk in the heavy cream and the gravy seasoning liquid.

3. Season with salt and pepper to taste, heat through, and serve.

YIELD: 8 servings of 2 tablespoons (28 ml), each with: 51 Calories; 4 g Fat (68.1% calories from fat); 3 g Protein; 1 g Carbohydrate; trace Dietary Fiber; 1 g net carbs

GINGER BEEF

This is my favorite thing to do with a chuck pot roast. It has a bright flavor full of tomato, fruit, and ginger.

3 tablespoons (45 ml) olive oil

3 pounds (1.4 kg) boneless chuck or round roast, about 2 inches (5 cm) thick

1 small onion

1 clove of garlic, crushed

1 can (14½ ounces, or 410 g) of diced tomatoes

Liquid stevia, monkfruit, or sucralose to equal 1 tablespoon (13 g) of sugar in sweetness

1 teaspoon ground ginger

¼ cup (60 ml) cider vinegar

1. Place the olive oil in a large, heavy skillet and brown the roast in it over medium-high heat. When both sides are well-seared, add the onion, garlic, and tomatoes.

2. In a bowl, stir the sweetener and ginger into the vinegar and add that mixture to the skillet, stirring to combine.

3. Cover the skillet, turn the burner to low, and let the whole thing simmer for about 1¼ hours.

4. Serve with the vegetables piled on top.

YIELD: 6 servings, each with: 556 Calories; 42 g Fat (69.3% calories from fat); 37 g Protein; 6 g Carbohydrate; 1 g Dietary Fiber; 5 g net carbs

YANKEE POT ROAST

This old-time favorite is just as good as you remember. Why use low-sodium beef broth? Not because we're afraid of salt, but because it's going to cook down some, and you don't want the final result to be too salty. Salt it when it's done.

3 pounds (1.4 kg) beef chuck roast or arm roast

¼ cup (60 ml) olive oil

8 ounces (225 g) mushrooms, sliced—buy 'em that way!

1 medium onion, sliced

1 large celery rib, sliced

2 small turnips, peeled and chunked

1 medium carrot, peeled and sliced

2 cups (475 ml) low-sodium beef broth

½ cup (30 g) chopped fresh parsley

1 teaspoon beef bouillon concentrate

Guar or xanthan

Salt and pepper

1. In a Dutch oven over medium heat, brown the beef on all sides in the olive oil. Remove the roast from the Dutch oven and reserve on a plate.

2. Cut up all the vegetables and put 'em in the Dutch oven. Set the roast on top and pour in the beef broth.

3. Cover the Dutch oven and put it over a very low burner. Let it simmer for 1½ to 2 hours. Stir in the parsley and let it cook 5 more minutes.

4. Remove the meat to a platter. Use a slotted spoon to scoop out about three-quarters of the vegetables and put them on the platter or in a serving dish, as you prefer.

5. Use a stick blender to blend the vegetables remaining in the pot into the broth. Blend in the bouillon concentrate and then use your guar shaker to thicken the gravy to the consistency of heavy cream. Season with salt and pepper to taste. Done!

YIELD: 6 servings, each with: 607 Calories; 45 g Fat (66.9% calories from fat); 41 g Protein; 9 g Carbohydrate; 2 g Dietary Fiber; 7 g net carbs

CHAPTER 10

Pork and Lamb

Americans eat more chicken and beef than any other meats, but pork is still quite popular, and with good reason: It's tasty and inexpensive. If you still think of pork as being very fatty, think again. The low-fat craze has dramatically affected pork breeding and feeding, and most pork is now very lean. This means you'll want to take care not to overcook your pork, or it may well end up dry. It also means that most pork is less flavorful than the pork of yore; you'll want to season it well. This chapter will show you how.

You also should take advantage of the low prices on fatty cuts of pork, such as shoulder, butt roast, and spare ribs! As I write this, a local grocery store has pork shoulder roasts at $1.49 per pound (455 g).

As for lamb, I've never understood why it isn't more popular in this country. It's one of the most widely eaten meats in the rest of the world. I grew up eating lamb, and I adore it. If you haven't tried it, you simply must. Unfortunately, because so little lamb is eaten in the United States, it is something of a specialty item, and the prices reflect this. If you love lamb—or learn to love it—keep an eye out for sales. When the price of lamb drops in the spring, I buy a leg or two and have it sliced into steaks about ¾ inch (2 cm) thick. They're cheaper and meatier than lamb chops, plus you get a little bonus of marrow in the bone—yum!

It's also good to know that virtually all lamb is grass-fed.

PORK CHOPS WITH MUSTARD CREAM SAUCE

Here's something good to do with pork chops, now that you're not breading them. How about cabbage or Brussels sprouts with these?

Salt or Vege-Sal	¼ cup (60 ml) dry white wine
Pepper	
4 pork chops (6 ounces, or 170 g each)	¼ cup (60 ml) heavy cream
	¼ cup (60 g) spicy brown mustard or Dijon mustard
¼ cup (60 ml) olive oil	

1. Salt and pepper the pork chops on both sides.
2. Heat the olive oil in a heavy skillet over medium heat. Sauté the chops until they're browned on both sides and done through. (Depending on the size of your skillet, this may take a couple of batches.) Put the chops on a serving platter and keep them warm.
3. Put the wine in the skillet and stir it around, scraping all the tasty brown bits off the pan as you stir. Stir in the heavy cream and mustard, blend well, and cook for a minute or two. Serve the chops with the sauce.

YIELD: 4 servings, each with: 458 Calories; 37 g Fat (74.0% calories from fat); 28 g Protein; 2 g Carbohydrate; trace Dietary Fiber; 2 g net carbs

ITALIAN HERB PORK CHOPS

Not all Italian food involves pasta, tomato sauce, or cheese. These take a little over an hour, but aren't much work. And you can use that time to make a salad or steam some asparagus, not to mention sip a little of the leftover wine.

4 cloves of garlic, crushed	2 teaspoons dried, powdered rosemary
4 pork chops, 1 inch (2.5 cm) thick	Salt or Vege-Sal
2 teaspoons dried, powdered sage	½ cup (60 ml) dry white wine

1. Rub the crushed garlic into both sides of your pork chops.
2. In a bowl, mix the sage and rosemary together and sprinkle this evenly over both sides of the pork chops, as well. Sprinkle lightly with the salt or Vege-Sal.
3. Place the chops in a heavy skillet and add water just up to the top edge of the pork chops. Cover the skillet, turn the burner to low, and let the chops simmer for about 1 hour or until the water has all evaporated.
4. Once the water is gone, the chops will start to brown. Turn them once or twice to get them browned on both sides. The pork chops will be very tender, so use a spatula and be careful. If they break a little, they will still taste great.
5. Remove the pork chops to a serving platter and pour the wine into the skillet. Turn up the burner to medium-high and stir the wine around, scraping up the stuck-on brown bits from the pan. Bring this to a boil and let it boil hard for a minute or two to reduce it just a little. Pour this sauce over the pork chops and serve.

YIELD: 4 servings, each with: 290 Calories; 17 g Fat (57.3% calories from fat); 26 g Protein; 2 g Carbohydrate; trace Dietary Fiber; 2 g net carbs

PORK CHOPS AND SAUERKRAUT

If you have a can of sauerkraut in the cupboard, this is a handy sort of a meal. You can substitute chicken broth for the wine if you prefer.

3 slices of bacon

3 pork chops, 1 inch (2.5 cm) thick

1 small onion, chopped

1 can (14½ ounces, or 410 g) of sauerkraut, drained

36 drops of liquid stevia–English toffee

¼ teaspoon dry mustard

2 tablespoons (28 ml) dry white wine

1. Fry the bacon until just barely crisp in a heavy skillet over medium heat. Drain and set aside.

2. Pour off all but about 2 tablespoons (28 ml) of the grease and brown the chops in it over medium heat. (You want them to have just a little color on each side.) Remove from the skillet and set aside.

3. Put the onion, sauerkraut, liquid stevia, dry mustard, and wine in the skillet and stir for a moment to blend. Crumble in the bacon and stir again, just for a moment.

4. Place the chops on top of the sauerkraut mixture, turn the burner to low, and cover the pan. Simmer for 45 minutes.

YIELD: 3 servings, each with: 346 Calories; 20 g Fat (53.7% calories from fat); 30 g Protein; 9 g Carbohydrate; 4 g Dietary Fiber; 5 g net carbs

APPLE-GLAZED PORK CHOPS

My mom always served applesauce with pork chops, and it was a great combination. Ever since I stopped eating applesauce, I've been looking for a way to have this combination of flavors again. The combination of cider vinegar and sweetener does a great job.

2 tablespoons (28 ml) olive oil

2 pork chops, 1 inch (2.5 cm) thick (about 6 ounces, or 170 g each)

¼ cup (60 ml) cider vinegar

2 teaspoons erythritol/ stevia or erythritol/ monkfruit blend OR 2 teaspoons erythritol PLUS liquid stevia, monkfruit, or sucralose to equal 2 teaspoons of sugar in sweetness

½ teaspoon soy sauce

1 small onion, thinly sliced

1. Put the olive oil in a heavy skillet and brown the pork chops in the oil.

2. When both sides are brown, stir together the vinegar, sweetener, and soy sauce and pour the mixture over the chops. Scatter the onion on top.

3. Cover and turn the burner to low. Let the chops simmer, turning at least once, for 45 minutes or until the pan is almost dry.

4. Serve the chops with the onions and scrape all the nice, syrupy pan liquid over them.

YIELD: 2 servings, each with: 408 Calories; 30 g Fat (67.0% calories from fat); 27 g Protein; 7 g Carbohydrate; 1 g Dietary Fiber; 6 g net carbs

PORK AND LAMB

PORK CHOPS WITH GARLIC AND BALSAMIC VINEGAR

The balsamic vinegar gives these a tangy-sweet flavor. These are big chops, so they're big servings!

2 tablespoons (28 ml) olive oil

3 pork rib chop, sometimes called pork rib eyes, 2 inches (5 cm) thick

¾ cup (175 ml) chicken broth

3 tablespoons (45 ml) balsamic vinegar

3 cloves of garlic, crushed

¼ teaspoon guar or xanthan

1. Put the olive oil in a large, heavy skillet over medium-high heat and sear the chops in the oil until well-browned on both sides. Add the chicken broth, vinegar, and garlic.

2. Cover the skillet, turn the burner to low, and let the chops simmer for 1 hour. Remove the chops to a serving platter or serving plates.

3. Use your guar shaker to thicken the sauce a little and serve with the chops.

YIELD: 3 servings, each with: 443 Calories; 31 g Fat (65.1% calories from fat); 36 g Protein; 2 g Carbohydrate; trace Dietary Fiber; 2 g net carbs

ARTICHOKE-MUSHROOM PORK

This is wonderful, and it cooks quite quickly because you pound the pork thin. If you prefer, you can make this out of 4 pork chops with the bones cut out. Feel free to use olive oil if you want to make this dairy-free.

1½ pounds (680 g) boneless pork loin, cut into 4 slices across the grain

4 tablespoons (55 g) butter

1 small onion, sliced

1 clove of garlic, crushed

8 ounces (225 g) sliced mushrooms

1 can (14 ounces, or 395 g) of quartered artichoke hearts, drained

½ cup (120 ml) chicken broth

2 teaspoons Dijon or spicy brown mustard

1. Put a piece of pork into a heavy zipper-lock bag and pound with a meat tenderizer, hammer, dumbbell, or whatever blunt, heavy object comes to hand, until it is ¼ inch (6 mm) thick. Repeat for the remaining pieces of pork.

2. Melt 2 tablespoons (28 g) of the butter in a large, heavy skillet over medium heat and brown the meat on both sides, (about 4 minutes per side). You'll have to do them one or two at a time. Set the browned pork on a plate and keep it warm.

3. Add the rest of the butter to the skillet and add the onion, garlic, and mushrooms. Sauté until the mushrooms and onion are limp. Add the artichokes, chicken broth, and mustard and stir around to dissolve the tasty brown bits on the bottom of the skillet.

4. Add the pork back into the skillet (you'll have to stack it a bit), cover, and let simmer for about 5 minutes. Serve the pork with the vegetables spooned over the top.

YIELD: 4 servings, each with: 316 Calories; 18 g Fat (51.4% calories from fat); 26 g Protein; 12 g Carbohydrate; 1 g Dietary Fiber; 11 g net carbs

LOOED PORK

This is a great way to add a lot of flavor to the usually bland boneless pork loin. It's quite low fat, so serve it with a salad or vegetable dish with butter, oil, or mayonnaise.

1½ pounds (680 g) boneless pork loin, sliced about 1½ inches (4 cm) thick (You can also use tenderloin or even shoulder.)	**1 batch of Looing Sauce (page 281)** **Scallions, sliced** **Toasted sesame oil**

1. Put the pork in a slow cooker and pour the Looing Sauce over it. Cover the cooker and set it to Low. Forget about it for 8 to 9 hours.

2. At dinnertime, remove the pieces of pork from the Looing Sauce. Put each piece on a serving plate, scatter a few scallions over each serving, and top with a few drops of toasted sesame oil.

YIELD: 4 servings, each with: 145 Calories; 6 g Fat (37.9% calories from fat); 21 g Protein; 0 g Carbohydrate; 0 g Dietary Fiber; 0 g net carbs

MU SHU PORK

I hear from lots of people that they miss Chinese food, so here's a Chinese restaurant favorite, decarbed. Low-carb tortillas stand in here for mu shu pancakes, and they work fine. The carb count will, to a large degree, depend on that of your low-carb tortillas. This count is based on La Tortilla Factory brand low-carb tortillas. If you want to decarb this even further, just eat it with a fork and forget the tortillas.

Make sure you have everything cut up and ready to go before you cook a thing, and this recipe will be a breeze.

3 eggs, beaten	**3 scallions, sliced**
Peanut oil	**1 cup (104 g) bean sprouts**
½ cup (35 g) slivered mushrooms	**3 tablespoons (45 ml) soy sauce**
8 ounces (225 g) boneless pork loin, sliced across the grain and then cut into matchsticks	**2 tablespoons (28 ml) dry sherry** **4 low-carb tortillas**
1 cup (75 g) shredded napa cabbage	**Hoisin Sauce (page 274)**

1. First, in a wok or heavy skillet over high heat, scramble the eggs in a few tablespoons (45–60 ml) of the peanut oil until they're set but still moist. Remove and set aside.

2. Wipe the wok out if there's much egg clinging to it. Add another ¼ cup (60 ml) or so of peanut oil and heat. Add the pork and stir-fry until it's mostly done. Add the cabbage, scallions, and bean sprouts and stir-fry for 3 to 4 minutes. Add the eggs back into the wok and stir them in, breaking them into small pieces. Now, add the soy sauce and sherry and stir.

3. To serve, take a warmed, low-carb tortilla and smear about 2 teaspoons of Hoisin Sauce on it. Put about a quarter of the stir-fry mixture on the tortilla and wrap it up.

YIELD: 2 servings, each with: 362 Calories; 15 g Fat (32.4% calories from fat); 37 g Protein; 33 g Carbohydrate; 19 g Dietary Fiber; 14 g net carbs. The analysis does not include Hoisin Sauce.

ROBINSKY'S CABBAGE & SAUSAGE

Robin Wilkins says this makes a great one-plate meal. Just make sure you read the labels on the kielbasa carefully, as they vary widely in carb count. You can shortcut this by using bagged coleslaw mix instead of chopping your own cabbage.

2–3 tablespoons (28–45 g) butter, divided

1 medium onion, chopped

1 pound (455 g) Polska Kielbasa or similar low-carb sausage, sliced

1 head of cabbage, chopped

1. Divide the butter between two skillets. Sauté the onion and sausage in one and sauté the cabbage in the other. The cabbage will overwhelm your frying pan at first, but it will reduce in volume as it fries.

2. When cooked to the texture you like (I like mine tender-crisp), combine the contents of both skillets and toss.

YIELD: 3 servings, each with: 660 Calories; 53 g Fat (71.6% calories from fat); 25 g Protein; 23 g Carbohydrate; 8 g Dietary Fiber; 15 g net carbs

COUNTRY SAUSAGE SKILLET SUPPER

This is ridiculously simple—quick, too! And the family is likely to enjoy it. Feel free to substitute turkey sausage, if you prefer it, but you'll need to add a little oil or fat to the pan.

1 pound (455 g) bulk pork sausage, hot or mild

1 small onion, chopped

¾ cup (86 g) shredded Cheddar cheese

1. Crumble the sausage in a heavy skillet over medium heat. As the grease starts to cook out of it, add the onion.

2. Cook until the sausage is no longer pink and the onion is translucent. Pour off the grease, spread the sausage mixture evenly in the pan, and scatter the Cheddar cheese over the top.

3. Cover and return to the heat for a minute or two, until the cheese is melted, and serve.

YIELD: 3 servings, each with: 759 Calories; 70 g Fat (84.0% calories from fat); 25 g Protein; 5 g Carbohydrate; 1 g Dietary Fiber; 4 g net carbs

KIELBASA AND BRUSSELS SPROUTS

My sister Kim, who tested this recipe, just loved it. Sadly, this is the one recipe sent in by a reader that I can't credit–the original email is lost. My apologies to the inventor and my thanks. There is gluten-free kielbasa available; Johnsonville is one such brand.

1 pound (455 g) frozen Brussels sprouts	**1 pound (455 g) kielbasa, sliced into 1-inch (2.5 cm) pieces**

1. Preheat the oven to 350°F (180°C, or gas mark 4). Spray an 8- x 8-inch (20 x 20 cm) glass baking dish with nonstick cooking spray.

2. Place the frozen sprouts on the bottom of the prepared baking dish. Arrange the kielbasa over the sprouts, to let the juices flow over them.

3. Cover with foil and bake for 40 minutes. Remove the cover and bake for 15 additional minutes, if you like your kielbasa browned.

YIELD: 3 servings, each with: 531 Calories; 42 g Fat (69.7% calories from fat); 26 g Protein; 15 g Carbohydrate; 6 g Dietary Fiber; 9 g net carbs. This was analyzed for the average kielbasa, so you could knock off a few extra grams by choosing the lowest-carb kielbasa available.

POLYNESIAN PORK

This marinade works well with a pork roast, too, but of course it will take longer to roast. Be aware: Most soy sauce contains wheat and is therefore neither grain-nor gluten-free. I use San-J brand soy sauce, which is wheat-free. If you're avoiding even this form of soy, you can substitute coconut aminos, which are remarkably similar to soy sauce, though a little higher carb. If you're unafraid of artificial sweeteners and want to give this even more island flavor, use ¼ cup (60 ml) DaVinci pineapple flavor sugar-free syrup in place of the sweetener!

5 large pork chops, 1 to 1½ inches (2.5 to 4 cm) thick	**3 tablespoons (45 g) erythritol/stevia or erythritol/monkfruit blend OR erythritol, plus liquid stevia, monkfruit, or sucralose to equal 3 tablespoons (39 g) of sugar in sweetness**
½ cup (120 ml) soy sauce	
4 cloves of garlic, crushed	
	½ teaspoon molasses
	1½ teaspoons grated fresh ginger

1. Preheat the oven to 325°F (170°C, or gas mark 3).

2. Put the pork chops in a large zipper-lock bag.

3. Combine the soy sauce, garlic, sweetener, molasses, and ginger, mixing them in a blender for a second or two, if possible.

4. Pour the mixture into the bag with the pork. Seal the bag and let it sit for 20 minutes or so, turning once.

5. Remove the pork from the marinade, reserving the marinade in a small sauce pan. Bring the marinade to a complete, roilling boil for a few minutes.

6. Place the chops in a shallow roasting pan and bake for 60 to 90 minutes or until done through. Brush once or twice with the boiled marinade while cooking.

YIELD: 5 servings, each with: 371 Calories; 22 g Fat (55.4% calories from fat); 37 g Protein; 4 g Carbohydrate; trace Dietary Fiber; 4 g net carbs

SAUSAGE SKILLET MIX-UP

This is yet another recipe adapted from one in a Peg Bracken book. Hers had rice, of course, and fewer vegetables. This version is a super-yummy one-dish meal.

1 pound (455 g) bulk pork sausage, hot or mild

1 small onion, chopped

2 ribs of celery, chopped

1 green pepper, chopped

1 cup (235 ml) chicken broth

2 teaspoons chicken bouillon concentrate

2 tablespoons (28 ml) Worcestershire sauce

½ teaspoon pepper

3 cups (300 g) Cauliflower Rice (page 113), uncooked

1. Brown and crumble the sausage in a heavy skillet over medium-high heat. When the sausage is no longer pink, pour off the grease, add the remaining ingredients, and give the mixture a stir.

2. Turn the burner to low, cover the skillet, and let it simmer for 15 to 20 minutes or until the cauliflower is tender.

YIELD: 3 servings, each with: 710 Calories; 62 g Fat (78.3% calories from fat); 23 g Protein; 16 g Carbohydrate; 4 g Dietary Fiber; 12 g net carbs

Swap the cauliflower for 2 packets of Miracle Rice, prepared according to the instructions on page 33, and you'll get: 3 servings, each with: 685 Calories; 62 g Fat (80.9% calories from fat); 21 g Protein; 12 g Carbohydrate; 3 g Dietary Fiber; 9 g net carbs

COCIDO DE PUERCO

This Mexican-style pork stew is simply marvelous. Do use bony cuts of meat, as they're more flavorful—and cheaper, too.

3 pounds (1.4 kg) bony cuts of pork (Meaty pork neck bones are ideal.)

2 tablespoons (28 ml) olive oil

1 clove of garlic, crushed

1 large onion, sliced

1 large green pepper, diced

2 medium zucchini, cut into chunks

1 can (14½ ounces, or 410 g) of diced tomatoes

2 teaspoons cumin

2 teaspoons dried oregano

½ teaspoon red pepper flakes (optional)

1. In a heavy skillet over medium-high heat, sear the pork bones in the olive oil until they're brown all over.

2. Turn the heat to low and add the garlic, onion, green pepper, zucchini, tomatoes, cumin, oregano, and red pepper flakes.

3. Cover the skillet and let it simmer for 1 hour.

YIELD: 6 servings, each with: 476 Calories; 38 g Fat (72.1% calories from fat); 25 g Protein; 9 g Carbohydrate; 2 g Dietary Fiber; 7 g net carb. I could not find nutritional statistics for pork neck bones, so I calculated this based on ribs.

HAM SLICE WITH MUSTARD SAUCE

Baking a ham takes hours! A ham slice or ham steak is a great way to enjoy ham on a busy weeknight. How about broccoli with Cheese Sauce (page 273) with this? If you want this to be gluten-free, read the label on your ham.

Note that you need either the unflavored sweetener plus molasses or the English toffee stevia, not both.

2-3 tablespoons (28-45 ml) coconut oil, olive oil, or MCT oil

Ham steak, about 2 pounds (910 g)

½ cup (120 ml) water

3 tablespoons (33 g) prepared mustard–yellow hot dog mustard will serve, or (45 g) brown mustard

1½ tablespoons (23 g) erythritol OR 1½ tablespoons (23 g) erythritol plus liquid stevia, monkfruit, or sucralose to equal 1½ tablespoons (20 g) of sugar in sweetness flavor PLUS ¼ teaspoon blackstrap molasses OR 24 drops of liquid stevia–English toffee

Salt and pepper

1. Put the oil in a heavy skillet over medium heat and fry the ham steak until it is golden on both sides. Remove the ham from the skillet, set it on a platter, and keep it warm.

2. Pour the water into the skillet and stir it around, scraping up all the brown bits from the ham. Stir in the mustard, sweetener, molasses if using, and salt and pepper to taste.

3. Pour the sauce over the ham and serve.

YIELD: 5 servings, each with: 437 Calories; 31 g Fat (65.7% calories from fat); 36 g Protein; 1 g Carbohydrate; trace Dietary Fiber; 1 g net carbs

JERK PORK

This recipe is packed with hot, bright island flavor! I like a cold beer with this. I'd go with Corona Light (5 g) or Corona Premier (2.6 g), both gluten-free.

1 recipe Jerk Marinade (page 280)

6 pork chops, 1 inch (2.5 cm) thick (about 8 ounces, or 225 g each)

1. Smear the Jerk Marinade all over the chops, put the chops in a large zipper-lock bag, and refrigerate. Now, wash your hands really well—that marinade is hot!

2. Let the chops marinate for at least several hours or overnight.

3. When you're ready to cook, grill these chops slowly, well above a low charcoal fire or a gas grill set on Low. Broil them only if you must.

YIELD: 6 servings, each with: 426 Calories; 29 g Fat (62.9% calories from fat); 35 g Protein; 3 g Carbohydrate; 1 g Dietary Fiber; 2 g net carbs

WINTER NIGHT LAMB STEW

On a raw winter's night, sometimes you just want stew. Here's one with no potatoes, and you can make it in your big skillet.

3 tablespoons (45 ml) olive oil

1½ pounds (680 g) lean lamb stew meat, cut into chunks

1 cup (160 g) chopped onion

1½ cups (225 g) diced turnip

1½ cups (225 g) diced rutabaga

¾ cup (175 ml) beef broth

½ teaspoon guar or xanthan

½ teaspoon salt or Vege-Sal

¼ teaspoon pepper

1 bay leaf

3 cloves of garlic, crushed

1. Put the olive oil in a heavy skillet over medium-high heat and brown the lamb in the oil. Add the onion, turnip, and rutabaga.

2. Put the beef broth and guar in a blender and blend for a few moments. Pour the mixture into the skillet. (If you choose not to use a thickener, just add the broth directly to the skillet.) Add the salt, pepper, bay leaf, and garlic and stir.

3. Cover, turn the burner to low, and let simmer for 1 hour. Remove the bay leaf before serving.

YIELD: 4 servings, each with: 497 Calories; 39 g Fat (71.1% calories from fat); 26 g Protein; 10 g Carbohydrate; 2 g Dietary Fiber; 8 g net carbs

QUICK CURRIED LAMB

I invented this for a quick lunch for my husband one day when there just happened to be a hunk of lamb in the fridge that needed to be used. It was so good, I decided it was worth repeating.

3 tablespoons (45 g) butter

1 tablespoon (6 g) curry powder

1 clove of garlic

1 large onion

1 pound (455 g) lean lamb, cut in ½-inch (1.3 cm) cubes

Salt and pepper

1. Melt the butter in a heavy skillet over medium heat. Add the curry powder and stir for a minute or so.

2. Add the garlic, onion, and lamb. Sauté, stirring frequently, for 7 minutes or so, or until the lamb is done through. Salt and pepper to taste and serve.

YIELD: 3 servings, each with: 436 Calories; 37 g Fat (77.5% calories from fat); 21 g Protein; 4 g Carbohydrate; 1 g Dietary Fiber; 3 g net carbs

LAMB KEBABS

This is very simple and very Greek. Add a Greek salad, and there's dinner.

2 pounds (910 g) lean lamb, cut into 1-inch (2.5 cm) cubes	**1 clove of garlic, crushed**
	½ teaspoon dried oregano
½ cup (120 ml) olive oil	**2 small onions, quartered and divided into sections 2 layers thick**
¼ cup (60 ml) lemon juice	

1. Put the lamb cubes into a large, zipper-lock bag.

2. Mix together the olive oil, lemon juice, garlic, and oregano. Pour it over the lamb cubes in the bag and refrigerate it for an hour or two (or overnight, if possible).

3. When it's time to cook dinner, pour off the marinade into a sauce pan, and bring to a complete, rolling boil for a few minutes. Thread your lamb chunks on skewers, alternating the pieces of meat with a "layer" or two of the onion. You can grill these, if you like, or broil them 8 inches (20 cm) or so from the broiler. Turn the kebabs while they're cooking and brush once or twice with the boiled marinade.

4. Check for doneness by cutting into a chunk of meat after 10 minutes; they should be thoroughly cooked within 15 minutes.

YIELD: 6 servings, each with: 452 Calories; 38 g Fat (76.8% calories from fat); 22 g Protein; 4 g Carbohydrate; 1 g Dietary Fiber; 3 g net carbs

THYME-PERFUMED LAMB STEAKS

When leg of lamb goes on sale, I buy one or two and get them sliced ½ inch (1.3 cm) thick into steaks. This is one of the millions of quick and delicious ways to cook them!

1 lamb steak (6 to 8 ounces, or 170 to 225 g)	**2 teaspoons lemon juice**
2 teaspoons olive oil	**1 tablespoon (2 g) fresh thyme leaves, stripped from their stems**

1. Rub the lamb steak with the olive oil and then the lemon juice. Cover the lamb with the thyme leaves, letting it sit for at least a couple of hours so the thyme flavor permeates the lamb.

2. Broil close to the heat for 4 to 5 minutes per side or grill.

YIELD: 1 serving with: 433 Calories; 36 g Fat (76.2% calories from fat); 24 g Protein; 1 g Carbohydrate; trace Dietary Fiber; 1 g net carbs

MEDITERRANEAN LEG OF LAMB

Lamb makes a wonderful Sunday dinner roast. If you don't want to roast a whole leg of lamb at once because it's a lot of meat, ask the butcher to cut one leg into two roasts. Make half now and freeze the other half for another day. Make Lamb Gravy (page 224) to go with your roast lamb and serve it with some Cauliflower Rice (page 113). Or, try roasting halved radishes in the drippings around the lamb. They're so good and so very different from raw radishes.

(continued)

Leg of lamb (with or without the bone in)

1 cup (235 ml) dry red wine

1 cup (235 ml) olive oil, divided

5 cloves of garlic, crushed

3 tablespoons (45 ml) lemon juice

1 tablespoon (3 g) dried rosemary

1 tablespoon (3 g) dried oregano

1. Place your leg of lamb in a nonreactive pan large enough to hold it.

2. Combine the wine, ½ cup (120 ml) of the olive oil, 3 cloves of the garlic, and the lemon juice, rosemary, and oregano. Pour this marinade over the lamb and let the lamb sit in it for at least 5 to 6 hours, turning it from time to time.

3. When the time comes to cook your lamb, preheat the oven to 425°F (220°C, or gas mark 7). Remove the meat from the marinade and place it on a rack in a roasting pan. Leave the rosemary needles and bits of oregano clinging to it.

4. Combine the remaining olive oil and cloves of garlic and spoon this mixture over the lamb, coating the whole leg. Position the leg with the fat side up and insert a meat thermometer deep into the center of the thickest part of the meat, but don't let it touch the bone.

5. When the oven is up to temperature, put your roast in and set the timer for 10 minutes. After 10 minutes, turn the oven down to 350°F (180°C, or gas mark 4) and roast for about 30 minutes per pound of meat or until the meat thermometer registers 170° to 180°F (77 to 82°C).

6. Remove the lamb from the oven and let it sit for 15 to 20 minutes before carving.

YIELD: Assuming an 8-pound (3.6 kg) bone-in leg or a 6-pound (2.7 kg) boneless leg, figure 16 servings, each with: 546 Calories; 44 g Fat (74.9% calories from fat); 32 g Protein; 1 g Carbohydrate; trace Dietary Fiber; 1 g net carbs

LAMB GRAVY

The easiest way to skim drippings is to pour them into a large, heavy, zipper-lock bag. Seal the bag and tip it so one corner points down over the roasting pan. Let it hang this way for a minute or two until you see the fat float to the top and the good, flavorful, dark-colored pan juices at the bottom. Snip a tiny triangle off the bottom corner of the bag and let the juices run out. Grab the corner of the bag to stop the flow before the fat runs into the pan and either throw the bag and the grease away or let the grease flow into a clean jar to use for cooking.

Drippings from Mediterranean Leg of Lamb (page 243)

1 cup (235 ml) chicken broth, divided

¾ teaspoon guar or xanthan

Salt and pepper

1. Skim the fat off of the drippings from the roast. (Fat will ruin the texture of your gravy.)

2. Pour ½ cup (120 ml) of the chicken broth into the roasting pan with the skimmed drippings and stir it around, scraping up the yummy browned bits from the rack and the bottom of the pan. When most of the stuck-on stuff is dissolved into the broth, put the roasting pan over medium-high heat.

3. Put the rest of the chicken broth in a blender with the guar and run the blender for a few seconds to dissolve all of the thickener. Pour the thickened broth into the roasting pan and stir until all the gravy is thickened. (If it gets too thick, add a little more chicken broth; if it's not quite thick enough, let it simmer for a few minutes to cook down.)

4. Salt and pepper the gravy to taste and serve with the leg of lamb.

YIELD: Number of servings, calories, and fat will depend on how many drippings you have, but the whole batch will have: only 1 g carbs, all of them from fiber, so essentially 0 net carbs

CHAPTER 11

Main Dish Salads

I n the first edition of this book, I wrote: "I think main dish salads are one of the very best things for a low-carber to eat, because they offer infinite variety. Of course, they contain enough vegetables that you probably won't want to eat much else in the way of carbohydrates at that particular meal, but with all the flavor and eye appeal these salads offer, who needs anything else?"

I still love main dish salads, but they are a clear illustration that you can eat enough vegetables to take your carb count above ketogenic limits, depending, of course, on your body chemistry. So enjoy as your own personal body permits.

On the other hand, if you choose the lowest carb of these salads and make them with mayonnaise containing MCT oil, you're likely to find yourself in some pretty deep ketosis!

CHICKEN WALDORF SALAD

Measure your apple carefully, as it's the main source of carbs here. Want to make this into 3 to 4 servings, with fewer carbs and more fat? Add a package of Miracle Rice prepared according the instructions on page 23 and double the mayo.

1½ cups (210 g) diced cooked chicken	½ cup (60 g) chopped walnuts
½ cup (75 g) diced apple	⅓ cup (75 g) mayonnaise
2 big ribs of celery, diced	Salt to taste

Combine all the ingredients, mix well, and serve.

YIELD: 2 servings, each with: 841 Calories; 75 g Fat (77.2% calories from fat); 40 g Protein; 9 g Carbohydrate; 3 g Dietary Fiber; 6 g net carbs

CAJUN CHICKEN SALAD

This is not your average mayonnaise-based chicken salad. Serve on lettuce-lined plates and it'll present prettily, too.

2 boneless, skinless chicken breasts (a generous pound [455 g])	3 tablespoons (45 ml) tarragon vinegar
1 teaspoon Cajun Seasoning (store-bought, or see page 276)	1 teaspoon spicy brown or Dijon mustard
1 sweet red pepper, cut into small strips	1 clove of garlic, crushed
1 green pepper, cut into small strips	⅓ cup (80 ml) olive oil
¼ of a sweet red onion, thinly sliced	1 teaspoon dried tarragon
	Salt and black pepper

1. Place a chicken breast in a large, heavy zipper-lock bag and pound with a meat tenderizer, hammer, or whatever you have available until it's ¼ inch (6 mm) thick. Repeat with the second breast.

2. Sprinkle both sides of each pounded chicken breast with the Cajun Seasoning. Grill or sauté until cooked through.

3. Cut both chicken breasts in strips about ¼ inch (6 mm) wide. Combine with the red and green peppers and onion.

4. In a small bowl, combine the tarragon vinegar, mustard, garlic, olive oil, dried tarragon, and salt and pepper to taste; mix well. Pour over the chicken and vegetables and toss.

5. Serve right away or let it chill for several hours for the flavors to blend.

YIELD: 3 servings, each with: 385 Calories; 27 g Fat (63.6% calories from fat); 27 g Protein; 8 g Carbohydrate; 2 g Dietary Fiber; 6 g net carbs

DANA'S TUNA SALAD

My recipe for tuna salad has changed over the years! This is how I'm making it now. Do pop for the good tuna canned in olive oil! Again, if you want to stretch this, you can add shirataki—either Miracle Rice or tofu shirataki macaroni—and up the mayo.

2 large ribs of celery, or 3 small ones

¼ of a medium, sweet red onion

1 sugar-free bread-and-butter pickle spear

5 ounces (140 g) canned tuna in olive oil

⅓ cup (75 g) mayonnaise

1. Dice up the vegetables. I like them fairly chunky, so I get lots of crunchy texture.

2. Add the tuna and mayo and mix it up. Sometimes, I stuff it into a tomato, but it's awfully good just eaten with a fork, right out of the mixing bowl. (Hey, I'm home alone at lunchtime; I'm allowed to eat out of the mixing bowl.)

YIELD: This could feed 2, but most of the time I treat it as 1 serving. If you're nice enough to share, each serving will have: 417 Calories; 37 g Fat (77.2% calories from fat); 22 g Protein; 3 g Carbohydrate; 1 g Dietary Fiber; 2 g net carbs

CLASSIC EGG SALAD

Here's your lunch for the week after Easter. When the dye has soaked through the shell we call it Technicolor Egg Salad.

4 hard-boiled eggs, peeled and chopped

1 rib of celery, diced

5 or 6 scallions, sliced

½ of a green pepper, diced

⅓ cup (75 g) mayonnaise

½ teaspoon prepared mustard

Lettuce

Combine all the ingredients and serve on lettuce.

YIELD: 2 servings, each with: 447 Calories; 43 g Fat (83.4% calories from fat); 14 g Protein; 5 g Carbohydrate; 2 g Dietary Fiber; 3 g net carbs

JANE'S EGG SALAD

Jane was my mom, and this is how she made her egg salad. The olives give a whole new flavor, plus add healthy fats.

4 hard-boiled eggs, peeled and chopped

1 rib of celery, diced

5–6 scallions, sliced

5 green olives, chopped

⅓ cup (75 g) mayonnaise

Lettuce

Combine all the ingredients and serve on lettuce.

YIELD: 2 servings, each with: 446 Calories; 43 g Fat (83.5% calories from fat); 14 g Protein; 5 g Carbohydrate; 2 g Dietary Fiber; 3 g net carbs

CHICKEN PECAN SALAD

This is a good reason to cook an extra couple of pieces of chicken every time you're roasting some. It will keep you full for hours.

1½ cups (210 g) diced cooked chicken

2 big ribs of celery, diced

¼ of a medium, sweet red onion, diced

¼ cup (28 g) chopped pecans

⅓ cup (75 g) mayonnaise

Salt

Toss the chicken, celery, onion, pecans, and mayonnaise together. Salt to taste and serve.

YIELD: 2 servings, each with: 742 Calories; 67 g Fat (79.2% calories from fat); 34 g Protein; 6 g Carbohydrate; 2 g Dietary Fiber; 4 g net carbs

DILLED CHICKEN SALAD

This is wonderful when made with leftover turkey, too. You can serve this with lettuce leaves for wrapping, stuff it into a tomato, or just eat it straight.

1½ cups (210 g) diced cooked chicken

1 large rib of celery, diced

½ of a green pepper, diced

¼ of a medium, sweet red onion, diced

3 tablespoons (42 g) mayonnaise

3 tablespoons (45 g) sour cream

1 tablespoon (4 g) snipped fresh dill weed or 1 teaspoon dried dill weed

Salt

1. Combine the chicken, celery, green pepper, and onion in a bowl.
2. In a separate bowl, mix together the mayonnaise, sour cream, and dill. Pour the mixture over the chicken and veggies and toss.
3. Salt to taste and serve.

YIELD: 2 servings, each with: 579 Calories; 48 g Fat (73.6% calories from fat); 33 g Protein; 5 g Carbohydrate; 1 g Dietary Fiber; 4 g net carbs

CHEF'S SALAD

This is infinitely variable, of course. If you don't like something, skip it. I just needed fixed quantities to analyze. Also, you don't have to use deli meats. If, the week after Thanksgiving, you have leftover turkey and ham, why not make a chef's salad? Or the week after Easter, when you have ham and boiled eggs?

10 cups (470 g) romaine, (720 g) iceberg, (280 g) red leaf, or any other favorite lettuce

¼ pound (115 g) deli turkey breast

¼ pound (115 g) deli ham

¼ pound (115 g) deli roast beef

¼ pound (115 g) Swiss cheese

1 green pepper, cut into strips or rings

½ of a sweet red onion, cut into rings

4 hard-boiled eggs, halved or quartered

2 ripe tomatoes, cut vertically into 8 wedges each

Salad dressing

1. Make nice beds of the lettuce on 4 serving plates.
2. Cut the turkey, ham, roast beef, and Swiss cheese into strips. (It's nice, by the way, to get fairly thickly sliced meat and cheese for this.) Arrange all of this artistically on the beds of lettuce.
3. Garnish with the green pepper, onion, eggs, and tomatoes. Let each diner add his or her own dressing.

YIELD: 4 servings, each with: 405 Calories; 25 g Fat (54.3% calories from fat); 34 g Protein; 13 g Carbohydrate; 4 g Dietary Fiber; 9 g net carbs. These numbers do not include whatever salad dressing you choose, so the fat percentage will be higher—and it's already 54%.

MAIN DISH SALADS

CHICKEN CAESAR SALAD

In the 1990s, I was calling this "the ubiquitous chicken Caesar salad" because it was the one low-carb dish you could get at almost any restaurant. If you haven't had one recently, you'll be surprised at how much better it is made at home!

1 boneless, skinless chicken breast

2–3 cups (94–141 g) romaine lettuce, washed, dried, and broken up

2 tablespoons (28 ml) Caesar Dressing (bottled, or see page 169)

2 tablespoons (10 g) Parmesan cheese, shredded or in very thin slivers

1. Grill the chicken breast. (I do mine in an electric tabletop grill for about 5 minutes, but you could sauté it, if you prefer.)
2. While the chicken cooks, put the lettuce in a bowl, pour the Caesar Dressing over it, and toss well. Pile it on your serving plate.
3. Slice the cooked chicken breast into thin strips and pile it on top of the lettuce. Scatter the Parmesan cheese on top and dig in.

YIELD: 1 serving with: 480 Calories; 29 g Fat (55.5% calories from fat); 45 g Protein; 7 g Carbohydrate; 3 g Dietary Fiber; 4 g net carbs

Shrimp Caesar Salad

Make this just like Chicken Caesar Salad (above), but substitute 6 ounces (170 g) cooked shrimp for the chicken breast. Frozen, precooked, shelled shrimp are handy for this because they thaw quickly.

YIELD: 1 serving with: 460 Calories; 27 g Fat (55.2% calories from fat); 41 g Protein; 9 g Carbohydrate; 3 g Dietary Fiber; 6 g net carbs

SOUVLAKI SALAD

This skewered lamb is usually served as a sandwich in pita bread, but it makes a fabulous salad for a lot fewer carbs. If you don't have skewers, you can just lay the lamb cubes on your broiler pan, but it's a whole lot easier to turn them on skewers. Skip the yogurt or sour cream to make this dairy-free.

2 pounds (910 g) lamb shoulder or leg, in 1-inch (2.5 cm) cubes

½ cup (120 ml) olive oil

1 cup (235 ml) dry red wine

1 teaspoon salt

¼ teaspoon pepper

1 teaspoon oregano

3 cloves of garlic, crushed

1 head of romaine lettuce

¼ of a sweet red onion, sliced paper-thin

24 cherry tomatoes, halved

⅔ cup (160 ml) Greek Lemon Dressing (page 163)

6 tablespoons (90 g) plain, full-fat Greek yogurt or sour cream (The yogurt is more authentic.)

1. Put the lamb cubes in a large, zipper-lock bag.
2. Combine the olive oil, wine, salt, pepper, oregano, and garlic. Pour the mixture over the lamb cubes in the bag. Let this marinate in the fridge for at least a few hours.
3. When you're ready to cook the lamb, pour off the marinade and thread the cubes onto skewers. You can grill these or broil them 8 inches (20 cm) or so from the broiler. Turn the kebabs while they're cooking and check for doneness by cutting into a chunk of meat after 10 minutes. They should be thoroughly cooked in 15 minutes.
4. While the meat is cooking, wash and dry your lettuce and arrange it on serving plates.
5. Push the cooked meat off the skewers and onto the prepared beds of lettuce. Scatter some red onion over each plate and arrange 8 cherry tomato halves on each. Drizzle each plate with a couple of tablespoons (28 ml) of Greek Lemon Dressing and top each with a tablespoon (15 g) of yogurt.

YIELD: 6 servings, each with: 706 Calories; 62 g Fat (81.2% calories from fat); 23 g Protein; 10 g Carbohydrate; 4 g Dietary Fiber; 6 g net carbs. The carb and fat counts are actually a bit lower than this, since you'll discard most of the marinade.

SIRLOIN SALAD

I admit it: I copied this directly from a salad I had at Applebee's. It was so good and so easy, I just had to tell you about it.

8 ounces (225 g) sirloin steak, 1 inch (2.5 cm) thick

2 cups (94 g) romaine lettuce, washed, dried, and broken up

½ of a medium, ripe tomato, cut into thin wedges

⅛ of a medium, sweet red onion, thinly sliced

Salad dressing of your choice (Vinaigrette [page 162] and Blue Cheese Dressing [page 164] are both good with this.)

1. Grill or broil the steak to your preferred degree of doneness. While the steak is cooking, arrange the lettuce on a serving plate.

2. Cut the cooked steak into thin slices across the grain and pile it on top of the lettuce. Arrange the tomato wedges around the edge and scatter the onion over the top.

3. Serve with the dressing of your choice.

YIELD: 1 generous serving with: 804 Calories; 64 g Fat (70.8% calories from fat); 47 g Protein; 12 g Carbohydrate; 3 g Dietary Fiber; 9 g net carbs

ASIAN CHICKEN SALAD

This is a wonderful salad, different from any I've ever tried. Do use rice vinegar instead of another kind and napa cabbage instead of regular. They may seem like small distinctions, but they make all the difference.

We generally only have two people to eat all this salad, so I set half of the vegetable mixture aside, undressed, in a container in the refrigerator and save half of the dressing and walnuts, as well. This is wonderful to have on hand for a quick, gourmet lunch—just grill a chicken breast, toss the salad with the dressing, and presto, lunch is served.

2 tablespoons (28 ml) olive oil, coconut oil, or MCT oil

½ cup (60 g) walnuts, chopped

4 boneless, skinless chicken breasts

3 cups (210 g) thinly sliced bok choy

3 cups (225 g) thinly sliced napa cabbage

¼ cup (28 g) grated carrots

1 cucumber, thinly sliced

½ cup (50 g) sliced scallions

½ cup (8 g) chopped fresh cilantro

⅓ cup (80 ml) soy sauce

¼ cup (60 ml) rice vinegar

1 tablespoon (15 ml) lime juice

2 tablespoons (30 ml) liquid stevia, monkfruit, or sucralose to equal 2 tablespoons (26 g) of sugar in sweetness

3 cloves of garlic, crushed

½ teaspoon red pepper flakes, or to taste

MAIN DISH SALADS

(continued)

1. Put the oil in a heavy skillet over medium heat and toast the walnuts, stirring for about 4 to 5 minutes or until they're brown and crisp. Set aside.

2. Grill your chicken breasts and slice them into strips. I use my electric tabletop grill, but you can use whatever method you prefer.

3. Combine the bok choy, napa cabbage, carrots, cucumber, scallions, and cilantro in a big bowl.

4. In a separate bowl, combine the soy sauce, rice vinegar, lime juice, sweetener, garlic, and red pepper flakes. Pour about two-thirds of this dressing over the salad and toss well, coating all the vegetables.

5. Heap the salad onto four serving plates, top each with a sliced chicken breast, and drizzle the rest of the dressing over them. Sprinkle with chopped walnuts and serve.

YIELD: 4 generous servings, each with: 428 Calories; 20 g Fat (45.9% calories from fat); 45 g Protein; 9 g Carbohydrate; 3 g Dietary Fiber; 6 g net carbs

NICER NIÇOISE

Salad niçoise is traditionally made with green beans and cold, boiled potatoes, but of course, we're not going to be eating those potatoes. I thought I'd try it with cauliflower, and sure enough, it worked great!

½ of a head of cauliflower

1 bag (1 pound, or 455 g) frozen, crosscut green beans, thawed but not cooked

1 clove of garlic, crushed

¼–½ cup (15–30 g) fresh parsley, minced

¼ of a medium, red onion, diced

8 to 10 olives, sliced plus more for optional garnish (I used stuffed olives, but use whatever you like best.)

½–¾ cup (120–175 ml) vinaigrette dressing, divided

Lettuce (to line plate)

15 ounces (about 425 g) tuna canned in olive oil, lightly drained

6 hard-boiled eggs, sliced

3 tomatoes, sliced

1. Slice your cauliflower quite thin. Put it in a microwave-safe bowl with about 1 tablespoon (15 ml) of water, cover, and cook it for 4 to 5 minutes. (We're looking for it to be just tender.)

2. Combine the green beans, garlic, parsley, onion, and olives in a good-sized bowl. When the cauliflower is done, add that as well and pour ½ cup (120 ml) of dressing over the whole thing.

3. Stir well and stick it in the fridge. Let it marinate for several hours to a day, stirring now and then when you think of it.

4. When you're ready to eat the salad, put a few nice lettuce leaves on each plate, and spoon a mound of the marinated mixture on top. Put the tuna on top and surround it with slices of hard-boiled egg and tomato. Garnish it with more olives and drizzle more dressing on top, if you like.

YIELD: 6 servings, each with: 420 Calories; 28 g Fat (59.1% calories from fat); 30 g Protein; 13 g Carbohydrate; 5 g Dietary Fiber; 8 g net carbs

DINNER SALAD ITALIANO

This could as easily be called "Grocery Store Salad." Grab the lettuce, mushrooms, cucumber, and onion from the salad bar. Grab the meat and cheese at the deli counter. All you need to do at home is toss it with dressing and cut the tomatoes.

1 head of romaine lettuce, washed, dried, and broken up

1 cup (70 g) sliced fresh mushrooms

½ of a cucumber, sliced

¼ of a sweet red onion, thinly sliced

½ pound (225 g) sliced salami, cut into strips

½ pound (225 g) sliced provolone cheese, cut into strips

Italian or Italian Vinaigrette dressing (bottled, or see page 163)

2 ripe tomatoes, cut into wedges

1. Make a big tossed salad from the lettuce, mushrooms, cucumber, onion, salami, and provolone cheese.

2. Toss with the dressing and then add the sliced tomatoes and serve.

YIELD: 3 servings, each with: 671 Calories; 52 g Fat (68.7% calories from fat); 36 g Protein; 18 g Carbohydrate; 6 g Dietary Fiber; 12 g net carbs

TACO SALAD

Is your family taco-prone? Oh, c'mon, whose family isn't? Here's a great salad for them. Since you're making the taco filling and Ranch Dressing, how about buying the vegetables and shredded cheese from the grocery store salad bar? You'll still have to cut up the avocado and chop the cilantro, but that's a cinch.

8 cups (440 g) romaine or iceberg lettuce, washed, dried, and broken up

1 cup (150 g) diced green pepper

½ of a medium cucumber, sliced

1 medium tomato, sliced into thin wedges, or 15 cherry tomatoes, halved

½ cup (80 g) diced sweet red onion

½ of a ripe avocado, peeled, seeded, and cut into small chunks

½ cup (8 g) cilantro, chopped (optional)

1 can (4 ounces, or 115 g) of sliced black olives, drained (optional)

⅔ cup (173 g) salsa, plus additional for topping

½ cup (120 ml) Ranch Dressing (page 165)

1 batch of Chicken or Beef Taco Filling (page 184 and 218)

1 cup (115 g) shredded Cheddar or Monterey Jack cheese

Sour cream

1. Put the lettuce, green pepper, cucumber, tomato, onion, avocado, cilantro (if using), and olives (if using) in a large salad bowl.

2. Stir together the salsa and the Ranch Dressing, pour it over the salad, and toss.

3. Divide the salad between the serving plates and top each one with the taco filling and shredded cheese. Put the extra salsa and sour cream on the table, so folks can add their own.

YIELD: 6 servings, each with: 372 Calories; 21 g Fat (51.0% calories from fat); 34 g Protein; 13 g Carbohydrate; 4 g Dietary Fiber; 9 g net carbs

SWEET 'N' NUTTY TUNA SALAD

Here's something a little different for when you get tired of your usual tuna salad. That's actually how I invented this recipe. The tricky bit is those grapes—you don't want to go through a whole bunch! If you don't have someone in the house who will eat the rest, look for grapes on the salad bar or in little cups in the produce section, so you don't have to buy far more than you need.

1 rib of celery, diced

2 tablespoons (20 g) chopped pecans, walnuts, or almonds

10 red, seedless grapes, quartered

2 tablespoons (20 g) diced red onion

1 can (6 ounces, or 170 g) of tuna

⅓ cup (75 g) mayonnaise

Combine all the ingredients and enjoy! I eat the whole thing by myself, but then, I'm a glutton.

YIELD: This could easily be 2 servings, each with:
476 Calories; 42 g Fat (76.4% calories from fat); 22 g Protein; 7 g Carbohydrate; 1 g Dietary Fiber; 6 g net carbs

MOZZARELLA SALAD

This is rich and filling. The texture will be quite different, depending on whether you use shredded or cubed cheese, but they're both good.

1½ cups (173 g) shredded or (198 g) diced mozzarella cheese

¼ cup (25 g) sliced scallions

½ cup (60 g) diced celery

¼ cup (60 g) mayonnaise

2 tablespoons (28 ml) wine vinegar

½ teaspoon oregano

½ teaspoon basil

1. Combine the mozzarella cheese, scallions, and celery in a mixing bowl.

2. In a separate bowl, combine the mayonnaise, vinegar, oregano, and basil.

3. Pour the mayonnaise mixture over the salad, stir to combine, and serve.

YIELD: 3 servings, each with: 586 Calories; 61 g Fat (88.7% calories from fat); 13 g Protein; 4 g Carbohydrate; 1 g Dietary Fiber; 3 g net carbs

MEDITERRANEAN CHICKEN AND "RICE" SALAD

This would make a nice summer lunch with a gal pal, especially if you put a cold glass of Pinot Grigio beside it. Can't you see it?

2 cups (200 g) Cauliflower Rice (page 113)

1 clove of garlic, crushed

3 tablespoons (45 ml) wine vinegar

2 tablespoons (28 ml) olive oil

1 tablespoon (14 g) mayonnaise

¼ teaspoon salt

¼ teaspoon pepper

1 cup (140 g) diced cooked chicken

⅓ cup (55 g) diced red onion

½ cup (60 g) diced celery

½ cup (75 g) diced green pepper

⅓ cup (20 g) chopped fresh parsley

1. Steam your Cauliflower Rice until just tender. For this small amount, I put it in a bowl, add about 1 tablespoon (15 ml) of water, cover it, and microwave it on High for 5 minutes. Put it in the refrigerator to cool. Use the time while you wait for the cauliflower to cool to do all the dicing and chopping for the rest of the recipe.

2. Mix together the garlic, vinegar, olive oil, mayonnaise, salt, and pepper and blend well.

3. Toss the chicken, onion, celery, green pepper, and parsley with the cooled cauliflower. Pour the dressing on the mixture and toss. This is good served right away, but even better the next day.

YIELD: 2 servings, each with: 472 Calories; 37 g Fat (68.6% calories from fat); 24 g Protein; 14 g Carbohydrate; 5 g Dietary Fiber; 9 g net carbs

If you substitute 2 packets of Miracle Rice, prepared according to the instructions on page 23, for the Cauliflower Rice, you'll get 2 servings, each with: 447 Calories; 37 g Fat (71.5% calories from fat); 22 g Protein; 10 g Carbohydrate; 3 g Dietary Fiber; 7 g net carbs

SUMMER TUNA SALAD

Cool and fresh, this is a great summer lunch or supper. Want to make it super easy? Stop at the grocery store salad bar to grab just about everything but the parsley and the olive oil–packed tuna.

1 medium cucumber, cut into chunks

⅓ cup (60 g) sweet red onion, sliced

⅓ cup (20 g) chopped fresh parsley

½ of a large green pepper, cut into small strips

15 cherry tomatoes, quartered

1 can (6 ounces, or 170 g) of tuna, drained

¼ cup (60 ml) extra-virgin olive oil

2 tablespoons (28 ml) wine vinegar

1 clove of garlic, crushed

¼ teaspoon salt

⅛ teaspoon pepper

1. Put the cucumber, onion, parsley, green pepper, tomatoes, and tuna in a salad bowl.

2. In a separate bowl, combine the olive oil, vinegar, garlic, salt, and pepper.

3. Pour the mixture over the salad, toss, and serve.

YIELD: 2 servings, each with: 452 Calories; 34 g Fat (65.4% calories from fat); 24 g Protein; 16 g Carbohydrate; 4 g Dietary Fiber; 12 g net carbs

COTTAGE CHEESE SALAD

You always thought of cottage cheese as diet food, right? This makes a nice, light lunch that would carry well in a snap-top container.

1 scallion, sliced, including the crisp part of the green

2 radishes, thinly sliced

½ cup (60 g) cucumber, quartered lengthways and thinly sliced

½ cup (115 g) full-fat (4%) cottage cheese

2 tablespoons (30 g) sour cream

A few lettuce leaves

1. Mix together the scallion, radishes, cucumber, cottage cheese, and sour cream.
2. Place a few leaves of lettuce on a serving dish and scoop the cottage cheese mixture onto it. Serve.

YIELD: 1 serving with: 177 Calories; 8 g Fat (42.4% calories from fat); 17 g Protein; 8 g Carbohydrate; 1 g Dietary Fiber; 7 g net carbs

TUNA EGG WALDORF

What to do with that half-an-apple? If you don't have a child to hand it to, coat the cut side with lemon juice, put it in a zipper-lock bag, seal it most of the way, and then suck out the air and finish sealing. It should be fine for a couple of days.

2 large ribs of celery, diced

½ cup (80 g) diced red onion

½ cup (75 g) diced red apple

½ cup (55 g) chopped pecans

5 ounces (140 g) tuna canned in olive oil, lightly drained

3 hard-boiled eggs, chopped

¾ cup (175 g) mayonnaise

Salt

Lettuce (for serving)

1. Put the celery, onion, apple, pecans, tuna, and hard-boiled eggs in a big bowl. Toss with the mayonnaise until it's all coated.
2. Salt to taste and serve on a lettuce-lined plate. (Or not; if you want to just eat it by itself, I won't tell.)

YIELD: 4 servings, each with: 545 Calories; 52 g Fat (82.2% calories from fat); 17 g Protein; 8 g Carbohydrate; 2 g Dietary Fiber; 6 g net carbs

CHAPTER 12

Soups

Soup is the stuff of legend! Sadly, way too many people think of soup as something that comes out of a can or a packet, yet the vast majority of packaged soups have added corn syrup or cornstarch, rice, noodles, potatoes, beans, and other ingredients we don't want.

So make soup! Most of these soups are quite simple to make, and many of them are filling, nutritious, one-dish meals. Making a big batch (or even a double batch) of soup over the weekend is one of the greatest things you can do to save cooking time all week long.

If you want to make a soup as an appetizer or snack, choose one of the soups with lowest carb counts. On the other hand, if you want a lunch or supper, keep an eye on the protein content and figure that the vegetables in the soup will be all your carbs for that meal.

Bone broth

Bone broth is trendy and with good reason; it's highly nutritious stuff. It's also dead simple to make, as I will explain in a moment. You don't have to use bone broth for these recipes, though it will improve their nutritional profile. Just plain broth or stock will do, but—do I need to repeat it?—*read the labels!* Here's the ingredient list from one popular brand:

Chicken Broth, Chicken Broth Flavor (Salt, Monosodium Glutamate, Sugar, Autolyzed Yeast Extract, Chicken Fat, Natural Flavor, Onion Powder, Hydrolyzed Soy Protein, Spice Extractives), Salt, Monosodium Glutamate, Beta Carotene, Chicken Stock Flavor (Autolyzed Yeast Extract, Dextrose, Maltodextrin, Partially Hydrogenated Soybean Oil).

I mostly make my own chicken broth, but I do keep boxed stock on hand. I buy Kitchen Basics or Costco's Kirkland brand. They're both nationally distributed, though of course you need to go to Costco to get the Kirkland broth. If you are gluten-free, be especially careful about labels.

Note: You'll find that packaged broth generally comes in two sizes: 1-quart (946 ml) boxes and 14½-ounce (410 ml) cans. Why this should be, I have no idea. But in any of these recipes, if you substitute two 14½-ounce (410 ml) cans for 1 quart (946 ml) of broth, no harm will come to your soup, you'll just get slightly less volume. You can make up the difference with water, if you really want to, but I don't see why you'd bother.

CHICKEN BONE BROTH OR SOMETHING FOR NOTHING

Bone broth is liquid gold, one of the most valuable foods you can add to your diet—heck, supplement companies are now selling canisters of pricey "bone broth protein" supplements. Skip it! You can make this with stuff you would otherwise discard.

This is a rule, rather than a recipe, but it is one of the most valuable in the book. Whenever you eat chicken on the bone—wings, a rotisserie chicken, or just roasted thighs—stash the bones, no matter how naked, in a plastic bag in your freezer. Add any onion trimmings, scallion tops, parsley stems, or bits of celery you might have—go easy on celery leaves, though; they can get bitter in concentration.

When you have enough bones to fill your slow cooker—I use my big 5-quart (4.7 L) Crock-Pot—dump them in. Cover with water and add 1 teaspoon salt and a tablespoon or two (15 to 28 ml) of cider or wine vinegar. (The vinegar draws calcium out of the bones, making for a more nutritious broth.) Lid it, set it to Low, and let it sit for a minimum of 24 hours, and 48 isn't excessive.

You can also do this in a stockpot on your stovetop, but you probably won't want to leave it on while you're asleep or out of the house. If you're with the current electric pressure cooker trend, I believe they have instructions for making broth, too. They can also be used as slow cookers.

Let your broth cool, strain, toss the bones, and you're done. You can make soup immediately, or stash your broth in snap-top containers in the freezer.

If you're short on freezer space or dislike the idea of using packaged bouillon concentrate, or both, put your strained broth back in the slow cooker, set it to Low again, and leave the lid off. Do this on a day when you'll be puttering around the house, so you can keep an eye on it. Let your broth cook down until it's syrupy, scrape it into a container, and freeze. Use just as you would commercial bouillon concentrate, though you'll want to add a little salt along with it.

Obviously, I can't give exact serving or nutrition counts for this, but it will be darned close to zero carb. Simply drinking a hot cup of this broth every day will do you good!

Should you be lucky enough to eat enough steak to assemble a whole sack of steak bones, you can make beef bone broth exactly the same way.

CALIFORNIA SOUP

This makes a quick and elegant first course. If you like curry, try this: Melt a tablespoon or so (about 14 g) of butter and add ½ teaspoon or so of curry powder. Cook for just a minute and add the mixture to the blender with the broth and avocados. Or, you could spike this with a dash or two of hot sauce and a touch of garlic.

1 large or 2 small, very ripe avocados, pitted, peeled, and cut into chunks

1 quart (946 ml) chicken broth, heated

Put the avocados through the blender with the chicken broth, puree until very smooth, and serve.

YIELD: 6 appetizer-sized servings, each with: 80 Calories; 6 g Fat (66.1% calories from fat); 4 g Protein; 3 g Carbohydrate; 1 g Dietary Fiber; 2 g net carbs

CORNER-FILLING CONSOMMÉ

It's an old trick: serve soup before an expensive roast, and you're likely to have leftover meat to eat tomorrow. Obviously, use the olive oil instead of the butter if you want this dairy-free.

2 tablespoons (28 g) butter or (28 ml) olive oil

4 ounces (115 g) sliced mushrooms

1 small onion, sliced paper-thin

1 quart (946 ml) beef broth

2 tablespoons (28 ml) dry sherry

¼ teaspoon pepper

1. Melt the butter in a skillet and sauté the mushrooms and onions in the butter until they're limp.
2. Add the beef broth, sherry, and pepper. Let it simmer for 5 minutes or so, just to blend the flavors a bit, and serve.

YIELD: 6 appetizer-sized servings, each with: 91 Calories; 4 g Fat (41.0% calories from fat); 8 g Protein; 5 g Carbohydrate; 1 g Dietary Fiber; 4 g net carbs

CROCK-POT TOMATO SOUP

This is a delicious tomato soup from *Splendid Low-Carbing* by Jennifer Eloff. It's so easy! I've published Jen's recipe as she wrote it. However, I would probably use 3 cups (700 ml) of beef broth in place of the 2½ cups (570 ml) of water and then use the beef bouillon concentrate if I felt the final results needed more salt. Plus, I've offered alternatives for the Splenda.

This is very low in fat. How about serving it with buttery grilled cheese sandwiches on Soul Bread (page 91)?

2½ cups (570 ml) V8 or other mixed vegetable juice

2½ cups (570 ml) boiling water

8 ounces (225 g) canned tomato sauce

1 small onion, thinly sliced

1 bay leaf

3 tablespoons (5 g) Splenda OR liquid stevia, monkfruit, or sucralose to equal 3 tablespoons (39 g) sugar in sweetness

1 tablespoon (8 g) beef bouillon granules or (15 ml) liquid beef-broth concentrate

⅛ teaspoon pepper

¼ teaspoon dried basil

1. Combine all the ingredients in a slow cooker and stir.
2. Cover and cook on Low for 4 hours.
3. Strain and serve.

YIELD: 6 servings, each with: 43 Calories; trace Fat (5.0% calories from fat); 2 g Protein; 10 g Carbohydrate; 2 g Dietary Fiber; 8 g net carbs

MULLIGATAWNY

This is a curried soup that came out of the British Colonial times in India. That Nice Boy I Married calls this Smell-i-ga-yummy because it smells so good! Feel free to make this with a turkey carcass or leftover lamb bone, too. Stick with coconut oil and coconut milk if you're dairy-free.

2 quarts (1.9 L) chicken broth

2 cups (280 g) or more diced cooked chicken or diced boneless, skinless chicken breast

3 tablespoons (45 g) butter or coconut oil

1 medium onion, chopped

1 clove of garlic, crushed

1 small carrot, shredded

2 ribs of celery, diced

2 teaspoons to 2 heaping tablespoons (4–13 g) curry powder (I like it with lots of curry!)

1 bay leaf

½ of a tart apple, chopped fine

1–2 teaspoons salt or Vege-Sal

½ teaspoon pepper

½ teaspoon dried thyme

Rind of 1 fresh lemon, grated, or ½ to 1 teaspoon dried

1 cup (235 ml) heavy cream OR 14 fluid ounces (410 ml) canned coconut milk

1. Put the chicken broth and diced chicken in a large stockpot and set the stockpot over low heat.

2. Melt the butter in a heavy skillet and add the onion, garlic, carrot, celery, and curry powder. Sauté until the vegetables are limp and add them to the stockpot.

3. Add the bay leaf, apple, salt, pepper, thyme, and lemon zest to the pot and simmer for ½ hour.

4. Just before serving, stir in the heavy cream and remove the bay leaf.

YIELD: 6 servings, each with: 494 Calories; 41 g Fat (74.9% calories from fat); 22 g Protein; 9 g Carbohydrate; 2 g Dietary Fiber; 7 g net carbs

SOPA AZTECA

That's soup made by Aztecs, not soup made from Aztecs! The totals on this soup may sound like a lot when you add them all up, but don't forget that this is a whole meal in a bowl: meat, vegetables, melted cheese, and lovely ripe avocado in each bite! You don't need to serve another thing with it, although you could serve tortillas or quesadillas for the carb-eaters in the crowd.

3 quarts (2.8 L) chicken broth

2 cups (280 g) diced cooked chicken or boneless, skinless chicken breast

¼ cup (60 ml) olive oil

1 medium onion, chopped

4 or 5 cloves of garlic, crushed

2 or 3 ribs of celery, diced

1 green pepper, diced

1 small carrot, shredded

1 small zucchini, diced

2 tablespoons (6 g) dried oregano

2 tablespoons (4 g) dried basil

2 teaspoons pepper

2 cans (14½ ounces, or 410 g each) of diced tomatoes, including juice

1 package of frozen chopped spinach

At least 8 ounces (225 g) Mexican Queso Quesadilla or Monterey Jack cheese, shredded, or packaged Mexican Cheese Blend

Chipotle peppers in adobo sauce (These come canned.)

5 ripe avocados

1. Heat the chicken broth and the diced chicken in a large pot over low heat.

2. Heat the olive oil in a skillet over medium heat and sauté the onion, garlic, celery, green pepper, carrot, and zucchini together until they're limp. Stir the oregano, basil, and pepper into the vegetables and sauté for another minute and add them to the soup, along with the tomatoes and spinach. Let the whole thing simmer for ½ to 1 hour, to let the flavors blend.

3. When you're ready to serve the Sopa Azteca, put at least ¼ to ½ cup (30 to 58 g) of cheese (more won't hurt) in the bottom of each bowl and anywhere from 1 to 3 chipotles, depending on how spicy you like your food. (If you don't like spicy food at all, leave the chipotles out entirely.) Ladle the hot soup over the cheese and chipotles.

4. Use a spoon to scoop chunks of half of a ripe avocado onto the top of each bowl of soup.

YIELD: 10 servings, each with: 398 Calories; 30 g Fat (64.3% calories from fat); 19 g Protein; 18 g Carbohydrate; 6 g Dietary Fiber; 12 g net carbs

¼ cup (30 g) of shredded cheese adds: 105 Calories; 9 g Fat (73.0% calories from fat); 7 g Protein; trace Carbohydrate; 0 g Dietary Fiber; trace net carbs

Each chipotle pepper adds: 1 Calories; trace Fat (5.0% calories from fat); 1 g Protein; trace Carbohydrate; trace Dietary Fiber; 0 g net carbs

¼ of an avocado has: 81 Calories; 8 g Fat (78.6% calories from fat); 1 g Protein; 4 g Carbohydrate; 1 g Dietary Fiber; 3 g net carbs

HOT-AND-SOUR SOUP

Really authentic Hot-and-Sour Soup uses Chinese mushrooms, but this is mighty good with any variety—especially when you have a cold!

2 quarts (1.9 L) chicken broth	**½ cup (120 ml) white vinegar**
1 piece of fresh ginger about the size of a walnut, peeled and thinly sliced	**2 cans (6½ ounces each, or 185 g) of mushrooms, including liquid**
½ pound (225 g) lean pork (I use boneless loin.)	**1 package (about 10 ounces, or 280 g) of firm tofu**
3 tablespoons (45 ml) soy sauce	**1 can (8 ounces, or 225 g) of bamboo shoots**
1–1½ teaspoons pepper	**5 eggs**

1. Put the chicken broth in a large pot and set it over medium heat. Add the ginger to the broth and let it simmer for a few minutes.

2. While the broth simmers, slice the pork into small cubes or strips. Stir the soy sauce, pork, pepper, vinegar, and mushrooms into the broth. Let it simmer for 10 minutes or so until the pork is done through.

3. Cut the tofu into small cubes. If you like, you can also cut the canned bamboo shoots into thinner strips. Stir the tofu and bamboo shoots into the soup and let it simmer another few minutes. Taste the soup; it won't be very hot—spicy-hot, that is, not temperature-hot—so if you like it hotter, add more pepper and some hot sauce. If you like, you can also add a little extra vinegar.

4. Beat the eggs in a bowl and then pour them in a thin stream over the surface of the soup. Stir them in and you'll get a billion little shreds of cooked egg in your soup. Who needs noodles?

Note: This is good served with a few finely sliced scallions on top (include some of the green part) and a few drops of toasted sesame oil. Since I like my soup hotter than my husband does, I use hot toasted sesame oil, rather than putting hot sauce in the whole batch. You could add a squirt of sriracha, for that matter.

YIELD: 6 servings, each with: 206 Calories; 9 g Fat (39.5% calories from fat); 22 g Protein; 10 g Carbohydrate; 2 g Dietary Fiber; 8 g net carbs

PEANUT SOUP

If you miss split pea or bean soup, try this. Try it even if you don't miss other legume soups—you may find you have a new favorite.

3 tablespoons (45 g) butter

2 or 3 ribs of celery, finely chopped

1 medium onion, finely chopped

2 quarts (1.9 L) chicken broth

½ teaspoon salt or Vege-Sal

1¼ cups (325 g) natural peanut butter (I use smooth.)

1 teaspoon guar gum (optional)

1 cup (235 ml) heavy cream

1 cup (235 ml) pourable unsweetened coconut milk

Salted peanuts, chopped

1. Melt the butter in a skillet and sauté the celery and onion in the butter. Add the chicken broth, salt, and peanut butter and stir. Cover and simmer on the lowest temperature for at least 1 hour, stirring now and then.

   TIP: If your slow cooker will hold this quantity of ingredients (mine will), it's ideal for cooking this soup. Set it on High, cover it, and let it go for 2 to 3 hours.

2. If you're using guar gum (it makes the soup thicker without adding carbs; most peanut soup is thickened with flour), a stick blender is ideal for blending it in quickly, with the soup still in the pot.

3. Stir in the heavy cream and coconut milk and simmer for another 15 minutes. Garnish with the chopped peanuts.

YIELD: 5 servings, each with: 665 Calories; 56 g Fat (76.1% calories from fat); 22 g Protein; 18 g Carbohydrate; 4 g Dietary Fiber; 14 g net carbs

SPRING CHICKEN SOUP

This soup is a great way to use up leftovers—just substitute 1 cup (140 g) of diced leftover chicken for the chicken breast listed with the ingredients. Using the canned mushrooms and asparagus, this is super-quick. If you like, use fresh mushrooms and asparagus and cook it a tad longer.

6 cups (1.4 L) chicken broth

1 can (6½ ounces, or 185 g) of mushrooms

1 can (6½ ounces, or 185 g) of cut asparagus

1 boneless, skinless chicken breast, diced into small cubes

¼ cup (60 ml) dry sherry

1 tablespoon (15 ml) soy sauce

Pepper

Sliced scallions

1. Combine the chicken broth, mushrooms, asparagus, chicken, sherry, and soy sauce in a pot and heat.

2. If you're using raw chicken, let it cook for 5 to 10 minutes (that's all it should take to cook small cubes of chicken through).

3. Add pepper to taste and serve with a scattering of scallions on top.

YIELD: 4 servings, each with: 161 Calories; 4 g Fat (23.6% calories from fat); 22 g Protein; 5 g Carbohydrate; 2 g Dietary Fiber; 3 g net carbs

JUDIE'S CHICKEN "NOODLE" SOUP

Judie Edwards created this when she was craving chicken noodle soup, and it's a cinch to make. The numbers on this assume you're using La Choy Fancy Chinese Vegetables, but I'm sure whatever your grocery store has will do. (Indeed, the La Choy vegetables are not gluten-free—I called the company—so you may want to do some label reading.) Since discovering tofu shirataki, I've taken to using the fettuccini style to make chicken noodle soup. Try it!

2 cups (475 ml) chicken broth

1 can (14 ounces, or 395 g) of Chinese vegetables, drained

Simply combine, heat, and serve.

YIELD: 1 serving with: 106 Calories; 3 g Fat (24.0% calories from fat); 12 g Protein; 8 g Carbohydrate; 2 g Dietary Fiber; 6 g net carbs

EASY TOMATO-BEEF SOUP

This recipe is super-quick and easy! If you want it extra hearty, use 1 pound (455 g) of ground beef. If you want noodles, throw in some tofu shirataki. If you like it spicy, use tomatoes with green chilies. If you're a dairy-eater, consider a sprinkle of shredded cheese!

¼–1½ pounds (115–680 g) ground beef

2 cans (14½ ounces, or 410 g each) of beef broth

1 can (14½ ounces, or 410 g) of diced tomatoes

Salt and pepper

1. In a skillet, brown the ground beef. Pour off the grease and add the beef broth and tomatoes.

2. Heat through, salt and pepper to taste, and serve.

YIELD: 4 servings, each with: 314 Calories; 15 g Fat (44.0% calories from fat); 32 g Protein; 12 g Carbohydrate; 1 g Dietary Fiber; 11 g net carbs

263

ITALIAN TUNA SOUP

Okay, it's not authentically Italian, but it's a lot like minestrone. It's easy, too. Check the frozen foods section of your supermarket for mixed bags of broccoli and cauliflower and substitute 1 cup (69 g) of the mix for the separate cauliflower and broccoli. That way, you'll only have one partially eaten bag of veggies in the freezer to use up, rather than two.

1 quart (946 ml) chicken broth

1 can (14½ ounces, or 410 g) of diced tomatoes

1 can (14½ ounces, or 410 g) of Italian green beans or 1 package (10 ounces, or 280 g) of frozen Italian green beans

½ cup (38 g) frozen broccoli cuts

½ cup (66 g) frozen cauliflower florets

1 cup (120 g) thinly sliced zucchini, frozen or fresh

3 tablespoons (48 g) tomato paste

1 teaspoon Italian seasoning

2 cans (5 ounces, or 140 g each) of tuna canned in olive oil

Tabasco

1. Combine the chicken broth, tomatoes, green beans, broccoli, cauliflower, zucchini, tomato paste, Italian seasoning, and tuna.

2. Add a few drops of Tabasco (more if you like it hotter, less if you just want a little zip) and simmer until the vegetables are tender.

Note: If you're a dairy-eater, a sprinkle of Parmesan cheese would be nice on this, but hardly necessary.

YIELD: 5 servings, each with: 194 Calories; 6 g Fat (27.9% calories from fat); 23 g Protein; 12 g Carbohydrate; 4 g Dietary Fiber; 8 g net carbs

ZESTY SEAFOOD SOUP

Marilee Wellersdick came up with this. Just make sure you use real crab, not the high-carb fake crab that's widely available these days, when you make this soup. Since Marie sent me this recipe, Kitchen Basics brand seafood stock has become widely available. I'd sub it for the chicken broth, here, but it's up to you.

2 tablespoons (28 ml) olive oil

1 medium onion, chopped

2 cloves of garlic, minced

1 cup (100 g) chopped celery

2 tablespoons (8 g) fresh or (3 g) dried parsley, chopped

1 teaspoon dried basil

½ teaspoon dried rosemary

½ teaspoon dried thyme

Dash of cayenne

3 cans (8 ounces, or 225 g each) of tomato sauce

8 ounces (235 ml) no-carb clam juice (Read the labels! Some have sugar.)

1 can (14½ ounces, or 410 g) of chicken broth

1 pound (455 g) firm fish (such as cod, halibut, or snapper), cut into 1-inch (2.5 cm) cubes

4½ ounces (130 g) small canned, fresh, or frozen shrimp

1 can (8 ounces, or 225 g) of crabmeat, or 1 fresh crab

Salt

1. Heat the olive oil in a Dutch oven. Add the onion, garlic, and celery and sauté until the onion is limp.

2. Stir in the parsley, basil, rosemary, thyme, cayenne, tomato sauce, clam juice, and chicken broth. Cover and simmer for about 10 minutes.

3. Add the fish; cover and simmer until the fish flakes (about 7 minutes). Stir in the shrimp and crab. Cover and cook for a few minutes until everything is thoroughly heated. Salt to taste.

YIELD: 8 servings, each with: 165 Calories; 5 g Fat (26.3% calories from fat); 22 g Protein; 9 g Carbohydrate; 2 g Dietary Fiber; 7 g net carbs

CREAM OF CAULIFLOWER

You'll be surprised by how much this tastes like Cream of Potato!

3 tablespoons (45 g) butter

¾ cup (120 g) diced onion

¾ cup (90 g) diced celery

1 quart (946 ml) chicken broth

1 package (10 ounces, or 280 g) of frozen cauliflower

½ teaspoon guar or xanthan (optional)

½ cup (120 ml) heavy cream

Salt and pepper

1. In a large saucepan, melt the butter over low heat and sauté the onion and celery in it until they're limp. Add the chicken broth and cauliflower, bring to a simmer, and cook until the cauliflower is tender.

2. Use your stick blender to puree the soup right in the pan, adding the optional guar as you do. If you lack a stick blender, use a slotted spoon to transfer the vegetables into a blender and then pour in as much of the broth as will fit. Add the guar (if using), puree the ingredients, and then return them to the saucepan.

3. Stir in the heavy cream and salt and pepper to taste.

YIELD: 4 servings, each with: 249 Calories; 21 g Fat (75.0% calories from fat); 7 g Protein; 8 g Carbohydrate; 3 g Dietary Fiber; 5 g net carbs

SKYDANCER'S ZUCCHINI SOUP

Jo Pagliassotti, an artist who works under the name Skydancer, came up with this savory and versatile soup. She sent many notes! "Want even more variety and some more protein along with it? Leftover flaked salmon and chunks of cold leftover chicken are both great in this. You can garnish the soup with some sliced scallions or shallots, and that's also wonderful.

This soup lends itself to many variations—be creative. Oh, and it freezes well! The cream cheese seems to hold up to this just fine."

4 cups (480 g) chopped zucchini, cut into chunks

2 cups (320 g) chopped Spanish onion

4 cups (946 ml) chicken stock, homemade or canned (if homemade, salt to taste)

1 to 2 teaspoons dry summer savory or ¼ cup (7 g) fresh summer savory leaves, chopped

1 tablespoon (2 g) dry basil or ½ cup (12 g) fresh leaves, lightly packed

8 ounces (225 g) cream cheese, at room temperature

1. Place the zucchini, onion, chicken stock, summer savory, and basil into a large saucepan. Bring to a simmer and cook over low heat until the vegetables are soft (30 minutes minimum). It won't hurt this soup a bit if you turn the burner to low, cover the pan, and forget it for a couple of hours. You want it to be squashy (pun intended!).

2. Put the cream cheese and a small quantity of the cooked mixture into a blender and blend until smooth. (Add more liquid if needed to get the cheese smooth.) Pour that into another pan. Add more of the cooked squash-and-onion mixture to the blender and blend until smooth (or as smooth as you like it). Blend the rest of the cooked mixture, pouring each blended batch into the soup and cheese mixture as you go. (These were Jo's original instructions, but this was before stick blenders were common. I see no reason not to simply puree everything right in the pan if you have a stick blender. That's what I'd do. Saves you washing an extra saucepan.)

3. Once everything is pureed, stir it well to mix in the initial cheese and zucchini blend and rewarm over low heat if necessary.

YIELD: 9 servings, each with: 128 Calories; 10 g Fat (65.5% calories from fat); 5 g Protein; 6 g Carbohydrate; 2 g Dietary Fiber; 4 g net carbs

JODEE'S ZUCCHINI SOUP

Here's another take on zucchini soup, from reader Jodee Rushton. She says this is satisfying as a quick between-meals snack, not to mention versatile: "In the summer, pour it into a mug and drink it cold. In the winter, you might microwave it."

¼ cup (55 g) butter

1 medium onion, chopped

1½ pounds (680 g) zucchini, washed and sliced

1 quart (946 ml) chicken broth

⅛ teaspoon salt

⅛ teaspoon pepper

½ teaspoon ground nutmeg

½ cup (120 ml) half-and-half

1. In a large saucepan, melt the butter and sauté the onion in it until golden. Add the zucchini and sauté over medium-high heat until limp (10 to 15 minutes).

2. Add the chicken broth, salt, pepper, and nutmeg. Simmer for 15 minutes, add the half-and-half, and let the mixture cool.

3. Puree your soup right in the pan with your stick blender or in a stand blender. (Do this in batches, if necessary.)

4. Refrigerate for a minimum of 4 hours, to allow the flavors to blend. Serve hot or cold.

YIELD: 8 servings, each with: 104 Calories; 8 g Fat (69.0% calories from fat); 4 g Protein; 5 g Carbohydrate; 1 g Dietary Fiber; 4 g net carbs

JAMAICAN PEPPERPOT SOUP

This soup is unbelievably hearty, almost like a stew, and very tasty! If you'd like this to be dairy-free, I see no reason not to use canned coconut milk in place of the cream.

½ pound (225 g) bacon, diced

2 pounds (910 g) boneless beef round or chuck, cut into ½-inch (1.3 cm) cubes

1 large onion, chopped

4 cups (946 ml) water

1 cup (235 ml) canned beef broth

2 packages (10 ounces, or 280 g each) of frozen chopped spinach

½ teaspoon dried thyme

1 green pepper, diced

1 can (14½ ounces, or 410 g) of sliced tomatoes

1 bay leaf

2 teaspoons salt

½ teaspoon pepper

1 teaspoon hot sauce, or to taste

1 package (10 ounces, or 280 g) of frozen sliced okra, thawed

3 tablespoons (45 g) butter

½ cup (120 ml) heavy cream

Paprika

1. Place the bacon, beef cubes, onion, water, and beef broth in a large, heavy soup pot. Bring to a boil, turn the burner to low, and let the mixture simmer for 1 hour.

2. Add the spinach, thyme, green pepper, tomatoes, bay leaf, salt, pepper, and hot sauce. Let it simmer for another 30 minutes.

3. Sauté the okra in the butter over the lowest heat for about 5 minutes, add to the soup, and simmer just 10 minutes more.

4. Just before serving, remove the bay leaf and stir in the heavy cream. Sprinkle just a touch of paprika on each serving. Pass the hot sauce!

YIELD: 8 servings, each with: 544 Calories; 42 g Fat (69.0% calories from fat); 32 g Protein; 11 g Carbohydrate; 4 g Dietary Fiber; 7 g net carbs

EGG DROP SOUP

This is quick and easy, but filling, and it can practically save your life when you've got a cold. You don't have to use the guar, but it gives the broth the same rich quality that the cornstarch-thickened Chinese broths have.

1 quart (946 ml) chicken broth	**1 tablespoon (15 ml) rice vinegar**
¼ teaspoon guar or xanthan (optional)	**½ teaspoon grated fresh ginger**
1 tablespoon (15 ml) soy sauce	**1 scallion, sliced**
	2 eggs

1. Put a cup (235 ml) or so of the chicken broth in your blender, turn it on Low, and add the guar (if using). Let it blend for a second and then put it in a large saucepan with the rest of the broth. (If you're not using the guar, just put the broth directly in a saucepan.)

2. Add the soy sauce, rice vinegar, ginger, and scallion. Heat over medium-high heat and let it simmer for 5 minutes or so to let the flavors blend.

3. Beat your eggs in a glass measuring cup or small pitcher—something with a pouring lip. Use a fork to stir the surface of the soup in a slow circle and pour in about one-quarter of the eggs, stirring as they cook and turn into shreds (which will happen almost instantaneously). Repeat three more times, using up all the egg, and then serve!

YIELD: 3 servings, each with: 101 Calories; 5 g Fat (44.6% calories from fat); 11 g Protein; 3 g Carbohydrate; trace Dietary Fiber; 3 g net carbs

STRACCIATELLA

This is the Italian take on egg drop soup, and it's delightful. Don't expect this to form long shreds like Chinese egg drop soup; because of the Parmesan cheese, it makes small, fluffy particles, instead.

1 quart (946 ml) chicken broth	**½ teaspoon lemon juice**
2 eggs	**Pinch of nutmeg**
½ cup (50 g) grated Parmesan cheese	**½ teaspoon dried marjoram**

1. Put ¼ cup (60 ml) of the chicken broth in a glass measuring cup or small pitcher. Pour the rest into a large saucepan over medium heat.

2. Add the eggs to the broth in the measuring cup and beat with a fork. Then, add the Parmesan cheese, lemon juice, and nutmeg and beat with a fork until well blended.

3. When the broth in the saucepan is simmering, stir it with a fork as you add small amounts of the egg-and-cheese mixture until it's all stirred in.

4. Add the marjoram, crushing it a bit between your fingers, and simmer the soup for another minute or so before serving.

YIELD: 4 servings, each with: 117 Calories; 7 g Fat (52.5% calories from fat); 12 g Protein; 2 g Carbohydrate; trace Dietary Fiber; 2 g net carbs

MANHATTAN CLAM CHOWDER

I wish I didn't have to say this, but read the labels on your clams. Yes, there are canned clams with sugar in them. Why, I cannot say.

4 slices of bacon, diced

1 large onion, chopped

2 ribs of celery, diced

1 green pepper, chopped

2½ cups (375 g) diced white turnip

1 grated carrot

1 can (14½ ounces, or 410 g) of diced tomatoes

3 cups (720 ml) seafood stock OR no-sugar-added clam juice and water, 50/50, OR water

1 teaspoon dried thyme

4 cans (6½ ounces, or 185 g each) of minced clams, including liquid

Tabasco

1 teaspoon salt or Vege-Sal

1 teaspoon pepper

1. In a large, heavy-bottomed stockpot, start the bacon cooking. As the fat cooks out of it, add the onion, celery, and green pepper and sauté them in the bacon fat for 4 to 5 minutes.

2. Add the turnip, carrot, tomatoes, stock or other liquid, and thyme and let the whole thing simmer for 30 minutes to 1 hour.

3. Add the clams, including the liquid, a dash of Tabasco, the salt, and pepper.

4. Simmer for another 15 minutes and serve.

YIELD: 10 servings, each with: 44 Calories; 3 g Fat (21.9% calories from fat); 14 g Protein; 8 g Carbohydrate; 2 g Dietary Fiber; 6 g net carbs

LO-CARB CLAM CHOWDER

New England Clam Chowder fans will want to try this recipe from reader Tricia Hudgins. This is how Tricia wrote the recipe, but now that it's widely available, I'd substitute boxed seafood stock for that chicken broth. Also, Tricia warns, "The sharp or bitter part of the turnip is the outside layer near the skin. Peel your turnips with a paring knife, being careful to get all of the outer layer."

8 slices of bacon

½ cup (80 g) finely chopped onion

½ cup (60 g) finely chopped celery

2 cans (6½ ounces, or 185 g each) of clams, drained and with the juice reserved

1 cup (235 ml) chicken broth

2 large turnips, peeled and chopped into small cubes

½ teaspoon pepper

½ teaspoon dried thyme

Salt

1 cup (235 ml) heavy cream

1. Fry the bacon and set it aside, reserving the bacon grease. Sauté the onion and celery in 3 tablespoons (45 ml) of the bacon grease until they're soft.

2. Remove the onion and celery from the heat and add the clam juice, chicken broth, turnips, pepper, thyme, and salt. Cover and cook over medium heat, stirring occasionally, until the turnips are soft (about 15 minutes).

3. Remove from the heat and stir in the heavy cream and clams. Crumble the bacon and add it to the soup. Reheat over a low flame and serve.

YIELD: 4 servings, each with: 315 Calories; 30 g Fat (67.9% calories from fat); 22 g Protein; 10 g Carbohydrate; 2 g Dietary Fiber; 8 g net carbs

QUICK GREEN CHOWDER

Our tester, Christina Robertson, says "A definite ten! I was expecting more of a bland flavor, but this was delicious with a fabulous flavor! I used fresh ground sea salt and fresh ground pepper and although that might have added to the flavor, I think it would be just as good with regular salt and pepper."

10 ounces (280 g) frozen chopped spinach, thawed

13 ounces (365 g) no-sugar-added canned clams (2 cans, including liquid)

1 cup (235 ml) half-and-half

1 cup (235 ml) heavy cream

1 cup (235 ml) clam juice, no-carb

Salt and pepper

1. This is super easy: Combine everything but the salt and pepper in your blender or food processor and puree.

2. Pour into a saucepan and bring to just below a simmer for 5 minutes—don't boil.

3. Salt and pepper to taste and serve.

Note: If you prefer, you can puree everything but the clams and then add them when you pour the puree into the saucepan.

YIELD: 4 servings, each with: 305 Calories; 31 g Fat (69.9% calories from fat); 21 g Protein; 9 g Carbohydrate; 2 g Dietary Fiber; 7 g net carbs

ARTICHOKE SOUP

This soup doesn't have a lot of protein, so serve it in cup-sized (235 ml) portions as a first course. It would go nicely before a roasted chicken, I think.

3–4 tablespoons (45–55 g) butter

1 small onion, finely chopped

2 stalks of celery, finely chopped

1 clove of garlic, crushed

1 can (14 ounces, or 395 g) of quartered artichoke hearts

4 cups (946 ml) chicken stock, divided

½ teaspoon guar or xanthan

1 cup (235 ml) half-and-half

Juice of ½ of a lemon

Salt or Vege-Sal

Pepper

1. In a heavy skillet, melt the butter and sauté the onion, celery, and garlic over low to medium heat. Stir from time to time.

2. Drain the artichoke hearts and trim off any tough bits of leaf that got left on. Put the artichoke hearts in a food processor with the S-blade in position. Add ½ cup (120 ml) of the chicken stock and the guar and process until the artichokes are a fine puree.

3. Scrape the artichoke mixture into a saucepan, add the remaining chicken stock, and set over medium-high heat to simmer.

4. When the onion and celery are soft, stir them into the artichoke mixture. When it comes to a simmer, whisk in the half-and-half. Bring it back to a simmer, squeeze in the lemon juice, and stir again. Add salt and pepper to taste.

5. You can serve this immediately, hot, or in the summer, you can serve it chilled.

YIELD: 6 servings, each with: 181 Calories; 13 g Fat (65.9% calories from fat); 6 g Protein; 9 g Carbohydrate; 1 g Dietary Fiber; 8 g net carbs. Much of the carbohydrates in artichokes is inulin, which remains largely undigested, so this carb count is actually misleadingly high.

OLIVE SOUP

Olives are so good for you that you should be eating more of them! This makes a fine first course. This would also make a great dish for Fat Fasting!

4 cups (946 ml) chicken stock

½ teaspoon guar or xanthan

1 cup (100 g) minced ripe olives (You can buy cans of minced ripe olives.)

1 cup (235 ml) heavy cream

¼ cup (60 ml) dry sherry

Salt or Vege-Sal

Pepper

1. Put ½ cup (120 ml) of the chicken stock in the blender with the guar gum and blend for a few seconds. Pour into a saucepan and add the rest of the stock and the olives.

2. Heat until simmering and then whisk in the heavy cream. Bring back to a simmer, stir in the sherry, and season with salt and pepper to taste.

YIELD: 6 servings, each with: 200 Calories; 18 g Fat (84.4% calories from fat); 4 g Protein; 3 g Carbohydrate; 1 g Dietary Fiber; 2 g net carbs

TURKEY MEATBALL SOUP

This makes a light, quick, and tasty supper all by itself. Don't want to be left with half-a-pound (225 g) of ground turkey? Double the batch and take it for lunch tomorrow.

½ pound (225 g) ground turkey

2 tablespoons (10 g) pork rind crumbs

2 tablespoons (8 g) minced fresh parsley

½ teaspoon salt or Vege-Sal

½ teaspoon poultry seasoning

⅛ teaspoon pepper

1 tablespoon (15 ml) olive oil

½ cup (55 g) grated carrot

2 cups (240 g) diced zucchini

1 tablespoon (10 g) minced onion

1 clove of garlic, crushed

1 quart (946 ml) chicken broth

1 teaspoon dried oregano

2 eggs, beaten

¼ cup (25 g) grated Parmesan cheese

1. In a mixing bowl, combine the ground turkey with the pork rind crumbs, parsley, ½ teaspoon of salt, poultry seasoning, and pepper. Mix well and form into balls the size of marbles or so. Set aside.

2. In a large, heavy-bottomed saucepan, heat the olive oil over a medium-high burner. Add the carrot and let it sauté for 2 to 3 minutes. Then, add the zucchini, onion, and garlic and sauté the vegetables for another 5 to 7 minutes.

3. Add the chicken broth and oregano and bring the soup to a simmer for 15 minutes. Drop the turkey meatballs into the soup one by one and let it simmer for another 10 to 15 minutes. Taste the soup at this point and add more salt and pepper to taste, if desired.

4. Just before you're ready to serve the soup, stir it slowly with a fork as you pour the beaten eggs in quite slowly. Simmer another minute and ladle into bowls.

5. Top each serving with 1 tablespoon (5 g) of Parmesan cheese and serve.

YIELD: 4 servings, each with: 241 Calories; 14 g Fat (53.3% calories from fat); 22 g Protein; 6 g Carbohydrate; 2 g Dietary Fiber; 4 g net carbs

KIM'S WEEK-AFTER-THANKSGIVING SOUP

This is what my sister did with the carcass from her Thanksgiving turkey. Our mother always made turkey and rice soup, but we low carbers needed a new tradition, and here it is.

1 turkey carcass

1 tablespoon (18 g) salt

2 tablespoons (28 ml) vinegar

5 small turnips, cut into largish cubes

4 ribs of celery, cut into ½-inch (1.3 cm) lengths

½ pound (225 g) mushrooms, sliced

1 large onion, chopped

2 zucchini, each about 6 inches (15 cm) long, diced into small chunks

2 cups (248 g) frozen, cut green beans

1 teaspoon chicken bouillon concentrate

2 tablespoons (4 g) dried basil

Salt and pepper

1. In a large pot, break up the turkey carcass with whatever meat is still on it. Cover it with water, add the salt and vinegar, and simmer on low until the water is reduced to about 4 quarts (3.8 L). Let cool.

2. Pour the whole thing through a strainer and return the broth to the pot. Pick the meat off the turkey bones. Discard the bones, cut up the meat, and return it to the pot.

3. Add the turnips, celery, mushrooms, onion, zucchini, green beans, bouillon concentrate, and basil. Simmer until the vegetables are soft.

4. Season with salt and pepper to taste and serve.

YIELD: 12 servings, each with: 12 grams of carbohydrates and 4 grams of fiber, for a total of 8 grams of net carbs. Your protein count will depend on how big your turkey carcass is and how much meat was left on it, but assuming 2 cups (280 g) of diced turkey total, you'll get 15 grams of protein per serving.

PORTUGUESE SOUP

If this were authentic, it would have potatoes in it. But this decarbed version is delicious, and it's a full meal in a bowl. Read the labels on the smoked sausage carefully—they range from 1 gram of carb per serving up to 5.

⅓ cup (80 ml) olive oil, divided

¾ cup (120 g) chopped onion

3 cloves of garlic, crushed

2 cups (300 g) diced turnip

2 cups (200 g) diced cauliflower

1 pound (455 g) kale

1½ pounds (680 g) smoked sausage

1 can (14½ ounces, or 410 g) of diced tomatoes

2 quarts (1.9 L) chicken broth

¼ teaspoon Tabasco

Salt and pepper

1. Put ¼ cup (60 ml) of the olive oil in a large soup pot and sauté the onion, garlic, turnip, and cauliflower over medium heat.

2. While that's cooking, chop the kale into bite-size pieces and add it to the pot as well. (You may need to cram it in at first, but don't worry—it cooks down quite a bit.) Let the vegetables sauté for another 10 minutes or so, stirring to turn the whole thing over every once and a while.

3. Slice the smoked sausage lengthwise into quarters, then crosswise into ½-inch (1.3 cm) pieces. Heat the remaining oil in a heavy skillet over medium heat and brown the smoked sausage a bit.

4. Add the browned sausage, tomatoes, and 7½ cups (1.8 L) of the chicken broth to the kettle. Use the last ½ cup (120 ml) of broth to rinse the tasty browned bits out of the frying pan and add that, too. Bring to a simmer and cook until the vegetables are soft (30 to 45 minutes).

5. Stir in the Tabasco, season with salt and pepper to taste, and serve.

YIELD: 10 servings, each with: 372 Calories; 29 g Fat (70.5% calories from fat); 16 g Protein; 12 g Carbohydrate; 3 g Dietary Fiber; 9 g net carbs

CHAPTER 13

Condiments, Seasonings, and Sauces

O nce you start reading labels, you'll be shocked at how many of your favorite seasonings, sauces, and especially condiments are simply loaded with sugar, corn syrup, cornstarch, flour, and other things you'd rather keep to a minimum. Most brands of ketchup have 4 grams of carbohydrates per tablespoon (15 g), for heaven's sake, and barbecue sauce tends to run even higher! You can carve significant chunks of carbohydrates out of your diet by making your own sauces at home, instead.

CHEESE SAUCE

Try this over broccoli or cauliflower. It's wonderful! It's good over tofu shirataki, too, for mac-and-cheese.

**½ cup (120 ml)
heavy cream**

**¾ cup (86 g) shredded
Cheddar cheese**

¼ teaspoon dry mustard

1. In a heavy-bottomed saucepan over the lowest heat, warm the heavy cream to just below a simmer.
2. Whisk in the cheese about 1 tablespoon (7 g) at a time, only adding the next tablespoonful (7 g) after the last one has melted. When all the cheese is melted in, whisk in the dry mustard and serve.

YIELD: 4 servings, each with: 189 Calories; 18 g Fat (85.2% calories from fat); 6 g Protein; 1 g Carbohydrate; trace Dietary Fiber; 1 g net carbs

STIR-FRY SAUCE

If you like Chinese food, make this up and keep it on hand. Then, you can just throw any sort of meat and vegetables in your wok or skillet and have a meal in minutes.

½ cup (120 ml) soy sauce

½ cup (120 ml) dry sherry

2 cloves of garlic, crushed

**2 tablespoons (16 g) grated
fresh ginger**

**Liquid stevia, monkfruit,
or sucralose to equal
2 teaspoons of sugar
in sweetness**

Combine all the ingredients in a container with a tight-fitting lid and refrigerate until you're ready to use.

YIELD: 8 servings, each with: 29 Calories; trace Fat (1.9% calories from fat); 1 g Protein; 2 g Carbohydrate; trace Dietary Fiber; 2 g net carbs

NOT-VERY-AUTHENTIC PEANUT SAUCE

This is inauthentic because I used substitutes for such traditional ingredients as lemongrass and fish sauce. I wanted a recipe that tasted good but could be made without a trip to a specialty grocery store.

1 piece of fresh ginger about the size of a walnut, peeled and thinly sliced across the grain

½ cup (130 g) natural peanut butter, creamy

½ cup (120 ml) chicken broth

1½ teaspoons lemon juice

1½ teaspoons soy sauce

¼ teaspoon sriracha or other hot sauce

1 large or 2 small cloves of garlic, crushed

Liquid stevia, monkfruit, or sucralose to equal 1½ teaspoons of sugar in sweetness

1. Put all the ingredients in a blender and run it until everything is well combined and smooth.
2. If you'd like it a little thinner, add another tablespoon (15 ml) of chicken broth.

YIELD: 16 servings, each with: 54 Calories; 4 g Fat (62.6% calories from fat); 2 g Protein; 3 g Carbohydrate; 1 g Dietary Fiber; 2 g net carbs

HOISIN SAUCE

This super-popular Chinese condiment sparks all sorts of dishes! Sadly, authentic hoisin contains sugar, but that needn't concern us. Try this as a dip for chicken wings or brushed on pork steaks. I like it in chicken salad, too! If you're gluten-free, be sure to check the ingredients on your tahini.

¼ cup (60 ml) MCT oil

4 cloves of garlic, crushed

⅔ cup (160 ml) soy sauce

Liquid stevia, monkfruit, or sucralose to equal ⅓ cup (67 g) of sugar in sweetness

¼ cup (60 ml) distilled vinegar

¼ cup (60 g) tahini (sesame butter)

4 teaspoons (20 g) chili garlic sauce

1. Put a nonreactive saucepan—stainless steel, enamelware, or ceramic nonstick—over medium-low heat.
2. Heat the oil and add the garlic. Saute until lightly golden, about 3 to 5 minutes.
3. Add everything else and stir, working in the tahini. Cook, stirring often, for about 5 minutes.
4. Store in a tight-lidded jar in the refrigerator.

YIELD: 12 servings, each with: 81 Calories; 7 g Fat (76.7% calories from fat); 2 g Protein; 3 g Carbohydrate; 1 g Dietary Fiber; 2 g net carbs

TACO SEASONING

Many store-bought seasoning blends include sugar or cornstarch—my food counter book says that several popular brands have 5 grams of carbs in 2 teaspoons! This is low-carb, very easy to put together, tastes great, and is even cheaper than the premixed stuff.

2 tablespoons (15 g) chili powder

1½ tablespoons (11 g) cumin

1½ tablespoons (11 g) paprika

1 tablespoon (11 g) onion powder

1 tablespoon (9 g) garlic powder

⅛ to ¼ teaspoon cayenne pepper (less makes a milder seasoning, more takes the spice up a notch)

1. Combine all the ingredients, blending well, and store in an airtight container.
2. Use 2 tablespoons (about 16 g) of this mixture to flavor 1 pound (455 g) of ground beef, turkey, or chicken.

YIELD: This should season about four 1-pound (455 g) batches of ground beef, turkey, or chicken, adding to each batch: 10 Calories; trace Fat (27.0% calories from fat); trace Protein; 2 g Carbohydrate; 1 g Dietary Fiber; 1 g net carbs

CHICKEN SEASONING

This is wonderful sprinkled over chicken before roasting. It's also good on roasted pecans!

⅓ cup (96 g) salt or (64 g) Vege-Sal

2 teaspoons paprika

2 teaspoons onion powder

2 teaspoons garlic powder

2 teaspoons curry powder

1 teaspoon black pepper

1. Combine all the ingredients well and store in a salt or spice shaker.
2. Sprinkle over chicken before roasting; I use it to season at the table, as well.

YIELD: The whole batch contains: 33 Calories; 1 g Fat (15.1% calories from fat); 1 g Protein; 7 g Carbohydrate; 2 g Dietary Fiber; 5 g net carbs. The carb load from sprinkling this on a piece of chicken is negligible.

CAJUN SEASONING

This New Orleans–style seasoning is good sprinkled over chicken, steak, pork, fish, or just about anything else you care to try it on.

2½ tablespoons (18 g) paprika

2 tablespoons (36 g) salt

2 tablespoons (18 g) garlic powder

1 tablespoon (6 g) black pepper

1 tablespoon (7 g) onion powder

1 tablespoon (5 g) cayenne pepper

1 tablespoon (3 g) dried oregano

1 tablespoon (3 g) dried thyme

Combine all the ingredients thoroughly and store in an airtight container.

YIELD: 32 servings, each with: 6 Calories; trace Fat (16.2% calories from fat); trace Protein; 1 g Carbohydrate; trace Dietary Fiber; 1 g net carbs

JERK SEASONING

Sprinkle this over chicken, pork chops, or fish before cooking for an instant hit of hot, sweet, and spicy flavor.

1 tablespoon (15 g) erythritol/stevia or erythritol/monkfruit blend

1 tablespoon (7 g) onion powder

2 teaspoons ground thyme

1 teaspoon ground allspice

¼ teaspoon ground cinnamon

1 teaspoon black pepper

1 teaspoon cayenne pepper

2 teaspoons salt

¼ teaspoon ground nutmeg

Combine all the ingredients and store in a shaker with a tight lid.

YIELD: Scant ⅓ cup (35 g). 16 servings, each with: 4 Calories; trace Fat (13.9% calories from fat); trace Protein; 1 g Carbohydrate; trace Dietary Fiber; 1 g net carb

DANA'S NO-SUGAR KETCHUP

Store-bought ketchup has more sugar in it per ounce (28 g) than ice cream does! Heinz no-sugar-added ketchup is quite good and even easier. But it's pricier and includes artificial sweeteners some people avoid. This is a cinch, tastes great, and has no artificial sweeteners

15 ounces (425 g) tomato sauce

½ cup (120 ml) cider vinegar

3 tablespoons (45 g) erythritol/stevia or erythritol/monkfruit sweetener OR

3 tablespoons (45 g) erythritol plus liquid stevia, monkfruit, or sucralose to equal 3 tablespoons (39 g) of sugar in sweetness

1 teaspoon salt

½ teaspoon onion powder

¼ teaspoon garlic powder

1. Simply combine everything in a nonreactive saucepan—stainless steel, ceramic nonstick, or enamelware—and bring to a simmer.
2. Let it cook for 15 minutes, let it cool, and it's done. I used a funnel to pour mine into an old squeeze-type ketchup bottle for ease of use, but a jar or snap-top container will do just fine.

YIELD: 24 servings of 2 teaspoons, each with: 6 Calories; trace Fat (3.5% calories from fat); trace Protein; 2 g Carbohydrate; trace Dietary Fiber; 2 g net carbs

LOW-CARB STEAK SAUCE

I love steak and eggs, but I want steak sauce with them! Sadly, both A.1. and Heinz 57 are pretty sugary. This isn't!

¼ cup (60 g) Dana's No-Sugar Ketchup

1 tablespoon (15 ml) Worcestershire sauce

1 teaspoon lemon juice

Combine everything well and store in an airtight container in the fridge.

YIELD: 5 servings of 1 tablespoon, each with: 6 Calories; 0 g Fat (0.0% calories from fat); trace Protein; 1 g Carbohydrate; trace Dietary Fiber; 1 g net carbs

COCKTAIL SAUCE

Use this for your cold, boiled shrimp, of course. Commercial cocktail sauce, like so many other condiments, is full of sugar.

¼ cup (60 g) Dana's No-Sugar Ketchup

1 teaspoon prepared horseradish

2 or 3 drops of Tabasco

½ teaspoon lemon juice

Just stir everything together and dip!

YIELD: The whole batch has: 10 Calories; trace Fat (1.7% calories from fat); trace Protein; 2 g Carbohydrate; trace Dietary Fiber; 2 g net carbs

AIOLI

This is just very garlicky mayonnaise. It's good on all kinds of vegetables and on fish, too. You can make this more ketogenic by using half MCT oil, if you like.

4 cloves of garlic, crushed very thoroughly

1 egg

¼ teaspoon salt

2 tablespoons (28 ml) lemon juice

½–⅔ cup (120–160 ml) olive oil

1. Put the garlic, egg, salt, and lemon juice in a blender.
2. Run the blender for 10 seconds and then pour in the olive oil in a very thin stream, as you would when making mayonnaise.
3. Turn off the blender when the sauce is thickened.

YIELD: 8 servings of 2 tablespoons, each with: 131 Calories; 14 g Fat (94.9% calories from fat); 1 g Protein; 1 g Carbohydrate; trace Dietary Fiber;1 g net carbs

WONDERFUL MEMPHIS-STYLE DRY RUB BBQ

The Mystery Chef sends this recipe. It's good on ribs, chops, or chicken and far lower carb than barbecue sauce.

1 tablespoon (7 g) paprika

2 teaspoons chili powder

¾ teaspoon salt

¼ teaspoon dry mustard

¼ teaspoon garlic powder

⅛ teaspoon pepper

1. Mix all the ingredients together and store the mixture in a salt shaker.
2. Sprinkle on both sides of whatever meat you're cooking and grill.

YIELD: Enough for 3½ pounds (1.6 kg) of ribs, or about 3 servings, each with: 13 Calories; 1 g Fat (31.1% calories from fat); 1 g Protein; 2 g Carbohydrate; 1 g Dietary Fiber; 1 g net carbs

REDUCED-CARB SPICY BARBECUE SAUCE

The first low-carb barbecue sauce I came up with and still a winner! Originally, this called for ¼ cup (6 g) of granular Splenda instead of the erythritol-based sweetener, and you can still make it that way if you prefer—or use liquid sucralose to equal ¼ cup (50 g) sugar in sweetness. If you're dairy-free, use MCT or coconut oil instead of butter.

If you're wondering whether it's worth it to make your own barbecue sauce from scratch, chew on this for a moment: Your average commercial barbecue sauce has between 10 and 15 grams of carbs per 2-tablespoon (32 g) serving—and do you know anyone who ever stopped at 2 tablespoons (32 g) of barbecue sauce?

1 clove of garlic, crushed

1 small onion, finely minced

¼ cup (55 g) butter or (60 ml) MCT or (55 g) bland coconut oil

2 tablespoons (30 g) erythritol/monkfruit or erythritol/stevia blend OR 2 tablespoons (30 g) erythritol PLUS 32 drops of liquid stevia–English toffee

1 teaspoon salt or Vege-Sal

1 teaspoon dry mustard

1 teaspoon paprika

1 teaspoon chili powder

½ teaspoon black pepper

2 teaspoons (14 g) molasses

1½ cups (355 ml) water

¼ cup (60 ml) cider vinegar

1 tablespoon (15 ml) Worcestershire sauce

1 tablespoon (15 g) prepared horseradish

1 can (6 ounces, or 170 g) of tomato paste

1 tablespoon (15 ml) liquid smoke

1. In a saucepan, sauté the garlic and onion in the butter for a few minutes.

2. Stir in the sweetener, salt, dry mustard, paprika, chili powder, and pepper. Add in the molasses, water, vinegar, Worcestershire sauce, and horseradish and stir to combine. Let the mixture simmer for 15 to 20 minutes.

3. Whisk in the tomato paste and liquid smoke and let the sauce simmer another 5 to 10 minutes.

4. Let the mixture cool, transfer it to a jar with a tight-fitting lid, and store in the refrigerator.

YIELD: 20 servings, each with: 34 Calories; 2 g Fat (59.8% calories from fat); trace Protein; 3 g Carbohydrate; 1 g Dietary Fiber; 2 g net carbs

TEQUILA LIME MARINADE

This is great for chicken, shrimp and other seafood, and even pork. If you like, you can boil the marinade at a complete, rolling boil for five minutes after draining it off and serve it as a sauce, too.

⅓ cup (80 ml) lime juice (Bottled is fine.)

⅓ cup (80 ml) water

3 tablespoons (45 ml) tequila

Liquid stevia, monkfruit, or sucralose to equal 1 tablespoon (13 g) of sugar in sweetness (I'd use lemon drop flavored stevia.)

1 tablespoon (15 ml) soy sauce

2 cloves of garlic, crushed

Combine all the ingredients and store in the refrigerator until ready to use.

YIELD: This is enough for a dozen servings of chicken or shrimp, and will add to each serving: 11 Calories; trace Fat (2.0% calories from fat); trace Protein; 1 g Carbohydrate; trace Dietary Fiber; 1 g net carbs. Keep in mind you'll only get all of that if you boil the marinade and use it as a sauce. Otherwise, quite a lot will drain off.

TERIYAKI SAUCE

This sauce is the perennial favorite! It's good on chicken, beef, fish—just about anything.

½ cup (120 ml) soy sauce

¼ cup (60 ml) dry sherry

1 clove of garlic, crushed

1 tablespoon (15 g) erythritol/monkfruit or erythritol/stevia blend

OR 1 tablespoon (15 g) erythritol PLUS liquid stevia, monkfruit, or sucralose to equal 1 tablespoon (13 g) of sugar in sweetness

1 tablespoon (8 g) grated fresh ginger

Combine all the ingredients and refrigerate until ready to use.

YIELD: 12 servings of 1 tablespoon (15 ml), each with: 14 Calories; trace Fat (1.4% calories from fat); 1 g Protein; 2 g Carbohydrate; trace Dietary Fiber; 2 g net carbs

JERK MARINADE

Jerk is a Jamaican way of life. Make it with one pepper if you want it just nicely hot or with two peppers if you want it traditional—also known as take-the-top-of-your-head-off hot.

If you just can't take the heat, you can chicken out and use a jalapeño or two instead of the habaneros or Scotch Bonnets, and your jerk marinade will be mild, as these things go. But remember: There is no such thing as a truly mild jerk sauce. If you just can't take heat, make something else.

1 or 2 Scotch bonnet or habanero peppers, with or without seeds and rib (The seeds and ribs are the hottest part.)

½ of a small onion

3 tablespoons (45 ml) MCT or melted bland coconut oil

1 tablespoon (6 g) ground allspice

2 tablespoons (18 g) grated fresh ginger

1 tablespoon (15 ml) soy sauce

1 teaspoon dried thyme

1 bay leaf, crumbled

¼ teaspoon cinnamon

1 tablespoon (15 g) erythritol PLUS a few drops of liquid stevia, monkfruit, or sucralose

2 cloves of garlic, crushed

1. Halve the pepper(s) and remove the seeds. If you're nervous about the heat, scrape out the ribs, as well—they're the hottest part.

2. Put the pepper or peppers in your food processor with the S-blade in place. Now WASH YOUR HANDS VERY THOROUGHLY WITH SOAP AND HOT WATER.

3. Add everything else to the food processor and run until it's fairly smooth.

YIELD: 4 servings, each with: 113 Calories; 11 g Fat (80.2% calories from fat); 1 g Protein; 5 g Carbohydrate; 1 g Dietary Fiber; 4 g net carbs

LOOING SAUCE

This is a Chinese sauce for "red cooking." You stew things in it, and it imparts a wonderful flavor to just about any sort of meat. Star anise is available in Asian markets, and my health food store carries it, too. It does look like a star, and it's essential to the recipe. Don't try to substitute regular anise. If you're gluten-free, be sure to check the label on your soy sauce.

2 cups (475 ml) soy sauce

1 star anise

½ cup (120 ml) dry sherry (The cheap stuff is fine.)

2 tablespoons (30 g) erythritol/monkfruit or erythritol/stevia blend OR 2 tablespoons (30 g) erythritol PLUS liquid stevia, monkfruit, or sucralose to equal 2 tablespoons (26 g) of sugar in sweetness

1 tablespoon (8 g) grated fresh ginger

4 cups (946 ml) water

---

1. Combine all the ingredients well and use the mixture to stew things in. (Specifically, see Looed Chicken on page 173, and Looed Pork on page 237.)

2. After using the Looing Sauce, you can strain it and refrigerate or freeze it to use again, if you like.

YIELD: The whole batch will have: 469 Calories; 2 g Fat (3.9% calories from fat); 31 g Protein; 55 g Carbohydrate; 6 g Dietary Fiber; 49 g net carbs. But that's misleading because only a tiny amount of the sauce actually penetrates the meat you cook in it.

CRANBERRY SAUCE

This is unbelievably easy and good with roast chicken or turkey—as though you needed to be told! Fresh cranberries are available only in fall, but they freeze beautifully. Just stick them in a plastic bag in the freezer and pull them out when you need them.

½ teaspoon plain gelatin (optional)

1 cup (235 ml) water

1 bag (12 ounces, or 340 g) of fresh cranberries

Liquid stevia, monkfruit, or sucralose to equal 1 cup (200 g) of sugar in sweetness (Use part Valencia orange stevia if you like cranberry-orange relish.)

---

1. Combine the water, cranberries, and sweetener in a saucepan over medium-high heat. (If you're using the gelatin, dissolve it in ½ cup [120 ml] of the water and then add it to the cranberries and sweetener in a saucepan over medium-high heat.)

2. Bring the mixture to a boil and boil it hard until the cranberries pop.

3. Keep it in a tightly covered jar in the fridge.

YIELD: 16 servings of 2 tablespoons (32 g), each with:
10 Calories; trace Fat (3.3% calories from fat); trace Protein; 3 g Carbohydrate; 1 g Dietary Fiber; 2 g net carbs

CRANBERRY CHUTNEY

Think of this as cranberry sauce with a kick. It's good with any curried poultry or even with plain old roast chicken. This recipe improves if you let the boiled mixture sit for a while before serving. Try it with a cinnamon stick added, too.

1 bag (12 ounces, or 340 g) of cranberries

1 cup (235 ml) water

¼ cup (60 g) erythritol/ stevia or erythritol/ monkfruit blend OR ¼ cup (60 g) erythritol PLUS liquid stevia, monkfruit, or sucralose to equal ¼ cup (50 g) of sugar in sweetness

2 cloves of garlic, crushed

1 tablespoon (6 g) pumpkin pie spice

⅛ teaspoon salt

1. Combine all the ingredients in a saucepan over medium heat.
2. Bring it to a boil and boil until the cranberries pop, about 7 to 8 minutes.

YIELD: 16 servings of 2 tablespoons (32 g), each with:
12 Calories; trace Fat (5.8% calories from fat); trace Protein; 3 g Carbohydrate; 1 g Dietary Fiber; 2 net carbs

HOLLANDAISE FOR SISSIES

This is an easy, unintimidating sauce for asparagus, artichokes, broccoli, or whatever you like. Since I wrote this recipe, tabletop induction burners have become available. I love mine, largely because it lets you set a specific temperature and it will hold it. You could do this on an induction burner set at about 130°F (54°C).

4 egg yolks

1 cup (230 g) sour cream

1 tablespoon (15 ml) lemon juice

½ teaspoon salt or Vege-Sal

Dash of Tabasco

1. You'll need either a double boiler or a heat diffuser for this; it needs very gentle heat. If you're using a double boiler, you want the water in the bottom hot, but not boiling. If you're using a heat diffuser, use the lowest possible heat under the diffuser.
2. Put all the ingredients in a heavy-bottomed saucepan or the top of a double boiler.
3. Whisk everything together well, let it warm through, and serve it over vegetables.

YIELD: 6 servings, each with: 122 Calories; 11 g Fat (83.4% calories from fat); 3 g Protein; 2 g Carbohydrate; trace Dietary Fiber; 2 g net carbs

NO-FAIL HOLLANDAISE

This recipe is courtesy of reader Linda Carroll-King. Make sure you follow her directions to use room-temperature eggs—that's what makes this recipe no-fail.

½ cup (112 g) butter

4 eggs yolks at room temperature

1 tablespoon (15 ml) fresh lemon juice

White pepper

1. Heat the butter to a bubble in a saucepan over low heat; don't let it burn.
2. While the butter is heating, put the egg yolks, lemon juice, and white pepper to taste in a blender.
3. When the butter is bubbling, start the blender. Without giving the butter time to cool, slowly pour it into the blender. Whir for several seconds and it's done.

YIELD: 4 servings of 2 tablespoons (28 g), each with: 264 Calories; 28 g Fat (94.5% calories from fat); 3 g Protein; 1 g Carbohydrate; trace Dietary Fiber; 1 g net carbs

GREEN TOMATO CHUTNEY

Most chutneys are full of sugar, so I invented my own. Now, I plant extra tomatoes in the summer to have enough to make this or buy up green tomatoes at the end-of-the-summer farmers' market. It's wonderful with anything curried.

I generally don't use the stevia/FOS blend anymore because I rarely used it up before it caked. But it's still available, under the name SweetLeaf.

4 quarts (2.8 kg) green tomatoes, cut into chunks

3 cups (700 ml) cider vinegar

1 whole ginger, sliced into very thin rounds

5 or 6 cloves of garlic, thinly sliced

1 tablespoon (6 g) whole cloves

5 or 6 sticks whole cinnamon

½ cup (120 g) erythritol

1 tablespoon (20 g) molasses

1 tablespoon (8 g) stevia/ FOS blend OR liquid stevia, monkfruit, or sucralose to equal ½ cup (100 g) of sugar in sweetness

Note: There are two things you need to know when buying and cooking with ginger. The first is that a whole ginger is also called a "hand" of ginger. The second is that you should always cut ginger across the grain, not along it, or you'll end up with woody ginger.

1. Combine all the ingredients in a large stainless steel or enamel kettle—no iron, no aluminum. (This is an acidic mixture, and if you use iron or aluminum, you'll end up with your chutney chock-full of iron, which will turn it blackish, or aluminum, which simply isn't good for you.)
2. Simmer on low for 3 to 4 hours.
3. Store in tightly closed containers in the refrigerator.

YIELD: 64 servings of 2 tablespoons (32 g), each with: 18 Calories; trace Fat (6.6% calories from fat); 1 g Protein; 5 g Carbohydrate; 1 g Dietary Fiber; 4 g net carbs

DUCK SAUCE

What will you eat duck sauce on, now that you're not eating egg rolls? Well, Crab and Bacon Bundles (page 64), for starters. It's good with chicken, too. This does have the sugar that's in the peaches, of course, but not all the added sugar of commercial duck sauce. And it tastes better, too. It's best to freeze this if you're not going to use it up right away.

1 bag (1 pound, or 455 g) unsweetened frozen peaches OR 2½ to 3 cups (425 to 510 g) sliced, peeled fresh peaches

½ cup (120 ml) water

2 tablespoons (28 ml) cider vinegar

1 tablespoon (15 g) erythritol

18 drops of liquid stevia–English toffee flavor

⅛ teaspoon salt

1 teaspoon soy sauce

1 clove of garlic, crushed

1. Put all the ingredients in a heavy-bottomed saucepan and bring them to a simmer. Cook, uncovered, until the peaches are soft (about 30 minutes).

2. Puree the duck sauce in a blender, if you like, or do what I do: simply mash the sauce with a potato masher or a fork. (I like the texture better this way.)

YIELD: 2 cups (620 g), or 16 servings of 2 tablespoons (32 g), each with: 11 Calories; trace Fat (0.1% calories from fat); trace Protein; 3 g Carbohydrate; trace Dietary Fiber; 3 g net carbs

TOOTSIE'S PESTO

Tootsie is my friend Kay's mother, and this is her recipe. Store-bought pesto is okay for us, but it's awfully expensive and not nearly so fresh and good! This makes a highly concentrated product; feel free to thin it a bit with olive oil before you use it.

Your can store your pesto by freezing it in an ice cube tray and then wrapping it in small pieces of plastic wrap, or you can keep it in a plastic container with a snap-on lid in the fridge. Kay says she particularly likes this thinned a bit with olive oil and served on cooked green beans—to quote her: "Yummy yum yum." Pesto is also good with chicken and seafood and of course, tossed with tofu shirataki!

2 cups (48 g) fresh basil leaves, washed and patted dry

4 good-sized garlic cloves

1 cup (100 g) shelled walnuts or (135 g) pine nuts (I generally use walnuts. I love pine nuts, but geez, they're expensive!)

1 cup (235 ml) extra-virgin olive oil

1 cup (100 g) freshly grated Parmesan cheese

¼ cup (25 g) freshly grated Romano cheese

Salt and pepper

1. Combine the basil, garlic, and nuts and chop in a food processor with the S-blade. Leave the motor running and add the olive oil in a slow steady stream.

2. Shut off the food processor and add the Parmesan cheese, Romano cheese, a big pinch of salt, and a liberal grinding of pepper. Process briefly to blend.

YIELD: 32 servings of 1 tablespoon (15 g), each with: 99 Calories; 10 g Fat (87.9% calories from fat); 2 g Protein; 1 g Carbohydrate; trace Dietary Fiber; 1 g net carbs

CHAPTER 14

Cookies, Cakes, and Other Sweets

I am of two minds about this chapter (a chapter which, by the way, contains recipes for treats as delicious as any sugary desserts you've ever made). On the one hand, I think it's a bad idea to get in the habit of eating these sugarless sweets with the same frequency with which you used to eat the sugary stuff. I feel strongly that weaning yourself away from wanting sweets all the time, from not considering a meal complete until you've had a dessert, is a very good and important thing.

On the other hand, I understand—boy, do I understand!—the lure of sweets. Heck, as a kid, I quite literally stole to get sugar. And I know that for some of you, these recipes will be the thing that lets you stick to your diet and break your sugar addiction altogether.

So, this is what I suggest: If you're fighting severe sugar cravings or if you're subject to frequent temptation, keep one or two of these desserts on hand. They really do taste great and satisfy your taste buds. However, they will not cause the blood sugar rush—or crash—of the sugary stuff, and therefore, with the help of these desserts, you should be able to slowly back away from sweets until they're just an occasional treat. And that, my friend, is where I would love for you to be.

BUTTER COOKIES

Our tester, Tammera Lowe, says to tell you that these don't spread much, so feel free to place them fairly close together on the baking parchment–also, that these are "addictive!"

You can play with the flavor of this recipe by using different flavors of liquid stevia. Vanilla, lemon drop, and English toffee would all be good. Tammera used English toffee. I wouldn't use cinnamon with lemon drop, but that's up to you.

1 cup (225 g) butter at room temperature

8 ounces (225 g) cream cheese at room temperature

3 tablespoons (45 g) erythritol/monkfruit or erythritol/stevia blend OR 3 tablespoons (45 g) erythritol plus liquid stevia, monkfruit, or sucralose to equal ⅓ cup (66 g) of sugar in sweetness

1 egg

1 cup (129 g) vanilla whey protein powder

1 cup (112 g) almond meal

½ teaspoon baking powder

¼ teaspoon guar or xanthan

½ teaspoon ground cinnamon (optional)

Erythritol, erythritol blend, or granular sucralose sweetener

1. Use an electric mixer to cream the butter and cream cheese together until well blended and soft. Add the sweetener(s) and cream until completely combined. Beat in the egg.

2. In another bowl, combine the protein powder, almond meal, baking powder, and guar. Stir together well.

3. Beat the dry ingredients into the butter–cream cheese mixture in 3 additions.

4. Make 1-inch (2.5 cm) balls of the dough and place them on baking parchment on cookie sheets. Chill for 15 minutes or so, while you preheat the oven to 375°F (190°C, or gas mark 5).

5. Mix 1 tablespoon (15 g) of erythritol or (2 g) of granular sucralose with the cinnamon (if using) on a small plate or saucer. Take a flat-bottomed glass, measuring cup, or something similar and butter the bottom. Pull the dough balls out of the fridge. Dip the buttered cup in the cinnamon and sweetener and use it to press the cookies flat. You'll need to dip your "pressing glass" in the cinnamon and sweetener for each cookie, but you won't have to rebutter the bottom each time. The butter just keeps the cup from sticking to the cookies and of course, puts yummy cinnamon and sweetener on each one!

6. Bake for about 9 minutes, checking at 8 minutes, to make sure the bottoms aren't browning too fast. The cookies are done when the bottoms are just starting to brown.

YIELD: 6 dozen cookies, each with: 55 Calories; 4 g Fat (68.4% calories from fat); 3 g Protein; 1 g Carbohydrate; trace Dietary Fiber; 1 net carb

CHOCOLATE WALNUT BALLS

These are great to make around Christmastime, when high-carb temptations abound. Christina Robertson, our tester, says, " very quick and easy. Just the right amount of chocolate, walnut, and sweetness." She also says that she served them with merlot for a company dessert, and they were much appreciated.

½ cup (112 g) butter at room temperature

2 ounces (55 g) cream cheese at room temperature

⅔ cup (160 g) erythritol

Liquid stevia to equal ⅔ cup (133 g) of sugar in sweetness–chocolate, vanilla, or a combination

1 egg

1 teaspoon vanilla extract

2 ounces (55 g) unsweetened baking chocolate, melted

1 cup (112 g) almond meal

½ cup (65 g) vanilla whey protein powder

1½ teaspoons baking powder

¼ teaspoon guar or xanthan

¼ teaspoon salt

½ cup (60 g) chopped walnuts

1. Preheat the oven to 375°F (190°C, or gas mark 5).

2. With an electric mixer, beat the butter and cream cheese until soft and well combined. Add the sweeteners and beat, scraping down the sides of the bowl a few times, until well combined. Add the egg and the vanilla and beat until well combined, again, scraping down the sides of the bowl a few times. Beat in the melted chocolate.

3. In another bowl, combine the almond meal, protein powder, baking powder, guar, and salt. Stir until everything is evenly distributed.

4. Beat the dry ingredients into the batter in 3 additions, incorporating each well before adding the next.

5. Stir in the walnuts.

6. Butter or spray cookie sheets with nonstick cooking spray. Roll the dough into small balls and place them on the sheets. Bake for 8 to 10 minutes. Cool on a wire rack.

YIELD: 40 cookies, each with: 69 Calories; 5 g Fat (65.9% calories from fat); 4 g Protein; 2 g Carbohydrate; trace Dietary Fiber; 2 g net carbs

PEANUT BUTTER COOKIES

I can't tell these from my mom's peanut butter cookies!

½ cup (112 g) butter at room temperature

½ cup (120 g) erythritol

1 teaspoon liquid stevia–English Toffee flavor

1 egg

1 cup (260 g) natural peanut butter

½ teaspoon salt

½ teaspoon baking soda

½ teaspoon vanilla extract

½ cup (56 g) almond meal

½ cup (65 g) vanilla whey protein powder

¼ teaspoon guar or xanthan

1. Preheat the oven to 375°F (190°C, or gas mark 5).

2. Use an electric mixer to beat the butter until creamy. Add the sweeteners and beat again until well combined.

3. Beat in the egg, peanut butter, salt, baking soda, and vanilla.

4. Measure the almond meal, protein powder, and guar into a separate bowl and stir together until they're evenly distributed.

5. Beat the dry ingredients into the wet ingredients in 3 separate additions.

6. Butter or spray cookie sheets with nonstick cooking spray or line with baking parchment. Roll the dough into 1-inch (2.5 cm) balls and place them on the sheets. Use the back of a fork to press the balls of dough flat, leaving those traditional peanut butter cookie crisscross marks.

7. Bake for 8 to 9 minutes or until the edges are just getting golden.

YIELD: About 50 cookies, each with: 62 Calories; 5 g Fat (67.5% calories from fat); 3 g Protein; 2 g Carbohydrate; trace Dietary Fiber; 2 g net carbs

HAZELNUT SHORTBREAD

Do you ILove Walkers Shortbread cookies? You have to try these! They are delicate, but then shortbread is supposed to be that way. If you'd like to make them a little sturdier, add ¼ to ½ teaspoon of guar or xanthan when grinding the hazelnuts. Oh, and you can make these from almond meal, instead, if you like.

2 cups (270 g) hazelnuts

1 cup (129 g) vanilla whey protein powder

¼ teaspoon guar or xanthan (optional, but improves texture)

½ teaspoon salt

¼ teaspoon baking powder

1 cup (225 g) butter at room temperature

¼ cup (60 g) erythritol

¼ teaspoon liquid stevia-plain or hazelnut

1 egg

2 tablespoons (28 ml) water

1. Preheat the oven to 325°F (170°C, or gas mark 3). Line a jelly roll pan with baking parchment.

2. Use your food processor to grind the hazelnuts to a fine meal. Add the protein powder, guar (if using), salt, and baking powder and pulse to combine.

3. Using an electric mixer, beat the butter until it's fluffy. Add the erythritol and liquid stevia and beat well again.

4. Add the egg and beat in thoroughly.

5. Beat in the dry ingredients in 3 additions, incorporating each addition thoroughly before adding more.

6. When all the dry ingredients are in, beat in the water.

7. You will now have a soft, sticky dough. Turn in out into the parchment-lined jelly roll pan. Cover with another sheet of baking parchment and press the dough out into an even layer covering the whole pan. It should be about ¼ inch (6 mm) thick.

8. Peel off the top sheet of parchment and score the dough into squares using a thin, straight-bladed, sharp knife in a straight up-and-down motion, rather than a slicing motion.

9. Bake for 25 to 30 minutes or until golden.

10. Re-score the lines before removing the shortbread from the pan. Use a straight up-and-down motion rather than drawing the knife across the shortbread and they'll be less likely to break. Store in a cookie can, of course!

YIELD: 48 cookies, each with: 91 Calories; 8 g Fat (75.3% calories from fat); 5 g Protein; 1 g Carbohydrate; trace Dietary Fiber; 1 g net carbs

ALMOND COOKIES

Our tester Nancy Loy says that these are big, adding that next time she'll make them a little smaller because the almond on top is "the bomb." She also says that they make great ice cream sandwiches, should you have any low-carb ice cream on hand.

If you add liquid stevia separately, use vanilla or English toffee.

1 cup (225 g) butter at room temperature

⅔ cup (160 g) erythritol/ monkfruit or erythritol/ stevia blend OR ½ cup (120 g) erythritol PLUS liquid stevia, monkfruit, or sucralose to equal ⅔ cup (133 g) of sugar in sweetness

1 egg

1 cup (260 g) almond butter

½ teaspoon salt

½ teaspoon baking soda

¾ cup (84 g) almond meal

¾ cup (97 g) vanilla whey protein powder

¼ teaspoon guar or xanthan

2 tablespoons (28 ml) water

30 shelled almonds

1. Preheat the oven to 375°F (190°C, or gas mark 5).

2. Use an electric mixer to beat the butter until smooth and fluffy. Add the sweeteners and beat again, scraping down the sides, until very well combined.

3. Beat in the egg and then add the almond butter, salt, and baking soda.

4. In a separate bowl, stir together the almond meal, protein powder, and guar.

5. Beat the combined dry ingredients into the butter-and-egg mixture in 3 additions, combining well.

6. Add the water and beat until everything is well combined.

7. Use a measuring tablespoon (15 ml) to scoop heaping tablespoons (15 ml) of dough onto greased cookie sheets. Each cookie should be made of about 2 tablespoons (28 ml) of dough. Press an almond into the center of each cookie. Bake for 10 to 12 minutes or until the cookies just begin to brown around the edges.

YIELD: Makes about 30 cookies: 143 Calories; 12 g Fat (71.0% calories from fat); 8 g Protein; 3 g Carbohydrate; 1 g Dietary Fiber; 2 net carbs

SESAME COOKIES

Tahini is sesame butter, made from ground sesame seeds just as peanut butter is made from ground peanuts. Keep in mind that it needs to be refrigerated once opened, and if it sits too long, it will separate, with oil on top and an intractable mass of sesame sludge at the bottom. So use it up.

½ cup (112 g) butter at room temperature

1 cup (240 g) tahini (roasted sesame butter)

½ cup (120 g) erythritol/ monkfruit or erythritol/ stevia blend

1 egg

¾ cup (84 g) almond meal

¾ cup (97 g) vanilla whey protein powder

½ teaspoon salt

½ teaspoon baking soda

¼ teaspoon guar or xanthan

¼ cup (36 g) sesame seeds

1. Preheat the oven to 350°F (180°C, or gas mark 4). Coat a couple of cookie sheets with cooking spray or line with baking parchment.

2. Use an electric mixer to beat the butter and tahini together, scraping down the sides of the bowl frequently, until smooth and completely blended.

3. Add sweetener and beat well. Next, beat in the egg.

4. In another bowl, combine all the dry ingredients, from almond meal through guar, and stir them together well. Crush any little lumps of baking soda you might see.

5. Beat the dry ingredients into the butter-tahini mixture in 3 additions until it's all well blended.

6. Beat in the sesame seeds last. Some are likely to fall to the bottom; use a rubber scraper to scrape them up and into the dough.

7. Form the dough into 1-inch (2.5 cm) balls and arrange on cookie sheets.

8. Bake for 10 to 12 minutes or until golden and just getting brown around the edges.

YIELD: 48 cookies: 58 Calories; 4 g Fat (55.5% calories from fat); 5 g Protein; 2 g Carbohydrate; 1 g Dietary Fiber; 1 g net carbs

MOM'S CHOCOLATE CHIP COOKIES

With this recipe, I assume the title of Low-Carb Cookie God.

I use Lily's brand sugar-free chocolate chips. I order them a case at a time from Sahara Mart, my health/international/gourmet grocery store. They're sweetened with erythritol and stevia and don't cause any gastric effect. If you can't get sugar-free chocolate chips, you need to make some from sugar-free chocolate bars. Break seven or eight of the bars, which are 1.3 to 1.5 ounces (36 to 42 g) each, into three or four pieces each and place the pieces in a food processor with the S-blade in place. Pulse the food processor until your chocolate bars are in pieces about the same size as commercial chocolate morsels and set them aside until you're ready to use them.

1 cup (225 g) butter at room temperature

¾ cup (180 g) erythritol

½ teaspoon liquid stevia–English Toffee

1 teaspoon molasses

2 eggs

1 cup (112 g) almond meal

1 cup (129 g) vanilla whey protein powder

1 teaspoon baking soda

1 teaspoon salt

¼ teaspoon guar or xanthan

1 cup (120 g) chopped walnuts or (110 g) pecans

12 ounces (340 g) sugar-free chocolate chips (I use Lily's brand.)

1. Preheat oven to 375°F (190°C, or gas mark 5). Coat 2 cookie sheets with cooking spray or line with baking parchment.

2. Use an electric mixer to beat the butter with the sweeteners until creamy and fluffy. Add the eggs, one at a time, beating well after each addition.

3. In a separate bowl, combine the almond meal, protein powder, baking soda, salt, and guar. Stir together until everything is evenly distributed.

4. Beat the dry ingredients into the butter mixture in 3 additions, making sure each is well-incorporated before adding the next.

5. Turn the mixer down to low speed and mix in the nuts and chocolate chips.

6. Drop dough by rounded tablespoonfuls (15 ml) onto the prepared cookie sheets. These will not spread and flatten as much as standard chocolate chip cookies, so if you want them flat, flatten them a bit now.

7. Bake for 10 minutes or until golden. Cool on the cookie sheets for a few minutes before transferring to wire racks to continue cooling. Store in a cookie can or snap-top container.

YIELD: 50 cookies, each with: 106 Calories; 8 g Fat (64.5% calories from fat); 6 g Protein; 4 g Carbohydrate; 1 g Dietary Fiber; 3 g net carbs

COCONUT SHORTBREAD

Tammera Lowe and Verna Haas, both of whom tested the new version of this recipe, loved it. Verna Haas adds, "I use the convection feature to bake cookies so I adjusted the temp to 300°F (150°C, or gas mark 2). I also added 1 minute to the 10 stated to achieve a golden brown color. The cookies were all slightly crisp and not too brown or white." She also said she added a teaspoon of coconut extract because her coconut oil was bland, not coconutty.

½ cup (115 g) butter at room temperature

½ cup (120 ml) extra-virgin coconut oil

1½ tablespoons (23 g) erythritol/monkfruit or erythritol/stevia blend OR 1½ tablespoons (23 g) erythritol plus liquid stevia, monkfruit, or sucralose to equal 1½ tablespoons (20 g) of sugar in sweetness

1½ cups (194 g) vanilla whey protein powder

1 cup (80 g) unsweetened shredded coconut meat

2 tablespoons (28 ml) water

1. Preheat the oven to 325°F (170°C, or gas mark 3).
2. Using an electric mixer, beat together the butter, coconut oil, and sweetener until light and creamy. Beat in the protein powder, coconut, and water, in that order, scraping down the sides of the bowl several times to make sure everything is well blended.
3. Line a jelly roll pan with baking parchment and turn the dough out onto it. Place another sheet of baking parchment on top and press the dough out into a thin, even sheet.
4. Use a sharp knife or pizza cutter to score the dough into small rectangles.
5. Bake for 7 to 10 minutes or until golden. Cool and break apart.

YIELD: 48 pieces, each with: 70 Calories; 5 g Fat (64.9% calories from fat); 5 g Protein; 1 g Carbohydrate; trace Dietary Fiber; 1 g net carbs

PECAN SANDIES

Peggy Witherow sent me a recipe for Pecan Sandies that she wanted decarbed, and this is the result. Our tester, Verna Haas, said she loved the flavor. I asked if she would make them again, and she gave an enthusiastic, "Yes!"

1 cup (225 g) butter at room temperature

½ cup (120 g) erythritol/monkfruit or erythritol/stevia blend OR ½ cup (120 g) erythritol plus Liquid stevia, monkfruit, or sucralose to equal ½ cup (100 g) of sugar

1 egg

¼ teaspoon guar or xanthan

1½ cups (194 g) vanilla whey protein powder

1½ cups (165 g) chopped pecans

½ teaspoon salt

1. Preheat the oven to 325°F (170°C, or gas mark 3).
2. Beat the butter and sweeteners together until light and creamy. Beat in the egg, mixing well. Then, beat in the guar, protein powder, pecans, and salt.
3. Spray a cookie sheet with nonstick cooking spray. Form the dough into balls about the size of a marble and flatten them slightly on the cookie sheet.
4. Bake for 10 to 15 minutes or until golden.

YIELD: 50 cookies, each with: 84 Calories; 7 g Fat (68.5% calories from fat); 6 g Protein; 1 g Carbohydrate; trace Dietary Fiber; 1 g net carbs

OATMEAL COOKIES

O.M.G. These are not grain-free, obviously, but still remarkably low carb and super-tasty! There are gluten-free rolled oats available, if you need them. Be sure your coconut oil is solid when you use it. If your kitchen is warm enough that it's liquid, stick your coconut oil in the refrigerator until it's solid before you use it.

1 cup (225 g) coconut oil

1 cup (225 g) butter at room temperature

¾ cup (180 g) erythritol/ monkfruit or erythritol/ stevia blend OR ¾ cup (180 g) erythritol plus Liquid stevia, monkfruit, or sucralose to equal ¾ cup (150 g) of sugar in sweetness

1 teaspoon molasses

2 eggs

1 cup (112 g) almond meal

1 cup (129 g) vanilla whey protein powder

1 teaspoon baking soda

1 teaspoon cinnamon

½ teaspoon salt

½ teaspoon guar or xanthan

1 cup (80 g) rolled oats (gluten-free)

1 cup (110 g) chopped pecans

1. Preheat the oven to 350°F (180°C, or gas mark 4). Coat a couple of cookie sheets with cooking spray or line with baking parchment.

2. With an electric mixer, beat together the coconut oil, butter, and sweetener until well combined, creamy, and fluffy.

3. Beat in the molasses and eggs, combining well.

4. In a separate bowl, combine the almond meal, protein powder, baking soda, cinnamon, salt, and guar, stirring until evenly combined.

5. Beat the almond meal–protein powder mixture into the wet ingredients in 3 additions, incorporating each one well before adding the next.

6. Beat in the oats and chopped pecans.

7. Drop the dough onto prepared cookie sheets by the scant tablespoonful (15 ml), leaving plenty of room for spreading.

8. Bake for 10 minutes, or until golden. Transfer the cookies carefully to wire racks to cool.

YIELD: About 60, each with: 104 Calories; 9 g Fat (74.9% calories from fat); 4 g Protein; 2 g Carbohydrate; trace Dietary Fiber; 2 g net carbs

COCOA-PEANUT PORKIES

The first time I tried this, I thought, "Dana, you have gone right 'round the bend, making pork rind cookies." Hah. They're fantastic. I have gotten more glowing feedback on this recipe than on almost any other. Try them. Really.

I first created this recipe using CarbSmart chocolate chips. Sadly, they are no longer with us. I now use Lily's stevia-and-erythritol-sweetened chocolate chips, which taste great, but melt a bit differently. I've altered the recipe to accommodate them. You could also melt 9 ounces (255 g) of sugar-free semisweet chocolate bars. ChocoPerfection are also erythritol and stevia sweetened.

We adore these as they are, but if your kids, just being weaned off of sugar, think they're not quite sweet enough, there's an easy fix: Add a glycerine-based liquid stevia extract to taste when you're stirring up the chocolate–peanut butter mixture. NOW dark chocolate flavor would be good; so would English toffee flavor. Go easy—think in drops, not spoonfuls.

1 cup (175 g) Lily's sugar-free chocolate chips

¾ cup (195 g) natural peanut butter

2 tablespoons (28 g) coconut oil

5 ounces (140 g) pork rinds (There are bags that hold just this amount.)

1. Line a 9 x 13-inch pan (23 x 33 cm) with nonstick foil. This is optional, but sure makes cleanup a breeze. Or, coat with nonstick spray if you prefer.

2. Originally, I microwaved the chocolate and peanut butter for these no-bake cookie bars, but my experiences microwaving Lily's chips have been . . . disappointing. So put your chocolate chips, peanut butter, and coconut oil in a saucepan over the very lowest heat you've got. If you have a heat diffuser, use it. You could also use a double boiler. The point is not to scorch your chocolate!

3. In the meanwhile, smash your pork rinds. Really. I just poke a hole in the bag to let the air out and bash 'em with my fists. You want bits somewhere between pea- and hazelnut-sized. Dump your broken-up pork rinds into your biggest mixing bowl.

4. When the chocolate–peanut butter mixture is all melted, stir it together well and then scrape it into the bowl with the pork rinds. Use your scraper to stir thoroughly, coating every bit of the pork rinds with the chocolate–peanut butter mixture.

5. Dump your chocolate-and-peanut-butter coated rinds into the prepared pan and use the scraper to spread and press them out into an even layer.

6. Chill thoroughly and then cut into bars. Store in the fridge.

YIELD: 24 bars, each with: 113 Calories; 8 g Fat (66.7% calories from fat); 6 g Protein; 4 g Carbohydrate; 1 g Dietary Fiber; 3 g net carbs

PEANUT BUTTER BROWNIES

This was the first recipe I tried from Diana Lee's *Baking Low-Carb*. I've updated the sweeteners and eliminated a tiny bit of oat flour. The peanut butter topping actually sinks, giving you a fudgy brownie layer on top and a chewy peanut butter cookie on the bottom.

BROWNIE LAYER

5 tablespoons (70 g) butter

¼ cup (20 g) unsweetened cocoa powder

2 eggs

¼ cup (60 ml) heavy cream

¼ cup (60 ml) water

1 teaspoon vanilla extract

½ cup (120 g) erythritol/ monkfruit or erythritol/ stevia blend

⅔ cup (86 g) vanilla whey protein powder

¼ cup (28 g) almond meal

1 tablespoon (5 g) baking powder

PEANUT BUTTER TOPPING

¼ cup (65 g) natural peanut butter

3 tablespoons (45 g) butter

1 tablespoon (15 g) erythritol/monkfruit or erythritol/stevia blend

1 egg

2 tablespoons (16 g) vanilla whey protein powder

---

1. Preheat the oven to 350°F (180°C, or gas mark 4). Coat an 8- x 8-inch (20 x 20 cm) baking pan with cooking spray.

2. Melt the butter and stir in the cocoa. Add the eggs, heavy cream, water, vanilla, and sweetener. Mix well.

3. Add the protein powder, almond meal, and baking powder and mix just until well moistened. Pour the batter into the prepared pan.

4. Mix the peanut butter, butter, sweetener, egg, and protein powder together. Spoon the mixture as evenly as you can over the top of the brownie batter.

5. Bake for 15 minutes—do not overbake.

YIELD: 16 servings, each with: 155 Calories; 11 g Fat (62.2% calories from fat); 12 g Protein; 4 g Carbohydrate; 1 g Dietary Fiber; 3 g net carbs

FUDGE TOFFEE

Jen Eloff says her husband Ian is mad for this candy. It's another winner from *Splendid Low-Carbing*.

2 cups (50 g) Splenda

1 cup (128 g) whole milk powder

1 cup (80 g) natural whey protein powder

½ cup (112 g) unsalted butter, melted

¼ cup (60 ml) whipping cream

2 tablespoons (28 ml) water

2 ounces (55 g) unsweetened baking chocolate, melted

1. In a large bowl, combine the Splenda, milk powder, and protein powder.

2. In a small bowl, combine the butter, cream, and water. Stir this into the dry ingredients. Stir in the melted chocolate until well combined.

3. Press the mixture into a 9 × 9-inch (23 x 23 cm) baking dish. Freeze for approximately 30 minutes and then refrigerate. Cut into squares and serve.

YIELD: 36 pieces, each with: 89 Calories; 7 g Fat (68.0% calories from fat); 5 g Protein; 2 g Carbohydrate; trace Dietary Fiber; 2 g net carbs

SUGAR-FREE CHOCOLATE MOUSSE TO DIE FOR!

This is the very first low-carb dessert I came up with, and it still blows people away. This is calculated on grocery store pudding mix—Jell-O, Royal, or the like. But if you prefer, there are stevia-and-erythritol sweetened pudding mixes on the market—Thrive Market carries one, and I'm sure Google could turn up more. And most plain instant coffee is gluten-free. Buy one that says it's 100% coffee and this mousse will be grain-free as well.

I like this made with the smaller amount of cream, for a sturdier texture, but I know folks who like it with the larger amount, for a fluffier texture. It's your choice.

1 package (4-serving size) of chocolate sugar-free instant pudding mix

1 package (about 10 ounces, or 280 g) of soft tofu

1 heaping tablespoon (5 g) unsweetened cocoa powder

¼–½ teaspoon instant coffee crystals (more, if you like mocha flavoring)

1–1½ cups (235–355 ml) heavy whipping cream, chilled

1. Use an electric mixer to beat the pudding mix, tofu, cocoa powder, and coffee crystals until very smooth.

2. In a separate bowl, whip the cream until just about stiff.

3. Turn the mixer to its lowest setting, blend in the pudding mixture, and turn off the mixer—quickly. (If you overbeat, you'll end up with chocolate butter.)

YIELD: Made with 1 cup (235 ml) of heavy cream, 6 servings, each with: 188 Calories; 17 g Fat (78.3% calories from fat); 5 g Protein; 6 g Carbohydrate; 1 g Dietary Fiber; 5 g net carbs

Made with 1½ cups (355 ml) of heavy cream, 8 servings, each with: 192 Calories; 18 g Fat (82.5% calories from fat); 4 g Protein; 5 g Carbohydrate; 1 g Dietary Fiber; 4 net carbs

Sugar-Free Vanilla Mousse To Die For!

Here's one for those non-chocoholics out there: Just use sugar-free vanilla instant pudding mix and a teaspoon of vanilla extract and omit the cocoa powder and the coffee crystals.

YIELD:

With 1 cup (235 ml) heavy cream, 6 servings, each with: 188 Calories; 17 g Fat (78.9% calories from fat); 5 g Protein; 6 g Carbohydrate; 1g Dietary Fiber; 5 g net carbs

With 1½ cups (355 ml) heavy cream, 7 servings, each with: 220 Calories; 21 g Fat (83.1% calories from fat); 4 g Protein; 5 g Carbohydrate; trace Dietary Fiber; 5 g net carbs

STRAWBERRY CUPS

This is a good make-ahead company dessert, and it's a really beautiful color. As with the previous recipe, these numbers are based on grocery store gelatin mix, but if you'd prefer, you can get erythritol/stevia sweetened "jel" mix from Thrive Market. It does not contain actual gelatin; apparently Thrive is appealing to the vegetarian market. I, on the other hand, consider gelatin a super-food. Up to you which issue is more important.

As for gluten, Jell-O sugar-free gelatin does not contain any direct gluten ingredients, but does not claim its product as gluten-free, I assume because of the possibility of cross-contamination. If you're gluten-free because, like me, you're convinced gluten isn't healthful, I wouldn't worry about it. If you have celiac disease, probably best to skip it.

1 cup (235 ml) water	**1 cup (235 ml) heavy cream, divided**
1 package (4-serving size) of sugar-free lemon gelatin	**½ teaspoon vanilla extract**
10 ounces (280 g) frozen unsweetened strawberries, partly thawed	**6 drops of liquid stevia, vanilla**

1. Bring the water to a boil. Put the gelatin and boiling water in a blender and whirl for 10 to 15 seconds to dissolve the gelatin. Add the strawberries and whirl again, just long enough to blend in the berries.

2. Put the blender container in the refrigerator for 10 minutes or just until the mixture starts to thicken a bit.

3. Add ¾ cup (175 ml) of the heavy cream and run the blender just long enough to mix it all in (10 to 15 seconds).

4. Pour into 5 or 6 pretty little dessert cups and chill. Whip the remaining cream with the vanilla and the liquid stevia, to garnish.

YIELD: If you make 5 servings, each will have: 200 Calories; 18 g Fat (81.1% calories from fat); 3 g Protein; 6 g Carbohydrate; 1 g Dietary Fiber; 5 g net carbs

MIXED BERRY CUPS

For you raspberry and blackberry lovers, here's a quick and tasty dessert. As with the previous recipe, these numbers are based on grocery store gelatin mix, but if you'd prefer, you can get erythritol/stevia sweetened "jel" mix from Thrive Market. It does not contain actual gelatin; apparently Thrive is appealing to the vegetarian market. I, on the other hand, consider gelatin a super-food. Up to you which issue is more important.

1 package (4-serving size) of sugar-free raspberry gelatin

1 cup (235 ml) boiling water

2 teaspoons lemon juice

Grated rind of ½ of an orange

¾ cup (113 g) frozen blackberries, partly thawed

1 cup (235 ml) heavy cream, divided

½ teaspoon vanilla extract

Liquid stevia, monkfruit, or sucralose to equal 1 teaspoon of sugar in sweetness. (Vanilla stevia is good.)

1. Put the gelatin, water, lemon juice, and orange zest in a blender and whirl for 10 to 15 seconds to dissolve the gelatin. Add the blackberries and blend again, just long enough to mix in the berries.

2. Put the blender container in the refrigerator for 10 minutes or just until the mixture starts to thicken a bit. Add ¾ cup (175 ml) heavy cream and run the blender just long enough to mix it all in (10 to 15 seconds).

3. Pour into 5 or 6 pretty little dessert cups and chill. Whip the remaining ¼ cup (60 ml) of cream with vanilla and sweetener (if using), to garnish.

YIELD: 5 servings, each with: 187 Calories; 18 g Fat (85.3% calories from fat); 1 g Protein; 6 g Carbohydrate; 1 g Dietary Fiber; 5 g net carbs

HAZELNUT CRUST

This is a great substitute for a graham cracker crumb crust with any cheesecake. And, I think it tastes even better than the original.

1½ cups (203 g) hazelnuts

⅓ cup (43 g) vanilla whey protein powder

5 tablespoons (70 g) butter, melted

1. Preheat the oven to 350°F (180°C, or gas mark 4).

2. Put the hazelnuts in a food processor with the S-blade in place. Pulse until the hazelnuts are ground to a medium-fine texture. Add the protein powder and butter and pulse to combine.

3. Spray the pie plate or springform pan, depending on which your recipe specifies, with nonstick cooking spray and press this mixture firmly and evenly into the pan. Don't try to build your crust too high up the sides, but if you're using a springform pan, be sure to cover the seam around the bottom and press the crust into place firmly over it.

4. Place your crust in a preheated oven on the bottom rack and bake for 12 to 15 minutes or until lightly browned and slightly pulling away from the sides of the pan.

5. Remove the crust from the oven and let it cool while you make the filling.

YIELD: 12 servings, each with: 178 Calories; 16 g Fat (77.8% calories from fat); 7 g Protein; 3 g Carbohydrate; 1 g Dietary Fiber; 2 g net carbs

Almond Crust

Here's another great nut crust for you to try. Just substitute 1½ cups (218 g) almonds for the hazelnuts in the Hazelnut Crust and decrease the protein powder to ¼ cup (32 g). Follow the directions to make the crust and bake for 10 to 12 minutes or until lightly golden. Cool.

It bears mentioning that while I like this crust this way, our tester, Christina Robertson, didn't like the flavor of her vanilla whey protein in this crust and preferred it with unflavored whey protein plus a teaspoon of vanilla extract and a few drops of liquid sucralose.

YIELD: 12 servings, each with: 165 Calories; 14 g Fat (74.2% calories from fat); 7 g Protein; 4 g Carbohydrate; 2 g Dietary Fiber; 2 g net carbs

CRISP CHOCOLATE CRUST

I put this here so you can use it for the Peanut Butter Silk Pie (page 307). But how many cheesecakes would be improved with a chocolate crust?

1½ cups (168 g) almond meal

¼ cup (60 g) erythritol, or to taste

2 ounces (55 g) unsweetened baking chocolate

3 tablespoons (45 g) butter

2 tablespoons (16 g) vanilla whey protein powder

1. Preheat the oven to 325°F (170°C, or gas mark 3).
2. Put the almond meal and erythritol in your food processor and pulse to combine. Melt the chocolate and butter together. With the processor running, pour into the almond meal mixture and run till evenly distributed. You may need to stop the processor and run the tip of a knife blade around the outer edge to get everything to combine properly. Then, add the protein powder and pulse again to combine.
3. Turn out into an 8-inch (20 cm) springform and press firmly into place, being sure to cover the seam at the bottom edge of the pan. Do not try to build it all the way up the walls.
4. Bake for 12 minutes and then cool before filling.

YIELD: 12 servings, each with: 164 Calories; 15 g Fat (75.3% calories from fat); 6 g Protein; 5 g Carbohydrate; 3 g Dietary Fiber; 2 g net carbs

CHOCOLATE CHEESECAKE

You'll be surprised how good a cheesecake you can make from cottage cheese! It's high in protein, too.

2 cups (450 g) cottage cheese, creamed (4% fat)

2 eggs

½ cup (115 g) sour cream

2 ounces (55 g) unsweetened baking chocolate, melted

Liquid stevia, monkfruit, or sucralose to equal ¼ cup (50 g) of sugar in sweetness

1 Hazelnut Crust (page 296) or Almond Crust (page 297), prebaked in a large, deep pie plate

Whipped cream (page 303) (for serving)

1. Preheat the oven to 375°F (190°C, or gas mark 5).
2. Put the cottage cheese, eggs, and sour cream in your blender. Run the blender, scraping down the sides now and then, until this mixture is very smooth. Add the melted chocolate and sweetener and blend again.
3. Pour into the prebaked crust.
4. Place the cheesecake on the top rack of the oven and place a flat pan of water on the bottom rack. Bake for 40 to 45 minutes.
5. Cool and then chill well before serving. Serve with Whipped Cream.

YIELD: 12 servings, each with: 261 Calories; 22 g Fat (72.2% calories from fat); 13 g Protein; 6 g Carbohydrate; 2 g Dietary Fiber; 4 g net carbs

CHEESECAKE TO GO WITH FRUIT

This lemon-vanilla cheesecake is wonderful with strawberries, blueberries, cherries—any fruit you care to use. It also makes a nice breakfast. Our tester, Christina Robertson, asked to rate it, said, "Solid 10! Super easy and quick to make. Really good, inexpensive, quick recipe! Perfect light dessert to follow a heavy meal."

2 cups (450 g) cottage cheese, creamed (4% fat)

2 eggs

½ cup (115 g) sour cream

¼ cup (32 g) vanilla whey protein powder

Liquid stevia–lemon drop or vanilla flavor, or both OR liquid monkfruit or sucralose to equal ¼ cup (50 g) of sugar in sweetness

1 lemon, grated zest and juice

1 teaspoon vanilla extract

Hazelnut Crust (page 296) made in a pie plate

1. Preheat the oven to 375°F (190°C, or gas mark 5).
2. Put the cottage cheese, eggs, sour cream, protein powder, sweetener, lemon zest and juice, and vanilla in a blender. Blend until very smooth.
3. Pour into the prebaked crust. Place the cheesecake on the top rack of the oven and place a flat pan of water on the bottom rack.
4. Bake for 30 to 40 minutes. Cool and then chill well before serving.

Note: Serve this cheesecake with the fruit of your choice. I like to serve it with thawed frozen, unsweetened strawberries, blueberries, or peaches, mashed coarsely with a fork and sweetened slightly. If you use 1½ cups (383 g) of strawberries for the whole cake, you'll add 2 grams of carbohydrates per slice, plus a trace of fiber and a trace of protein. Use 1½ cups (420 g) sour cherries—you can get these canned, with no added sugar—and sweeten them with sweetener to equal ⅓ cup (67 g) sugar in sweetness, and you'll add 3 grams per slice. I'm lucky enough to have a sour cherry tree, and cherry cheesecake is one of the joys of early summer around here!

YIELD: 12 servings, each with: 257 Calories; 20 g Fat (66.9% calories from fat); 16 g Protein; 6 g Carbohydrate; 1 g Dietary Fiber; 5 g net carbs. The analysis does not include fruit.

SUNSHINE CHEESECAKE

I originally made this with a hazelnut crust, and it's great that way. But having grown up on devil's food cake with orange icing, I'm now eying that Crisp Chocolate Crust on page 297.

1 cup (225 g) cottage cheese, creamed (4% fat)

8 ounces (225 g) cream cheese

1 cup (230 g) sour cream

4 eggs

2 teaspoons orange zest

1 tablespoon (15 ml) orange extract

Liquid stevia, monkfruit, or sucralose to equal 1 cup (200 g) of sugar in sweetness (I'd use lemon drop stevia.)

2 tablespoons (28 ml) lemon juice

1 tiny pinch of salt

Hazelnut Crust (page 296) or Almond Crust (page 297) prebaked in a springform pan

1. Put the cottage cheese, cream cheese, sour cream, eggs, orange zest, orange extract, sweetener, lemon juice, and salt in a blender. Run the blender until everything is well blended and a bit fluffy.

2. Pour into the prebaked crust. Place the cheesecake on the top rack of the oven and place a flat pan of water on the bottom rack.

3. Bake for 50 minutes. The cheesecake will still jiggle slightly in the center when you take it out.

4. Cool and then chill well before serving.

Note: This is wonderful with sugar-free chocolate syrup. Many grocery stores carry it; it's worth your while to take a look-see.

YIELD: 12 servings, each with: 318 Calories; 28 g Fat (77.2% calories from fat); 13 g Protein; 5 g Carbohydrate; 1 g Dietary Fiber; 4 g net carbs

BLACKBOTTOMED MOCKAHLUA CHEESECAKE

You'll have to make yourself some Mockahlua 2017 before you can make this. What better incentive could you have?

5 ounces (140 g) sugar-free dark or semisweet chocolate (I'd use Lily's chocolate chips.)

¼ cup (60 ml) heavy cream

Hazelnut Crust (page 296)

24 ounces (680 g) cream cheese, softened

Liquid stevia, monkfruit, or sucralose to equal ¾ cup (150 g) of sugar in sweetness

¾ cup (173 g) sour cream

1 tablespoon (15 ml) vanilla extract

4 eggs

⅓ cup (80 ml) Mockahlua 2017 (page 313)

1. Preheat the oven to 325°F (170°C, or gas mark 3).

2. Over the lowest possible heat, melt the chocolate (preferably in a heat diffuser or a double boiler, to keep the chocolate from burning). When the chocolate is melted, stir in the heavy cream, blending well. Pour over the crust and spread evenly.

3. In a large bowl, use an electric mixer to beat the cream cheese until smooth, scraping down the sides of the bowl often. Beat in the sweetener and sour cream and mix well. Add the vanilla and the eggs, one by one, beating until very smooth and creamy. Beat in the Mockahlua last and mix well.

4. Pour into the chocolate-coated crust. Place the cheesecake in the oven and on the rack below it or on the floor of the oven place a pie pan of water.

5. Bake for 1 hour.

6. Cool in the pan on a wire rack. Chill well before serving.

YIELD: 12 servings, each with: 500 Calories; 45 g Fat (82.0% calories from fat); 14 g Protein; 8 g Carbohydrate; 3 g Dietary Fiber; 5 g net carbs. The analysis does not include maltitol if your chocolate contains it.

COOKIES, CAKES, AND OTHER SWEETS

BUTTER-PECAN CHEESECAKE

All you butterscotch fans are going to love this one. Our tester, Verna Haas, says that "while it's rich, it's also light and fluffy." She also says the crust would stand alone as a cookie recipe and says it was quick and easy to prepare.

PECAN COOKIE CRUST

1 stick of butter at room temperature

¼ cup (60 g) erythritol/ stevia or erythritol/ monkfruit blend OR ¼ cup (60 g) erythritol plus liquid stevia, monkfruit, or sucralose to equal ¼ cup (50 g) of sugar in sweetness

¾ cup (97 g) vanilla whey protein powder

¾ cup (83 g) chopped pecans

½ teaspoon salt

BUTTERSCOTCH CHEESECAKE FILLING

24 ounces (680 g) cream cheese, at room temperature

¼ cup (60 g) erythritol/ monkfruit or erythritol/ stevia blend OR ¼ cup (60 g) erythritol plus liquid stevia, monkfruit, or sucralose

Liquid stevia, monkfruit, or sucralose to equal ½ cup (100 g) of sugar in sweetness

¾ cup (173 g) sour cream

2 teaspoons butter flavoring

1 tablespoon (15 ml) vanilla extract

1 tablespoon (20 g) molasses

4 eggs

1. Preheat the oven to 325°F (170°C, or gas mark 3).

2. Beat the butter and sweetener together until light and creamy. Then, beat in the protein powder, pecans, and salt. Spray a springform pan with nonstick cooking spray and press the crust evenly and firmly into the bottom of the pan, plus just far enough up the sides to cover the seam at the bottom.

3. Bake for 12 to 15 minutes until lightly golden. Set aside to cool while you make the filling.

4. In a large bowl, use an electric mixer to beat the cream cheese until smooth, scraping down the sides of the bowl often. Next, beat in the sweetener and the sour cream and mix well. Beat in the butter flavoring, vanilla, and molasses. Add the eggs one by one, beating until very smooth and creamy.

5. Pour the mixture into the crust. Place the cheesecake in the oven, and on the oven rack below it or on the floor of the oven place a pie pan of water.

6. Bake for 1 hour.

7. Cool in the pan on a wire rack. Chill well before serving.

Note: For a nice touch, decorate this with some pretty pecan halves.

YIELD: 12 servings, each with: 400 Calories; 35 g Fat (77.2% calories from fat); 18 g Protein; 5 g Carbohydrate; 1 g Dietary Fiber; 4 g net carbs

PUMPKIN CHEESECAKE

Vicki Cash gives us this elegant alternative to pumpkin pie for Thanksgiving dessert. It's from her *Low Carb Success Calendar*, and it's not to be missed.

Butter

½ cup (55 g) pecans, coarsely chopped

2 packages (8 ounces, or 225 g each) of cream cheese, softened

Liquid stevia, monkfruit, or sucralose to equal ½–¾ cup (100–150 g) of sugar in sweetness (I'd use English toffee stevia.)

2 teaspoons vanilla extract

1½ cups (368 g) pure canned pumpkin

½ cup (115 g) sour cream

4 eggs

1½ teaspoons cinnamon

1 teaspoon powdered ginger

½ teaspoon nutmeg

¼ teaspoon ground cloves

¼ teaspoon salt

1. Preheat the oven to 300°F (150°C, or gas mark 2).
2. Butter the bottom and sides of a 9½-inch (24 cm) springform cheesecake pan. Sprinkle the bottom of the pan with chopped pecans, distributing evenly.
3. In a large mixing bowl, use an electric mixer to beat the cream cheese, sweetener, and vanilla until fluffy, stopping occasionally to scrape the sides of the bowl and beaters.
4. Add the pumpkin and sour cream, mixing thoroughly on medium speed. Add the eggs one at a time, mixing thoroughly between each one. Mix in the cinnamon, ginger, nutmeg, ground cloves, and salt.
5. Pour the batter over the nuts in the pan.
6. Bake for 60 to 70 minutes or until a knife placed in center comes out clean.
7. Cool for 20 minutes before removing from the pan, and chill for at least 2 hours before serving.

YIELD: 12 servings, each with: 238 Calories; 22 g Fat (81.5% calories from fat); 6 g Protein; 6 g Carbohydrate; 1 g Dietary Fiber; 5 g net carbs

GRASSHOPPER CHEESECAKE

If you're a mint-chocolate chip ice cream fan, this is your cheesecake! Chocolate extract can be a little hard to find, but it's worth it for this. Order online, if need be.

CHOCOLATE LAYER

5 ounces (140 g) sugar-free dark or semisweet chocolate (I'd use Lily's chocolate chips.)

¼ cup (60 ml) heavy cream

1 Almond Crust (page 297) or Hazelnut Crust (page 296), prebaked in a springform pan

GRASSHOPPER FILLING

3 packages (8 ounces, or 225 g each) of cream cheese, softened

Liquid stevia, monkfruit, or sucralose to equal ¾ cup (150 g) of sugar in sweetness

¾ cup (173 g) sour cream

¾ teaspoon peppermint extract

1½ tablespoons (23 ml) chocolate extract

1 or 2 drops of green food coloring (optional, but pretty)

4 eggs

1. Preheat the oven to 325°F (170°C, or gas mark 3). In the top of a double boiler over hot water (or in a heavy-bottomed saucepan over the lowest possible heat), melt the chocolate and whisk in the heavy cream until smooth. Spread this mixture evenly over the crust and set aside.
2. In a large bowl, use an electric mixer to beat the cream cheese until smooth, scraping down the sides of the bowl often. Beat in the Splenda and the sour cream and mix well. Beat in the peppermint and chocolate extracts, food coloring (if using), and eggs, one by one, beating until very smooth and creamy.
3. Pour the mixture into the chocolate-coated crust. Place the cheesecake in the oven and on the oven rack below it or on the floor of the oven place a pie pan of water.
4. Bake for 1 hour.
5. Cool in the pan on a wire rack. Chill well before serving.

YIELD: 12 servings, each with: 490 Calories; 45 g Fat (82.2% calories from fat); 14 g Protein; 7 g Carbohydrate; 3 g Dietary Fiber; 4 grams net carbs

KATHY'S PEANUT BUTTER PROTEIN BARS

This recipe is from reader Kathy Miller. These would make a filling snack, or even breakfast or lunch. For storage, it's a good idea to package these in individual zipper-lock bags in the freezer.

¼ cup (55 g) butter

½ cup (130 g) natural peanut butter (preferably chunky), at room temperature

4 ounces (115 g) cream cheese, softened

1¾ cups (226 g) vanilla whey protein powder

1 tablespoon (15 ml) vanilla extract

Liquid stevia, monkfruit, or sucralose to equal 2 tablespoons (26 g) of sugar in sweetness

½ cup (75 g) chopped peanuts

1. Melt the butter (a microwave works well for this) and add the peanut butter and softened cream cheese to it. Mix together with a spoon (no need to drag out a blender or mixer). Add the protein powder, vanilla, sweetener, and peanuts. Stir well. (It will be very crumbly.)

2. Taste and see if it is sweet enough. If not, add a little more sweetener.

3. Press the mixture firmly into an 8- x 8-inch (20 x 20 cm) pan. Slice into 12 pieces and put the whole pan in the freezer. Remove when the bars are firm.

YIELD: 12 servings, each with: 295 Calories; 17 g Fat (51.7% calories from fat); 30 g Protein; 7 g Carbohydrate; 2 g Dietary Fiber; 5 g net carbs

GREAT BALLS OF PROTEIN!

You may recognize this updated version of an old health-food standby. These are great for active kids! They'll think it's a treat, and you won't be worried that they'll spoil their supper because this is just as nutritious.

1 jar (16 ounces, or 455 g) of natural peanut butter, oil and all

2 cups (258 g) vanilla whey protein powder

Splenda or powdered erythritol (optional) (Swerve confectioner's style is good.)

Sesame seeds (optional)

Unsweetened shredded coconut (optional)

Sugar-free chocolate bars (optional)

Unsweetened cocoa powder (optional)

Splenda (optional)

This is easiest to make if you have a powerful stand mixer or a heavy-duty food processor. If you don't, don't try to use a smaller appliance—you'll only burn it out. Rather than dooming your old mixer, just roll up your sleeves, scrub your hands, and dive in.

1. Thoroughly combine the peanut butter with the protein powder. (I find that working in about ⅓ cup [43 g] of the protein powder at a time is about right.) This should make a stiff, somewhat crumbly dough.

2. Work the sweetener of your choice (if using) into the dough. My whey protein powder is sweetened with stevia, and I find that that's enough sweetener for me. But if you want your Great Balls of Protein to be sweeter, simply add sweetener. (I've specified powdered sweetener because it's easier to work in evenly—you can sprinkle it in gradually. If you make these often and know you like a certain amount of additional sweetness, you can use liquid sweetener by beating it into the peanut butter first, before the protein powder.)

3. Roll into balls about 1 inch (2.5 cm) in diameter.

Note: It's nice, but hardly essential, to coat these with something. If you like sesame seeds, you can toast them by shaking them in a dry, heavy skillet over medium heat until they start popping and jumping around the pan and then roll the balls in them while they're still warm. You could roll them in shredded plain coconut, if you prefer. Again, you can toast it lightly in a dry frying pan and add a little sweetner. Or you could melt sugar-free chocolate bars and dip your Balls of Protein in chocolate—although it would probably be simpler to chop them up and mix them in. Another option is to roll them in unsweetened cocoa mixed with a little powdered sweetener.

YIELD: Makes about 50 balls, each with: 92 Calories; 5 g Fat (49.7% calories from fat); 9 g Protein; 3 g Carbohydrate; 1 g Dietary Fiber; 2 g net carbs. The analysis does not include optional ingredients.

WHIPPED CREAM

This may seem like a gimme, but I have had people react with surprise when I mention making whipped cream. They've always assumed it simply grows in plastic tubs or aerosol cans. Nope! This is so much better and takes maybe five minutes.

1 cup (235 ml) heavy cream, well chilled

1 teaspoon vanilla extract

Liquid stevia, or monkfruit or sucralose to equal 2–3 teaspoons (8–13 g) of sugar in sweetness (French vanilla stevia is great, here, but English toffee is wonderful, as well.)

1. Here's the deal: Your heavy cream must be chilled. You cannot use your blender or food processor; you'll just get butter. An electric mixer is best, but a whisk is fine, too. (Back in the Dark Ages, I used an egg beater.)

2. Put the heavy cream in a deep, narrow bowl along with the vanilla and the sweetener. Whip until it's . . . well, whipped cream; it should form soft peaks when you lift the mixer out. Then stop! Overbeat and you'll get sweetened butter.

YIELD: 16 servings, each with: 52 Calories; 6 g Fat (93.9% calories from fat); trace Protein; trace Carbohydrate; 0 g Dietary Fiber; trace net carbs

WHIPPED TOPPING

This is incredible with berries, as a simple but elegant dessert. I like to serve strawberries and whipped cream in my nice chip-and-dip; it looks so pretty, and it makes the whole thing engagingly informal. This whipped topping is also great on any dessert and terrific on Irish Coffee (page 315)!

The pudding adds a very nice texture to this topping, and it helps the whipped cream "stand up," as well as adding a slightly sweet vanilla flavor to the cream, of course. If you're avoiding artificial sweetener, try Thrive Market for instant pudding mixes with erythritol and stevia instead.

1 cup (235 ml) heavy cream, well chilled	**1 tablespoon (10 g) vanilla sugar-free instant pudding powder**

Whip the heavy cream and pudding mix together until the cream is stiff.

YIELD: 16 servings, each with: 52 Calories; 6 g Fat (93.4% calories from fat); trace Protein; 1 g Carbohydrate; 0 g Dietary Fiber; 1 g net carbs

LEMON SHERBET

You know how it goes: You're eating low carb, your sister is eating low fat, and your cousin is just watching calories. Voila! This is low carb, low fat, low calorie—and delicious! Obvious variation: Use orange gelatin and orange extract to make orange sherbet.

Jell-O brand does not contain any gluten ingredients, but is not labeled gluten-free, I assume because of the possibility of cross-contamination. It does contain corn-derived ingredients.

1 package (4-serving size) of sugar-free lemon gelatin	**Liquid stevia, monkfruit, or sucralose to equal 3 tablespoons (39 g) of sugar in sweetness (Lemon drop flavor stevia is a great choice.)**
2 cups (475 ml) boiling water	
2 cups (460 g) plain yogurt	
2 teaspoons lemon extract	**¼ cup (32 g) vanilla whey protein powder**

1. Put the gelatin powder in the blender and add the water. Blend for 20 seconds or just long enough to dissolve the gelatin.

2. Add all the other ingredients and blend well. Put the blender container in the refrigerator and let it chill for 10 to 15 minutes. Take it out and blend it again for about 10 seconds. Then, chill it for another 10 to 15 minutes and give it another quick blend it when it's done chilling.

3. Pour the sherbet mixture into a home ice cream freezer and freeze according to the directions for your freezer.

YIELD: 8 servings of ½ cup (70 g), each with: 77 Calories; 2 g Fat (35.3% calories from fat); 9 g Protein; 2 g Carbohydrate; trace Dietary Fiber; 2 g net carbs

CREAMY STRAWBERRY POPSICLES

From sweety.com's Jennifer Eloff and her terrific cookbook *Splendid Low-Carbing*, these popsicles are bound to liven up your summer.

1½ cups (345 g) plain yogurt

1 cup (235 ml) heavy cream

⅔ cup (16 g) Splenda, or liquid stevia, monkfruit, or sucralose to equal ²/₃ cup (133 g) of sugar in sweetness

½ cup (75 g) frozen, unsweetened strawberries

¼ teaspoon strawberry Kool-Aid powder

1. In a blender, blend the yogurt, heavy cream, Splenda, strawberries, and Kool-Aid powder until smooth.

2. Pour into popsicle molds and freeze.

YIELD: 13 pops, each with: 87 Calories; 8 g Fat (80.8% calories from fat); 1 g Protein; 3 g Carbohydrate; trace Dietary Fiber; 3 g net carbs

COCONUT BANANA CREAM POPSICLES

This is a tropical treat for a hot summer day! Just hand them to the kids and send them outside to drip. Don't tell them it's health food.

14 ounces (395 ml) canned coconut milk, unsweetened

1 cup (230 g) plain full-fat yogurt

⅔ cup (160 ml) heavy cream

1 cup (25 g) Splenda, OR liquid stevia, monkfruit, or sucralose to equal 1 cup (200 g) of sugar in sweetness

1 banana, sliced

½ teaspoon vanilla extract or banana flavoring

1. Simply run everything through the blender until it's smooth.

2. Pour into molds and freeze.

YIELD: 16 pops, each with: 103 Calories; 9 g Fat (78.4% calories from fat); 1 g Protein; 4 g Carbohydrate; trace Dietary Fiber; 4 g net carbs

Orange Popsicles

Make just like Creamy Strawberry Popsicles, only substitute 2 tablespoons (28 ml) of frozen orange juice concentrate for the strawberries and instead of the Kool-Aid powder, add 2 teaspoons of lemon juice and ¼ teaspoon of orange extract.

YIELD: 13 pops, each with: 90 Calories; 8 g Fat (78.5% calories from fat); 1 g Protein; 3 g Carbohydrate; trace Dietary Fiber; 3 g net carbs

FLAVORED WHIP

Reader David Drake Hunter sends this easy dessert recipe. If you prefer to choose your own sweetener, buy unflavored drink mix powder and add the liquid sweetener of your choice.

1 pint (475 ml) heavy cream, chilled

1 to 2 teaspoons sugar-free fruit-flavored drink mix powder (your choice of flavor)

1. Pour the heavy cream into a bowl and add the drink mix crystals to taste.
2. Beat into whipped cream.

YIELD: 8 servings, each with: 205 Calories; 22 g Fat (94.5% calories from fat); 1 g Protein; 2 g Carbohydrate; 0 g Dietary Fiber; 2 g net carbs

MARIA'S FLAN

My childhood friend Maria found me on the Internet a couple of years ago, and we got together. Her mom is Colombian, so Maria had grown up eating flan, a traditional Latin American dessert. Here's the version we came up with together. Traditionally, flan is made with caramelized sugar on the bottom of the pan, so that it has caramel sauce on top when inverted. I find it easier and just as satisfactory to pour a tablespoon (15 ml) or so of sugar-free caramel coffee-flavoring syrup over each serving.

1 cup (235 ml) heavy cream

1 cup (235 ml) half-and-half

6 eggs

1 teaspoon vanilla extract

Pinch of nutmeg

Pinch of salt

Liquid stevia, monkfruit, or sucralose to equal 2/3 cup (133 g) of sugar in sweetness

1. Preheat the oven to 350°F (180°C, or gas mark 4). Coat a glass pie plate with cooking spray.
2. Whisk together the heavy cream, half-and-half, eggs, vanilla, nutmeg, salt, and sweetener and pour into the pie plate.
3. Carefully place the pie plate in a large, flat baking dish. Place it in the oven and then pour water around it, not quite up to the brim of the pie plate. Bake for 45 minutes or until a knife inserted in the center comes out clean.
4. Cool and cut the flan into wedges. Traditionally, each piece is served inverted on a plate, with the syrup on top.

YIELD: 8 generous servings, each with: 193 Calories; 18 g Fat (82.8% calories from fat); 6 g Protein; 3 g Carbohydrate; trace Dietary Fiber; 3 g net carbs

LEMON-VANILLA CUSTARD

Don't save this just for dessert—it makes a lovely breakfast, too.

1 cup (235 ml) heavy cream

1 cup (235 ml) half-and-half

3 eggs

Liquid stevia, monkfruit, or sucralose to equal ⅓ cup (67 g) of sugar in sweetness (Lemon drop stevia and vanilla stevia are obvious choices, here.)

1 teaspoon lemon extract

½ teaspoon vanilla extract

2 tablespoons (16 g) vanilla whey protein powder

1 teaspoon lemon zest

Pinch of salt

1. Preheat the oven to 300°F (150°C, or gas mark 2).

2. Put all the ingredients in a blender and blend well.

3. Spray a 1-quart (946 ml) casserole with nonstick cooking spray and pour the mixture into it. (If you prefer, use individual custard cups.) Place the casserole or custard cups in a larger pan in the oven and then fill with hot water to within ½ inch (1.3 cm) of the rim of the casserole.

4. Bake for 2 hours. Cool and chill well.

YIELD: 4 generous servings, each with: 364 Calories; 33 g Fat (80.3% calories from fat); 13 g Protein; 6 g Carbohydrate; trace Dietary Fiber; 6 g net carbs

PEANUT BUTTER SILK PIE

This pie is incredible, decadent, outrageous, and utterly scrumptious. It's a real special-occasion dessert and a surefire crowd-pleaser. My darling friend Virginia, testing, called this "SO yummy!"

Crisp Chocolate Crust (page 297)

8 ounces (225 g) cream cheese at room temperature

1 teaspoon liquid stevia–English toffee

1 cup (260 g) creamy natural peanut butter

1 tablespoon (14 g) butter, melted

1 teaspoon vanilla extract

1 cup (235 ml) heavy cream

Walden Farms sugar-free chocolate syrup (for serving)

1. Make your Crisp Chocolate Crust first, pressing it into a 9-inch (23 cm) pie plate instead of a springform pan.

2. Using an electric mixer, beat the cream cheese, liquid stevia, peanut butter, butter, and vanilla together until creamy.

3. In a separate bowl, whip the heavy cream until stiff.

4. Turn the mixer to its lowest setting and beat the whipped cream into the peanut butter–cream cheese mixture in 3 additions.

5. Spread the peanut butter filling in the Crisp Chocolate Crust.

6. Serve with Walden Farms sugar-free chocolate syrup.

YIELD: 12 servings, each with: 433 Calories; 40 g Fat (79.4% calories from fat); 12 g Protein; 11 g Carbohydrate; 4 g Dietary Fiber; 7 g net carbs

HELEN'S CHOCOLATE BREAD PUDDING

Helen was my dad's mom, and this was our family's traditional Christmas dessert the whole time I was growing up. People have threatened to marry into the family to get the secret recipe, but since this is the decarbed version, it's not secret! It is still high-carb enough that you'll want to save it for a special occasion, though. Sadly, I can think of no way to make this both low-carb and gluten-free and certainly not grain-free.

2 cups (475 ml) half-and-half

1 cup (235 ml) heavy cream

1 cup (235 ml) pourable unsweetened coconut milk

6 slices of "lite" white bread (5 grams of net carbs per slice or fewer–the squishiest you can find)

3 ounces (85 g) unsweetened baking chocolate

Liquid stevia, monkfruit, or sucralose to equal ⅔ cup (133 g) of sugar in sweetness (Chocolate or vanilla stevia make sense here.)

2 eggs, beaten

1 teaspoon vanilla extract

Pinch of salt

1. Preheat the oven to 375°F (190°C, or gas mark 5). Coat a 2-quart (1.9 L) casserole with cooking spray.

2. Combine the half-and-half, heavy cream, and coconut milk and scald. Bring it just up to a simmer.

3. While the liquids are heating, tear the bread into small bits and put them in the casserole. Pour the hot half-and-half mixture over the bread and let it sit for 10 minutes.

4. Melt the chocolate over very low heat or in the microwave, according to package directions, and add it to the bread mixture. Use a little of the hot cream to rinse out the pan you melted the chocolate in, so you get all of it. Stir the cream, bread, and chocolate until the chocolate is well distributed. Now, stir in the sweetener, eggs, vanilla, and salt, mixing very well.

5. Bake for 1 hour or until firm. Serve with Not-So-Hard Sauce (page 308).

YIELD: 8 servings, each with: 305 Calories; 26 g Fat (72.0% calories from fat); 6 g Protein; 16 g Carbohydrate; 2 g Dietary Fiber; 14 g net carbs

NOT-SO-HARD SAUCE

Traditional hard sauce is made with sugar, butter, and egg, plus vanilla, rum, or brandy, and when it's refrigerated, it gets quite hard–hence the name. However, with Splenda instead of sugar, my hard sauce just didn't work–it fell apart in little globs. I added cream cheese, and it all came together, but it doesn't get quite so hard when refrigerated, which is why this is Not-So-Hard Sauce. It still tastes great, though!

5 tablespoons (70 g) butter at room temperature

Liquid stevia, monkfruit, or sucralose to equal 1 cup (200 g) of sugar in sweetness

⅛ teaspoon salt

1 teaspoon vanilla extract

1 egg

2 ounces (55 g) cream cheese at room temperature

Rum or brandy–optional, we never used 'em, but 1 tablespoon (15 ml) would be about right

Nutmeg

1. Use an electric mixer to beat the butter and sweetener together until well blended. Beat in the salt, vanilla extract, and egg. At this point, you'll be sure you've made a dreadful mistake.

2. Beat in the cream cheese and watch the sauce smooth out! Mix very well until light and fluffy.

3. Pile your Not-So-Hard Sauce into a pretty serving dish, sprinkle it lightly with nutmeg, and refrigerate until well chilled.

YIELD: 8 servings, each with: 98 Calories; 10 g Fat (93.1% calories from fat); 1 g Protein; trace Carbohydrate; 0 g Dietary Fiber; trace net carbs

COEUR À LA CRÈME

This is a classic French dessert, traditionally made in a heart-shaped mold. Coeur à la crème molds are hard to come by, but you can buy a regular 2-cup (475 ml) heart-shaped mold and stick three or four holes in it with a nail, which is what I did. Serve with fresh strawberries or Strawberry Sauce (page 309) for a truly beautiful Valentine's Day dessert. Warning: This is not a quick dessert to whip up before your sweetheart comes over. You need to start making this dessert at least 24 hours in advance, to give it plenty of time to chill.

2 packages (8 ounces, or 225 g each) of cream cheese, softened

Liquid stevia, monkfruit, or sucralose to equal 2 tablespoons (26 g) of sugar in sweetness

3 tablespoons (45 ml) heavy cream

2 tablespoons (30 g) sour cream

¼ teaspoon salt

1. Use an electric mixer to beat the cream cheese until it's very creamy. Beat in the sweetener, heavy cream, sour cream, and salt, mixing very well.

2. Line your mold with a double layer of dampened cheesecloth and pack the cheese mixture into it, pressing it in well. Place the mold on a plate to catch any moisture that drains out and chill for at least 24 hours.

YIELD: 8 servings, each with: 225 Calories; 23 g Fat (88.9% calories from fat); 5 g Protein; 2 g Carbohydrate; 0 g Dietary Fiber; 2 g net carbs

STRAWBERRY SAUCE

Traditionally, Coeur à la crème is served with fresh strawberries, but I make this for Valentine's Day, and I'm generally not impressed with the quality of the fresh strawberries I can get in February. I'd rather use frozen. This is good over the Cheesecake To Go With Fruit, page 298, too.

1 bag (1 pound, or 455 g) of frozen, unsweetened strawberries, thawed

1 tablespoon (15 ml) lemon juice

Liquid stevia, monkfruit, or sucralose to equal 2–3 tablespoons (26–39 g) of sugar in sweetness

1. Simply pour your strawberries and any liquid in the package into a bowl and stir in the lemon juice and sweetener.

2. Mash your strawberries a little with a fork, if you'd like; I like mine fairly chunky.

YIELD: 8 servings, each with: 20 Calories; trace Fat (2.1% calories from fat); trace Protein; 5 g Carbohydrate; 1 g Dietary Fiber; 4 g net carbs

COOKIES, CAKES, AND OTHER SWEETS

ZUCCHINI-CARROT CAKE

This doesn't need a darned thing—it's simply delicious exactly the way it is. However, I've supplied you with a Cream Cheese Frosting recipe on page 312, because why the heck not? This cake, by the way, makes a fabulous breakfast, and since it's loaded with protein and good fats, it should keep you going all morning.

Use regular, not Greek, yogurt for this. It contributes more moisture.

1½ cups (203 g) hazelnuts

½ cup (65 g) vanilla whey protein powder

⅓ cup (80 g) erythritol/ monkfruit or erythritol/ stevia blend OR ⅓ cup (80 g) erythritol plus liquid stevia, monkfruit, or sucralose to equal ½ cup (100 g) of sugar in sweetness

1½ teaspoons cinnamon

1¼ teaspoons baking soda

½ teaspoon salt

¼ teaspoon nutmeg

2 eggs

½ cup (120 ml) oil (I'd use MCT or melted coconut oil.)

½ cup (115 g) full-fat yogurt (Use regular yogurt, not Greek.)

¾ cup (90 g) shredded zucchini

¼ cup (28 g) shredded carrot

1. Preheat the oven to 350°F (180°C, or gas mark 4). Coat a Bundt pan with cooking spray or grease well.

2. In a food processor with the S-blade in place, use the pulse control to grind the hazelnuts to a mealy consistency. (You want 1½ cups [113 g] of ground hazelnuts when you're done, and for some inexplicable reason, they seem to actually grow a little rather than shrink a little when you grind them.) Remove and reserve 2 tablespoons (9 g) of the ground hazelnuts.

3. Add the protein powder, sweetener, cinnamon, baking soda, salt, and nutmeg to the ground hazelnuts in the food processor and pulse until everything is evenly distributed.

4. In a large mixing bowl, whisk the eggs until well blended. Add the oil and yogurt, whisking again.

5. Whisk in the dry ingredients in 3 additions, making sure each is incorporated before adding the next.

6. Add the zucchini and carrots last, mixing well.

7. Give your Bundt pan one more shot of spray or grease and then sprinkle in the reserved hazelnut meal, turning and tapping the pan until it is "floured."

8. Pour in the batter. Do not expect it to fill the Bundt pan all the way. It fills mine about halfway.

9. Bake for 45 minutes or until a toothpick inserted halfway between the walls of the pan comes out damp but clean. Turn out on a wire rack to cool.

YIELD: 8 generous servings, each with: 372 Calories; 33 g Fat (75.8% calories from fat); 16 g Protein; 7 g Carbohydrate; 2 g Dietary Fiber; 5 g net carbs

ADAM'S CHOCOLATE BIRTHDAY CAKE

I made a low-carb feast for my friend Adam's birthday, and this was the cake. It's not a layer cake, it's a snack-type cake: dense, moist, and fudgy—a lot like brownies. It's easy, too, because it needs no frosting, tasting great just as it is. My tester Soren Schreiber-Katz, says, "Flavor and moistness are a solid 10!" Oh, and that I should point out that this is a cake recipe with no egg, should you or any of your friends and family be allergic.

1 cup (112 g) almond meal

½ cup (65 g) vanilla whey protein powder

3 tablespoons (15 g) unsweetened cocoa powder

1 teaspoon baking soda

½ cup (120 g) erythritol/stevia or erythritol/monkfruit blend OR ½ cup (120 g) erythritol plus liquid stevia, monkfruit, or sucralose to equal ½ cup (100 g) of sugar in sweetness

½ teaspoon salt

5 tablespoons (75 ml) oil (I'd use MCT oil, but any bland oil should serve.)

1 tablespoon (15 ml) cider vinegar

1 cup (235 ml) cold water

1. Preheat the oven to 350°F (180°C, or gas mark 4).

2. In a bowl, combine the almond meal, protein powder, cocoa, baking soda, sweetener, and salt and stir them together quite well. (Make sure there are no lumps of baking soda!)

3. Spray an 8- x 8-inch (20 x 20 cm) baking dish with nonstick cooking spray and place the combined ingredients in it. Make two holes in this mixture. Pour the oil into one, the vinegar into the other, and the water over the whole thing. Mix with a spoon or fork until everything's well combined.

4. Bake for 30 minutes or until a toothpick inserted in the middle comes out clean.

YIELD: 9 servings, each with: 183 Calories; 11 g Fat (53.3% calories from fat); 16 g Protein; 7 g Carbohydrate; 1 g Dietary Fiber; 6 g net carbs

GINGERBREAD

I've always loved gingerbread, and this is as good as any high-carb gingerbread I've ever had! Don't worry about that zucchini; it completely disappears, leaving only moistness behind. Try serving this with Whipped Topping (page 304) or Whipped Cream (page 303).

1 cup (112 g) almond meal

½ cup (65 g) vanilla whey protein powder

1 teaspoon baking soda

½ teaspoon salt

2½ teaspoons (7 g) ground ginger

½ teaspoon cinnamon

¼ cup (60 g) erythritol/monkfruit or erythritol/stevia blend OR ¼ cup (60 g) erythritol PLUS ¼ teaspoon English Toffee liquid stevia

½ cup (115 g) plain, full-fat yogurt (not Greek)

¼ cup (60 ml) bland coconut oil, olive oil, or MCT oil

1 teaspoon molasses

1 egg

2 tablespoons (28 ml) water

½ cup (60 g) shredded zucchini

1. Preheat the oven to 350°F (180°C, or gas mark 4).

2. In a mixing bowl, combine the almonds, protein powder, baking soda, salt, ginger, cinnamon, and sweetener and mix them well.

3. In a separate bowl or measuring cup, whisk together the yogurt, oil, molasses, egg, and water. Pour into the dry ingredients and whisk until everything is well combined and there are no dry spots. Add the zucchini and whisk briefly to distribute evenly.

4. Spray an 8- x 8-inch (20 x 20 cm) baking pan with nonstick cooking spray and turn the batter into it.

5. Bake for 30 minutes or until a toothpick inserted in the middle comes out clean.

YIELD: 9 servings, each with: 186 Calories; 11 g Fat (50.2% calories from fat); 17 g Protein; 7 g Carbohydrate; 1 g Dietary Fiber; 6 g net carbs

CREAM CHEESE FROSTING

This is my sister's recipe. It's good on the Zucchini-Carrot Cake (see page 310) or the Gingerbread (page 311).

¾ cup (175 ml) heavy cream, chilled

1 package (8 ounces, or 225 g) of cream cheese, softened

Liquid stevia, monkfruit, or sucralose to equal ½ cup (100 g) of sugar in sweetness (I'd use vanilla stevia.)

1 teaspoon vanilla extract

1. Whip the heavy cream until it's stiff.
2. In a separate bowl, beat the cream cheese until very smooth, and then beat in the sweetener and vanilla. Turn the mixer to its lowest speed, blend in the whipped cream, and then turn off the mixer, quick!

YIELD: 9 servings, each with: 158 Calories; 16 g Fat (90.8% calories from fat); 2 g Protein; 1 g Carbohydrate; 0 g Dietary Fiber; 1 g net carbs

GINGERED MELON

The dish is light and elegant—and people following a low-fat diet can eat it, too. It looks so pretty in glass dishes!

½ of a ripe cantaloupe

½ of a ripe honeydew

⅓ cup (80 ml) lime juice

Liquid stevia, monkfruit, or sucralose to equal 2 tablespoons (26 g) of sugar in sweetness

1 teaspoon grated fresh ginger

1. Peel the cantaloupe and honeydew and cut it into bite-size chunks or if you have a melon baller, cut balls from it. Place in a serving dish.
2. Combine the lime juice, sweetener, and ginger. Pour over the melon, toss, and serve.

YIELD: 8 servings, each with: 43 Calories; trace Fat (3.4% calories from fat); 1 g Protein; 11 g Carbohydrate; 1 g Dietary Fiber; 10 g net carbs

STRAWBERRIES IN WINE

It's simple, and simply delicious. This is another dessert that works for low carbers and low-fat folks, both.

8 ounces (225 g) fresh strawberries

½ cup (120 ml) burgundy wine

Liquid stevia, monkfruit, or sucralose to equal 1 tablespoon (13 g) of sugar in sweetness (or to taste)

Cinnamon stick

1. Hull the strawberries and slice or cut them into quarters.

2. Mix the wine and the sweetener and pour the mixture over the berries.

3. Add the cinnamon stick and refrigerate, stirring from time to time, for at least 12 hours (but 2 days wouldn't hurt!). Remove the cinnamon stick before serving.

YIELD: 4 servings, each with: 37 Calories; trace Fat (8.0% calories from fat); trace Protein; 4 g Carbohydrate; 1 g Dietary Fiber; 3 g net carbs

MOCKAHLUA 2017

My sister, a longtime Kahlua fan, says this is addictive. And my husband demanded to know, "How did you do that?" You can make this with decaf if caffeine bothers you. The version in *500 Low-Carb Recipes* used Splenda and so included those maltodextrin carbs. With a liquid sweetener—sucralose, monkfruit, or stevia—we can eliminate them.

Technically, coffee does not contain gluten, but reportedly there are proteins in coffee that can trigger celiac disease. I'd say, "Okay for those avoiding gluten on principle, but not for those with celiac disease."

2½ cups (570 ml) water

3 tablespoons (9 g) instant coffee granules

1 teaspoon vanilla extract

Liquid sweetener to equal 3 cups (600 g) of sugar (I used 1 tablespoon [15 ml] Natural Mate liquid monkfruit/stevia.)

1 bottle (750 ml) of vodka

You'll need a clean 1.5 liter bottle with a cork. I used an old wine bottle.

1. Mix together the water, instant coffee granules, vanilla, and sweetener.

2. Use a funnel to pour this into your bottle.

3. Pour in the vodka. Cork it and shake. That's it!

YIELD: 32 servings, each with: 52 Calories; 0 g Fat (0.0% calories from fat); trace Protein; trace Carbohydrate; 0 g Dietary Fiber; trace net carbs

(continued)

Mochahlua

Try this one if you like a little chocolate with your coffee. Just cut the water back to 1½ cups (355 ml) and substitute a 12-ounce (355 ml) bottle of sugar-free chocolate coffee-flavoring syrup for the sweetner and vanilla. This has only a trace of carbohydrates per shot.

Mockahlua and Cream

This makes a nice "little something" to serve at the end of a dinner party, in lieu of a heavier dessert. For each serving, you'll need a shot of Mockahlua (or Mochalua) and 2 shots of heavy cream. Simply mix and sip!

YIELD: 1 serving with: 357 Calories; 33 g Fat (94.2% calories from fat); 2 g Protein; 3 g Carbohydrate; 0 g Dietary Fiber; 3 g net carbs

KAY'S HOT RUM TODDY

This is a delicious winter libation—for adults only! The rum is carb-free, but it will slow down your metabolism, so go easy. Kay says that one theory of hot-toddy making is that it is impossible to use too much batter and you should keep stirring more in until you are bored with stirring. Another theory of hot-toddy making is that it is impossible to use too much rum, and that you should keep stirring in more until your friends panic. Use your best judgment.

½ pound (225 g) butter, softened	1 teaspoon ground cinnamon
½ cup (120 g) erythritol/ monkfruit or erythritol/ stevia blend	1 teaspoon ground cloves
1 teaspoon liquid stevia, English Toffee flavor	1 teaspoon ground cardamom
1 teaspoon ground nutmeg	1 bottle (750 ml) top-quality dark rum

1. Put the butter, sweeteners, nutmeg, cinnamon, ground cloves, and cardamom in a food processor with the S-blade in place. Process until it's smooth and creamy, scraping down the sides of the processor once or twice to make sure everything combines evenly.

2. Scoop this "batter" mixture into a snap-top container and keep it in the fridge. (The batter will keep well, and that means you can make only a serving or two at a time, if you like.)

3. To serve the toddy, warm a coffee mug by filling it with boiling water and pouring it out. Then, fill it again, halfway, with more boiling water. Add 1 to 2 tablespoons (15 to 28 ml) of the batter and stir until it dissolves into the water (a small whisk works well for this). Add two shots of dark rum, stir, and sip.

YIELD: 12 servings, each with: 275 Calories; 15 g Fat (97.1% calories from fat); trace Protein; 1 g Carbohydrate; trace Dietary Fiber; 1 g net carbs

IRISH COFFEE

If you're having this after dinner, you may want to use decaf instead of regular coffee.

2 ounces (28 ml) Irish whiskey

6 ounces (175 ml) hot coffee

Liquid stevia, monkfruit, or sucralose to equal 1–2 teaspoons of sugar in sweetness

2 tablespoons (6 g) Whipped Topping (page 304) or Whipped Cream (page 303)

1. Put the whiskey into a stemmed Irish coffee glass or a mug.
2. Fill with coffee.
3. Stir in the sweetener and top with whipped cream.

YIELD: 1 serving with: 197 Calories; 6 g Fat (88.4% calories from fat); trace Protein; 1 g Carbohydrate; 0 g Dietary Fiber; 1 g net carbs

COCOA

There are some acceptably low-carb diet hot chocolate mixes in the grocery stores, but this is much better. The protein in this cocoa make a cup of it a good breakfast. And for grownups, this is very nice with a shot of Mockahlua 2017 (page 313) or Mochalua (page 314) in it—but not at breakfast!

1 cup (235 ml) heavy cream

1 cup (235 ml) water

2 tablespoons (10 g) unsweetened cocoa powder

Liquid stevia, monkfruit, or sucralose to equal 1½–2 tablespoons (20–26 g) of sugar in sweetness (Chocolate or vanilla stevia would make sense here.)

2 tablespoons (16 g) vanilla whey protein powder

Tiny pinch of salt

1. Over the lowest possible heat (it doesn't hurt to use a heat diffuser or a double boiler), combine the heavy cream and water.
2. When they're starting to get warm, add the cocoa powder, sweetener, protein powder, and salt. Whisk until well combined.
3. Bring just barely to a simmer and pour into cups.

YIELD: 2 servings, each with: 478 Calories; 46 g Fat (82.5% calories from fat); 14 g Protein; 7 g Carbohydrate; 2 g Dietary Fiber; 5 g net carbs

CREAMY VANILLA COFFEE

Reader Honey Ashton sends this sweet little treat and says it's also good iced. I analyzed this with vanilla whey protein, which should work fine.

1 hot cup (235 ml) decaffeinated coffee

2 tablespoons (16 g) low-carb vanilla shake meal-replacement powder

1 to 2 teaspoons sugar-free vanilla coffee-flavoring syrup

Cinnamon (optional)

Combine the coffee, vanilla shake powder, and coffee-flavoring syrup. Garnish with cinnamon (if using).

YIELD: 1 serving with: 116 Calories; 2 g Fat (14.2% calories from fat); 22 g Protein; 3 g Carbohydrate; 1 g Dietary Fiber; 2 g net carbs

CHAI

My darling friend Nicole is a devotee of this spiced Indian tea. She suggested I come up with a low-carb version for this book, and here it is. Make up a batch, and your whole house will smell wonderful. You can refrigerate this for a day or two and reheat it in the microwave whenever you want a cup.

1 tablespoon (6 g) fennel seed or (7 g) anise seed

6 green cardamom pods

12 whole cloves

1 cinnamon stick

¼ inch (6 mm) of fresh ginger, thinly sliced

¼ teaspoon whole black peppercorns

2 bay leaves

7 cups (1.6 L) water

2 tablespoons (12 g) loose Darjeeling tea

Liquid stevia, monkfruit, or sucralose to equal ⅓ cup (67 g) of sugar in sweetness—(If you use English toffee stevia, you can skip the molasses.)

⅛ teaspoon molasses

½ cup (120 ml) heavy cream

½ cup (120 ml) unsweetened pourable coconut milk

1. Combine the fennel seed, cardamom, cloves, cinnamon, ginger, peppercorns, bay leaves, and water. Bring to a simmer and let simmer for 5 minutes.

2. Add the tea, turn off the burner, cover, and let the mixture steep for 10 minutes.

3. Strain and stir in the sweetener, molasses if using, heavy cream, and coconut milk.

YIELD: 8 servings, each with: 94 Calories; 8 g Fat (62.8% calories from fat); 1 g Protein; 9 g Carbohydrate; 5 g Dietary Fiber; 4 g net carbs. Once again, an accurate count escapes us. Most of the carbs here are in the spices, and you strain them out.

EGGIWEGGNOG

This is for those of you who are unafraid of raw eggs. My husband would gladly have this for breakfast every day! If you wish to pasteurize eggs, instructions are on page 22.

3 eggs

½ cup (120 ml) heavy cream

½ cup (120 ml) half-and-half

Liquid stevia, monkfruit, or sucralose to equal 2 tablespoons (26 g) sugar in sweetness

1 teaspoon vanilla extract

Pinch of salt

Pinch of nutmeg

1. Put the eggs, heavy cream, half-and-half, sweetener, vanilla, and salt in a blender and run it for 30 seconds or so.
2. Pour into glasses, sprinkle a little nutmeg on top, and drink up.

YIELD: 2 servings, each with: 389 Calories; 36 g Fat (82.5% calories from fat); 11 g Protein; 6 g Carbohydrate; trace Dietary Fiber; 6 g net carbs

COOKED EGGNOG

This is for you safe-living folks who would never consider eating a raw egg—and it's mighty tasty, too. It just takes more work.

2 cups (475 ml) half-and-half

1 cup (235 ml) heavy cream

Liquid stevia, monkfruit, or sucralose to equal ¼ cup (50 g) of sugar in sweetness

1 teaspoon vanilla extract

¼ teaspoon salt

6 eggs

1 cup (235 ml) water

Nutmeg

1. In a big glass measuring cup, combine the half-and-half and heavy cream. Microwave it at 70 percent power for 3 to 4 minutes or until it's very warm through, but not boiling. (This is simply a time-saver, and is not essential; if you prefer, you can simply heat the half-and-half and cream over a low flame in the saucepan you'll use to finish the recipe.)
2. After microwaving, pour the half-and-half mixture into a heavy-bottomed saucepan and whisk in the sweetener, vanilla, salt, and eggs. Turn the burner to lowest heat (if you have a heat diffuser or a double boiler, this would be a good time to use it) and stand there and stir your eggnog constantly until it's thick enough to coat a metal spoon with a thin film. This will, I'm sorry to say, take at least 5 minutes and maybe as many as 20.
3. Stir in the water and chill. Sprinkle a little nutmeg on each serving and feel free to spike this, if you like!

YIELD: 6 servings of about 1 cup (235 ml), each with: 310 Calories; 28 g Fat (82.0% calories from fat); 9 g Protein; 5 g Carbohydrate; 0 g Dietary Fiber; 5 g net carbs

Acknowledgments

There were a great number of people whose collective efforts have made this cookbook possible in what seemed like an impossibly short time:

First, I'd like to thank my husband, Eric Schmitz, who has been my unfailing right hand all through this project, grocery shopping, recipe testing, eating my failures without complaint, and accepting the strain on the food budget. He also helped me run the nutritional calculations for these recipes, which is about the only reason this book was done by its deadline. I quite literally couldn't have done it without him.

Holly Schmidt was the editor who, reading my self-published book, recruited me to write for Fair Winds and guided me through the first several books. Jill Alexander is the editor who has been with me since Holly moved on several years ago and has been endlessly patient with me. Thanks to them both.

Three cookbook authors kindly allowed me to reprint recipes from their cookbooks. I do not know if any of these books are still in print, but I thank their authors:

Baking Low Carb and *Bread and Breakfast: Baking Low Carb II*, both by my pal Diana Lee. Recipes reprinted with permission from *Baking Low Carb*, 1999, Diana Lee. Recipes reprinted with permission from *Bread and Breakfast: Baking Low Carb II*, 2001, Diana Lee.

Splendid Low-Carbing, by Jennifer Eloff. Jen is the Splenda Queen, and since she lives in Canada, where Splenda's been available far longer than in the United States, Jen's had far more experience with it than I. Recipes reprinted with permission from *Splendid Low-Carbing*, 2001, Jennifer Eloff.

Recipes from *The Fat Fast Cookbook* appear by permission of Andrew DiMino of CarbSmart.com. *The Fat Fast Cookbook* May 24, 2014, CarbSmart Inc.

Lo-Carb Cooking, by Debra Rowland, is the source, among other things, for recipes for "cornbread" and cheese popovers—and there are many more great-sounding recipes in her book that I didn't have room for. Recipes reprinted with permission from *Lo-Carb Cooking*, 2001, Debra Rowland.

Also contributing greatly to this book is Vicki Cash, who allowed me to use the recipes from her 2002 *Low Carb Success Calendar*. If Vicki puts out a calendar again, I strongly suggest you snap it up! Recipes reprinted with permission from *The 2002 Low Carb Success Calendar*, 2001, Just Ducky Productions.

My readers responded to my requests with piles of great low-carb recipes for this book. The ones whose recipes have been used are named with their recipes. I thank them, but I also thank those folks who sent recipes I didn't use. Quite often it was because we already had a similar recipe or because the carb count was judged to be just a bit too high; it was very rarely because we just didn't like a recipe. So whether your recipe is here or not, thank you, thank you, from the bottom of my heart. And who knows? We may use your recipe in another book! I also thank all of you who have come up with ideas for recipes you wanted me to develop. My readers are one of the genuine joys of my life.

The first time through, I was far too busy coming up with recipes of my own to test all of the recipes coming in from readers, so I recruited a crack troop of recipe testers. Again, I couldn't have done it without them. My recipe testers were Kim Carpender, Deborah Crites, Jane Duquette, Julie McIntosh, Ray Todd Stevens, Carol Vandiver, Maria Vander Vloedt, and Kay Winefordner—not to mention their families and friends. Thank you, one and all.

I also recruited testers for this reboot and would like to thank them: Dawn, Sheryl, Christina Prentice Roberts, Tammern Lowe, Nancy Loy, Alan Blues, Cheryl Andrews Readio, and Verna Haas.

Finally, I'd like to thank my mom, the late Jane Carpender, for letting me help her cook from the time I was tiny. Because of her, I knew how to measure accurately, separate an egg, bake cookies, make gravy, knead bread, rice potatoes, and perform dozens of other cooking tasks by the time I was seven or eight years old. If I know my way around a kitchen, it's because of my mother. Thanks, Mom! (I should note: I write this on Mother's Day, 2018. I miss you, Mom. I always will.) All you parents out there, cook with your kids. Not only is it terrific quality time together and a great defense against junk food, but it also teaches kids skills that will serve them well for the rest of their lives.

About the Author

In retrospect, Dana Carpender's career seems inevitable: She's been cooking since she had to stand on a step stool to reach the stove. She was also a dangerously sugar-addicted child, eventually stealing from her parents to support her habit, and was in Weight Watchers by age eleven. At nineteen, Dana read her first book on nutrition and she recognized herself in a list of symptoms of reactive hypoglycemia. She ditched sugar and white flour and was dazzled by the near instantaneous improvement in her physical and mental health. A lifetime nutrition buff was born.

Unfortunately, in the late 1980s and early 1990s, Dana got sucked into the low-fat/high-carb mania, and whole-grain-and-beaned her way up to a size 20, with nasty energy swings, constant hunger, and borderline high blood pressure. In 1995, she read a nutrition book from the 1950s that stated that obesity had nothing to do with how much one ate, but was rather a carbohydrate intolerance disease. She thought, "What the heck, might as well give it a try." Three days later, her clothes were loose, her hunger was gone, and her energy level was through the roof. She never looked back and she has now been lowcarb for over twenty years—more than one-third of her life.

Realizing that this change was permanent and being a cook at heart, Dana set about creating as varied and satisfying a cuisine as she could with a minimal carb load. And being an enthusiastic, gregarious sort, she started sharing her experience. By 1997, she was writing about it. The upshot is more than 2,500 recipes published and more than a million books sold—and she still has ideas left to try! Dana lives in Bloomington, Indiana, with her husband, three dogs, and a cat, all of whom are well and healthily fed.

Index

THE NEW 500 LOW-CARB RECIPES

THE NEW 500 LOW-CARB RECIPES

INDEX